SUPERMAN
THE MEN OF TOMORROW

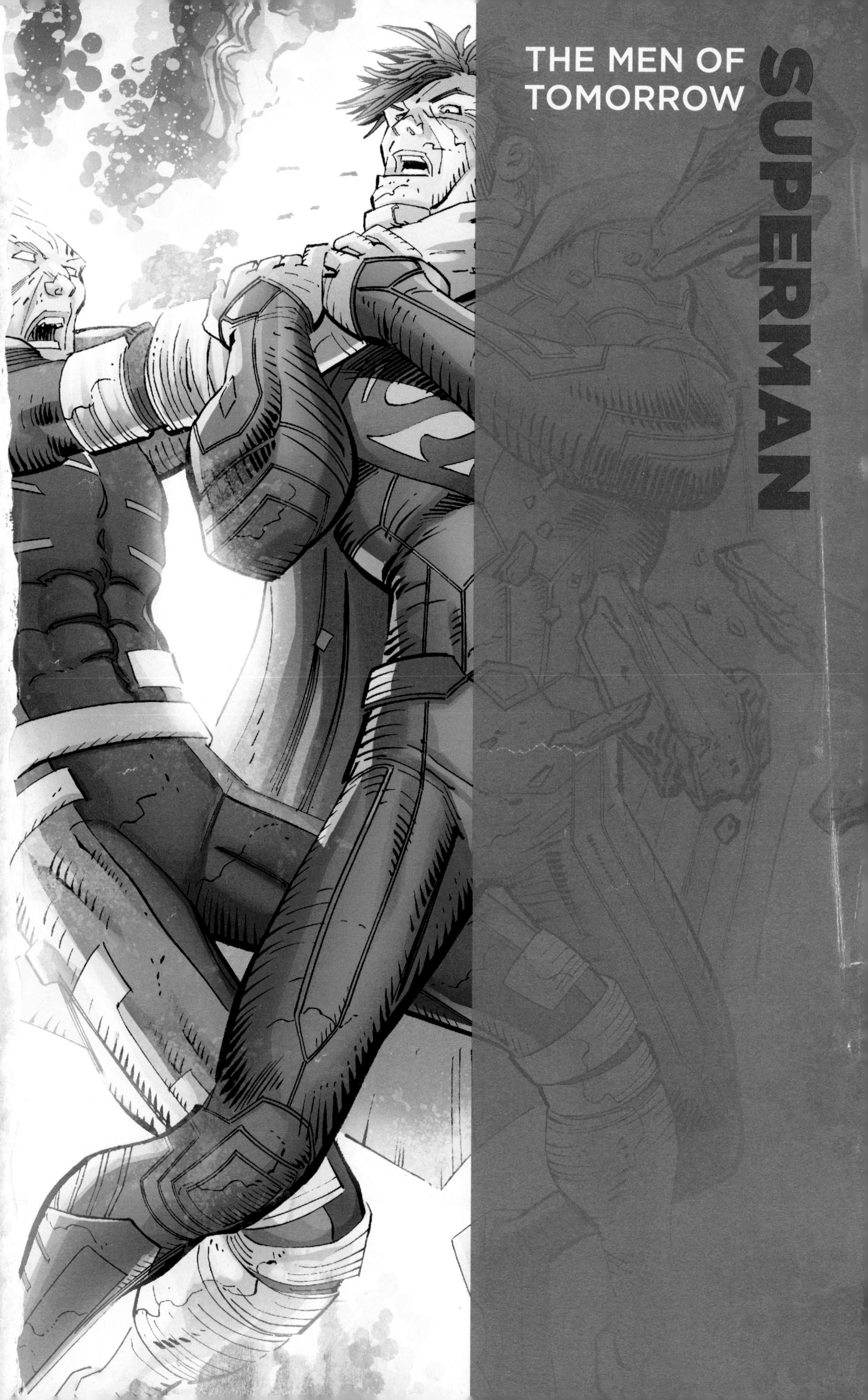

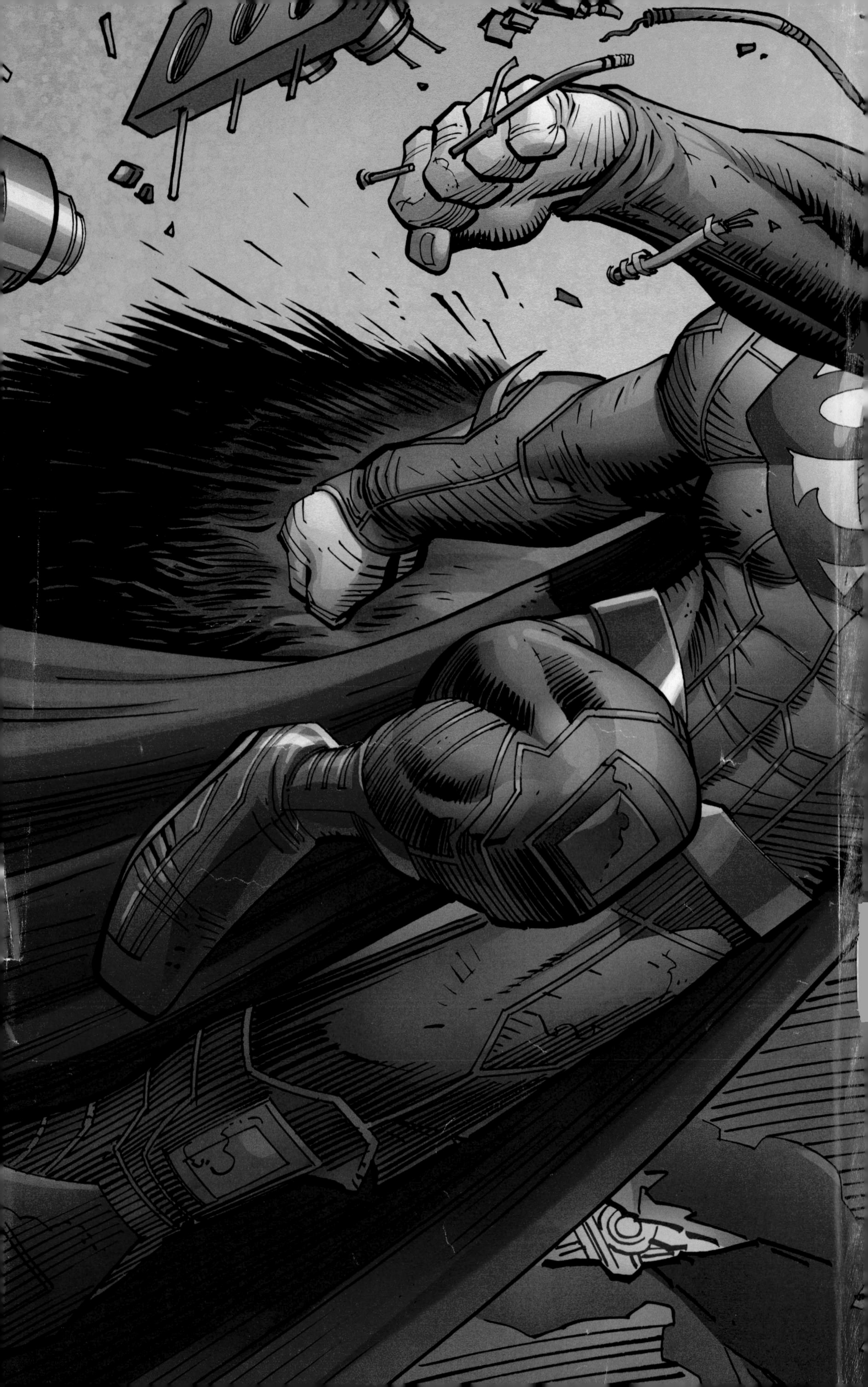

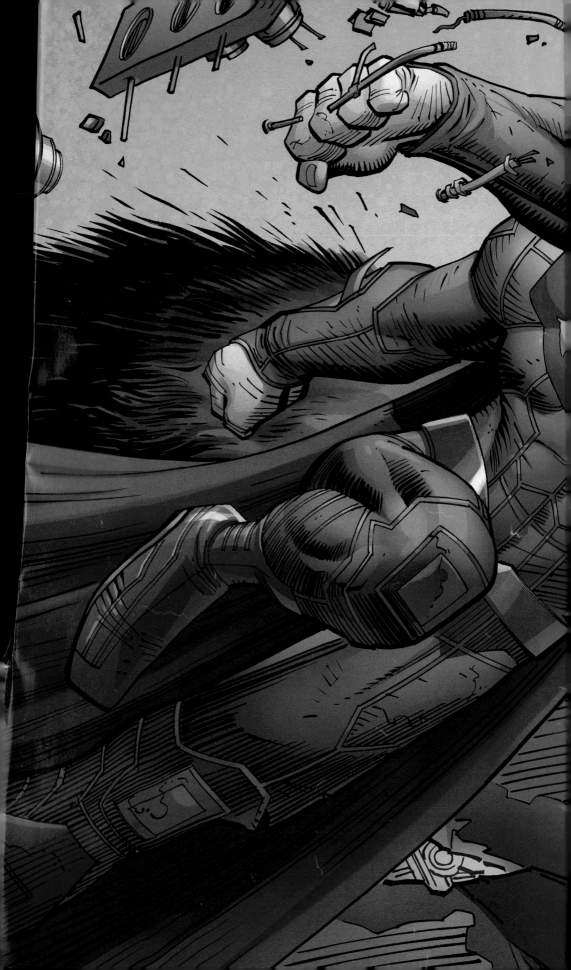

THE MEN OF TOMORROW

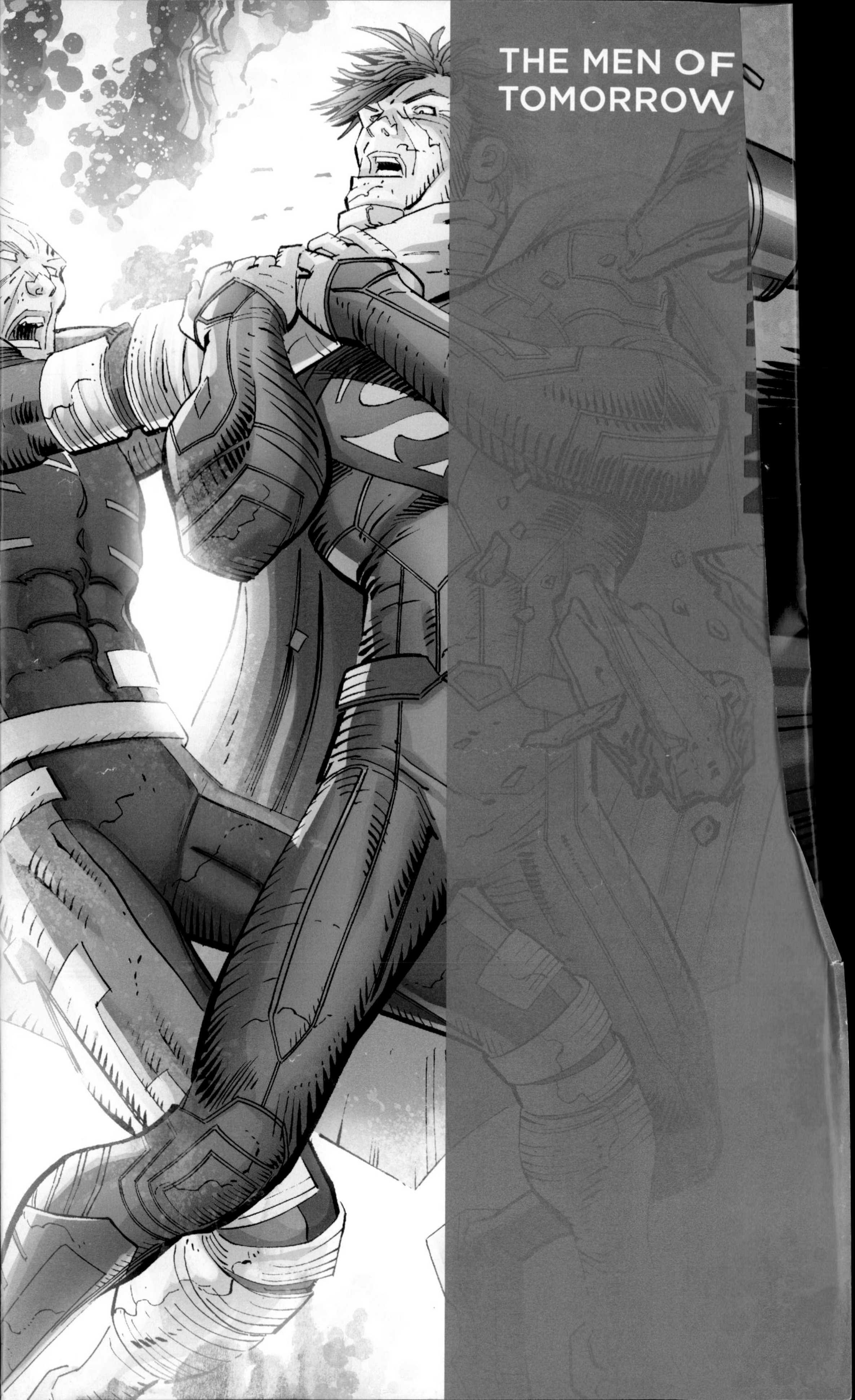

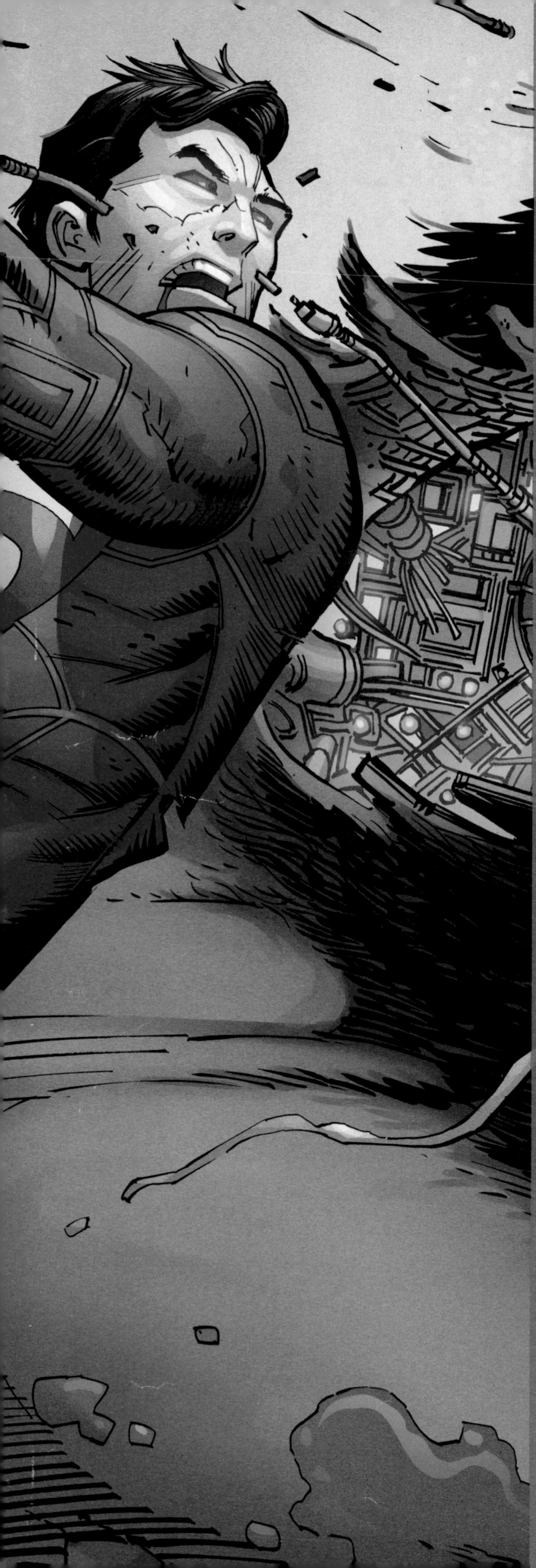

SUPERMAN

THE MEN OF TOMORROW

WRITTEN BY
GEOFF JOHNS

PENCILS BY
JOHN ROMITA JR.

INKS BY
KLAUS JANSON

COLOR BY
LAURA MARTIN
HI-FI
ULISES ARREOLA
DAN BROWN
WIL QUINTANA

LETTERS BY
SAL CIPRIANO
TRAVIS LANHAM

ORIGINAL SERIES &
COLLECTION COVER ART BY
JOHN ROMITA JR.,
KLAUS JANSON &
LAURA MARTIN

SUPERMAN CREATED BY
JERRY SIEGEL &
JOE SHUSTER
BY SPECIAL ARRANGEMENT
WITH THE JERRY SIEGEL FAMILY

EDDIE BERGANZA Editor – Original Series
RICKEY PURDIN Associate Editor – Original Series
ANTHONY MARQUES Assistant Editor – Original Series
ROBIN WILDMAN Editor
DAMIAN RYLAND Publication Design

BOB HARRAS Senior VP – Editor-in-Chief, DC Comics

DIANE NELSON President DAN DIDIO and JIM LEE Co-Publishers
GEOFF JOHNS Chief Creative Officer
AMIT DESAI Senior VP – Marketing and Franchise Management
AMY GENKINS Senior VP – Business and Legal Affairs
NAIRI GARDINER Senior VP – Finance
JEFF BOISON VP – Publishing Planning
MARK CHIARELLO VP – Art Direction and Design
JOHN CUNNINGHAM VP – Marketing
TERRI CUNNINGHAM VP – Editorial Administration
LARRY GANEM VP – Talent Relations and Services
ALISON GILL Senior VP – Manufacturing and Operations
HANK KANALZ Senior VP – Vertigo and Integrated Publishing
JAY KOGAN VP – Business and Legal Affairs, Publishing
JACK MAHAN VP – Business Affairs, Talent
NICK NAPOLITANO VP – Manufacturing Administration
SUE POHJA VP – Book Sales
FRED RUIZ VP – Manufacturing Operations
COURTNEY SIMMONS Senior VP – Publicity
BOB WAYNE Senior VP – Sales

SUPERMAN: THE MEN OF TOMORROW

DC Comics, 4000 Warner Blvd., Burbank, CA 91522
A Warner Bros. Entertainment Company
Printed by RR Donnelley, Salem, VA, USA. 7/3/15. First Printing.
ISBN: 978-1-4012-5239-7

Library of Congress Cataloging-in-Publication Data

Johns, Geoff, 1973- author.
Superman. Volume 6 / Geoff Johns, writer ; John Romita Jr, Klaus Janson, artists.
pages cm. — (The New 52!)
ISBN 978-1-4012-5239-7 (hardback)
1. Graphic novels. I. Romita, John, illustrator. II. Janson, Klaus,
illustrator. III. Title.
PN6728.S9J57 2015
741.5'973—dc23
2015008050

SUSTAINABLE
FORESTRY
INITIATIVE

Certified Chain of Custody
20% Certified Forest Content,
80% Certified Sourcing
www.sfiprogram.org
SFI-01042
APPLIES TO TEXT STOCK ONLY

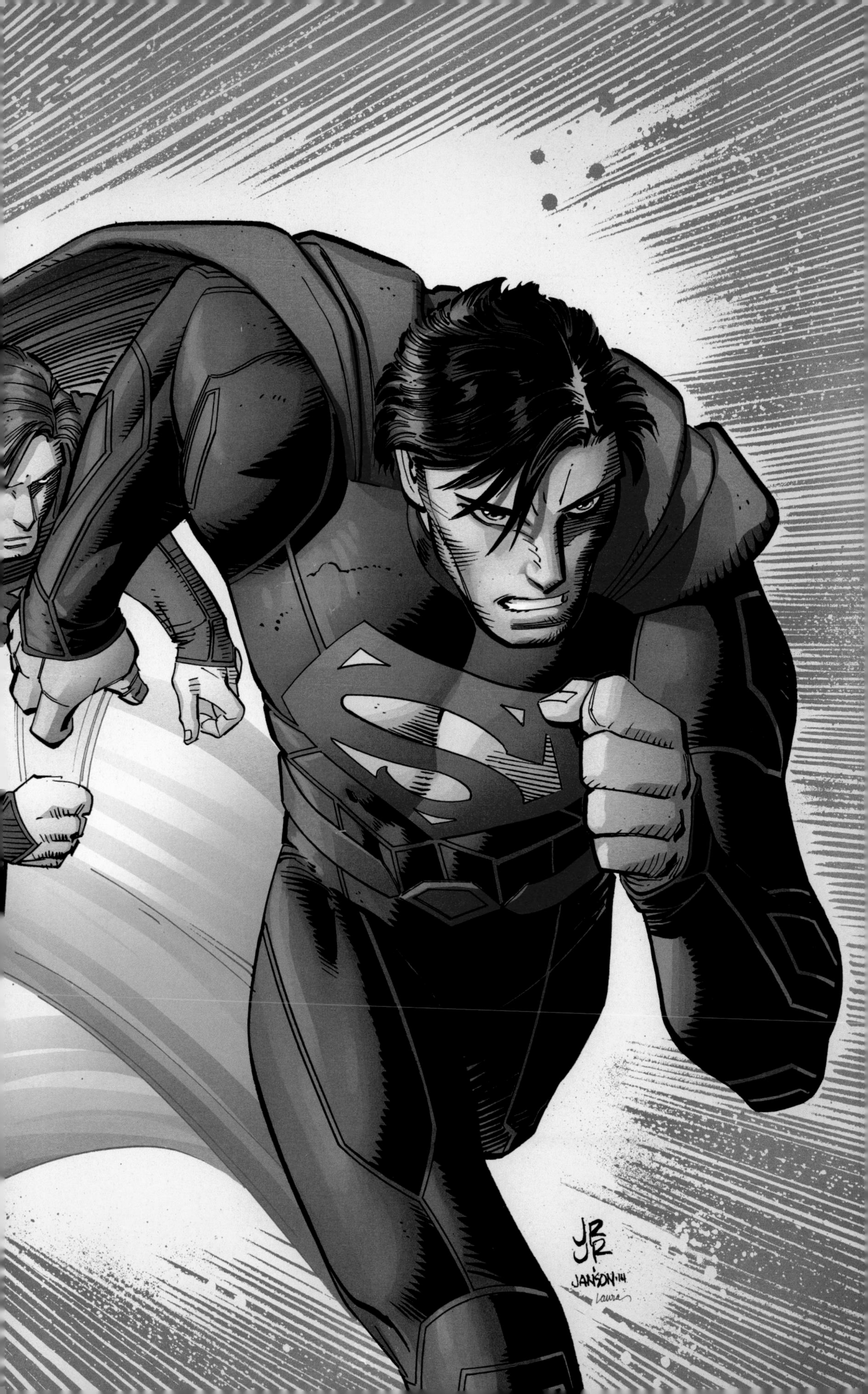
JANSON·14

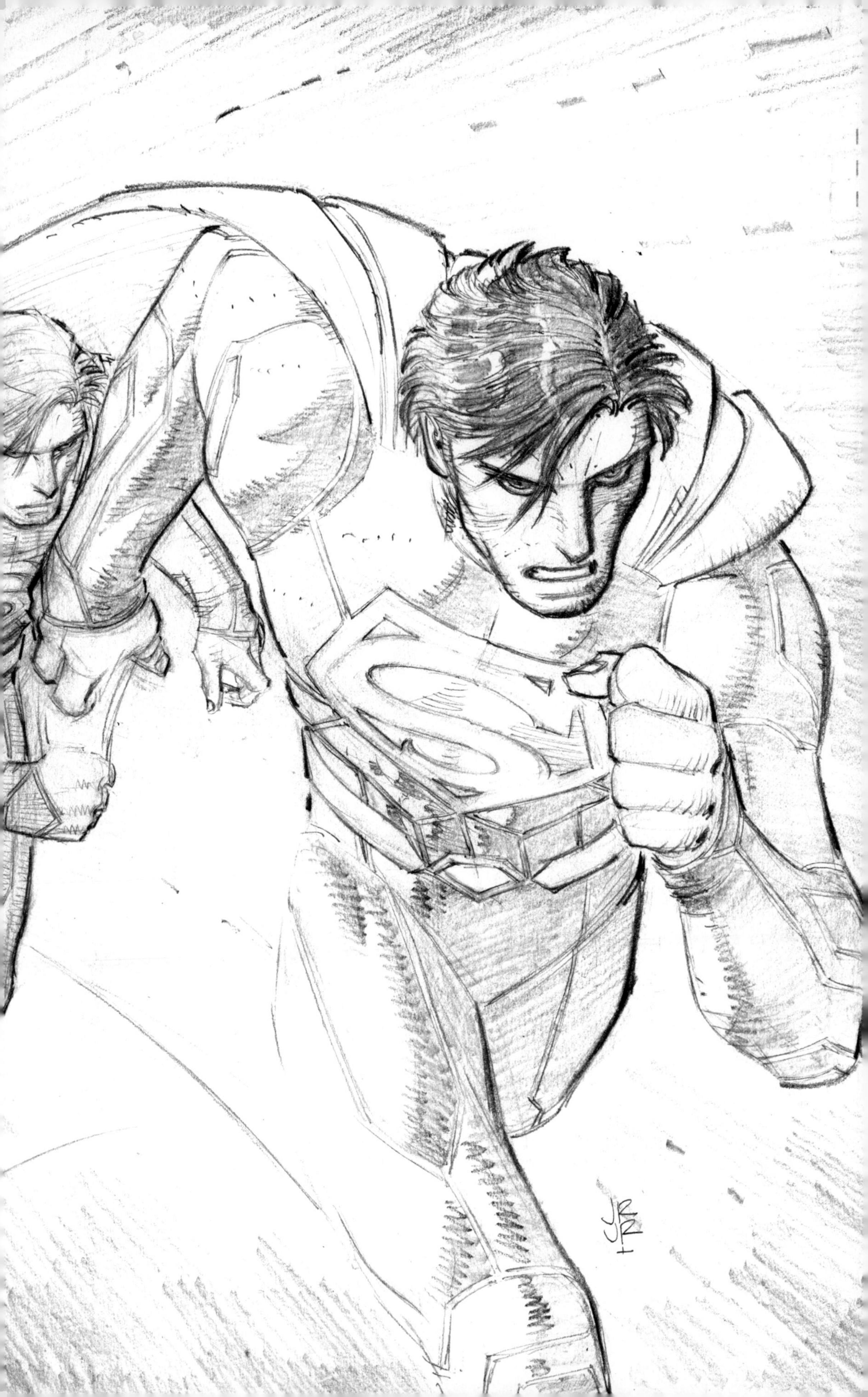
JR JR

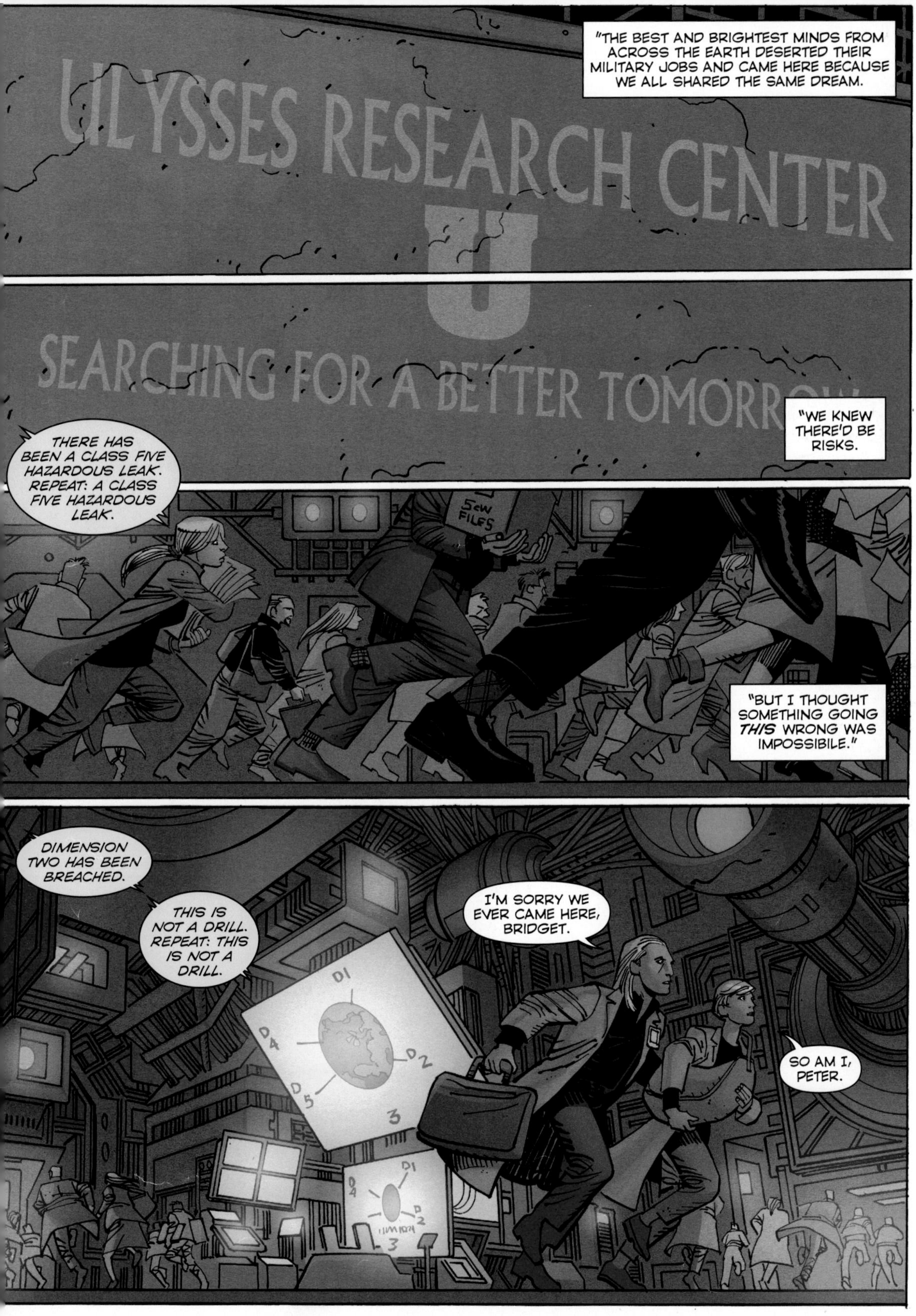

"THE BEST AND BRIGHTEST MINDS FROM ACROSS THE EARTH DESERTED THEIR MILITARY JOBS AND CAME HERE BECAUSE WE ALL SHARED THE SAME DREAM.
ULYSSES RESEARCH CENTER
U
SEARCHING FOR A BETTER TOMORROW
"WE KNEW THERE'D BE RISKS.
THERE HAS BEEN A CLASS FIVE HAZARDOUS LEAK. REPEAT: A CLASS FIVE HAZARDOUS LEAK.
5cw FILES
"BUT I THOUGHT SOMETHING GOING *THIS* WRONG WAS IMPOSSIBILE."
DIMENSION TWO HAS BEEN BREACHED.
THIS IS NOT A DRILL. REPEAT: THIS IS NOT A DRILL.
I'M SORRY WE EVER CAME HERE, BRIDGET.
SO AM I, PETER.
D1
D4
D2
D5
3

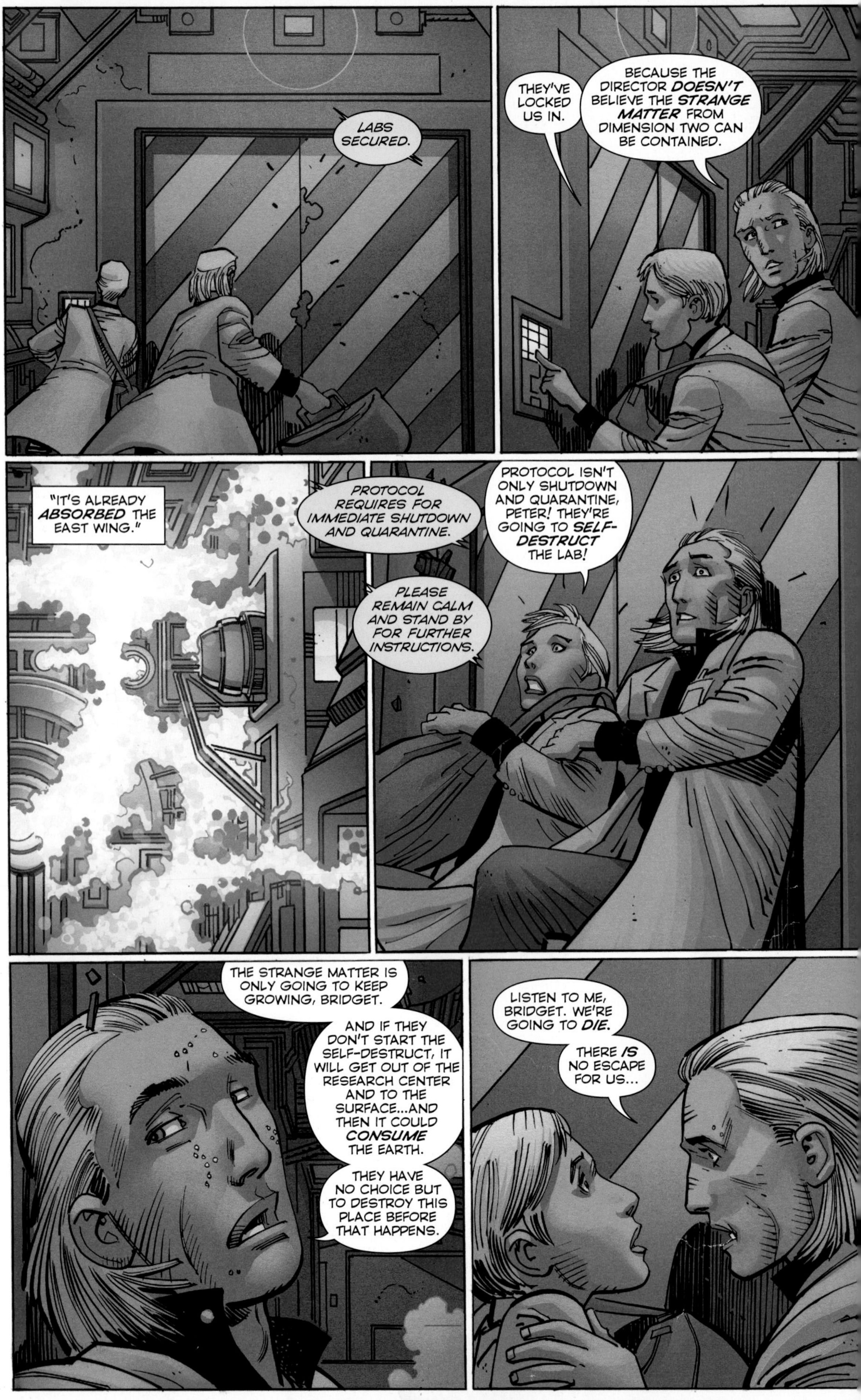
LABS SECURED.
THEY'VE LOCKED US IN.
BECAUSE THE DIRECTOR DOESN'T BELIEVE THE STRANGE MATTER FROM DIMENSION TWO CAN BE CONTAINED.
"IT'S ALREADY ABSORBED THE EAST WING."
PROTOCOL REQUIRES FOR IMMEDIATE SHUTDOWN AND QUARANTINE.
PROTOCOL ISN'T ONLY SHUTDOWN AND QUARANTINE, PETER! THEY'RE GOING TO SELF-DESTRUCT THE LAB!
PLEASE REMAIN CALM AND STAND BY FOR FURTHER INSTRUCTIONS.
THE STRANGE MATTER IS ONLY GOING TO KEEP GROWING, BRIDGET.
AND IF THEY DON'T START THE SELF-DESTRUCT, IT WILL GET OUT OF THE RESEARCH CENTER AND TO THE SURFACE...AND THEN IT COULD CONSUME THE EARTH.
THEY HAVE NO CHOICE BUT TO DESTROY THIS PLACE BEFORE THAT HAPPENS.
LISTEN TO ME, BRIDGET. WE'RE GOING TO DIE.
THERE IS NO ESCAPE FOR US...

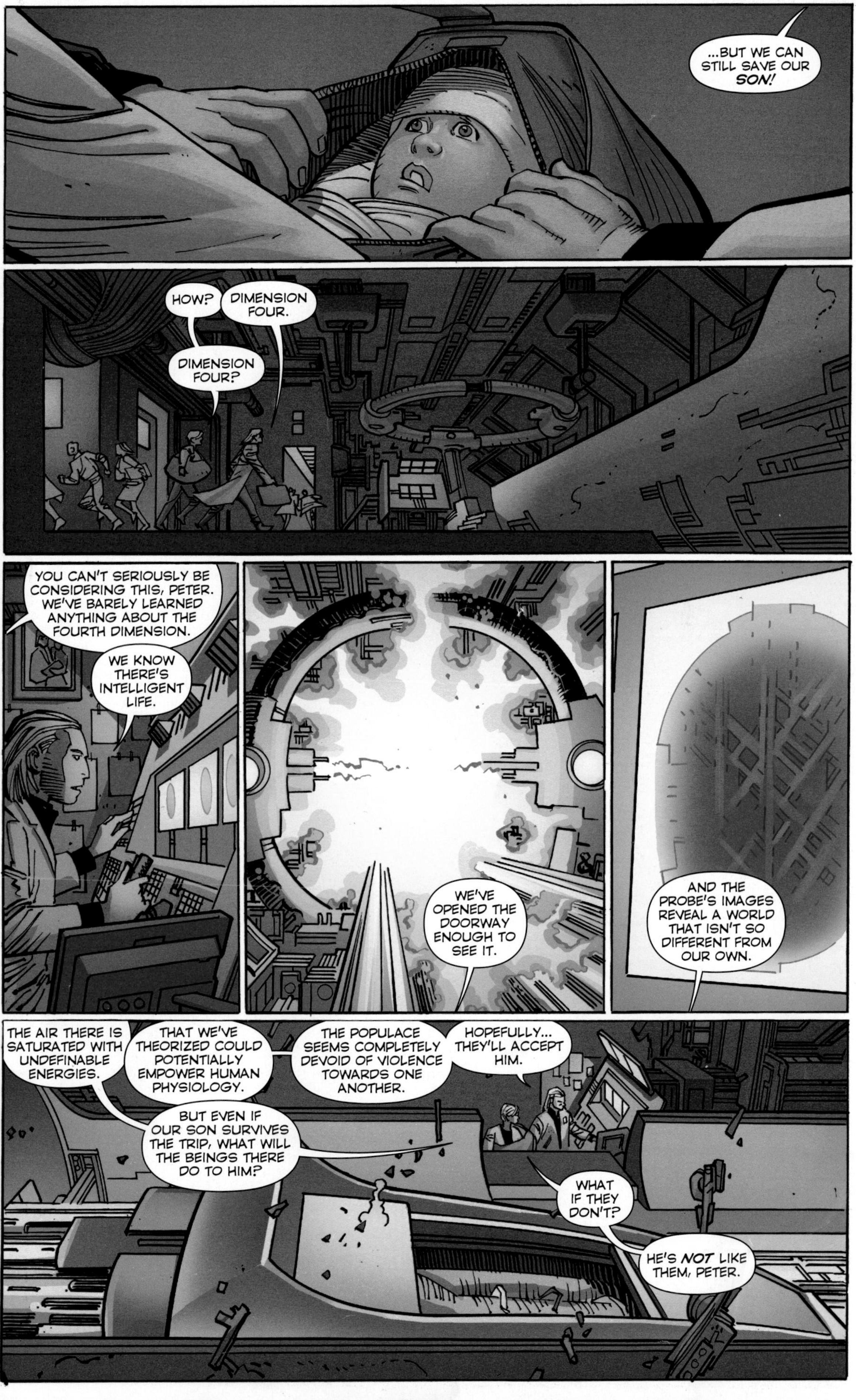
...BUT WE CAN STILL SAVE OUR *SON!*
HOW?
DIMENSION FOUR.
DIMENSION FOUR?
YOU CAN'T SERIOUSLY BE CONSIDERING THIS, PETER. WE'VE BARELY LEARNED ANYTHING ABOUT THE FOURTH DIMENSION.
WE KNOW THERE'S INTELLIGENT LIFE.
WE'VE OPENED THE DOORWAY ENOUGH TO SEE IT.
AND THE PROBE'S IMAGES REVEAL A WORLD THAT ISN'T SO DIFFERENT FROM OUR OWN.
THE AIR THERE IS SATURATED WITH UNDEFINABLE ENERGIES.
THAT WE'VE THEORIZED COULD POTENTIALLY EMPOWER HUMAN PHYSIOLOGY.
BUT EVEN IF OUR SON SURVIVES THE TRIP, WHAT WILL THE BEINGS THERE DO TO HIM?
THE POPULACE SEEMS COMPLETELY DEVOID OF VIOLENCE TOWARDS ONE ANOTHER.
HOPEFULLY... THEY'LL ACCEPT HIM.
WHAT IF THEY DON'T?
HE'S *NOT* LIKE THEM, PETER.

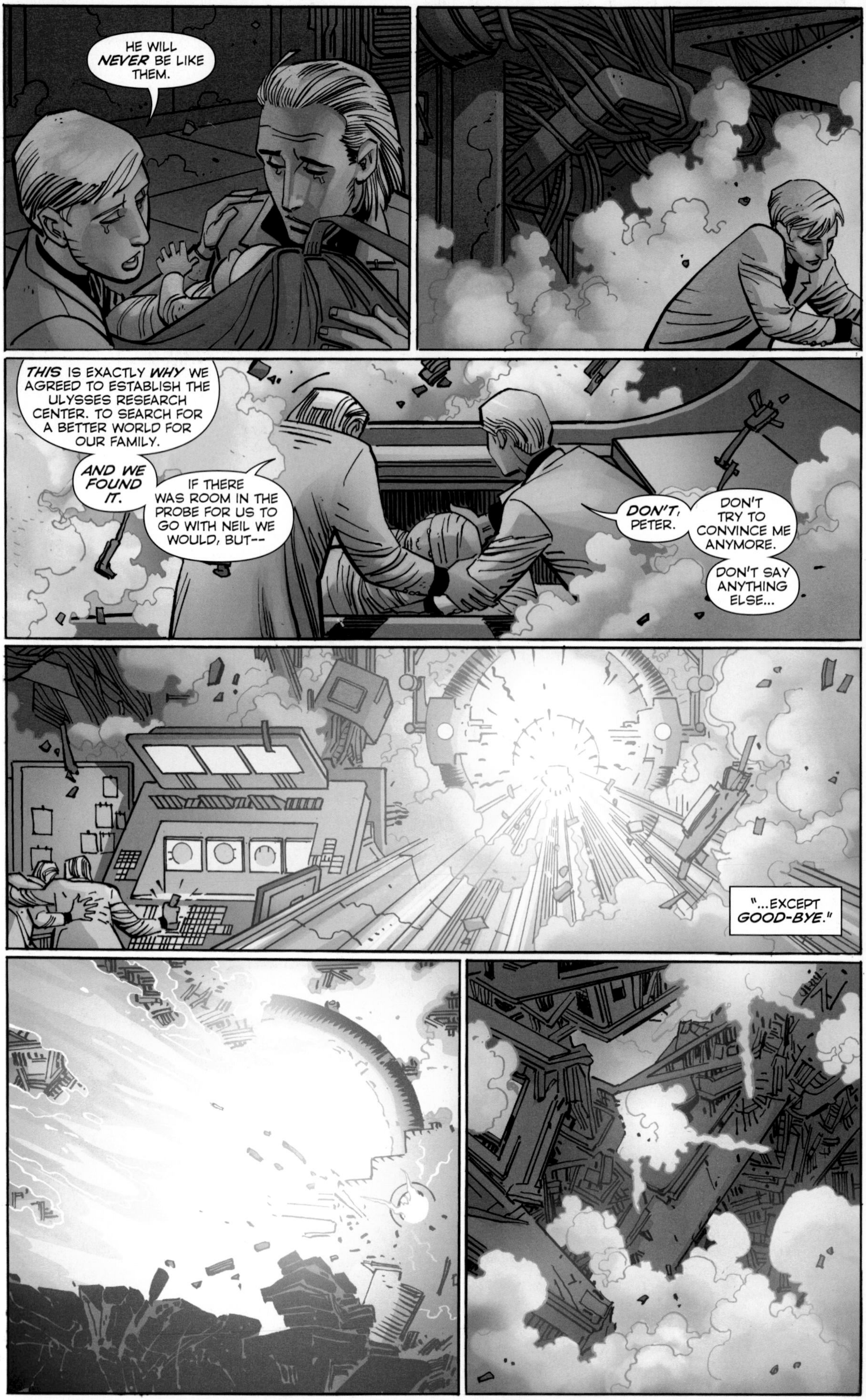
HE WILL *NEVER* BE LIKE THEM.
THIS IS EXACTLY *WHY* WE AGREED TO ESTABLISH THE ULYSSES RESEARCH CENTER. TO SEARCH FOR A BETTER WORLD FOR OUR FAMILY.
AND WE FOUND IT.
IF THERE WAS ROOM IN THE PROBE FOR US TO GO WITH NEIL WE WOULD, BUT--
DON'T, PETER.
DON'T TRY TO CONVINCE ME ANYMORE.
DON'T SAY ANYTHING ELSE...
"...EXCEPT *GOOD-BYE*."

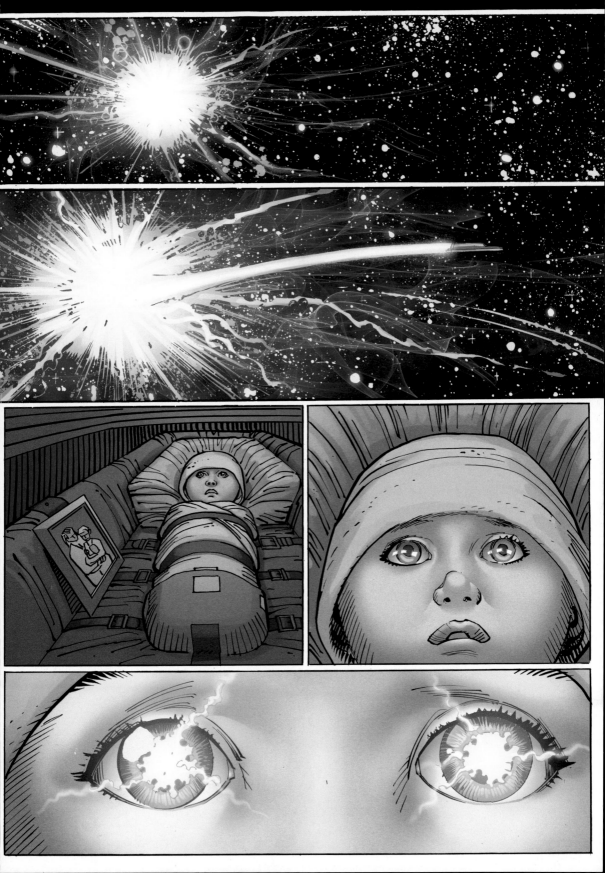

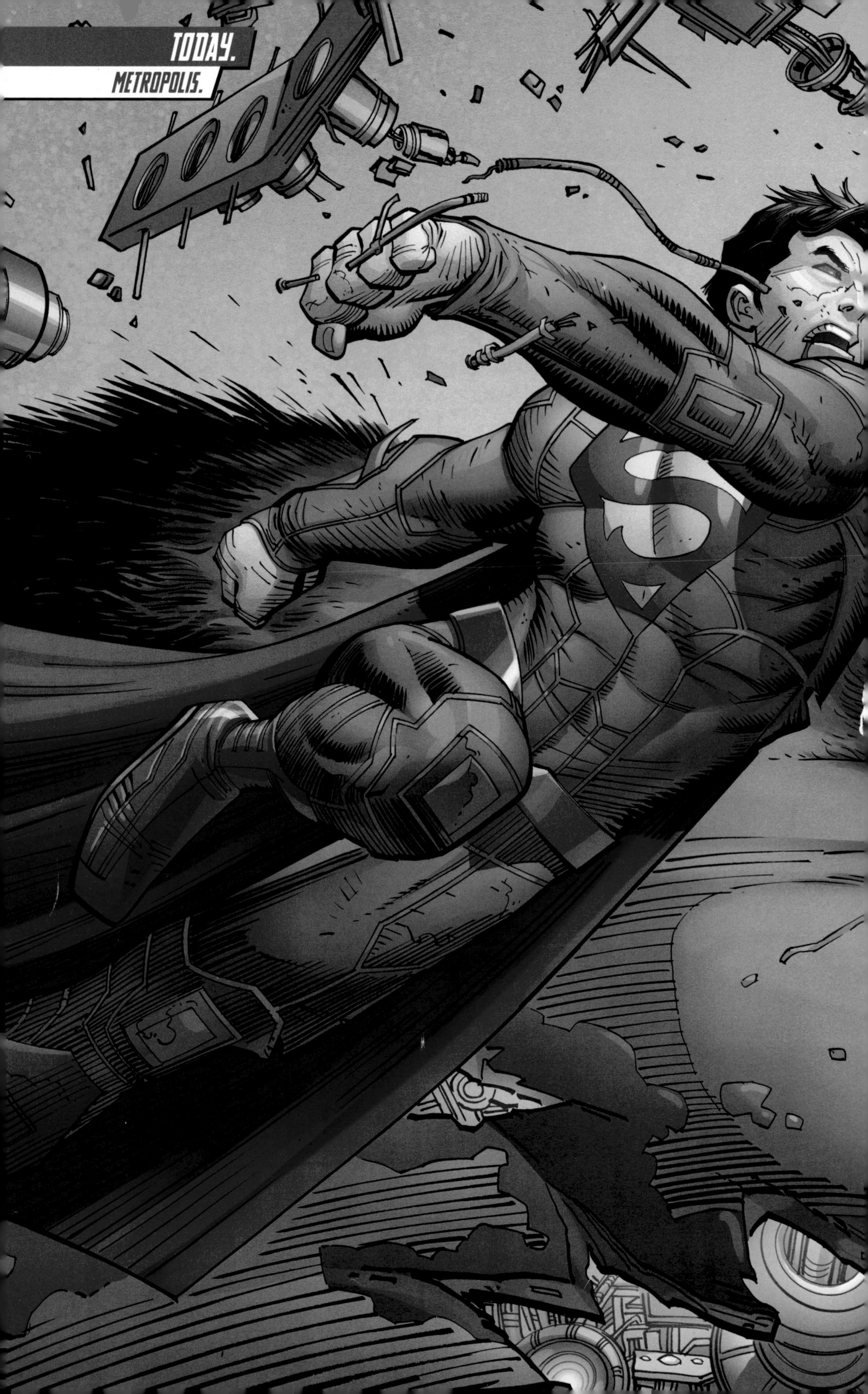
TODAY.
METROPOLIS.

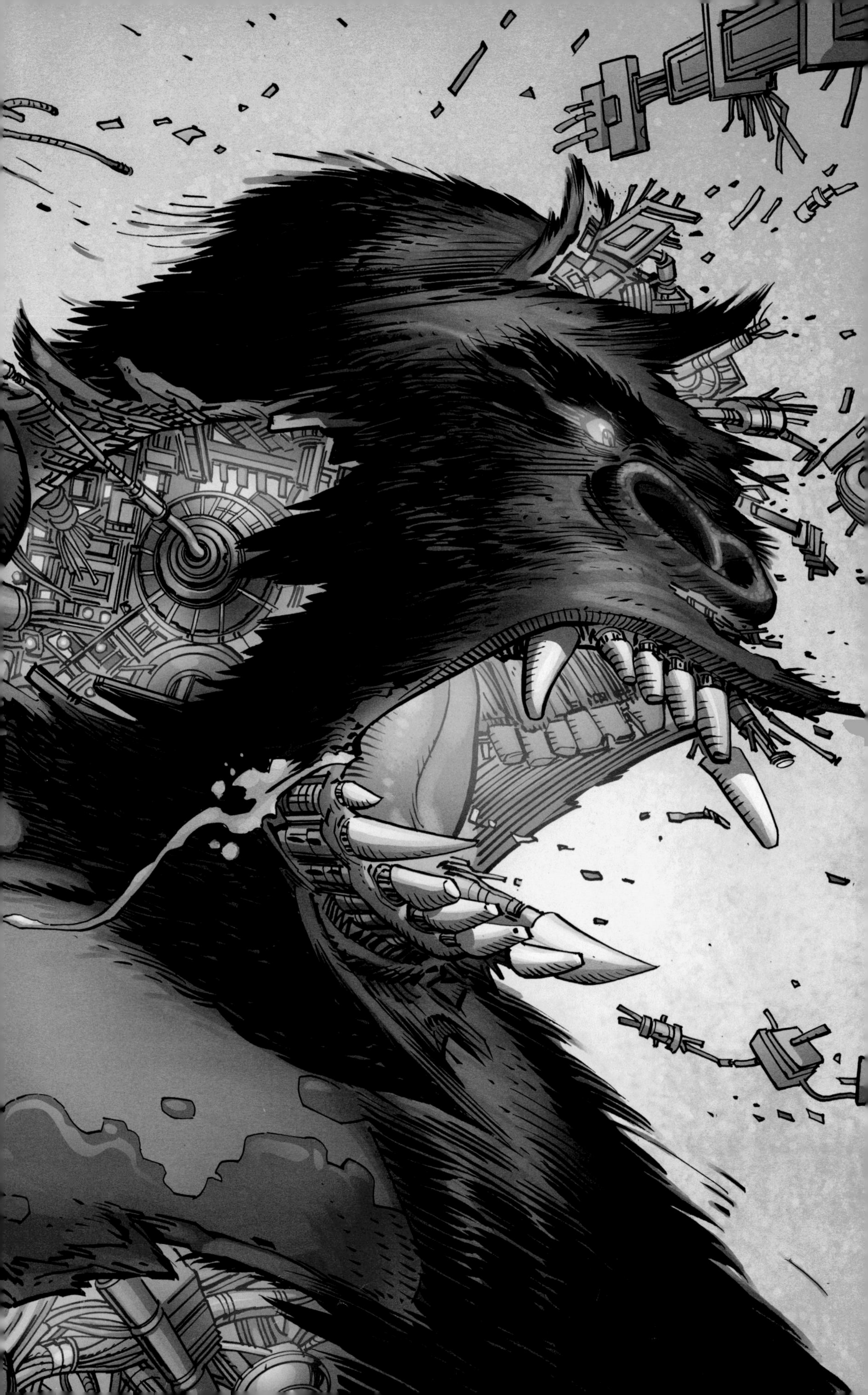

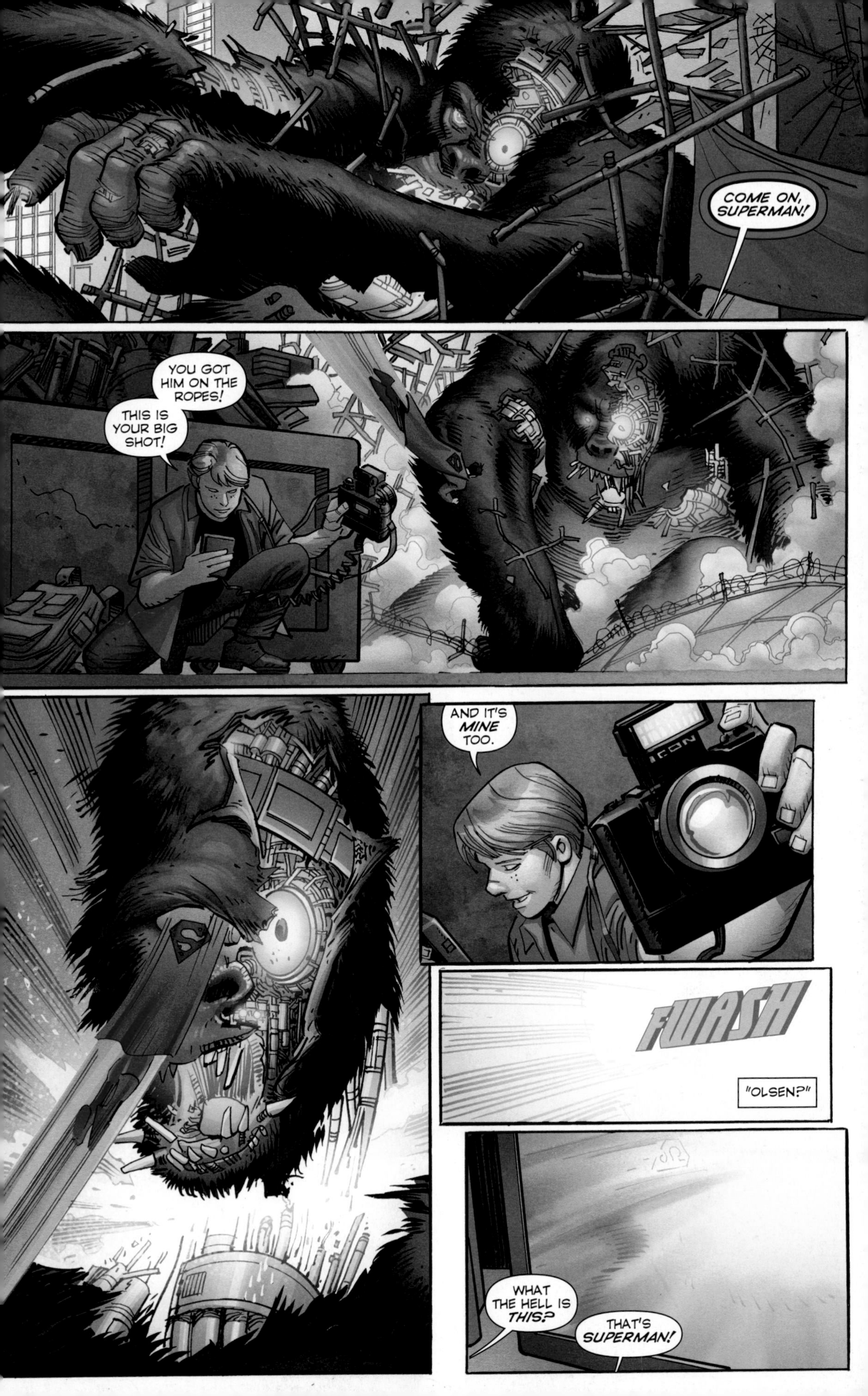
COME ON, SUPERMAN!
YOU GOT HIM ON THE ROPES!
THIS IS YOUR BIG SHOT!
AND IT'S MINE TOO.
FWASH
"OLSEN?"
WHAT THE HELL IS THIS?
THAT'S SUPERMAN!

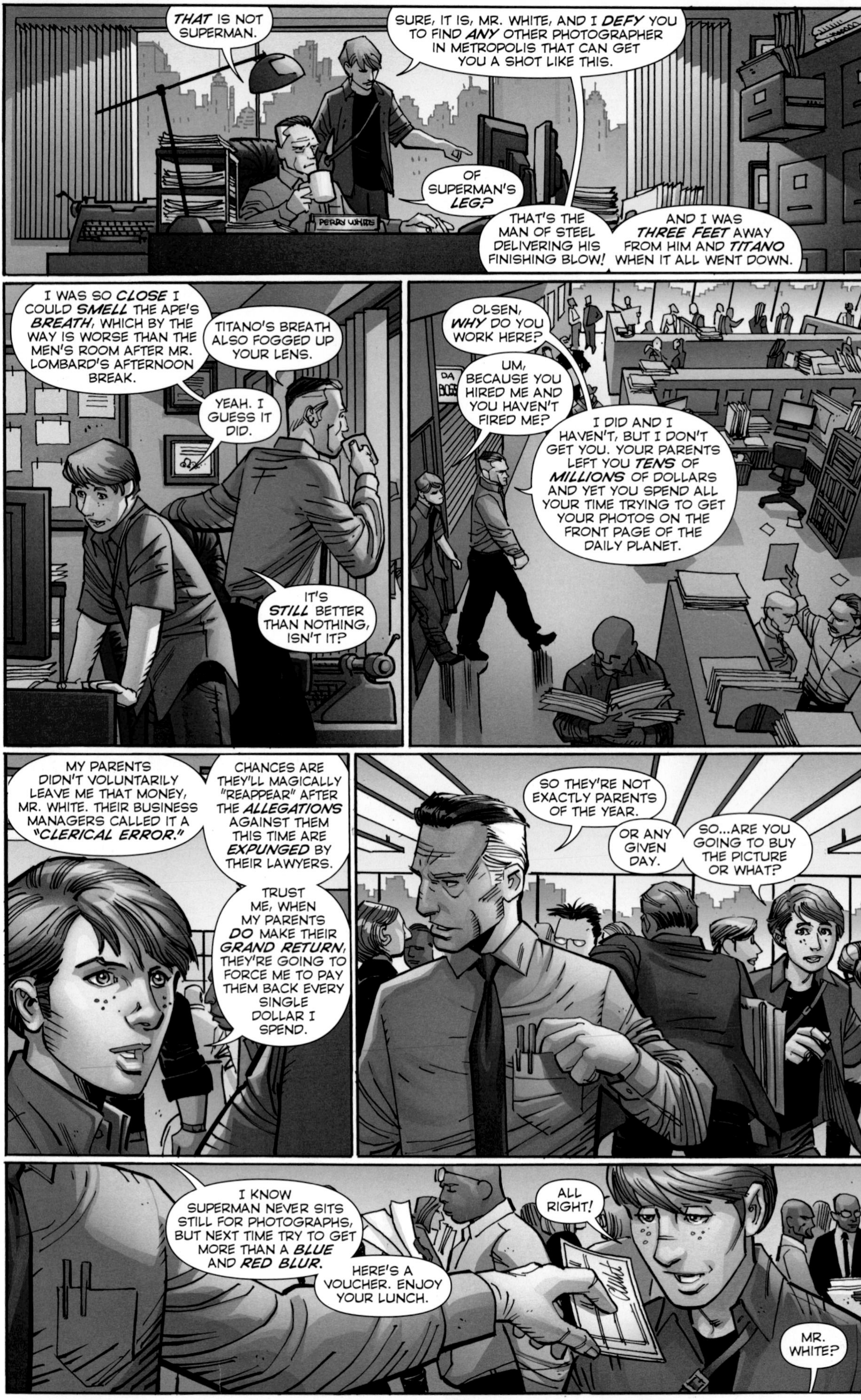
THAT IS NOT SUPERMAN.
SURE, IT IS, MR. WHITE, AND I DEFY YOU TO FIND ANY OTHER PHOTOGRAPHER IN METROPOLIS THAT CAN GET YOU A SHOT LIKE THIS.
PERRY WHITE
OF SUPERMAN'S LEG?
THAT'S THE MAN OF STEEL DELIVERING HIS FINISHING BLOW!
AND I WAS THREE FEET AWAY FROM HIM AND TITANO WHEN IT ALL WENT DOWN.
I WAS SO CLOSE I COULD SMELL THE APE'S BREATH, WHICH BY THE WAY IS WORSE THAN THE MEN'S ROOM AFTER MR. LOMBARD'S AFTERNOON BREAK.
TITANO'S BREATH ALSO FOGGED UP YOUR LENS.
YEAH. I GUESS IT DID.
IT'S STILL BETTER THAN NOTHING, ISN'T IT?
OLSEN, WHY DO YOU WORK HERE?
UM, BECAUSE YOU HIRED ME AND YOU HAVEN'T FIRED ME?
I DID AND I HAVEN'T, BUT I DON'T GET YOU. YOUR PARENTS LEFT YOU TENS OF MILLIONS OF DOLLARS AND YET YOU SPEND ALL YOUR TIME TRYING TO GET YOUR PHOTOS ON THE FRONT PAGE OF THE DAILY PLANET.
MY PARENTS DIDN'T VOLUNTARILY LEAVE ME THAT MONEY, MR. WHITE. THEIR BUSINESS MANAGERS CALLED IT A "CLERICAL ERROR."
CHANCES ARE THEY'LL MAGICALLY "REAPPEAR" AFTER THE ALLEGATIONS AGAINST THEM THIS TIME ARE EXPUNGED BY THEIR LAWYERS.
TRUST ME, WHEN MY PARENTS DO MAKE THEIR GRAND RETURN, THEY'RE GOING TO FORCE ME TO PAY THEM BACK EVERY SINGLE DOLLAR I SPEND.
SO THEY'RE NOT EXACTLY PARENTS OF THE YEAR.
OR ANY GIVEN DAY.
SO...ARE YOU GOING TO BUY THE PICTURE OR WHAT?
I KNOW SUPERMAN NEVER SITS STILL FOR PHOTOGRAPHS, BUT NEXT TIME TRY TO GET MORE THAN A BLUE AND RED BLUR.
HERE'S A VOUCHER. ENJOY YOUR LUNCH.
ALL RIGHT!
MR. WHITE?

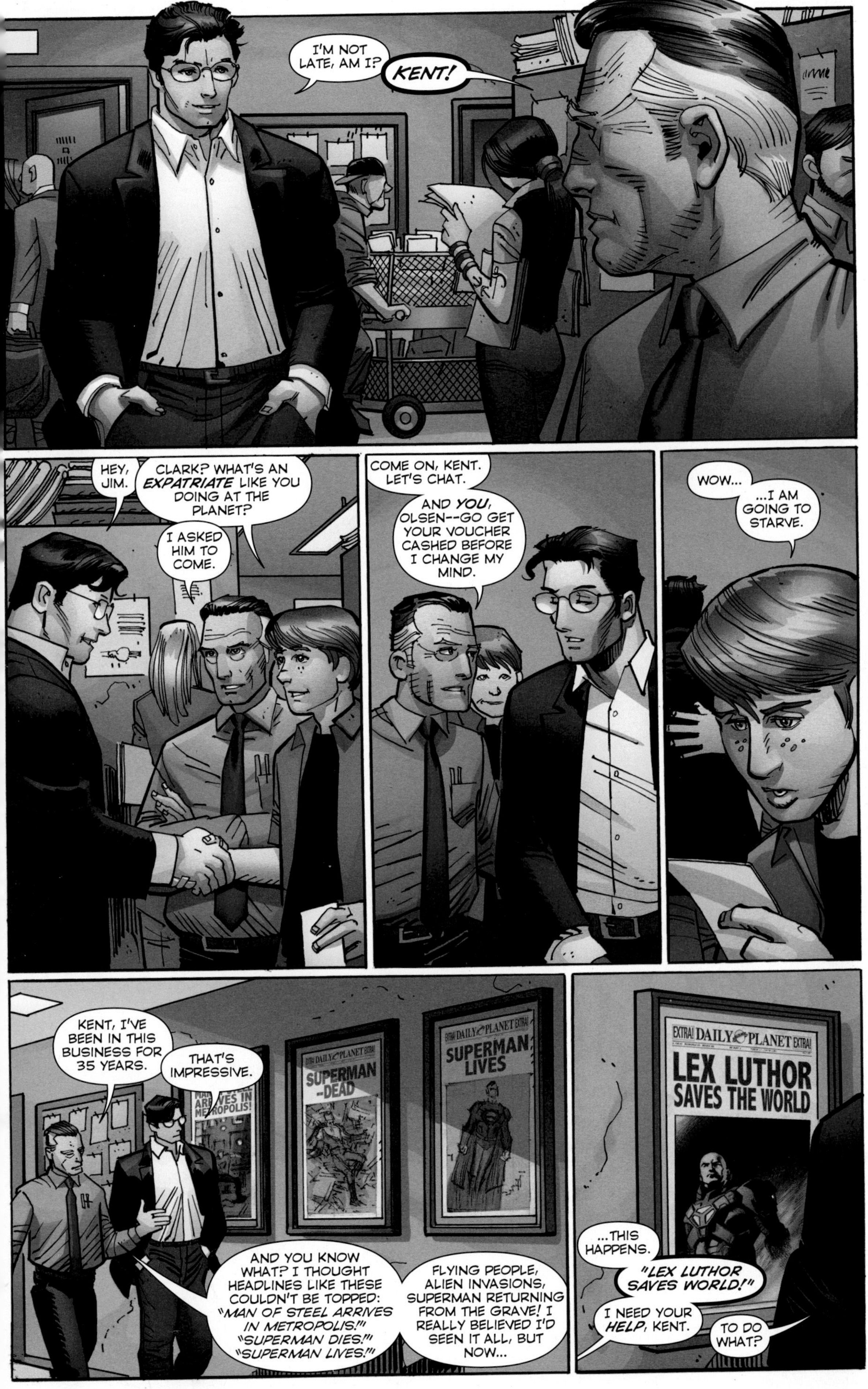
I'M NOT LATE, AM I?
KENT!
HEY, JIM.
CLARK? WHAT'S AN EXPATRIATE LIKE YOU DOING AT THE PLANET?
I ASKED HIM TO COME.
COME ON, KENT. LET'S CHAT.
AND YOU, OLSEN--GO GET YOUR VOUCHER CASHED BEFORE I CHANGE MY MIND.
WOW...
...I AM GOING TO STARVE.
KENT, I'VE BEEN IN THIS BUSINESS FOR 35 YEARS.
THAT'S IMPRESSIVE.
DAILY PLANET
SUPERMAN -DEAD
DAILY PLANET
SUPERMAN LIVES
AND YOU KNOW WHAT? I THOUGHT HEADLINES LIKE THESE COULDN'T BE TOPPED: "MAN OF STEEL ARRIVES IN METROPOLIS!" "SUPERMAN DIES!" "SUPERMAN LIVES!"
FLYING PEOPLE, ALIEN INVASIONS, SUPERMAN RETURNING FROM THE GRAVE! I REALLY BELIEVED I'D SEEN IT ALL, BUT NOW...
EXTRA! DAILY PLANET EXTRA!
LEX LUTHOR SAVES THE WORLD
...THIS HAPPENS.
"LEX LUTHOR SAVES WORLD!"
I NEED YOUR HELP, KENT.
TO DO WHAT?

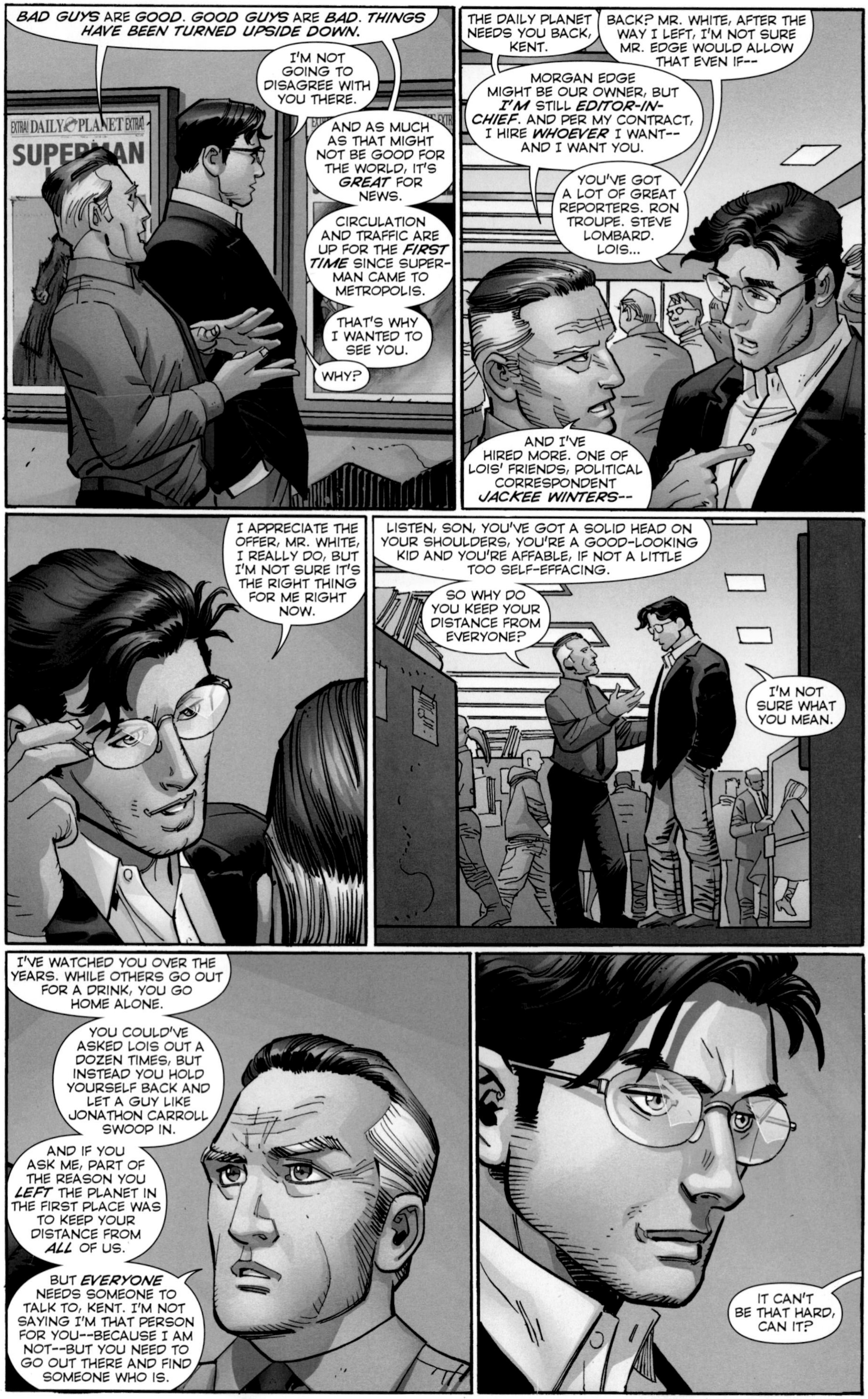

BAD GUYS ARE GOOD. GOOD GUYS ARE BAD. THINGS HAVE BEEN TURNED UPSIDE DOWN.
I'M NOT GOING TO DISAGREE WITH YOU THERE.
AND AS MUCH AS THAT MIGHT NOT BE GOOD FOR THE WORLD, IT'S GREAT FOR NEWS.
CIRCULATION AND TRAFFIC ARE UP FOR THE FIRST TIME SINCE SUPERMAN CAME TO METROPOLIS.
THAT'S WHY I WANTED TO SEE YOU.
WHY?
EXTRA! DAILY PLANET EXTRA!
SUPERMAN
THE DAILY PLANET NEEDS YOU BACK, KENT.
BACK? MR. WHITE, AFTER THE WAY I LEFT, I'M NOT SURE MR. EDGE WOULD ALLOW THAT EVEN IF--
MORGAN EDGE MIGHT BE OUR OWNER, BUT I'M STILL EDITOR-IN-CHIEF. AND PER MY CONTRACT, I HIRE WHOEVER I WANT--AND I WANT YOU.
YOU'VE GOT A LOT OF GREAT REPORTERS. RON TROUPE. STEVE LOMBARD. LOIS...
AND I'VE HIRED MORE. ONE OF LOIS' FRIENDS, POLITICAL CORRESPONDENT JACKEE WINTERS--
I APPRECIATE THE OFFER, MR. WHITE, I REALLY DO, BUT I'M NOT SURE IT'S THE RIGHT THING FOR ME RIGHT NOW.
LISTEN, SON, YOU'VE GOT A SOLID HEAD ON YOUR SHOULDERS, YOU'RE A GOOD-LOOKING KID AND YOU'RE AFFABLE, IF NOT A LITTLE TOO SELF-EFFACING.
SO WHY DO YOU KEEP YOUR DISTANCE FROM EVERYONE?
I'M NOT SURE WHAT YOU MEAN.
I'VE WATCHED YOU OVER THE YEARS. WHILE OTHERS GO OUT FOR A DRINK, YOU GO HOME ALONE.
YOU COULD'VE ASKED LOIS OUT A DOZEN TIMES, BUT INSTEAD YOU HOLD YOURSELF BACK AND LET A GUY LIKE JONATHON CARROLL SWOOP IN.
AND IF YOU ASK ME, PART OF THE REASON YOU LEFT THE PLANET IN THE FIRST PLACE WAS TO KEEP YOUR DISTANCE FROM ALL OF US.
BUT EVERYONE NEEDS SOMEONE TO TALK TO, KENT. I'M NOT SAYING I'M THAT PERSON FOR YOU--BECAUSE I AM NOT--BUT YOU NEED TO GO OUT THERE AND FIND SOMEONE WHO IS.
IT CAN'T BE THAT HARD, CAN IT?

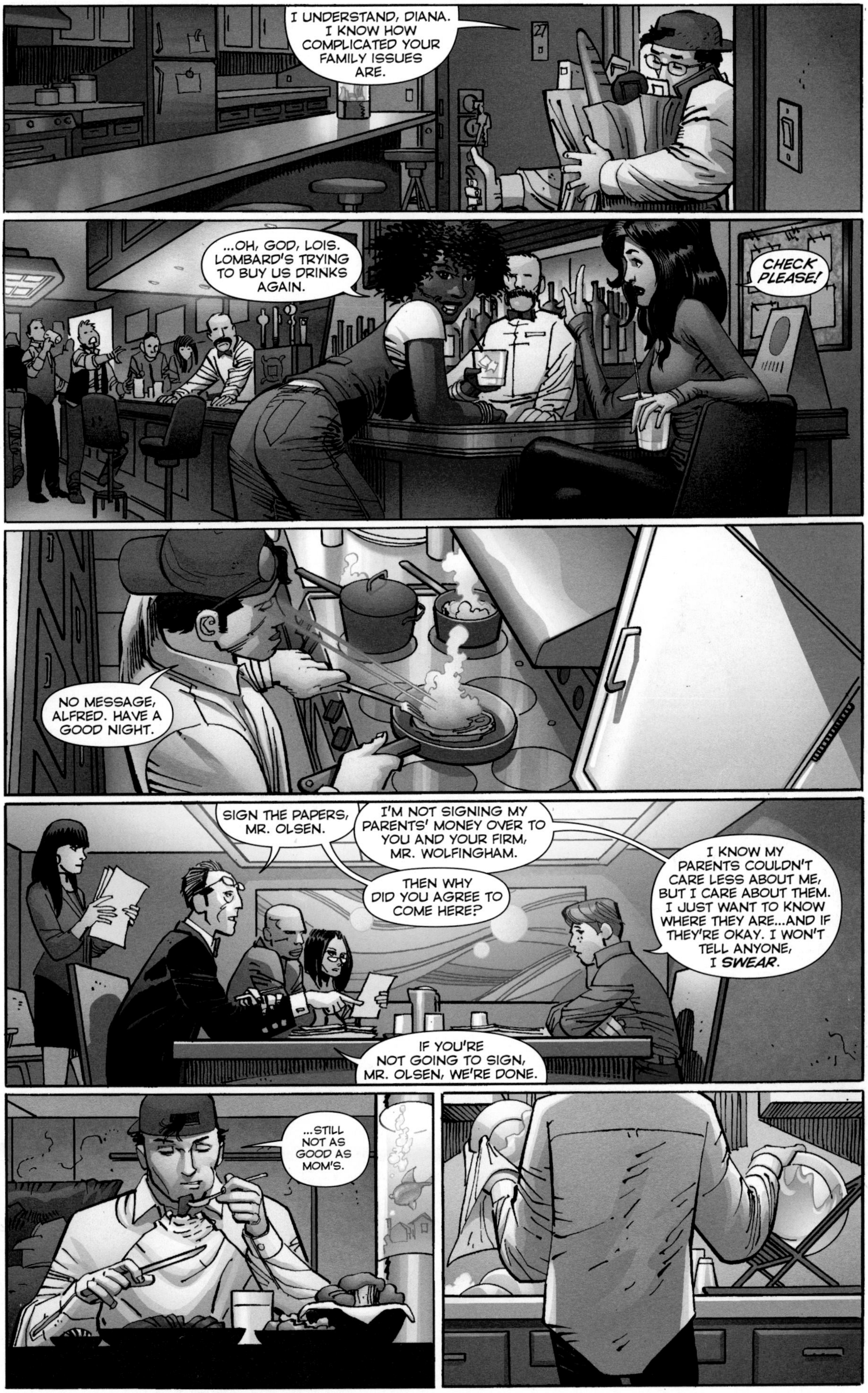

I UNDERSTAND, DIANA. I KNOW HOW COMPLICATED YOUR FAMILY ISSUES ARE.
27
...OH, GOD, LOIS. LOMBARD'S TRYING TO BUY US DRINKS AGAIN.
CHECK PLEASE!
NO MESSAGE, ALFRED. HAVE A GOOD NIGHT.
SIGN THE PAPERS, MR. OLSEN.
I'M NOT SIGNING MY PARENTS' MONEY OVER TO YOU AND YOUR FIRM, MR. WOLFINGHAM.
THEN WHY DID YOU AGREE TO COME HERE?
I KNOW MY PARENTS COULDN'T CARE LESS ABOUT ME, BUT I CARE ABOUT THEM. I JUST WANT TO KNOW WHERE THEY ARE...AND IF THEY'RE OKAY. I WON'T TELL ANYONE, I SWEAR.
IF YOU'RE NOT GOING TO SIGN, MR. OLSEN, WE'RE DONE.
...STILL NOT AS GOOD AS MOM'S.

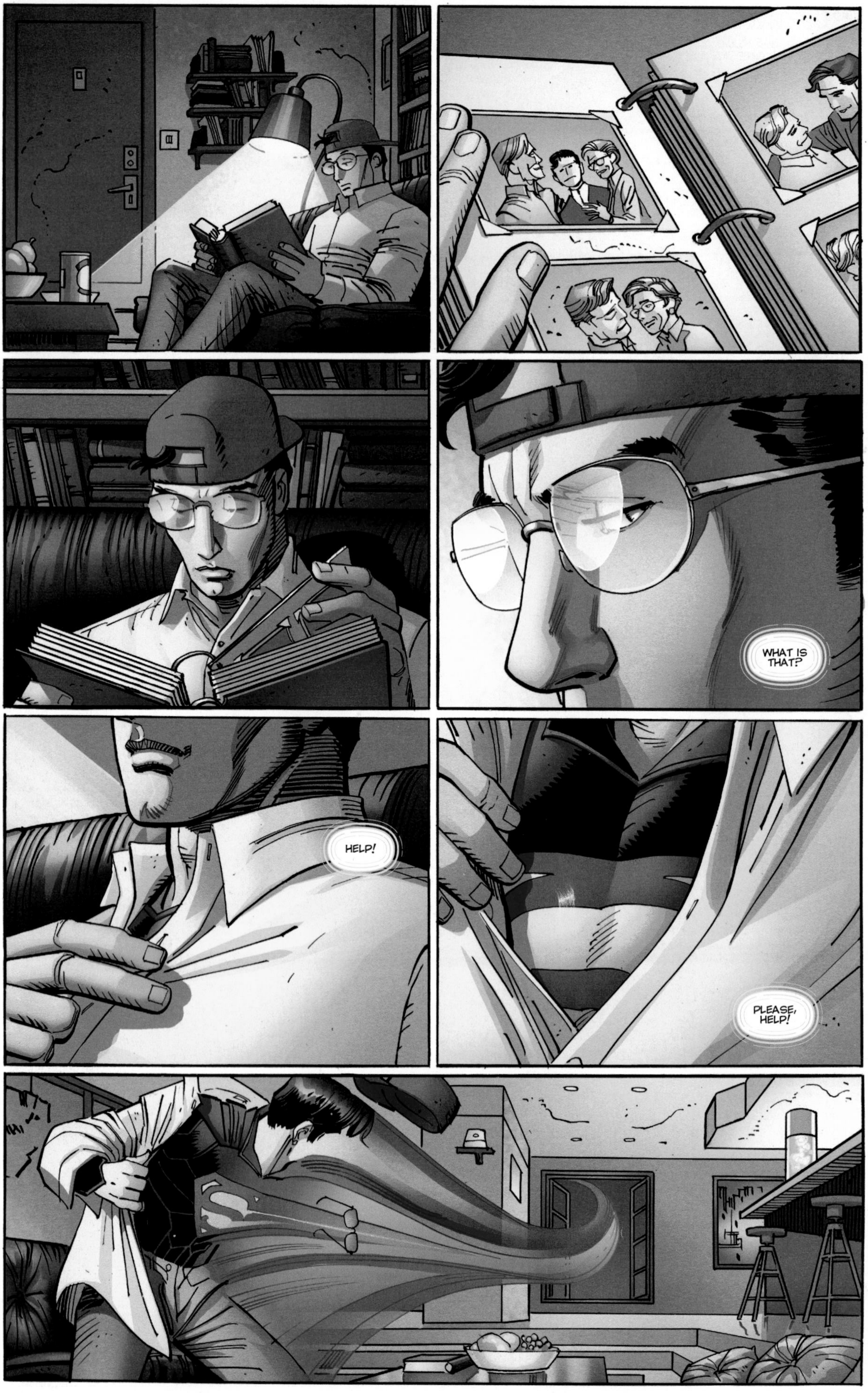
WHAT IS THAT?
HELP!
PLEASE, HELP!

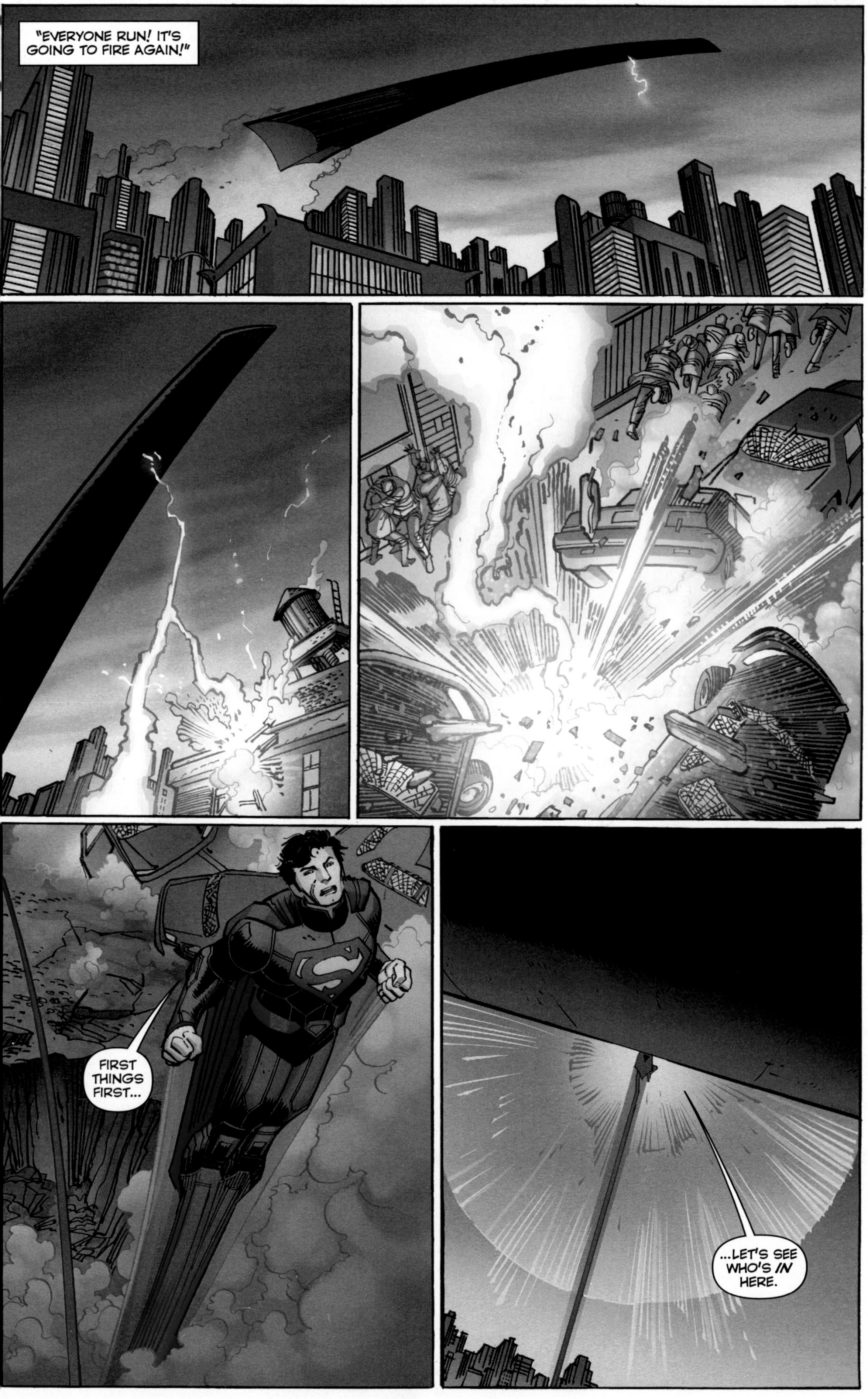
"EVERYONE RUN! IT'S GOING TO FIRE AGAIN!"
FIRST THINGS FIRST...
...LET'S SEE WHO'S *IN* HERE.

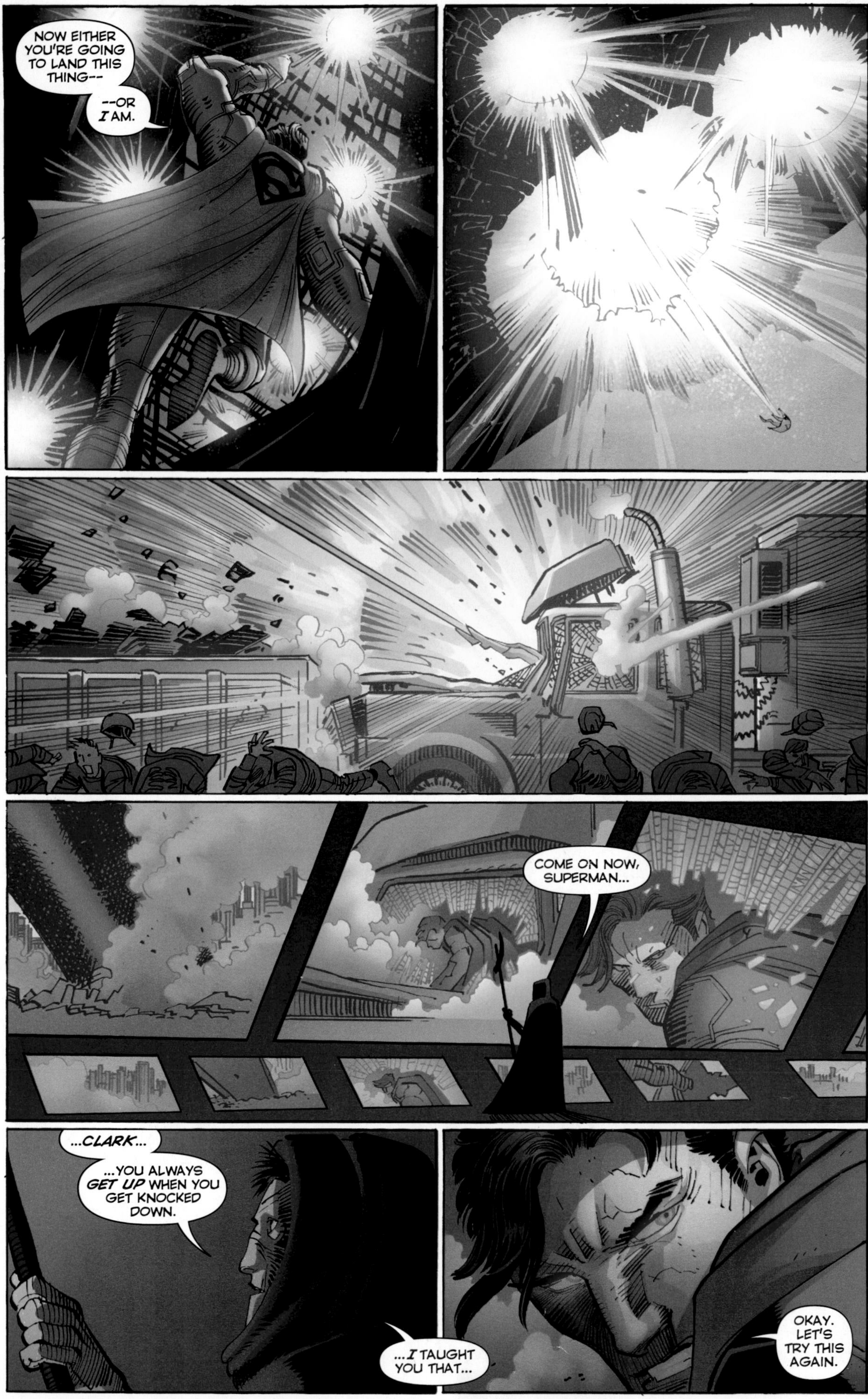
NOW EITHER YOU'RE GOING TO LAND THIS THING--
--OR *I* AM.
COME ON NOW, SUPERMAN...
...*CLARK*...
...YOU ALWAYS *GET UP* WHEN YOU GET KNOCKED DOWN.
...*I* TAUGHT YOU THAT...
OKAY. LET'S TRY THIS AGAIN.

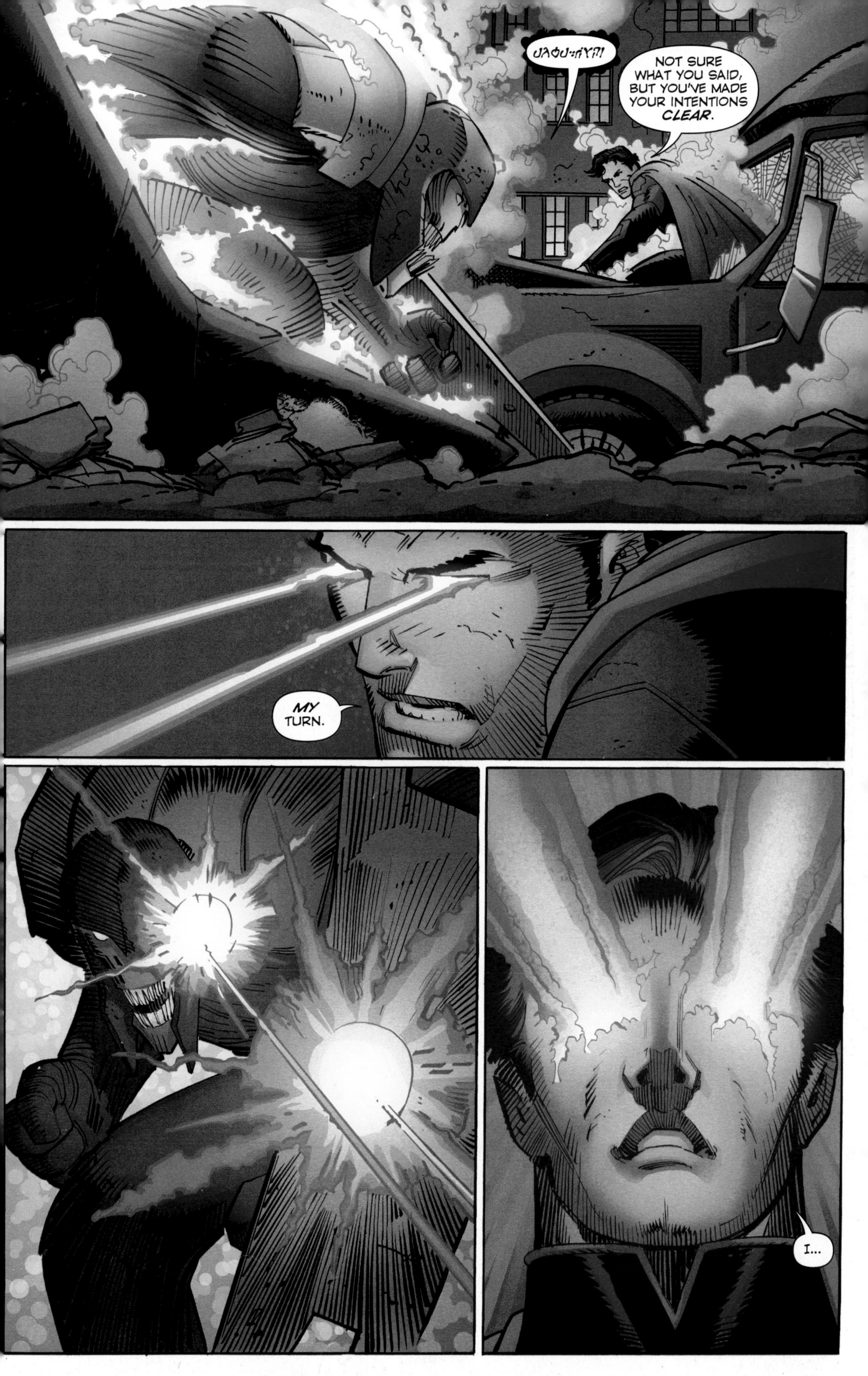
NOT SURE WHAT YOU SAID, BUT YOU'VE MADE YOUR INTENTIONS CLEAR.
MY TURN.
I...

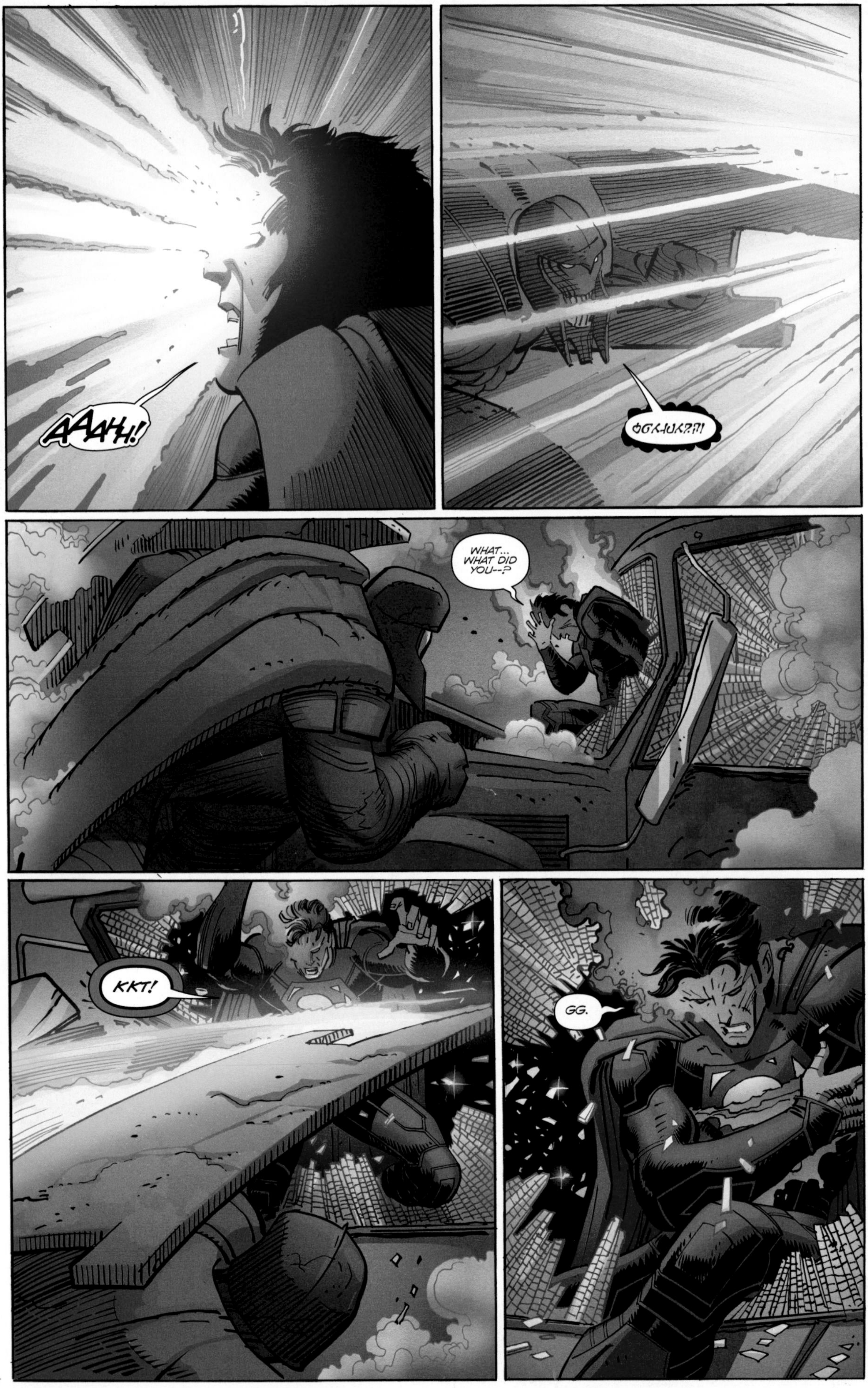
AAAHH!
WHAT... WHAT DID YOU--?
KKT!
GG.

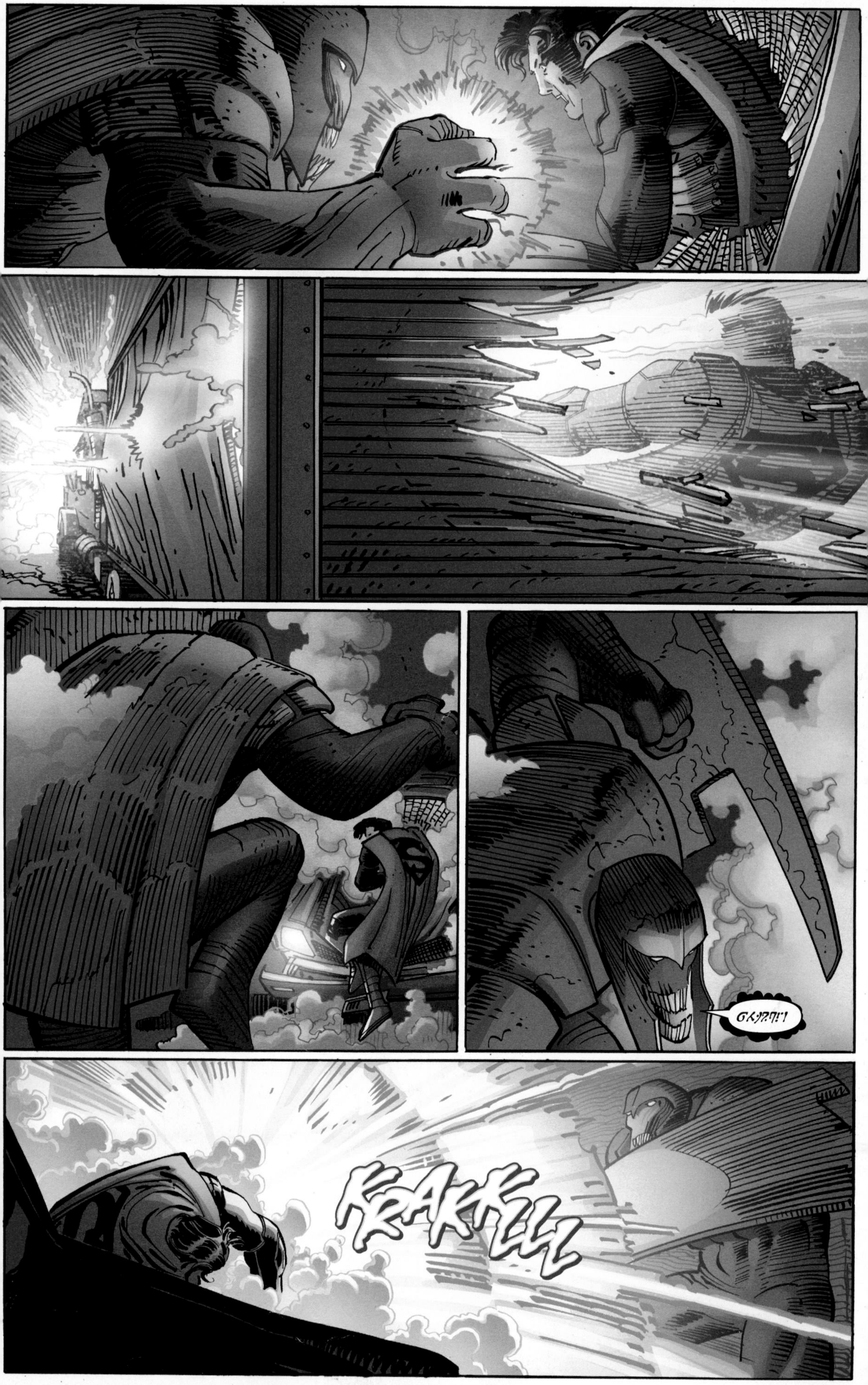
KRAKKLL

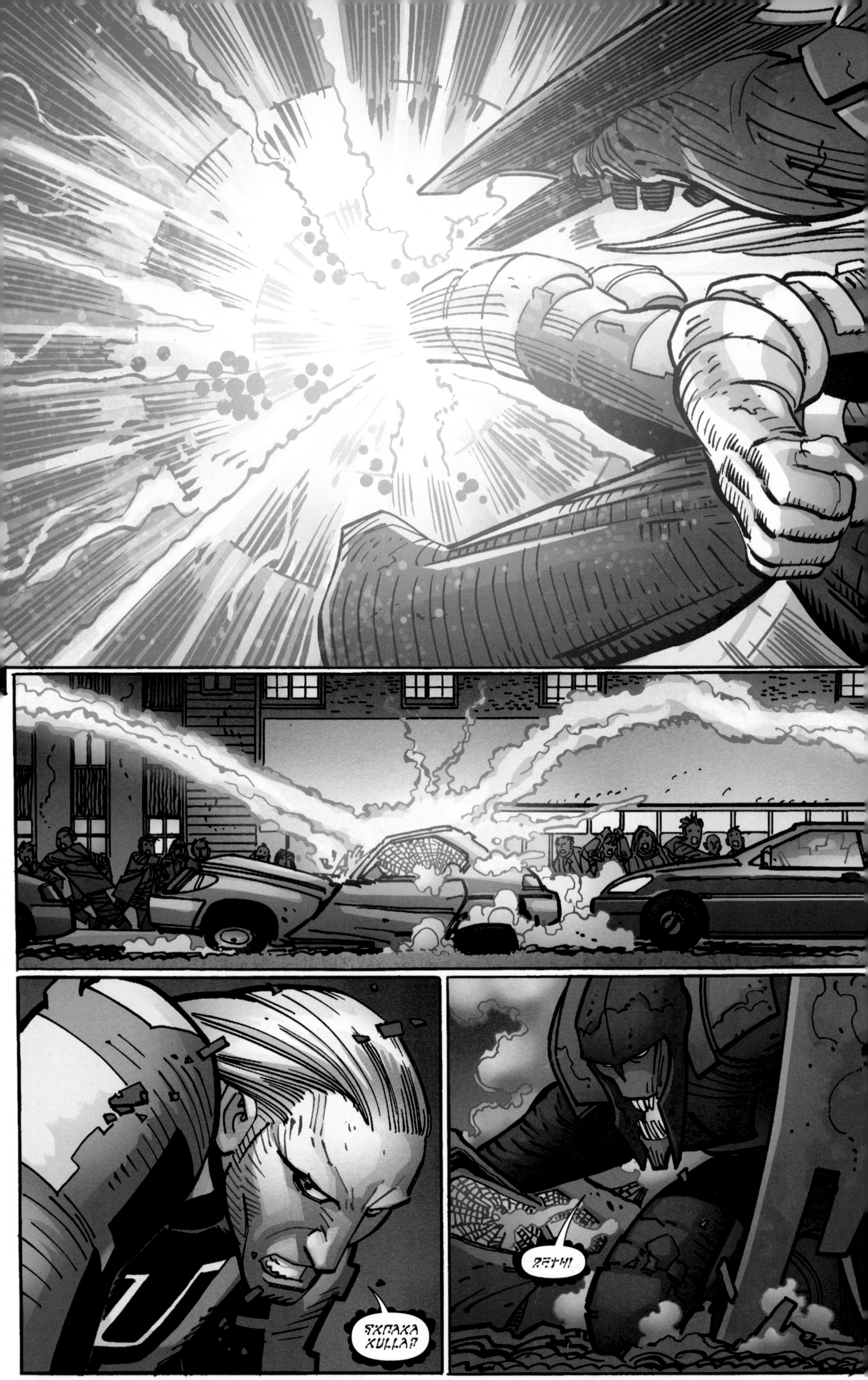

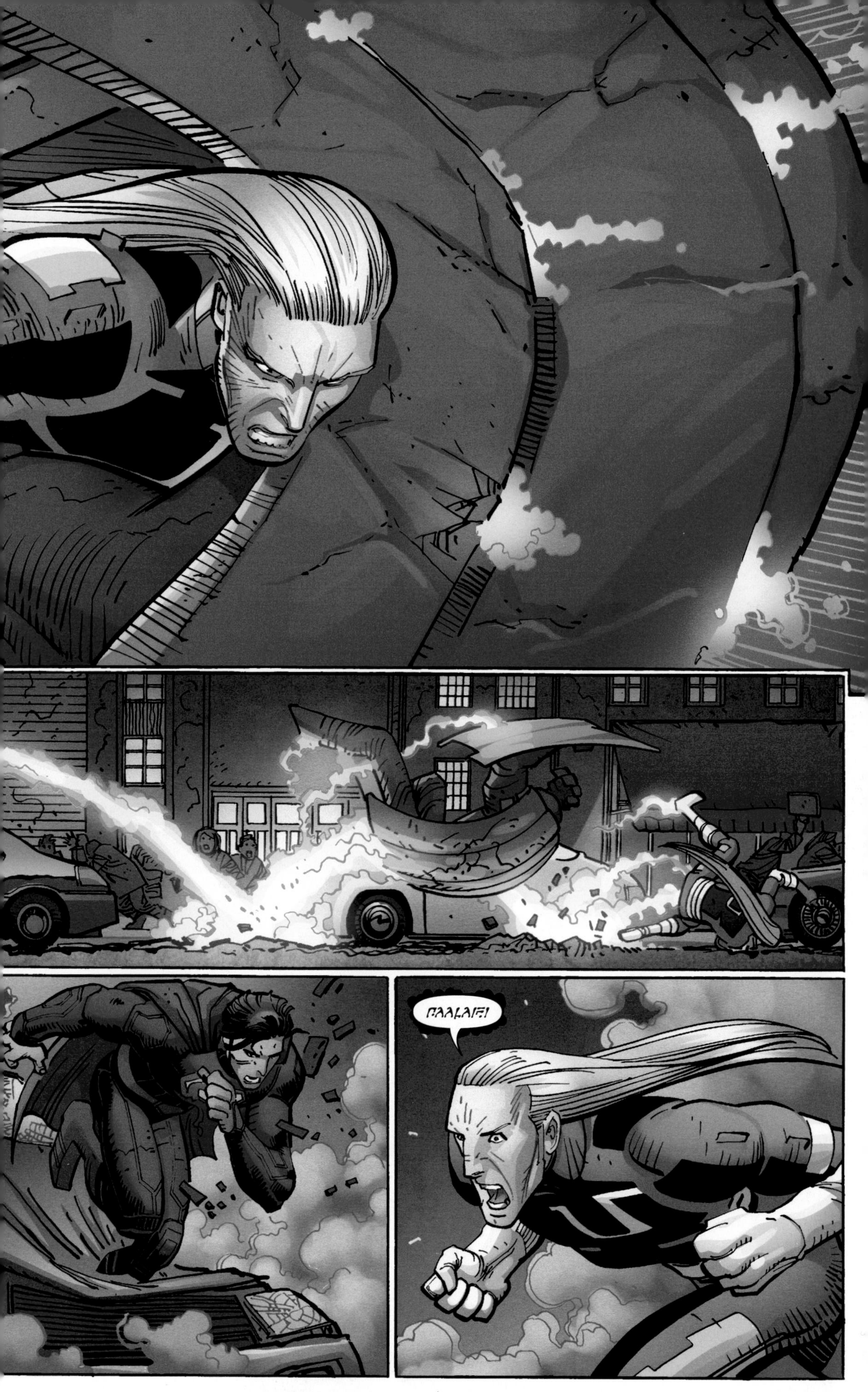

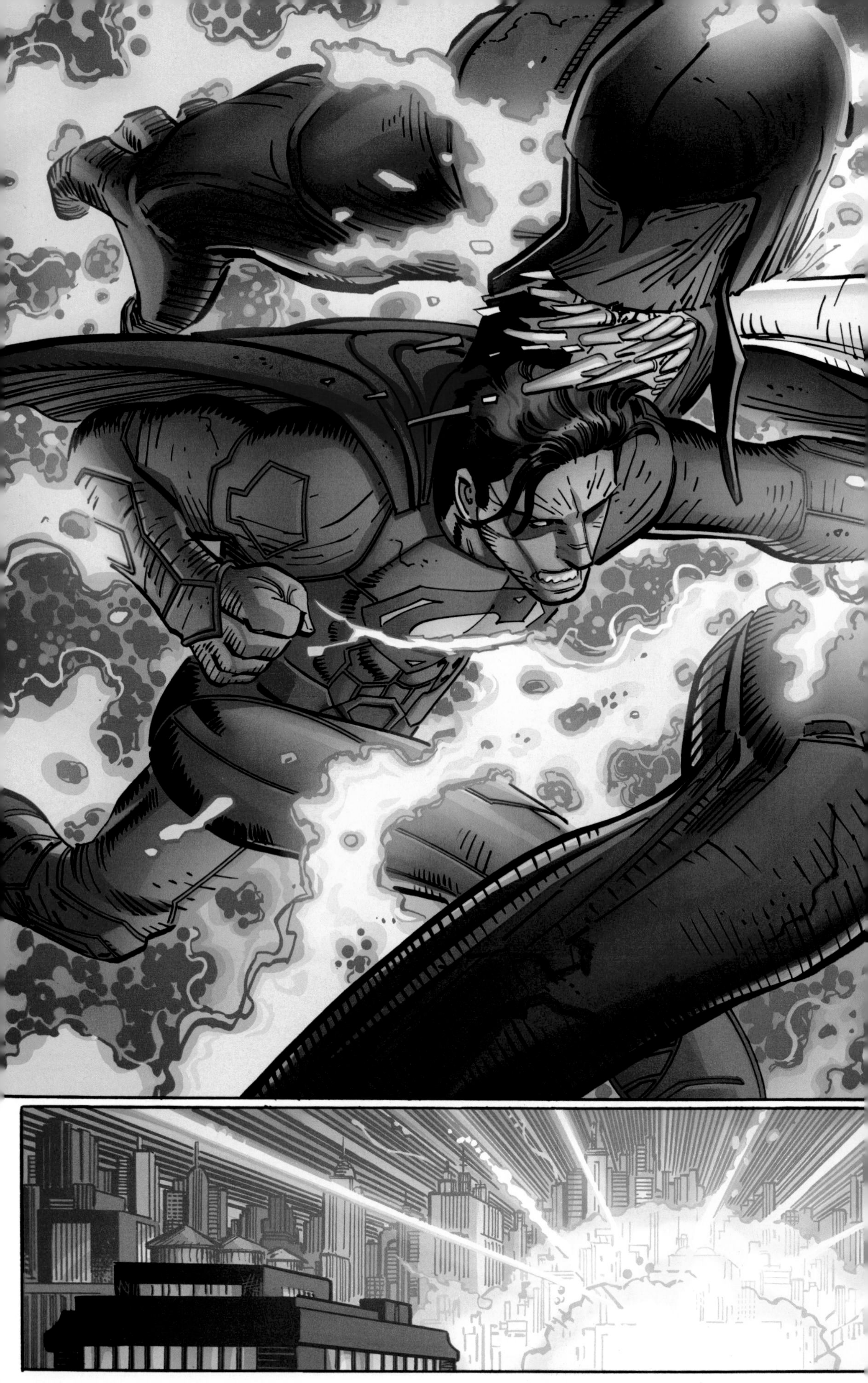

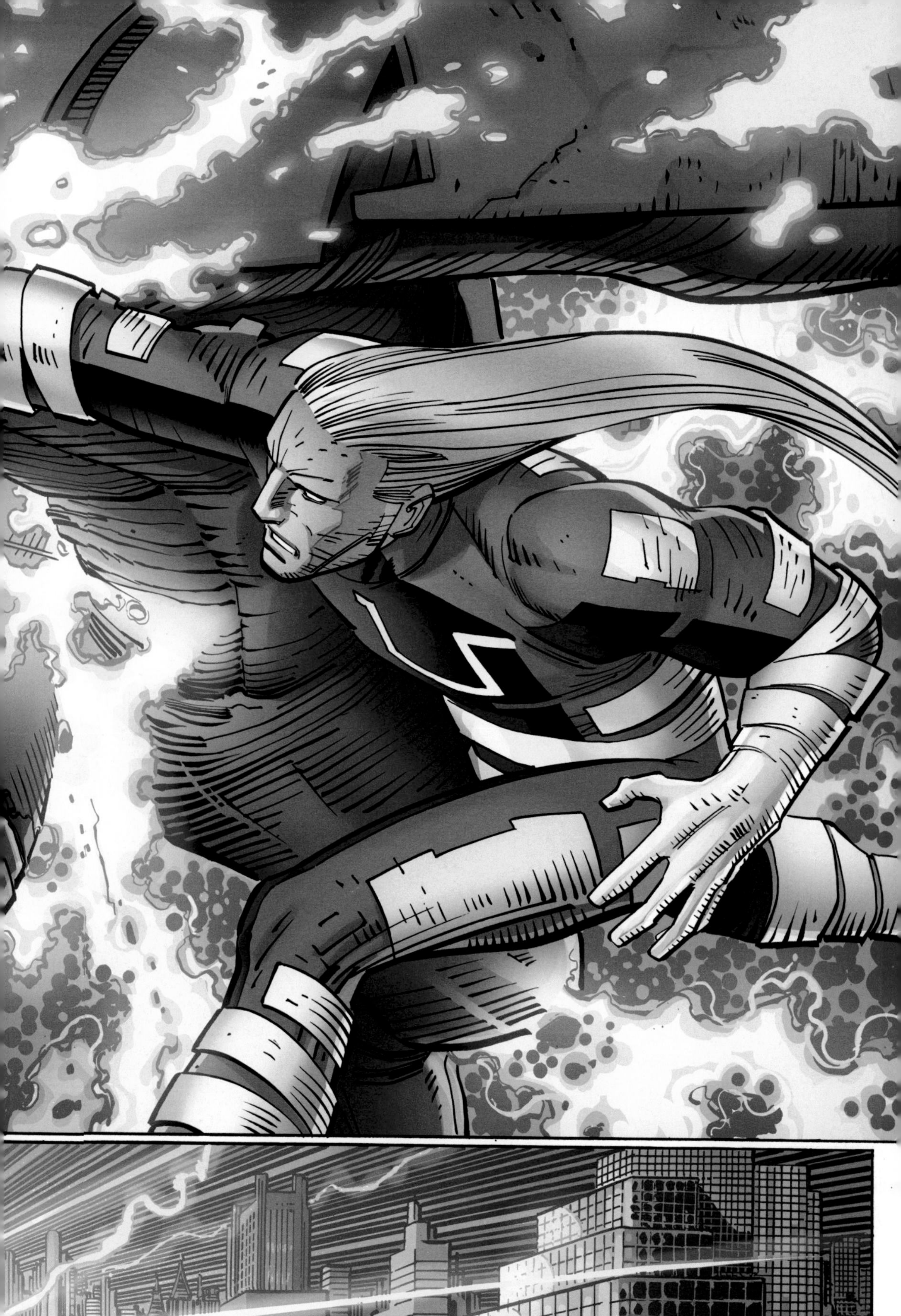
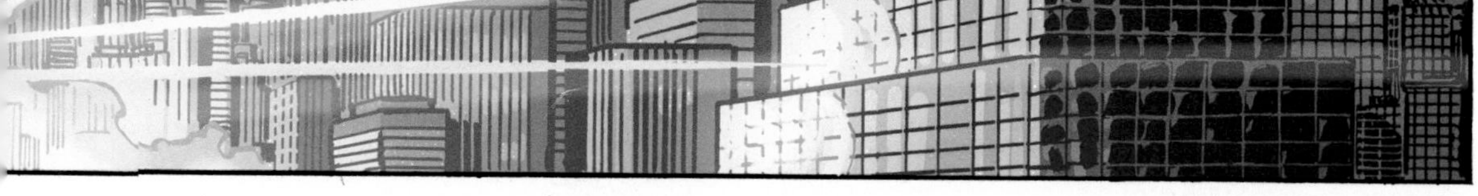

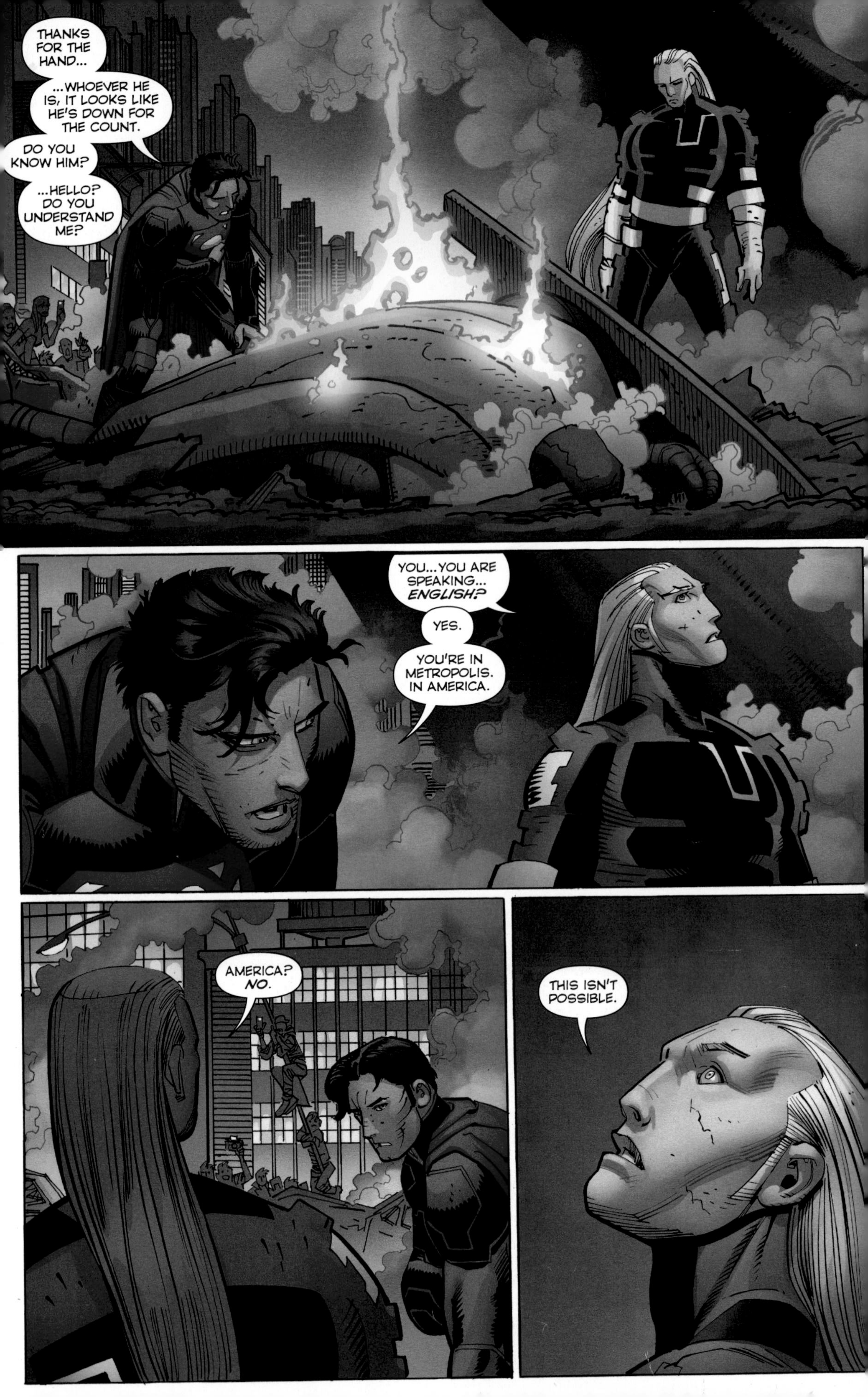
THANKS FOR THE HAND...
...WHOEVER HE IS, IT LOOKS LIKE HE'S DOWN FOR THE COUNT.
DO YOU KNOW HIM?
...HELLO? DO YOU UNDERSTAND ME?
YOU...YOU ARE SPEAKING... *ENGLISH?*
YES.
YOU'RE IN METROPOLIS. IN AMERICA.
AMERICA? *NO.*
THIS ISN'T POSSIBLE.

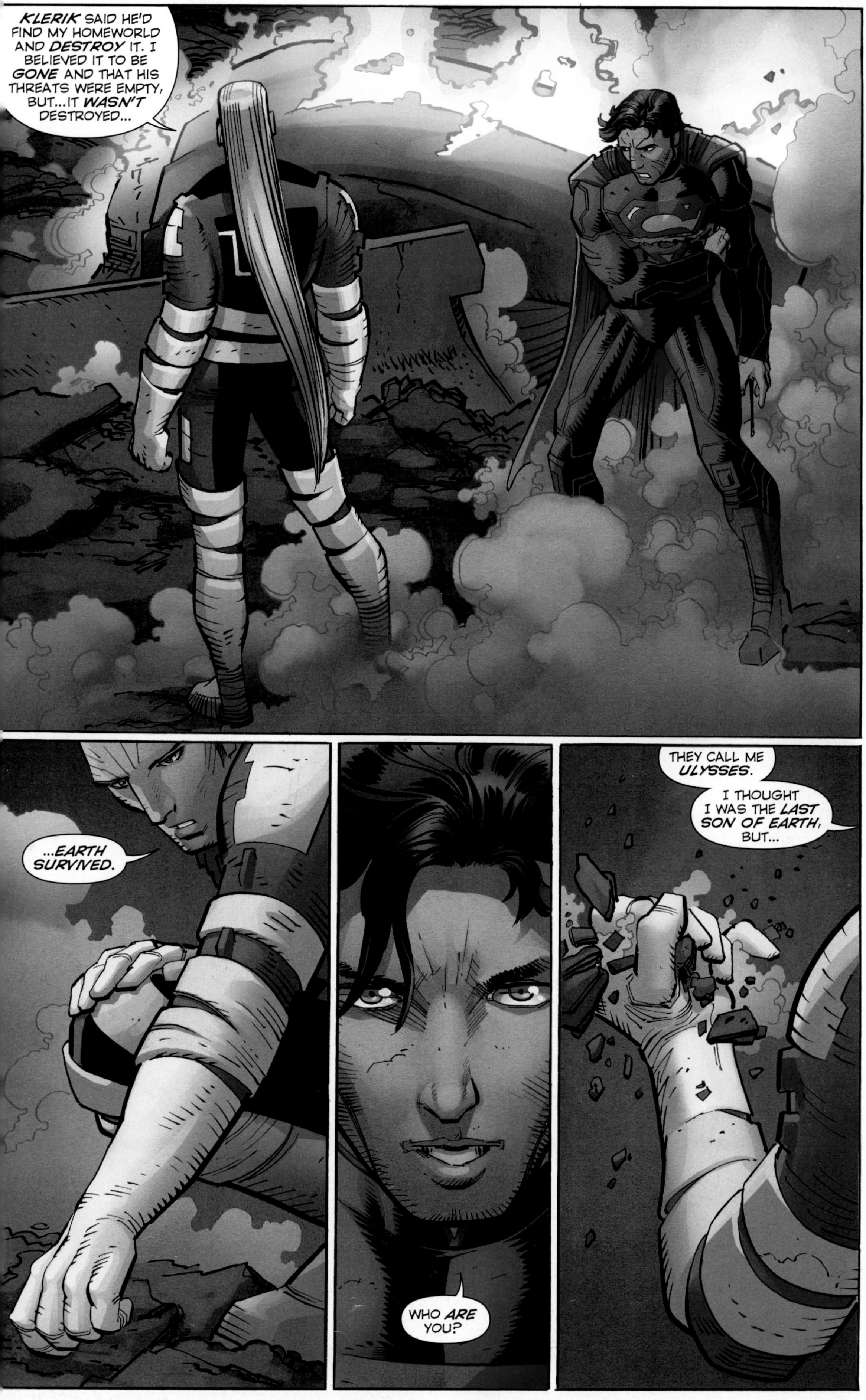
KLERIK SAID HE'D FIND MY HOMEWORLD AND DESTROY IT. I BELIEVED IT TO BE GONE AND THAT HIS THREATS WERE EMPTY, BUT...IT WASN'T DESTROYED...
...EARTH SURVIVED.
WHO ARE YOU?
THEY CALL ME ULYSSES.
I THOUGHT I WAS THE LAST SON OF EARTH, BUT...

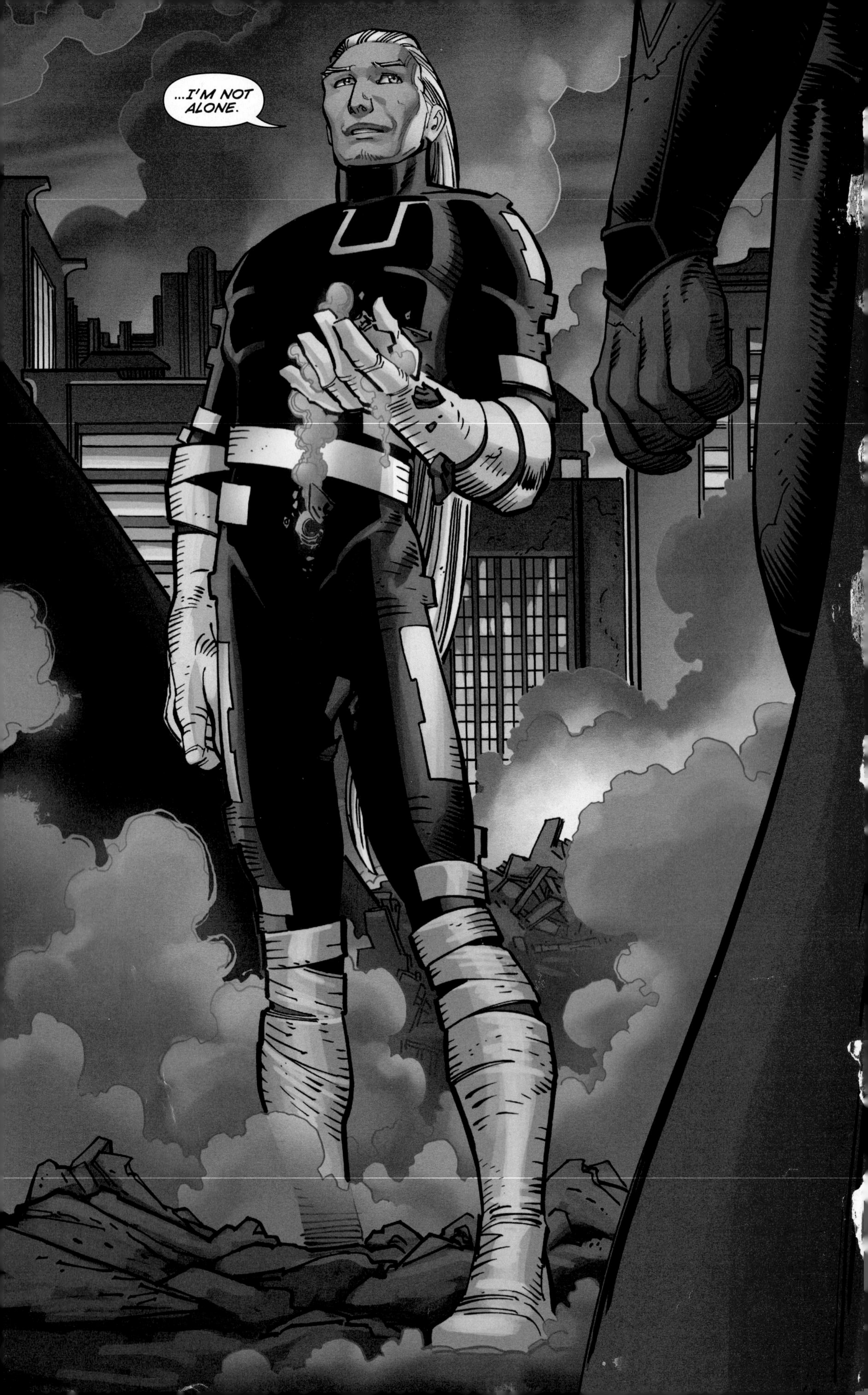
...I'M NOT ALONE.

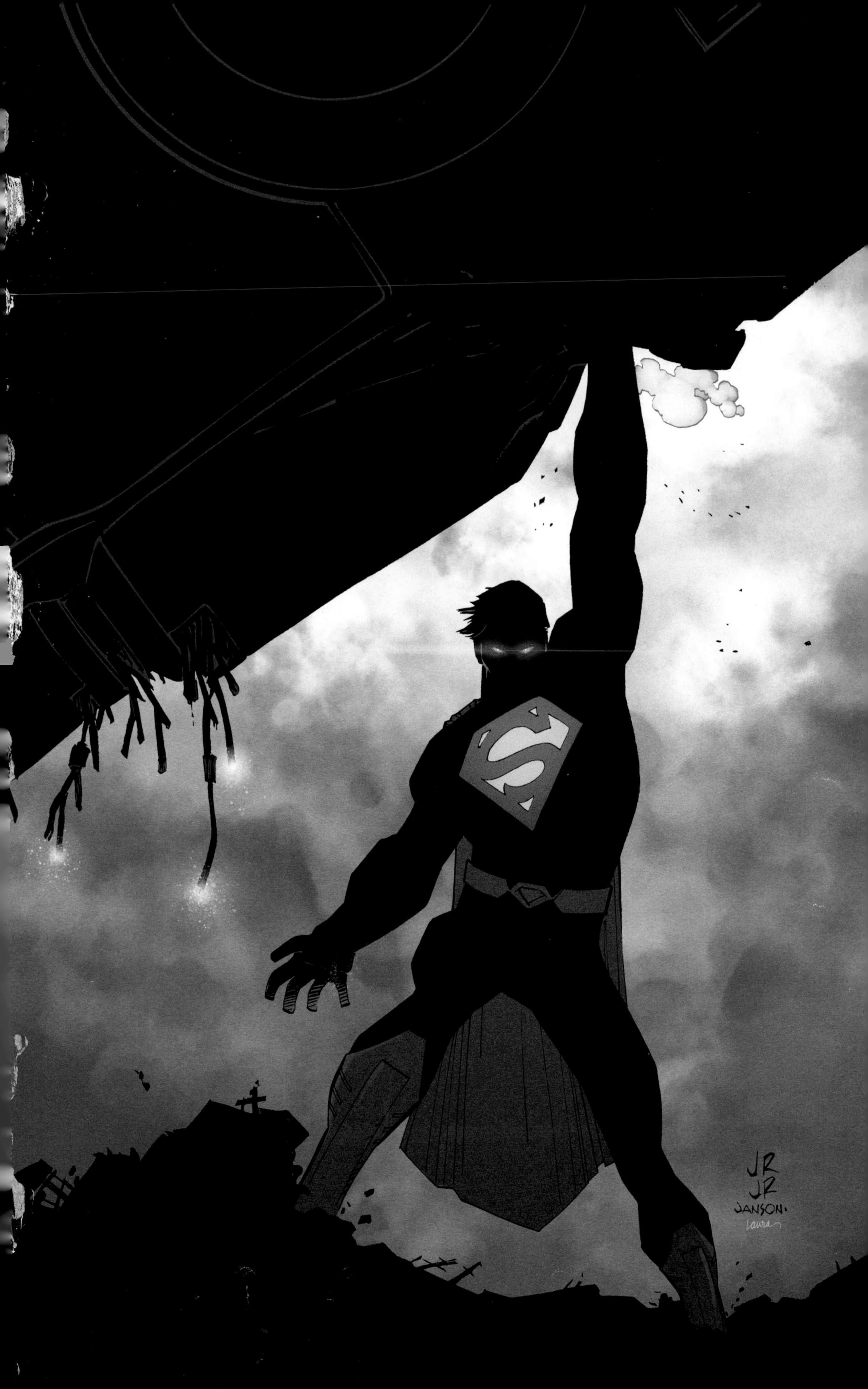
JR JR
JANSON
Laura

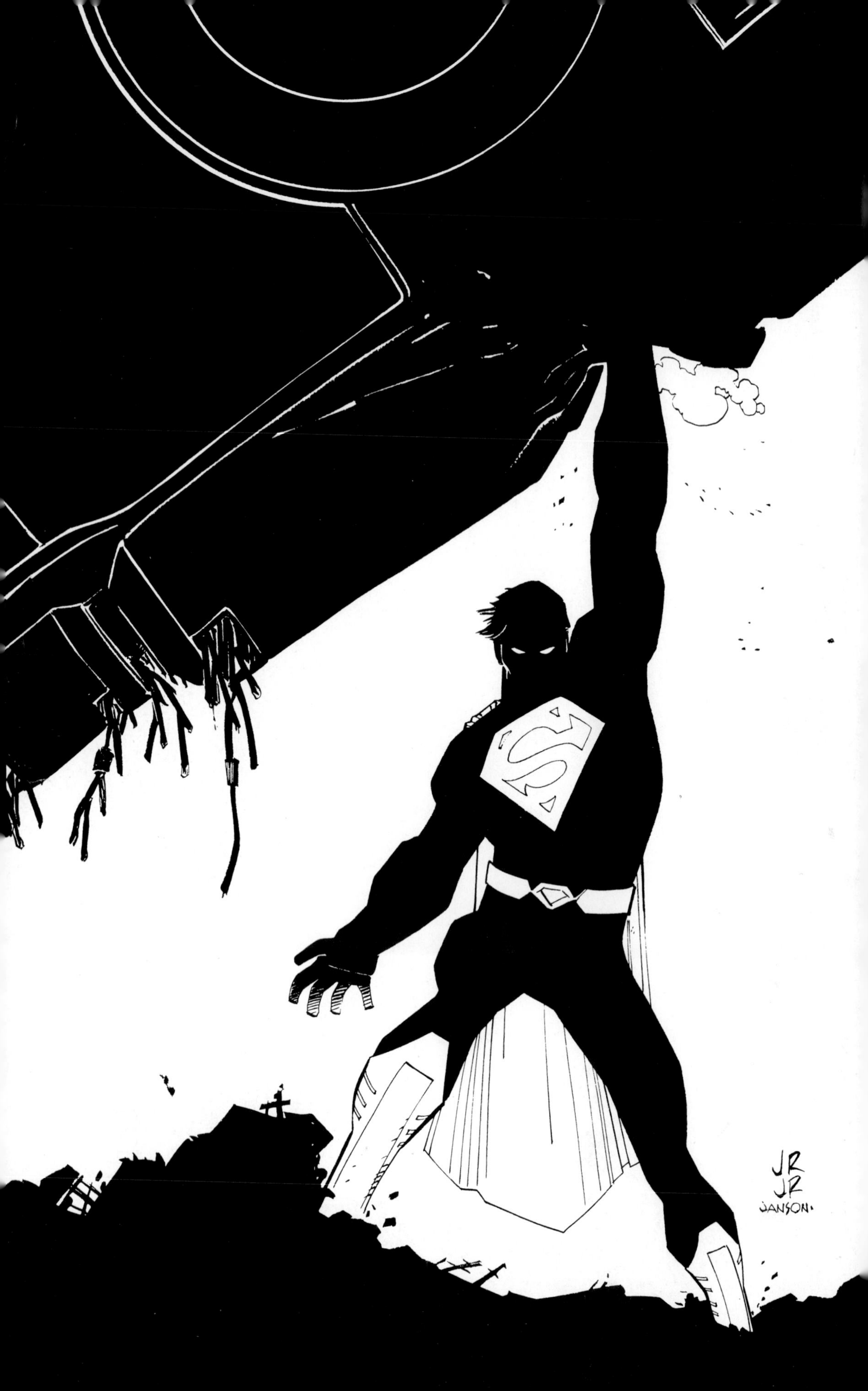
JR JR
JANSON.

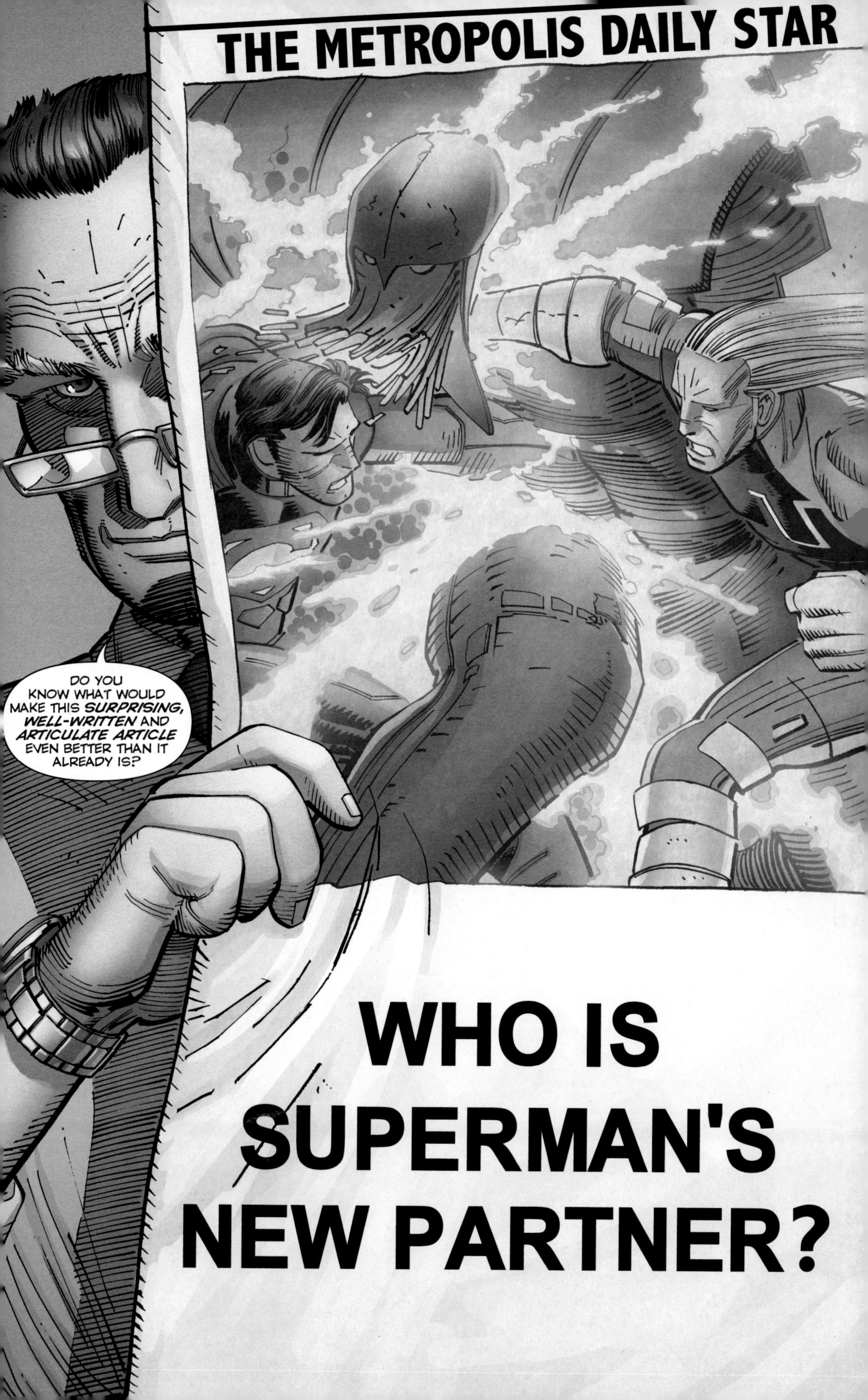
THE METROPOLIS DAILY STAR
DO YOU KNOW WHAT WOULD MAKE THIS SURPRISING, WELL-WRITTEN AND ARTICULATE ARTICLE EVEN BETTER THAN IT ALREADY IS?
WHO IS SUPERMAN'S NEW PARTNER?

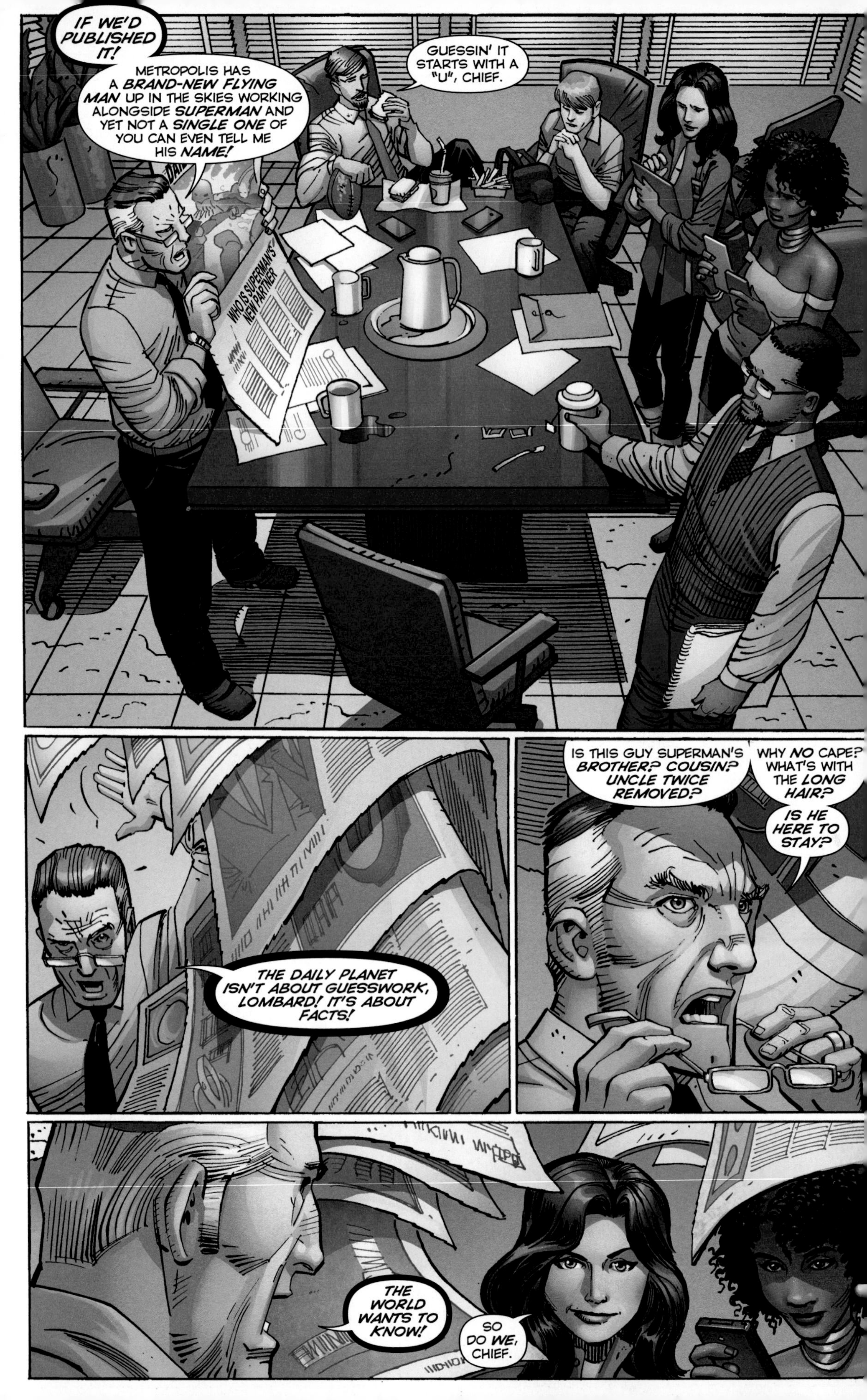
IF WE'D PUBLISHED IT!
METROPOLIS HAS A BRAND-NEW FLYING MAN UP IN THE SKIES WORKING ALONGSIDE SUPERMAN AND YET NOT A SINGLE ONE OF YOU CAN EVEN TELL ME HIS NAME!
GUESSIN' IT STARTS WITH A "U", CHIEF.
WHO IS SUPERMAN'S NEW PARTNER
THE DAILY PLANET ISN'T ABOUT GUESSWORK, LOMBARD! IT'S ABOUT FACTS!
IS THIS GUY SUPERMAN'S BROTHER? COUSIN? UNCLE TWICE REMOVED?
WHY NO CAPE? WHAT'S WITH THE LONG HAIR?
IS HE HERE TO STAY?
THE WORLD WANTS TO KNOW!
SO DO WE, CHIEF.

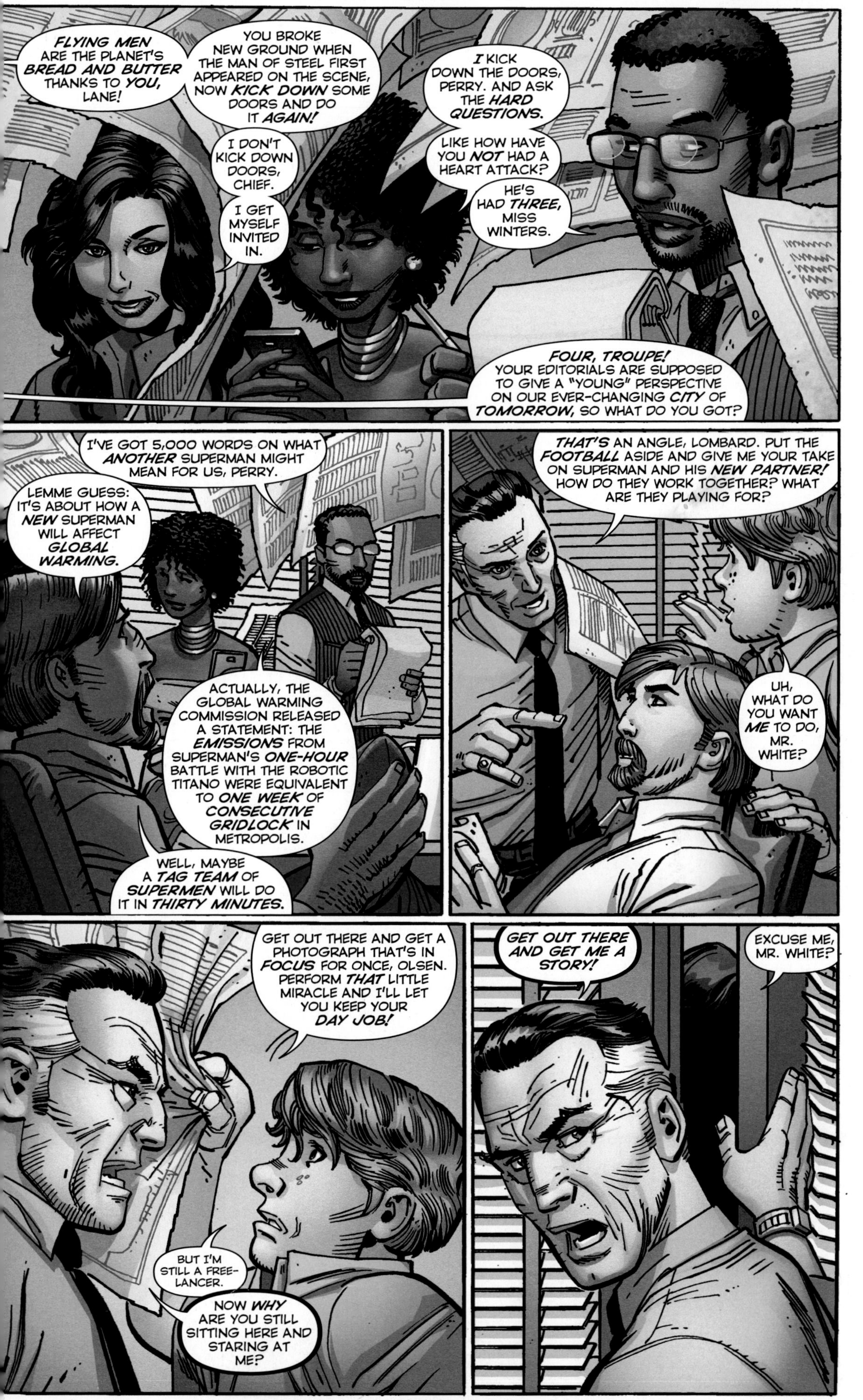
FLYING MEN ARE THE PLANET'S BREAD AND BUTTER THANKS TO YOU, LANE!
YOU BROKE NEW GROUND WHEN THE MAN OF STEEL FIRST APPEARED ON THE SCENE, NOW KICK DOWN SOME DOORS AND DO IT AGAIN!
I DON'T KICK DOWN DOORS, CHIEF.
I GET MYSELF INVITED IN.
I KICK DOWN THE DOORS, PERRY. AND ASK THE HARD QUESTIONS.
LIKE HOW HAVE YOU NOT HAD A HEART ATTACK?
HE'S HAD THREE, MISS WINTERS.
FOUR, TROUPE! YOUR EDITORIALS ARE SUPPOSED TO GIVE A "YOUNG" PERSPECTIVE ON OUR EVER-CHANGING CITY OF TOMORROW, SO WHAT DO YOU GOT?
I'VE GOT 5,000 WORDS ON WHAT ANOTHER SUPERMAN MIGHT MEAN FOR US, PERRY.
LEMME GUESS: IT'S ABOUT HOW A NEW SUPERMAN WILL AFFECT GLOBAL WARMING.
ACTUALLY, THE GLOBAL WARMING COMMISSION RELEASED A STATEMENT: THE EMISSIONS FROM SUPERMAN'S ONE-HOUR BATTLE WITH THE ROBOTIC TITANO WERE EQUIVALENT TO ONE WEEK OF CONSECUTIVE GRIDLOCK IN METROPOLIS.
WELL, MAYBE A TAG TEAM OF SUPERMEN WILL DO IT IN THIRTY MINUTES.
THAT'S AN ANGLE, LOMBARD. PUT THE FOOTBALL ASIDE AND GIVE ME YOUR TAKE ON SUPERMAN AND HIS NEW PARTNER! HOW DO THEY WORK TOGETHER? WHAT ARE THEY PLAYING FOR?
UH, WHAT DO YOU WANT ME TO DO, MR. WHITE?
GET OUT THERE AND GET A PHOTOGRAPH THAT'S IN FOCUS FOR ONCE, OLSEN. PERFORM THAT LITTLE MIRACLE AND I'LL LET YOU KEEP YOUR DAY JOB!
BUT I'M STILL A FREE-LANCER.
NOW WHY ARE YOU STILL SITTING HERE AND STARING AT ME?
GET OUT THERE AND GET ME A STORY!
EXCUSE ME, MR. WHITE?

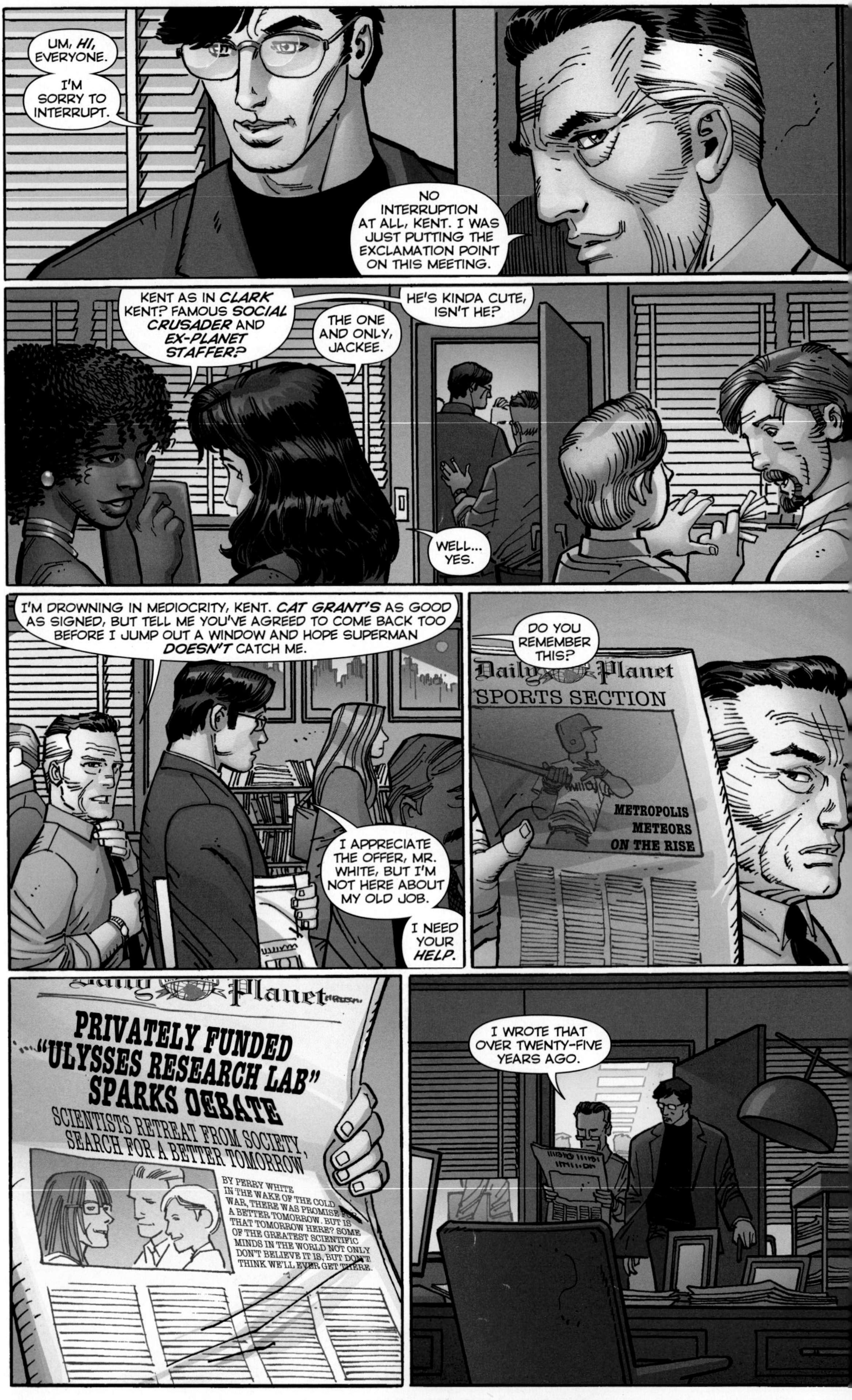
UM, *HI*, EVERYONE.
I'M SORRY TO INTERRUPT.
NO INTERRUPTION AT ALL, KENT. I WAS JUST PUTTING THE EXCLAMATION POINT ON THIS MEETING.
KENT AS IN *CLARK* KENT? FAMOUS *SOCIAL CRUSADER* AND *EX-PLANET STAFFER?*
THE ONE AND ONLY, JACKEE.
HE'S KINDA CUTE, ISN'T HE?
WELL... YES.
I'M DROWNING IN MEDIOCRITY, KENT. *CAT GRANT'S* AS GOOD AS SIGNED, BUT TELL ME YOU'VE AGREED TO COME BACK TOO BEFORE I JUMP OUT A WINDOW AND HOPE SUPERMAN *DOESN'T* CATCH ME.
I APPRECIATE THE OFFER, MR. WHITE, BUT I'M NOT HERE ABOUT MY OLD JOB.
I NEED YOUR *HELP*.
DO YOU REMEMBER THIS?
Daily Planet
SPORTS SECTION
METROPOLIS METEORS ON THE RISE
Planet
PRIVATELY FUNDED "ULYSSES RESEARCH LAB" SPARKS DEBATE
SCIENTISTS RETREAT FROM SOCIETY, SEARCH FOR A BETTER TOMORROW
BY PERRY WHITE
IN THE WAKE OF THE COLD WAR, THERE WAS PROMISE FOR A BETTER TOMORROW. BUT IS THAT TOMORROW HERE? SOME OF THE GREATEST SCIENTIFIC MINDS IN THE WORLD NOT ONLY DON'T BELIEVE IT IS, BUT DON'T THINK WE'LL EVER GET THERE.
I WROTE THAT OVER TWENTY-FIVE YEARS AGO.

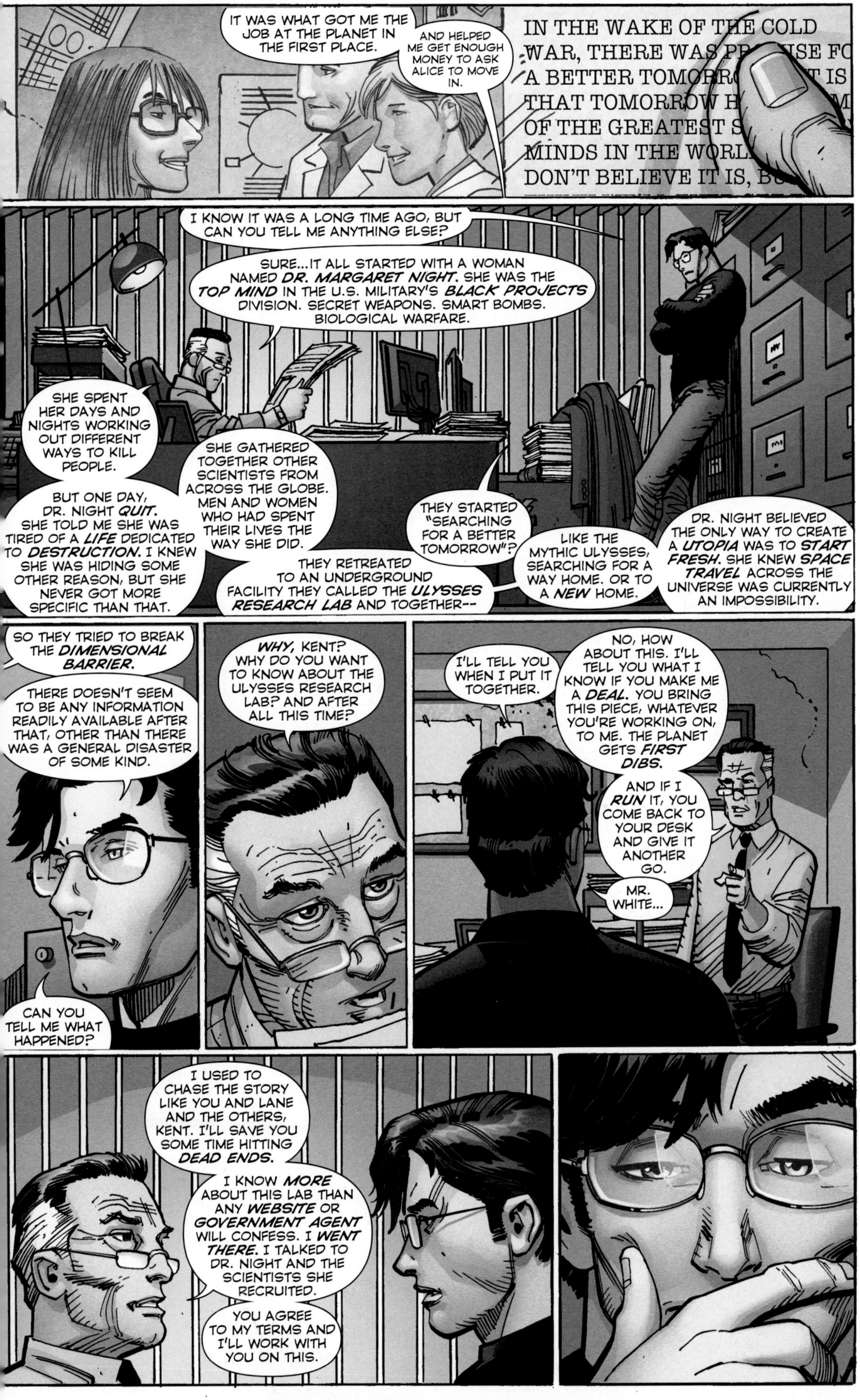
IT WAS WHAT GOT ME THE JOB AT THE PLANET IN THE FIRST PLACE.
AND HELPED ME GET ENOUGH MONEY TO ASK ALICE TO MOVE IN.
IN THE WAKE OF THE COLD
WAR, THERE WAS PR
A BETTER TOMORRO
THAT TOMORROW H
OF THE GREATEST S
MINDS IN THE WORL
DON'T BELIEVE IT IS, BU
I KNOW IT WAS A LONG TIME AGO, BUT CAN YOU TELL ME ANYTHING ELSE?
SURE...IT ALL STARTED WITH A WOMAN NAMED DR. MARGARET NIGHT. SHE WAS THE TOP MIND IN THE U.S. MILITARY'S BLACK PROJECTS DIVISION. SECRET WEAPONS. SMART BOMBS. BIOLOGICAL WARFARE.
SHE SPENT HER DAYS AND NIGHTS WORKING OUT DIFFERENT WAYS TO KILL PEOPLE.
BUT ONE DAY, DR. NIGHT QUIT. SHE TOLD ME SHE WAS TIRED OF A LIFE DEDICATED TO DESTRUCTION. I KNEW SHE WAS HIDING SOME OTHER REASON, BUT SHE NEVER GOT MORE SPECIFIC THAN THAT.
SHE GATHERED TOGETHER OTHER SCIENTISTS FROM ACROSS THE GLOBE. MEN AND WOMEN WHO HAD SPENT THEIR LIVES THE WAY SHE DID.
THEY RETREATED TO AN UNDERGROUND FACILITY THEY CALLED THE ULYSSES RESEARCH LAB AND TOGETHER--
THEY STARTED "SEARCHING FOR A BETTER TOMORROW"?
LIKE THE MYTHIC ULYSSES, SEARCHING FOR A WAY HOME. OR TO A NEW HOME.
DR. NIGHT BELIEVED THE ONLY WAY TO CREATE A UTOPIA WAS TO START FRESH. SHE KNEW SPACE TRAVEL ACROSS THE UNIVERSE WAS CURRENTLY AN IMPOSSIBILITY.
SO THEY TRIED TO BREAK THE DIMENSIONAL BARRIER.
THERE DOESN'T SEEM TO BE ANY INFORMATION READILY AVAILABLE AFTER THAT, OTHER THAN THERE WAS A GENERAL DISASTER OF SOME KIND.
CAN YOU TELL ME WHAT HAPPENED?
WHY, KENT? WHY DO YOU WANT TO KNOW ABOUT THE ULYSSES RESEARCH LAB? AND AFTER ALL THIS TIME?
I'LL TELL YOU WHEN I PUT IT TOGETHER.
NO, HOW ABOUT THIS. I'LL TELL YOU WHAT I KNOW IF YOU MAKE ME A DEAL. YOU BRING THIS PIECE, WHATEVER YOU'RE WORKING ON, TO ME. THE PLANET GETS FIRST DIBS.
AND IF I RUN IT, YOU COME BACK TO YOUR DESK AND GIVE IT ANOTHER GO.
MR. WHITE...
I USED TO CHASE THE STORY LIKE YOU AND LANE AND THE OTHERS, KENT. I'LL SAVE YOU SOME TIME HITTING DEAD ENDS.
I KNOW MORE ABOUT THIS LAB THAN ANY WEBSITE OR GOVERNMENT AGENT WILL CONFESS. I WENT THERE. I TALKED TO DR. NIGHT AND THE SCIENTISTS SHE RECRUITED.
YOU AGREE TO MY TERMS AND I'LL WORK WITH YOU ON THIS.

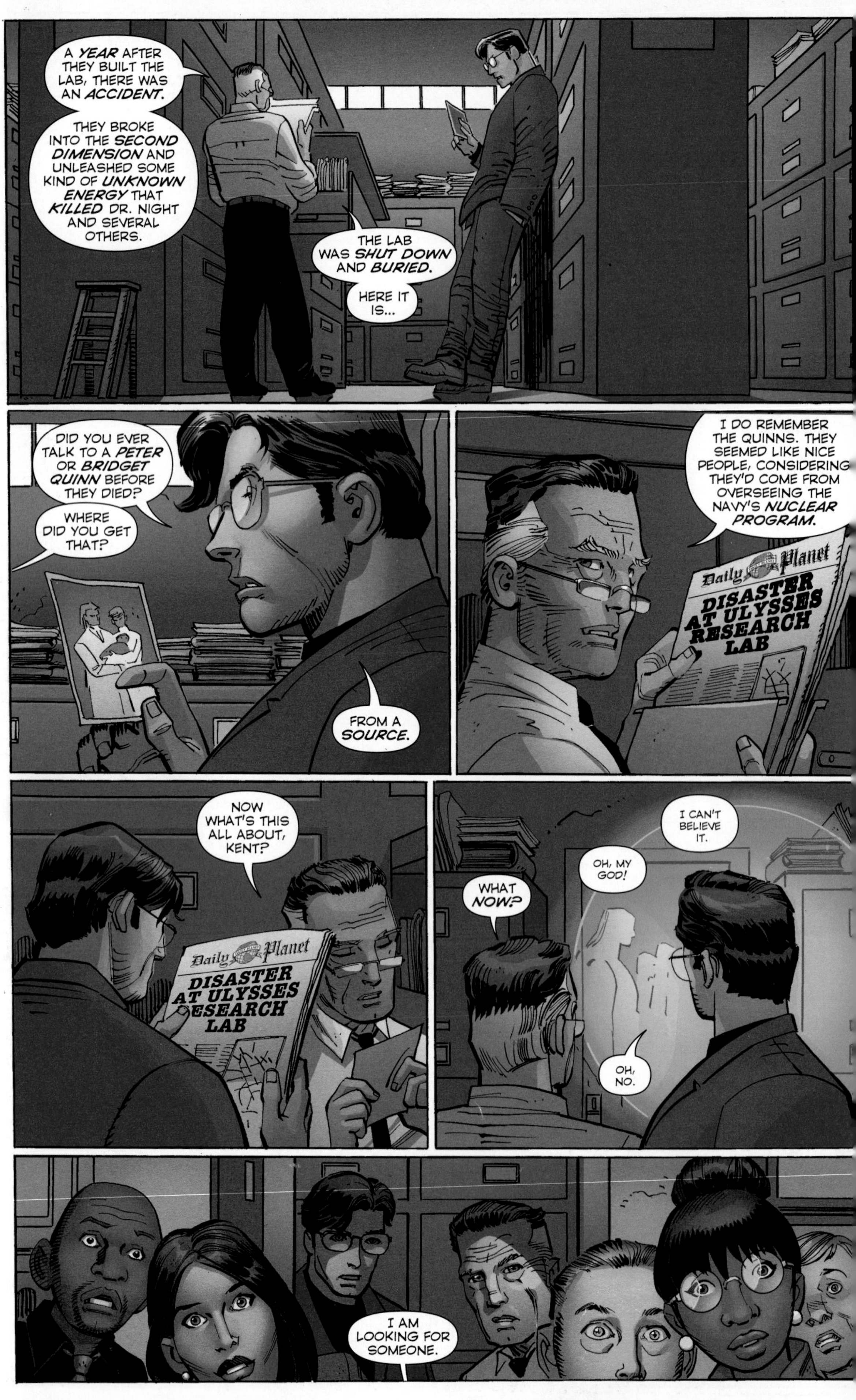
A YEAR AFTER THEY BUILT THE LAB, THERE WAS AN ACCIDENT.
THEY BROKE INTO THE SECOND DIMENSION AND UNLEASHED SOME KIND OF UNKNOWN ENERGY THAT KILLED DR. NIGHT AND SEVERAL OTHERS.
THE LAB WAS SHUT DOWN AND BURIED.
HERE IT IS...
DID YOU EVER TALK TO A PETER OR BRIDGET QUINN BEFORE THEY DIED?
WHERE DID YOU GET THAT?
FROM A SOURCE.
I DO REMEMBER THE QUINNS. THEY SEEMED LIKE NICE PEOPLE, CONSIDERING THEY'D COME FROM OVERSEEING THE NAVY'S NUCLEAR PROGRAM.
Daily Planet
DISASTER AT ULYSSES RESEARCH LAB
NOW WHAT'S THIS ALL ABOUT, KENT?
Daily Planet
DISASTER AT ULYSSES RESEARCH LAB
I CAN'T BELIEVE IT.
OH, MY GOD!
WHAT NOW?
OH, NO.
I AM LOOKING FOR SOMEONE.

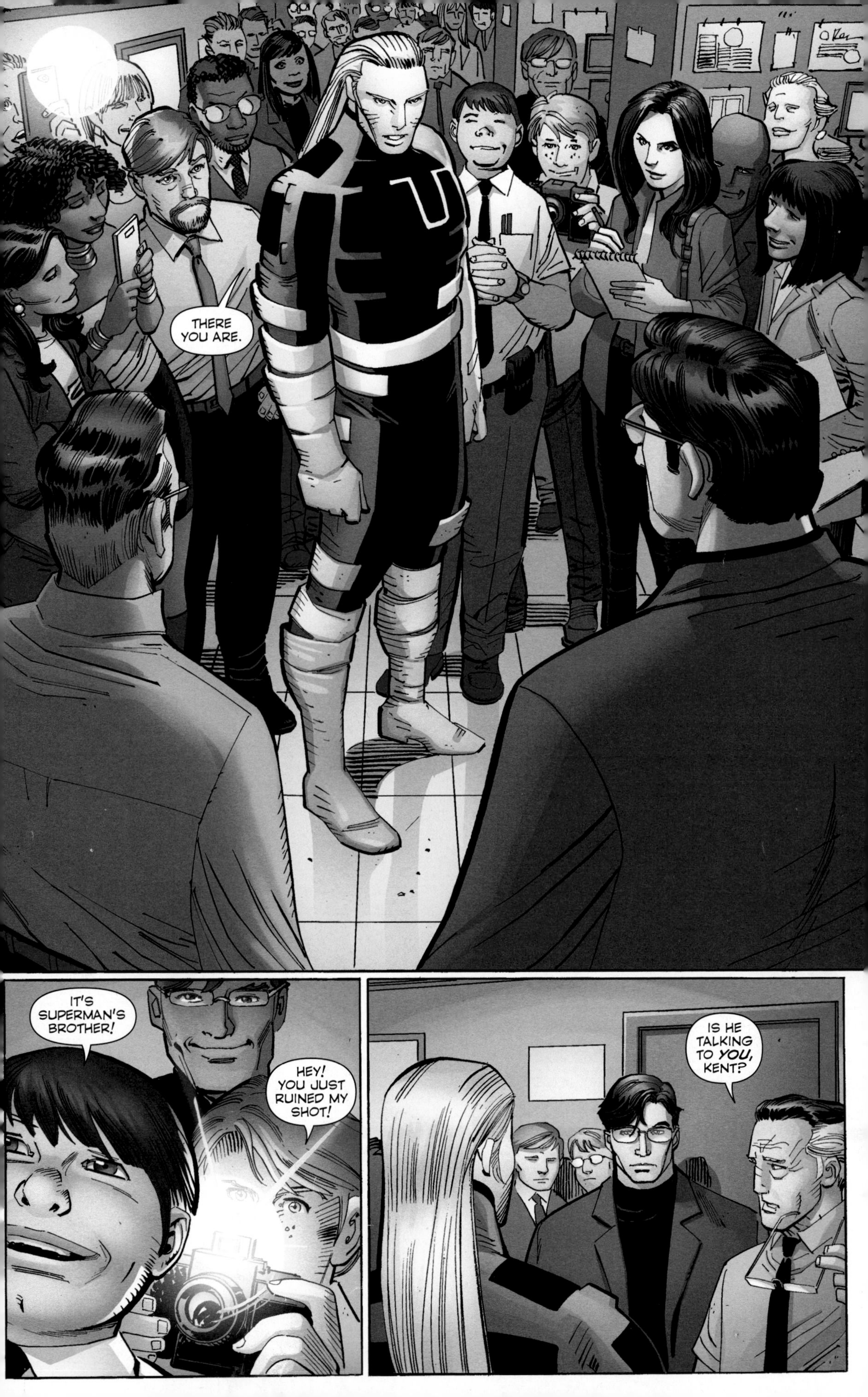
THERE YOU ARE.
IT'S SUPERMAN'S BROTHER!
HEY! YOU JUST RUINED MY SHOT!
IS HE TALKING TO *YOU*, KENT?

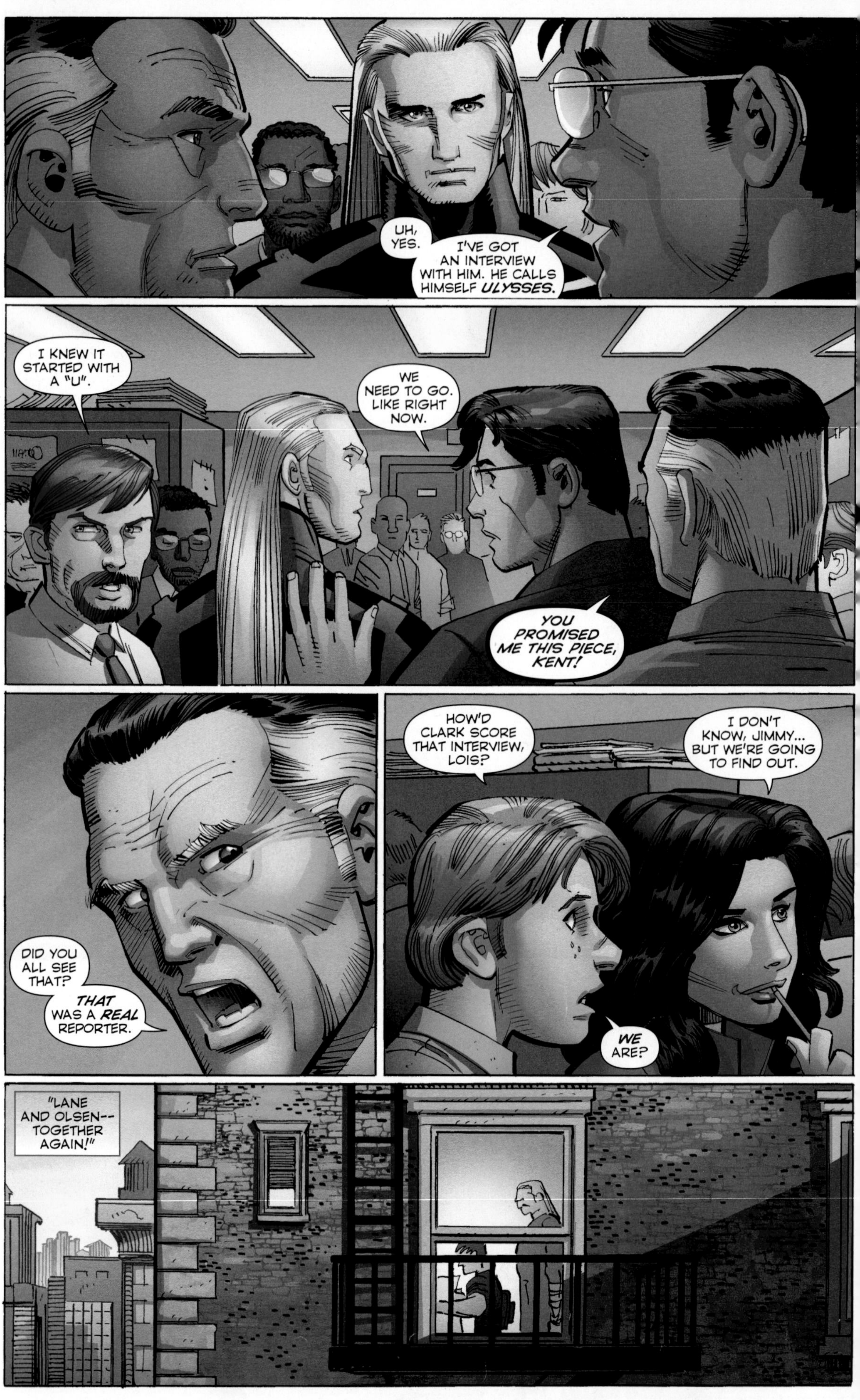
UH, YES.
I'VE GOT AN INTERVIEW WITH HIM. HE CALLS HIMSELF *ULYSSES.*
I KNEW IT STARTED WITH A "U".
WE NEED TO GO. LIKE RIGHT NOW.
YOU PROMISED ME THIS PIECE, KENT!
DID YOU ALL SEE THAT?
THAT WAS A *REAL* REPORTER.
HOW'D CLARK SCORE THAT INTERVIEW, LOIS?
I DON'T KNOW, JIMMY... BUT WE'RE GOING TO FIND OUT.
WE ARE?
"LANE AND OLSEN-- TOGETHER AGAIN!"

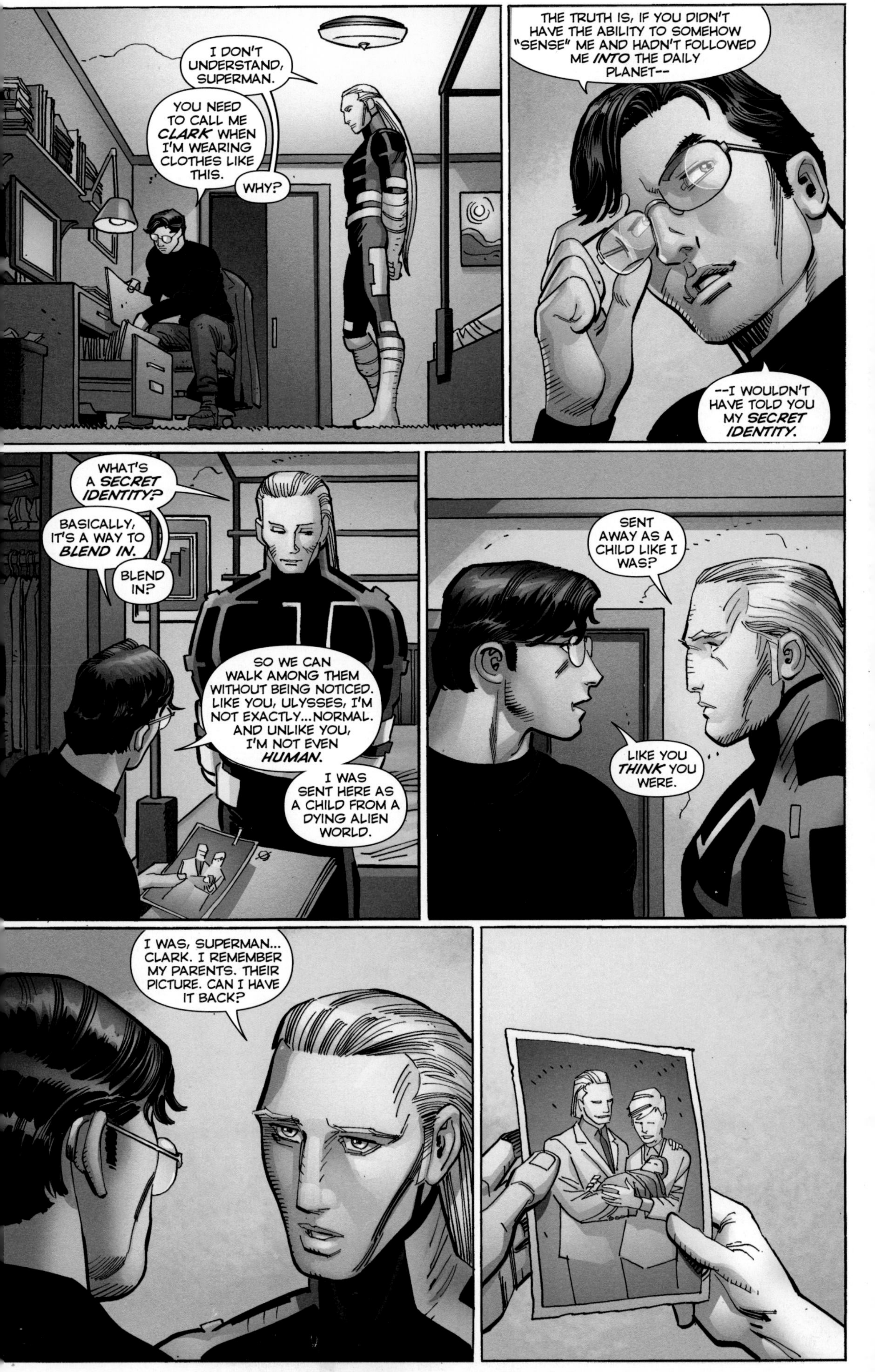
I DON'T UNDERSTAND, SUPERMAN.
YOU NEED TO CALL ME CLARK WHEN I'M WEARING CLOTHES LIKE THIS.
WHY?
THE TRUTH IS, IF YOU DIDN'T HAVE THE ABILITY TO SOMEHOW "SENSE" ME AND HADN'T FOLLOWED ME INTO THE DAILY PLANET--
--I WOULDN'T HAVE TOLD YOU MY SECRET IDENTITY.
WHAT'S A SECRET IDENTITY?
BASICALLY, IT'S A WAY TO BLEND IN.
BLEND IN?
SO WE CAN WALK AMONG THEM WITHOUT BEING NOTICED. LIKE YOU, ULYSSES, I'M NOT EXACTLY...NORMAL. AND UNLIKE YOU, I'M NOT EVEN HUMAN.
I WAS SENT HERE AS A CHILD FROM A DYING ALIEN WORLD.
SENT AWAY AS A CHILD LIKE I WAS?
LIKE YOU THINK YOU WERE.
I WAS, SUPERMAN... CLARK. I REMEMBER MY PARENTS. THEIR PICTURE. CAN I HAVE IT BACK?

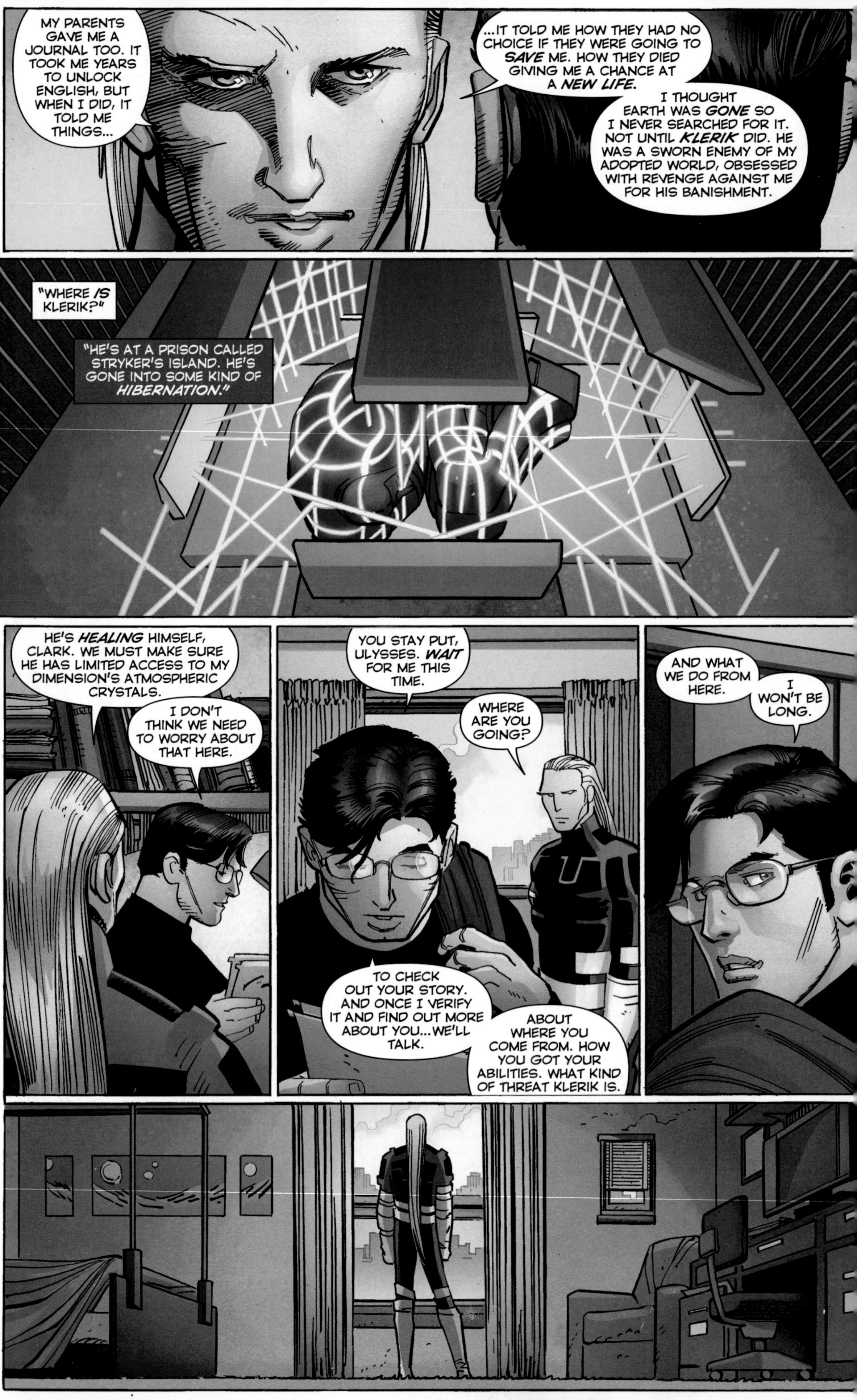

MY PARENTS GAVE ME A JOURNAL TOO. IT TOOK ME YEARS TO UNLOCK ENGLISH, BUT WHEN I DID, IT TOLD ME THINGS...
...IT TOLD ME HOW THEY HAD NO CHOICE IF THEY WERE GOING TO SAVE ME. HOW THEY DIED GIVING ME A CHANCE AT A NEW LIFE.
I THOUGHT EARTH WAS GONE SO I NEVER SEARCHED FOR IT. NOT UNTIL KLERIK DID. HE WAS A SWORN ENEMY OF MY ADOPTED WORLD, OBSESSED WITH REVENGE AGAINST ME FOR HIS BANISHMENT.
"WHERE IS KLERIK?"
"HE'S AT A PRISON CALLED STRYKER'S ISLAND. HE'S GONE INTO SOME KIND OF HIBERNATION."
HE'S HEALING HIMSELF, CLARK. WE MUST MAKE SURE HE HAS LIMITED ACCESS TO MY DIMENSION'S ATMOSPHERIC CRYSTALS.
I DON'T THINK WE NEED TO WORRY ABOUT THAT HERE.
YOU STAY PUT, ULYSSES. WAIT FOR ME THIS TIME.
WHERE ARE YOU GOING?
TO CHECK OUT YOUR STORY. AND ONCE I VERIFY IT AND FIND OUT MORE ABOUT YOU...WE'LL TALK.
ABOUT WHERE YOU COME FROM. HOW YOU GOT YOUR ABILITIES. WHAT KIND OF THREAT KLERIK IS.
AND WHAT WE DO FROM HERE.
I WON'T BE LONG.

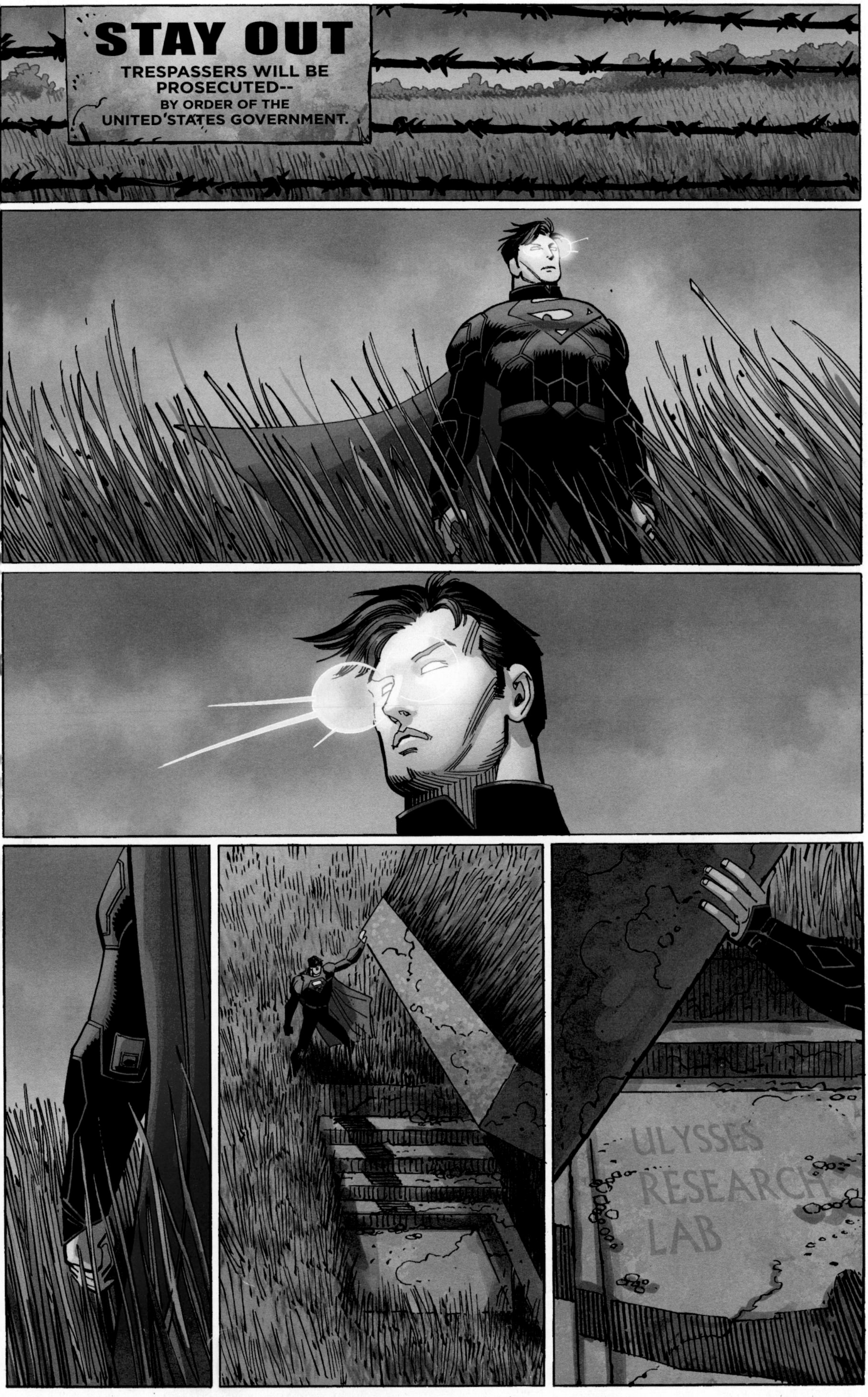
STAY OUT
TRESPASSERS WILL BE PROSECUTED--
BY ORDER OF THE UNITED STATES GOVERNMENT.
ULYSSES RESEARCH LAB

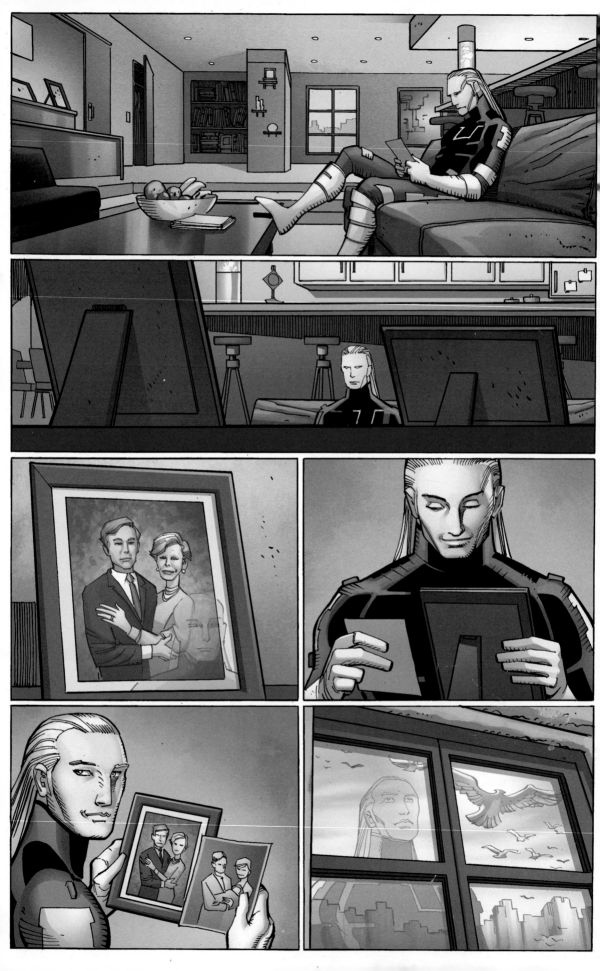

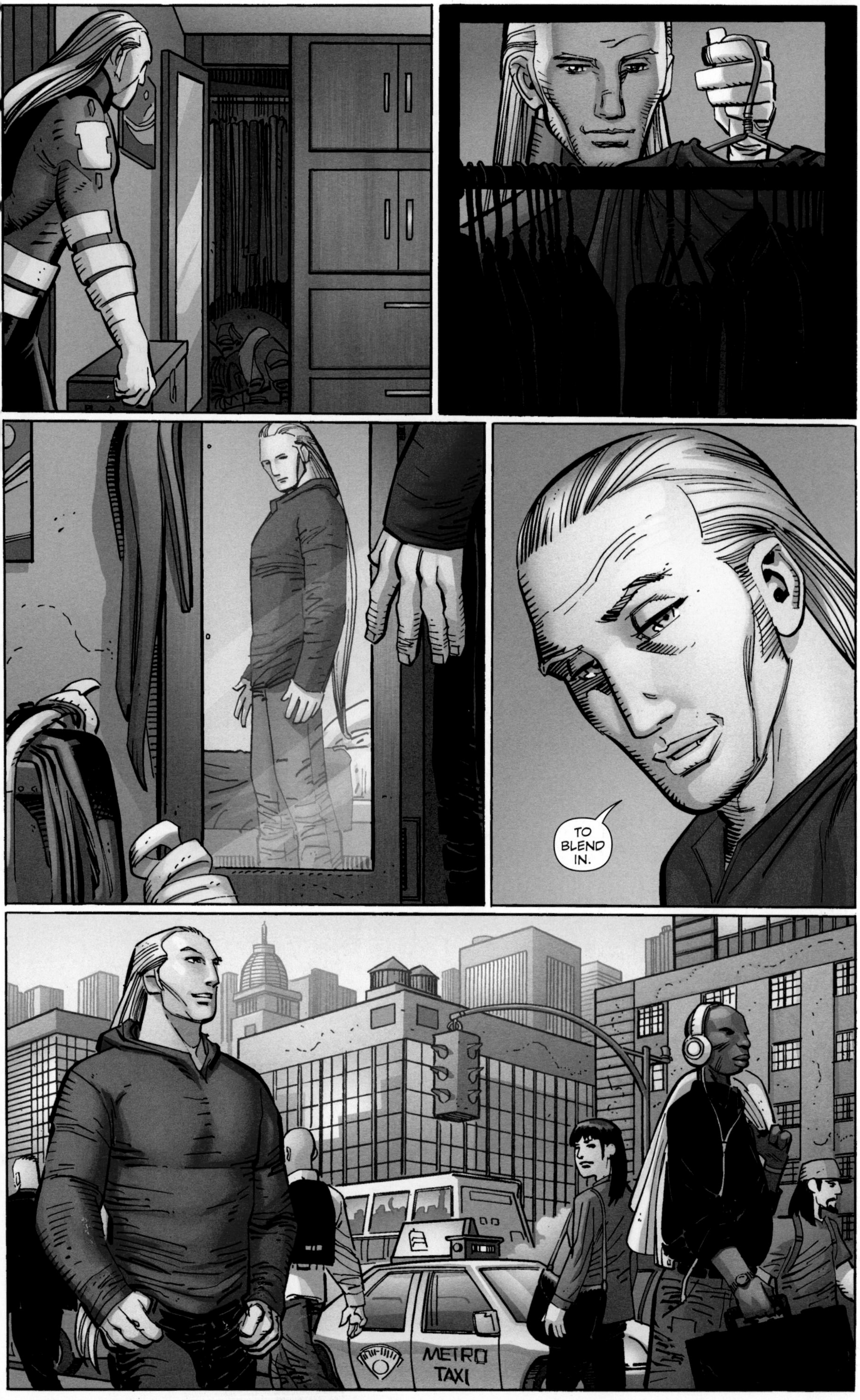
TO BLEND IN.
METRO TAXI

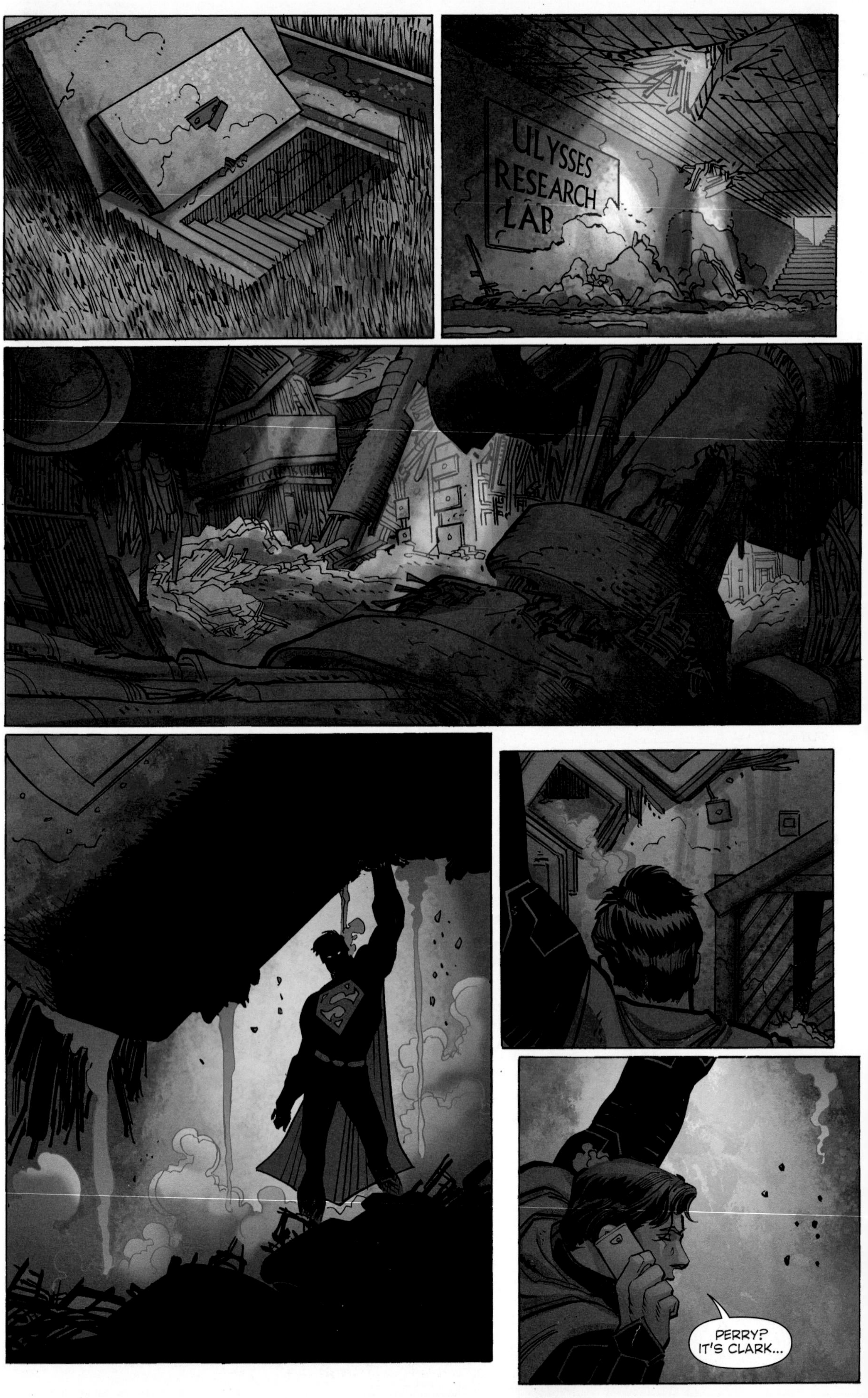
ULYSSES
RESEARCH
LAB
PERRY? IT'S CLARK...

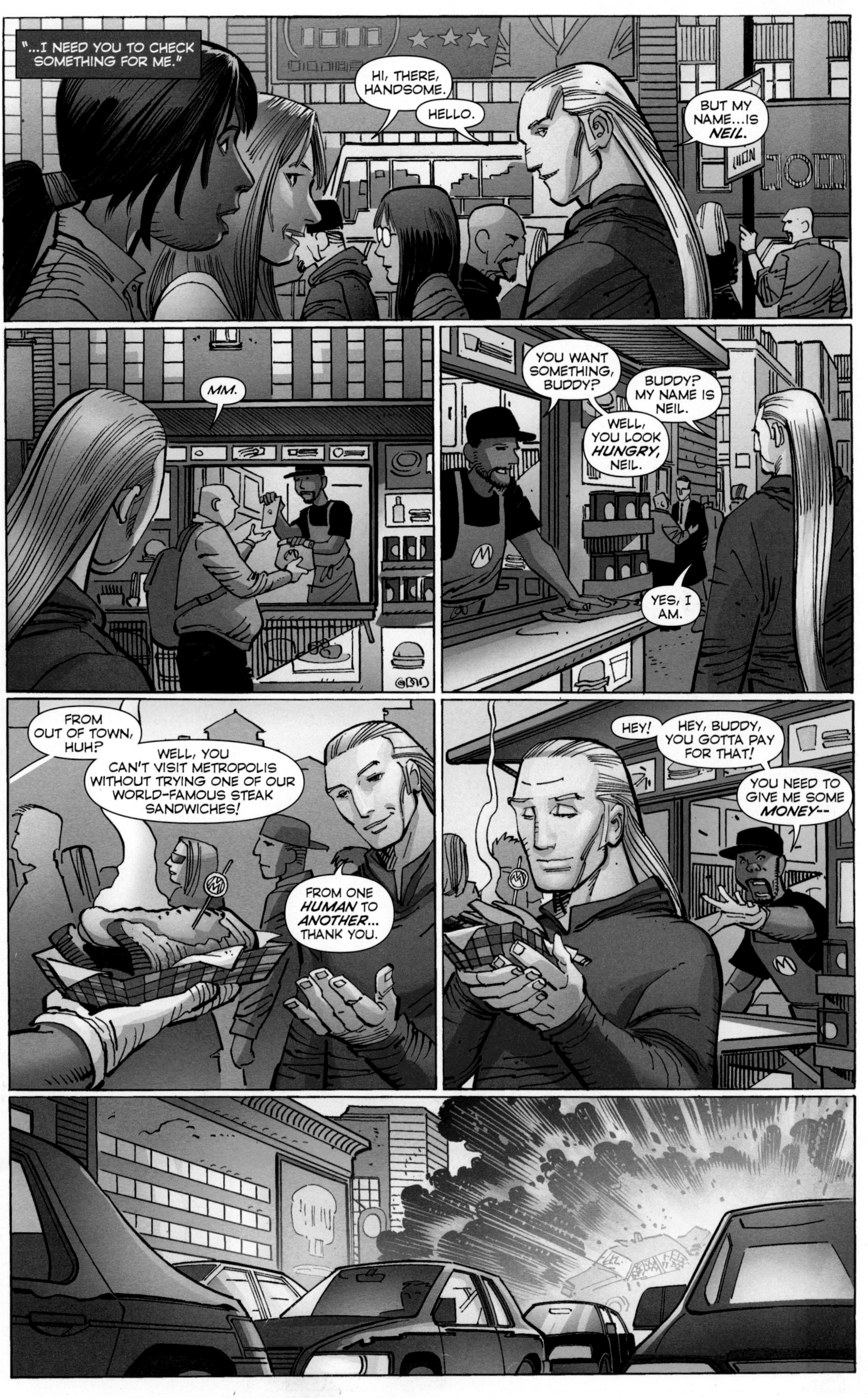
"...I NEED YOU TO CHECK SOMETHING FOR ME."
HI, THERE, HANDSOME.
HELLO.
BUT MY NAME...IS NEIL.
MM.
YOU WANT SOMETHING, BUDDY?
BUDDY? MY NAME IS NEIL.
WELL, YOU LOOK HUNGRY, NEIL.
YES, I AM.
FROM OUT OF TOWN, HUH?
WELL, YOU CAN'T VISIT METROPOLIS WITHOUT TRYING ONE OF OUR WORLD-FAMOUS STEAK SANDWICHES!
FROM ONE HUMAN TO ANOTHER... THANK YOU.
HEY!
HEY, BUDDY, YOU GOTTA PAY FOR THAT!
YOU NEED TO GIVE ME SOME MONEY--

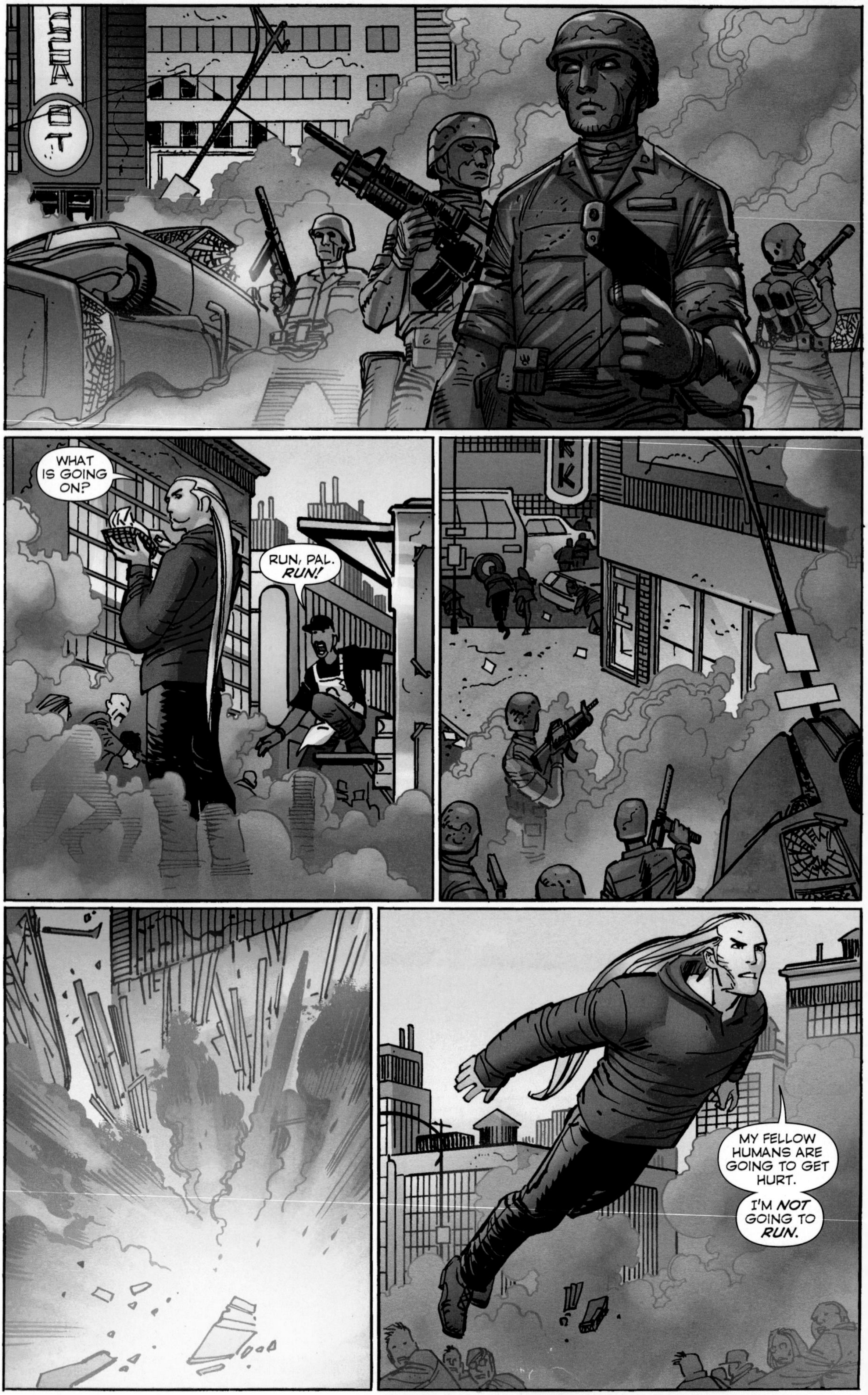
WHAT IS GOING ON?
RUN, PAL. *RUN!*
MY FELLOW HUMANS ARE GOING TO GET HURT.
I'M *NOT* GOING TO *RUN*.

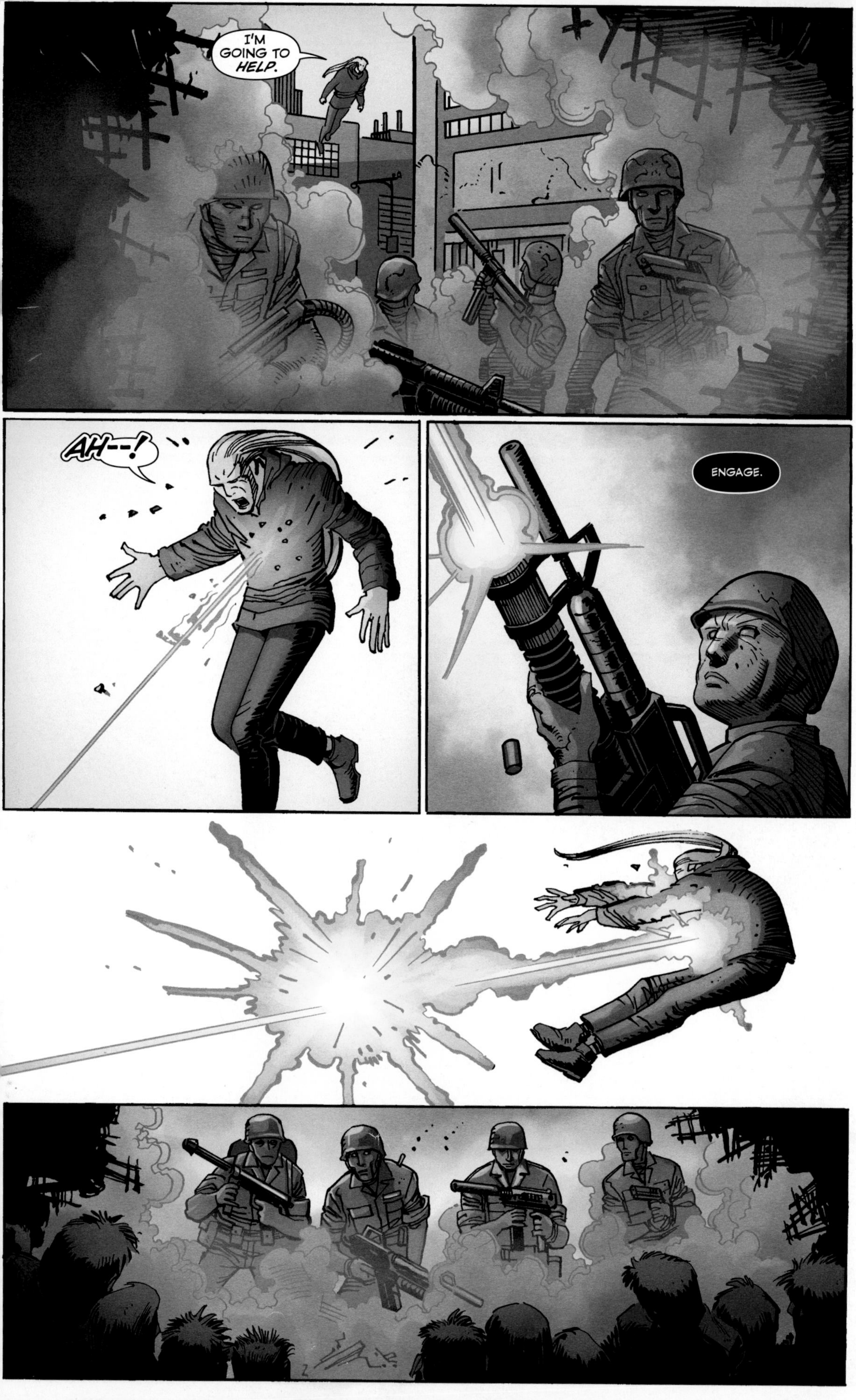
I'M GOING TO HELP.
AH--!
ENGAGE.

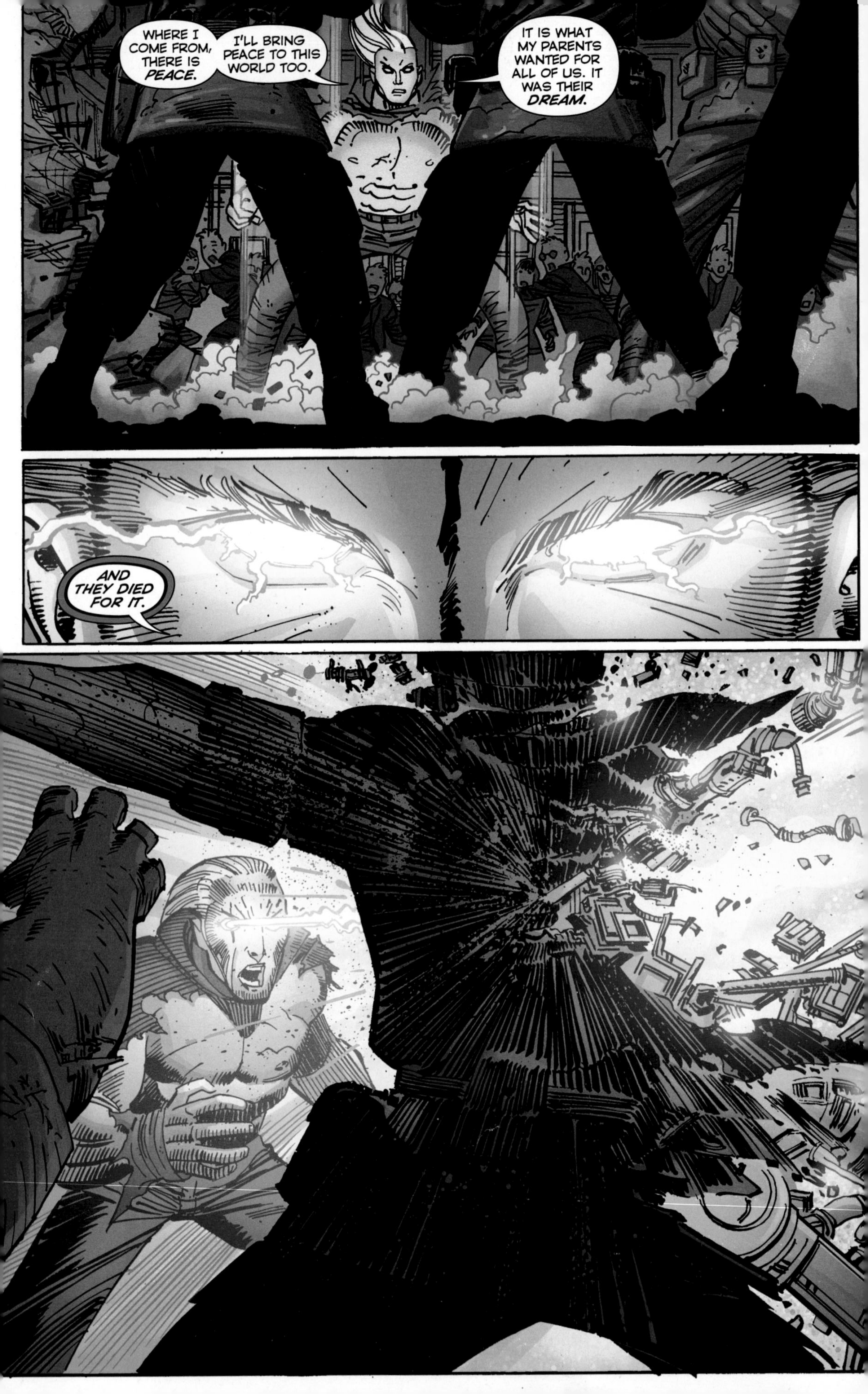
WHERE I COME FROM, THERE IS PEACE.
I'LL BRING PEACE TO THIS WORLD TOO.
IT IS WHAT MY PARENTS WANTED FOR ALL OF US. IT WAS THEIR DREAM.
AND THEY DIED FOR IT.

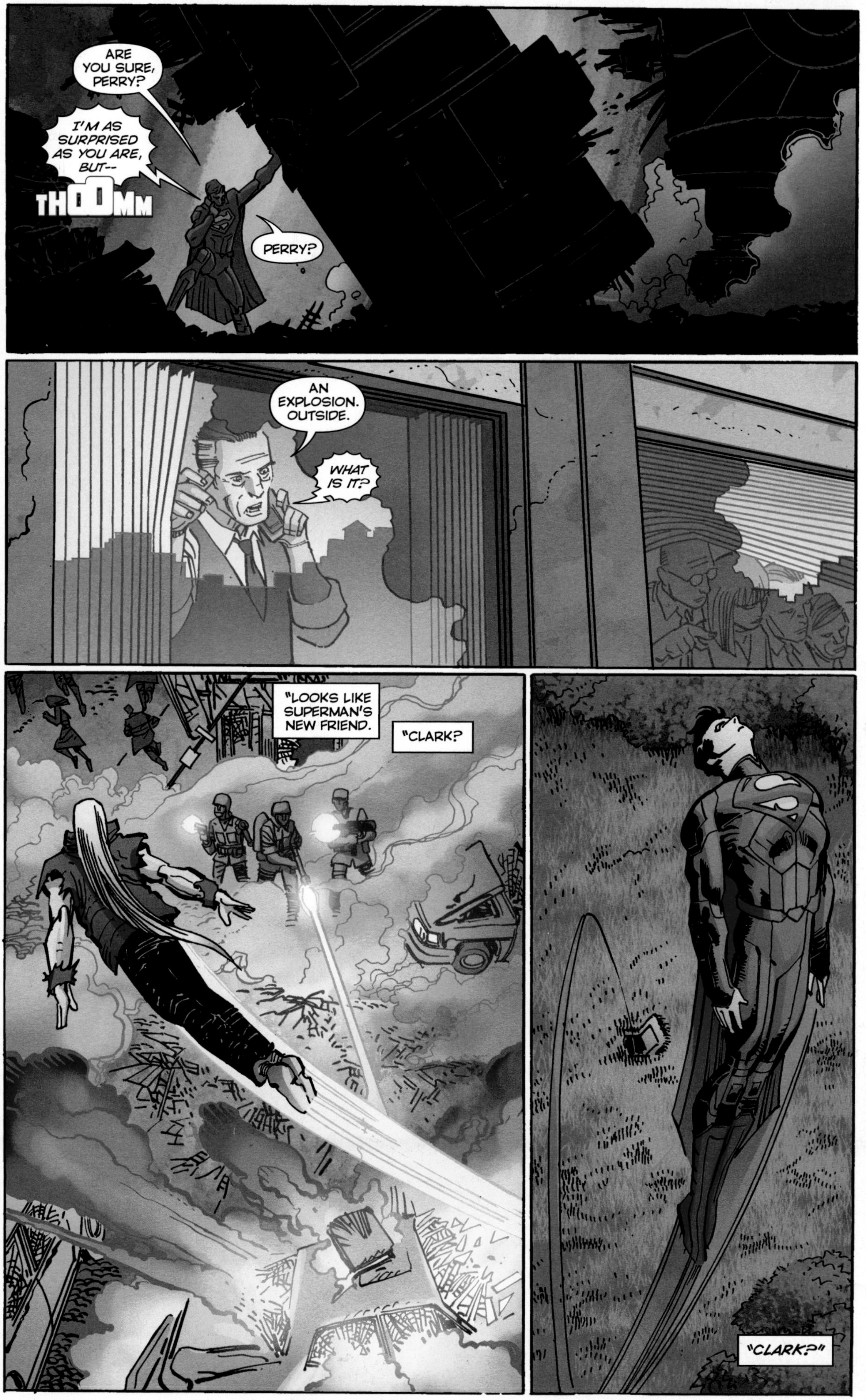

ARE YOU SURE, PERRY?
I'M AS SURPRISED AS YOU ARE, BUT--
THOOMM
PERRY?
AN EXPLOSION. OUTSIDE.
WHAT IS IT?
"LOOKS LIKE SUPERMAN'S NEW FRIEND.
"CLARK?
"CLARK?"

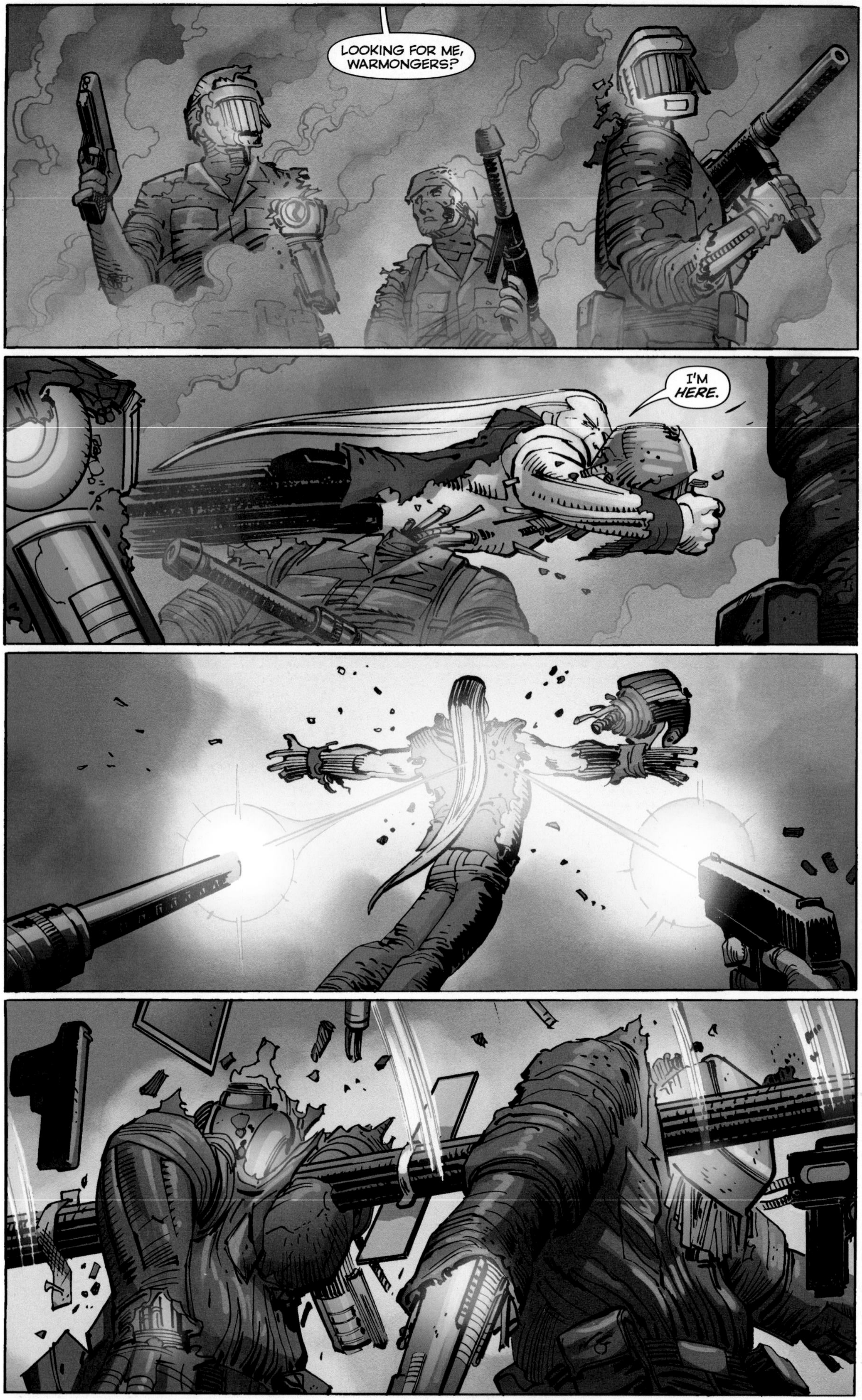
LOOKING FOR ME, WARMONGERS?
I'M *HERE.*

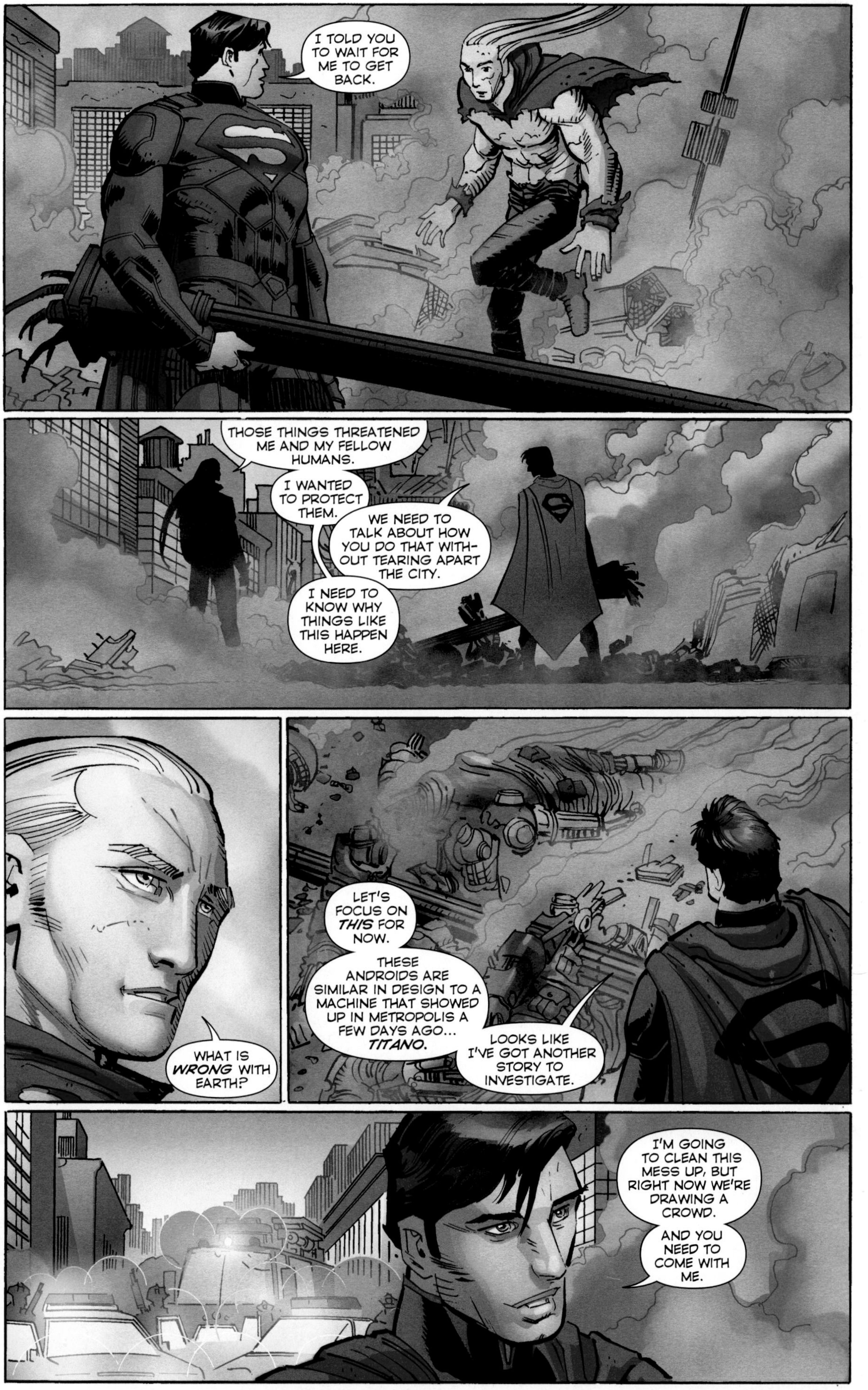
I TOLD YOU TO WAIT FOR ME TO GET BACK.
THOSE THINGS THREATENED ME AND MY FELLOW HUMANS.
I WANTED TO PROTECT THEM.
WE NEED TO TALK ABOUT HOW YOU DO THAT WITH-OUT TEARING APART THE CITY.
I NEED TO KNOW WHY THINGS LIKE THIS HAPPEN HERE.
WHAT IS *WRONG* WITH EARTH?
LET'S FOCUS ON *THIS* FOR NOW.
THESE ANDROIDS ARE SIMILAR IN DESIGN TO A MACHINE THAT SHOWED UP IN METROPOLIS A FEW DAYS AGO... *TITANO.*
LOOKS LIKE I'VE GOT ANOTHER STORY TO INVESTIGATE.
I'M GOING TO CLEAN THIS MESS UP, BUT RIGHT NOW WE'RE DRAWING A CROWD.
AND YOU NEED TO COME WITH ME.

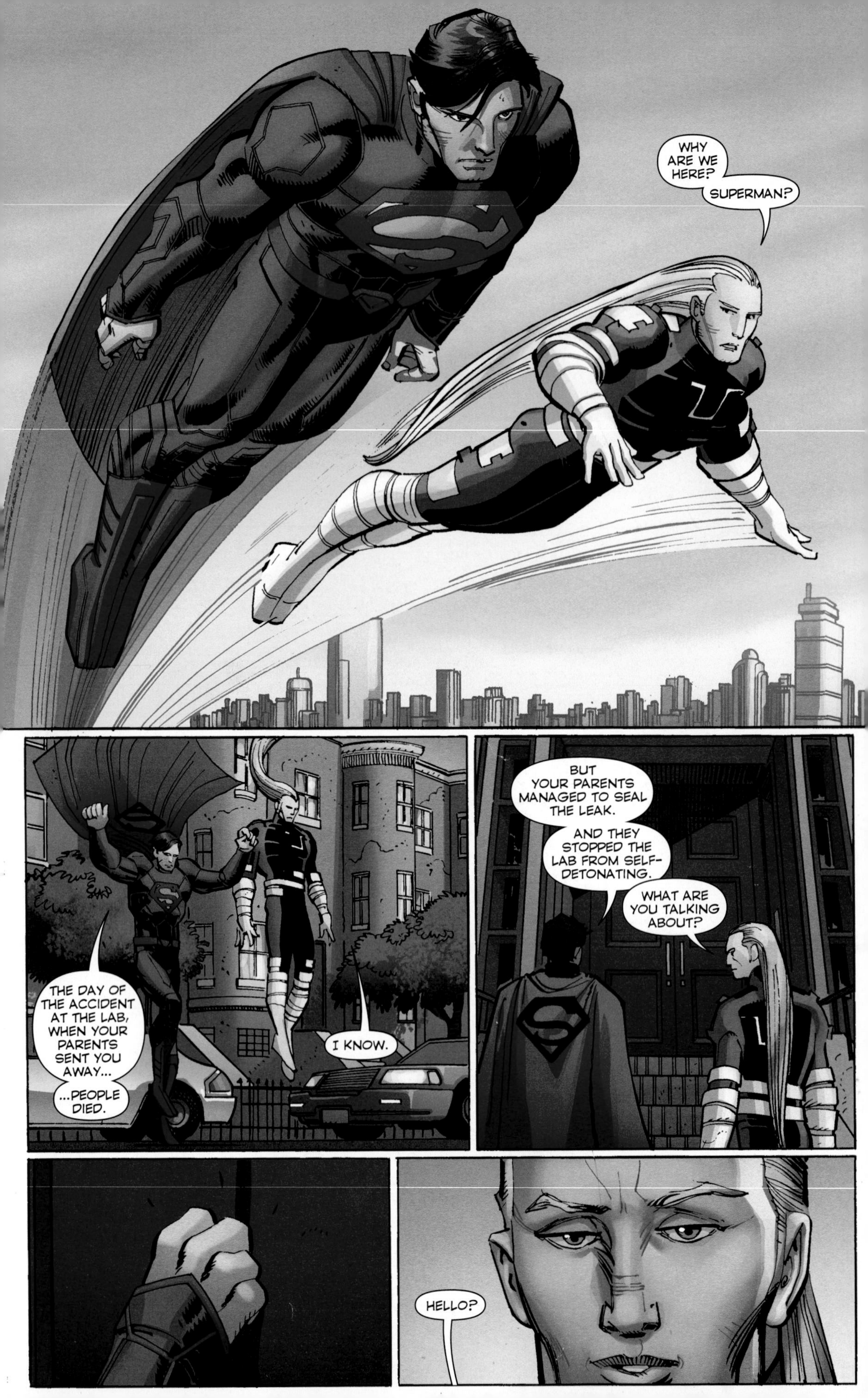
WHY ARE WE HERE?
SUPERMAN?
THE DAY OF THE ACCIDENT AT THE LAB, WHEN YOUR PARENTS SENT YOU AWAY...
...PEOPLE DIED.
I KNOW.
BUT YOUR PARENTS MANAGED TO SEAL THE LEAK.
AND THEY STOPPED THE LAB FROM SELF-DETONATING.
WHAT ARE YOU TALKING ABOUT?
HELLO?

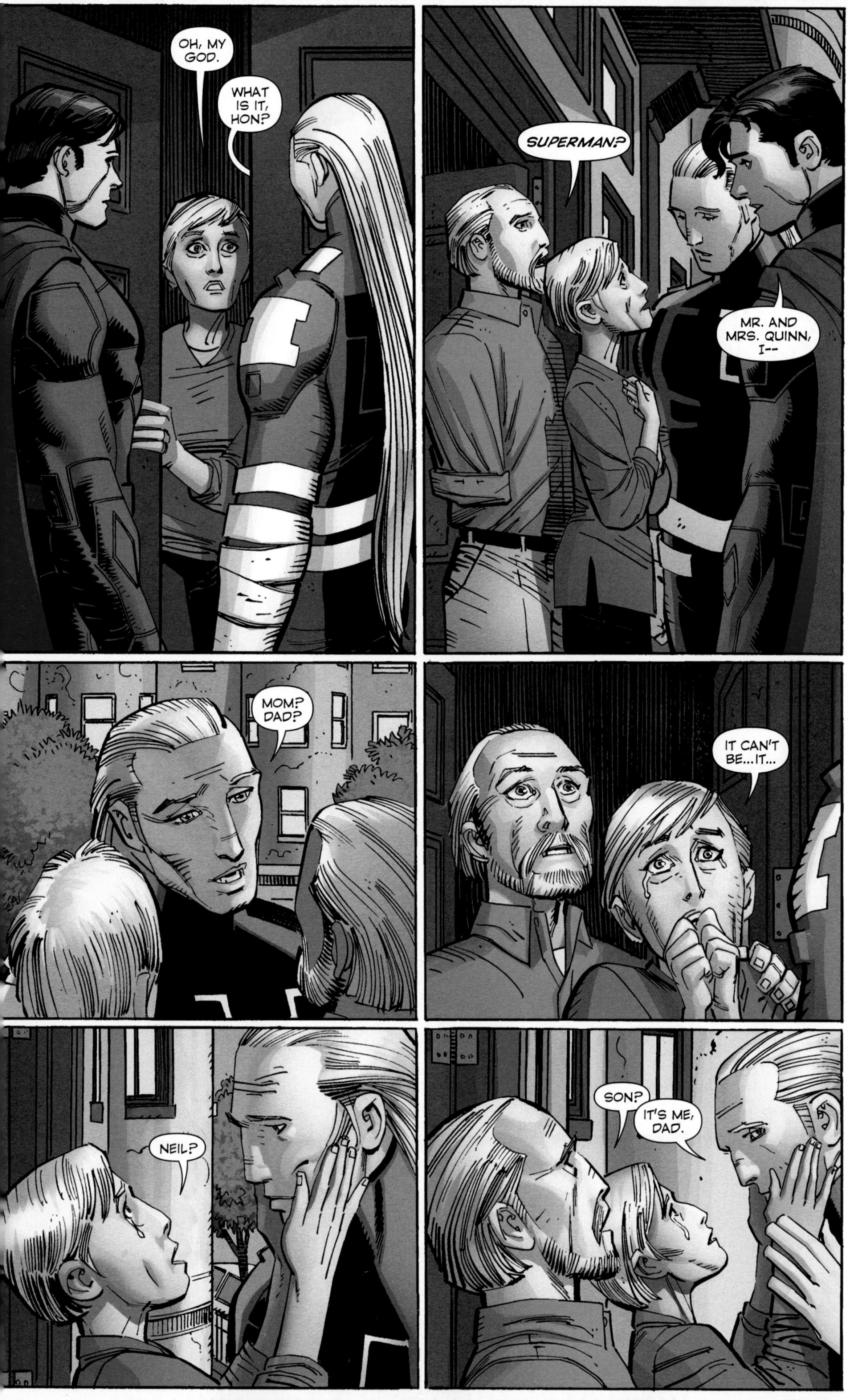
OH, MY GOD.
WHAT IS IT, HON?
SUPERMAN?
MR. AND MRS. QUINN, I--
MOM? DAD?
IT CAN'T BE...IT...
NEIL?
SON?
IT'S ME, DAD.

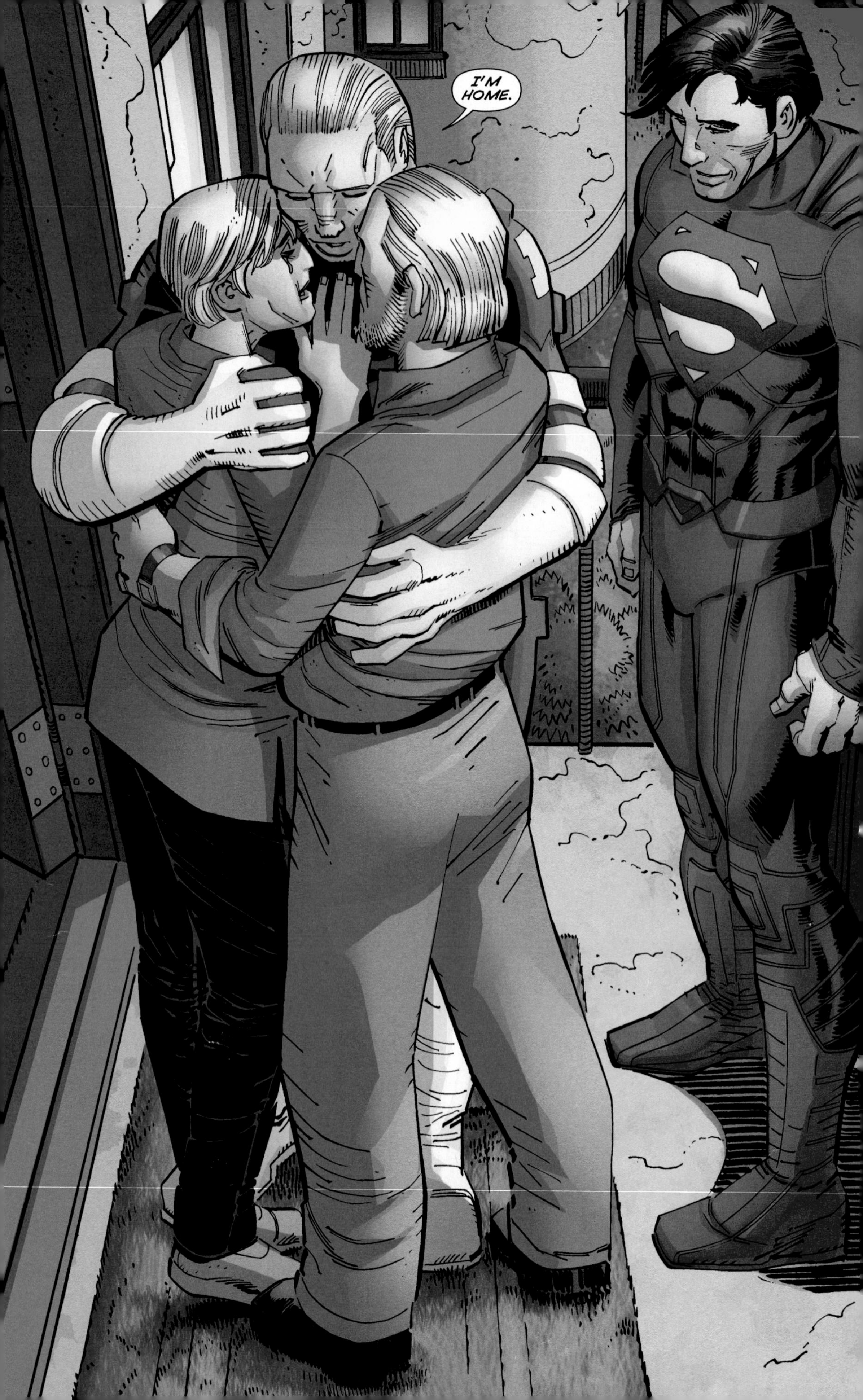
I'M HOME.

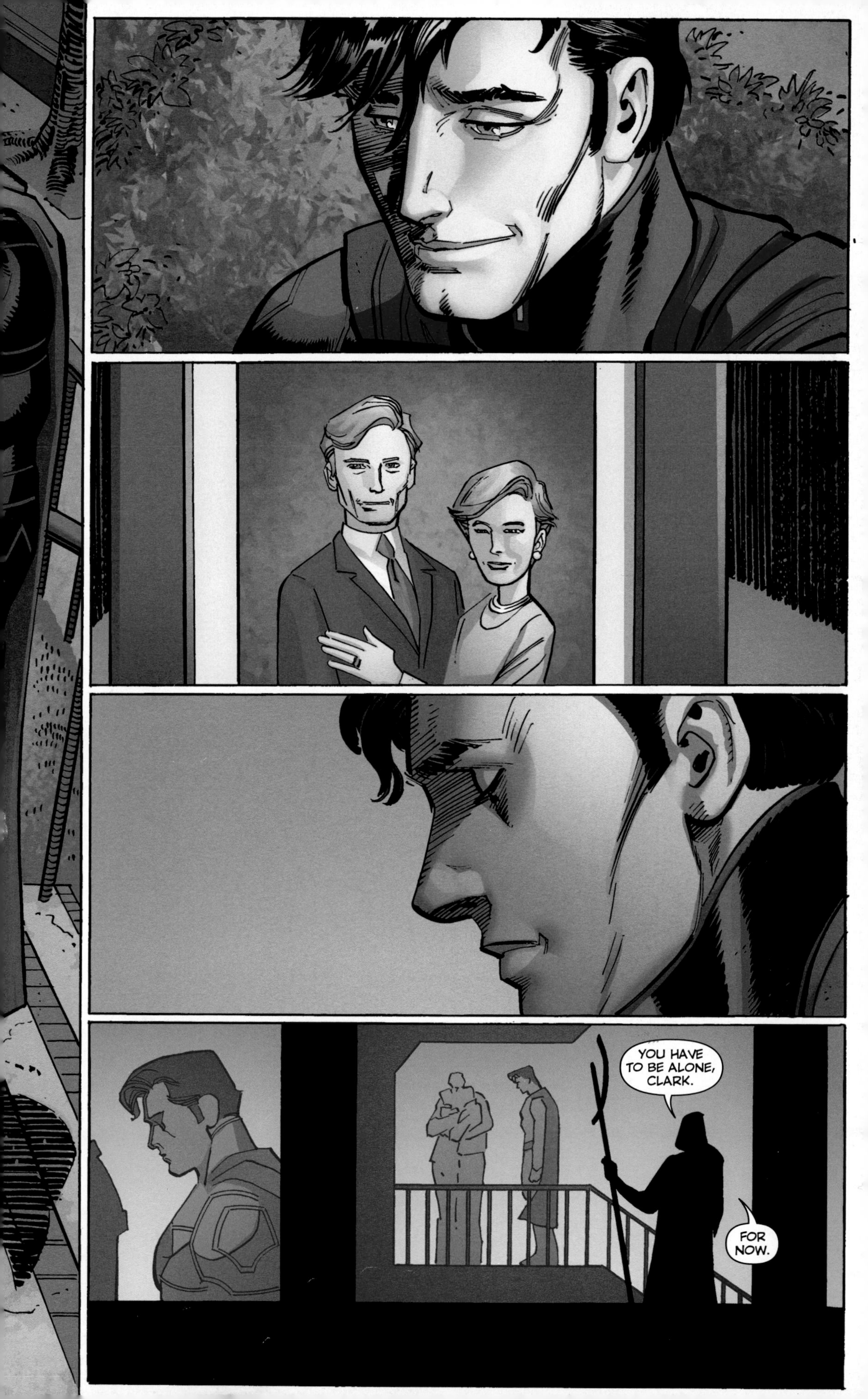
YOU HAVE TO BE ALONE, CLARK.
FOR NOW.

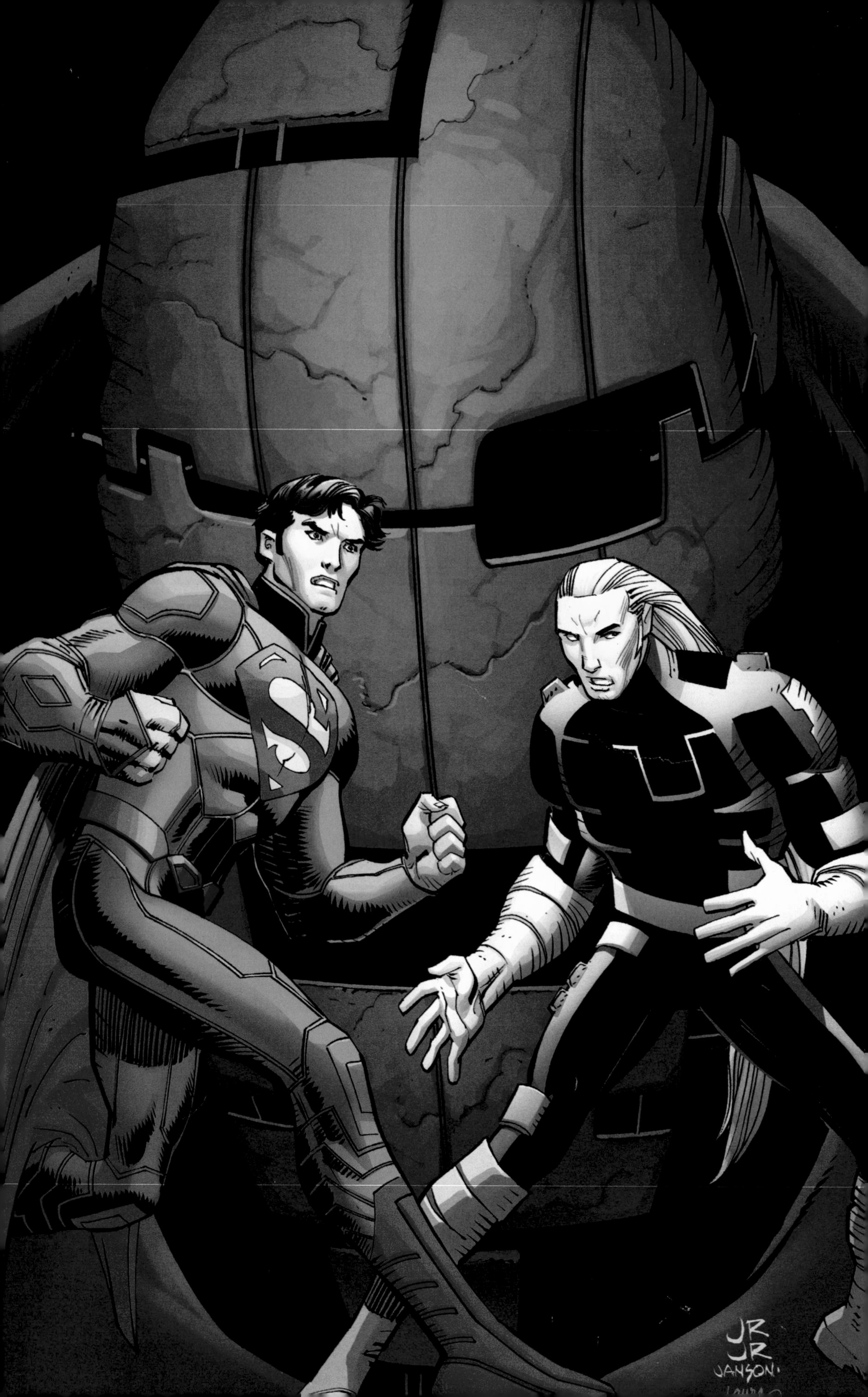
JR
JR
JANSON

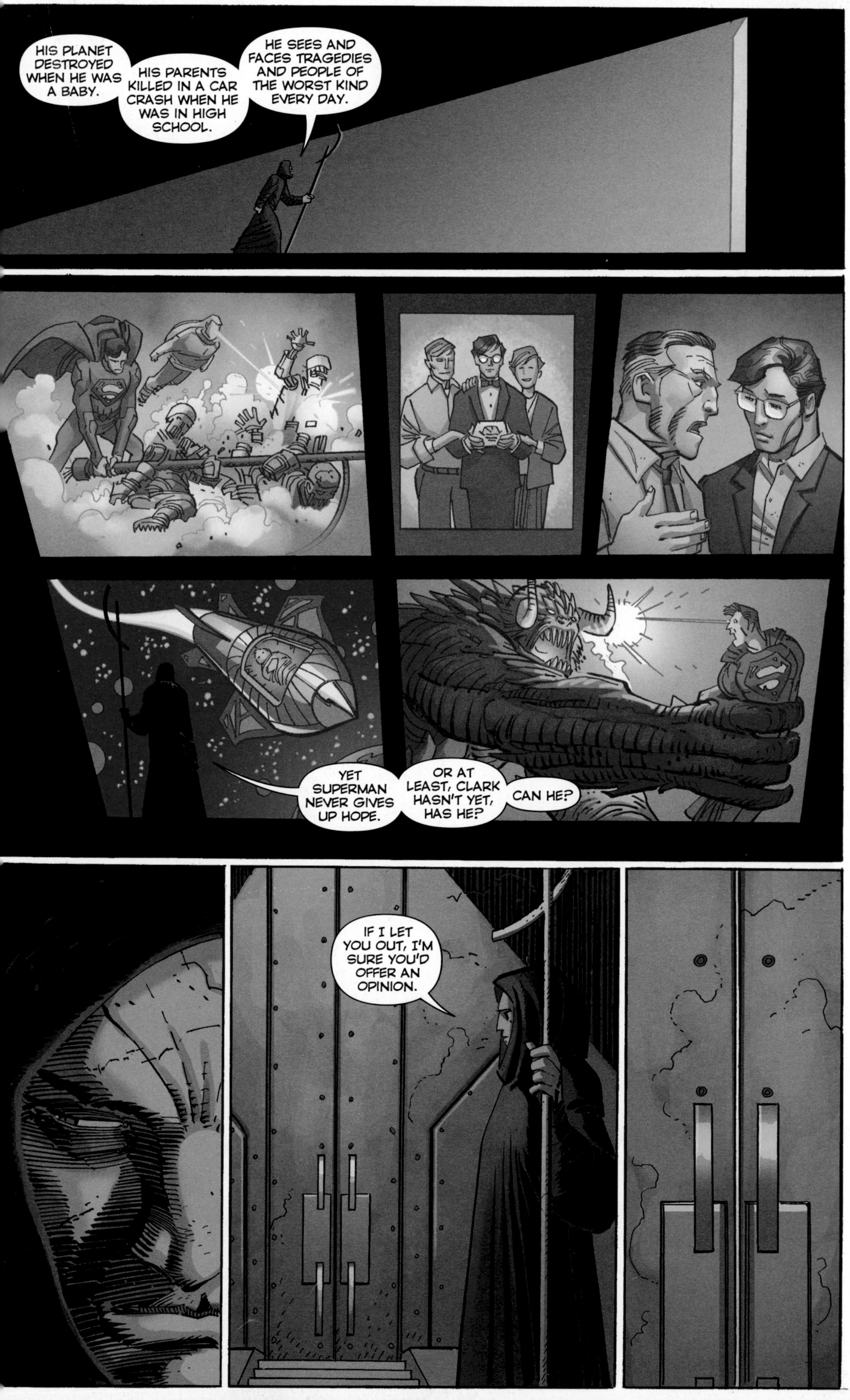
HIS PLANET DESTROYED WHEN HE WAS A BABY.
HIS PARENTS KILLED IN A CAR CRASH WHEN HE WAS IN HIGH SCHOOL.
HE SEES AND FACES TRAGEDIES AND PEOPLE OF THE WORST KIND EVERY DAY.
YET SUPERMAN NEVER GIVES UP HOPE.
OR AT LEAST, CLARK HASN'T YET, HAS HE?
CAN HE?
IF I LET YOU OUT, I'M SURE YOU'D OFFER AN OPINION.

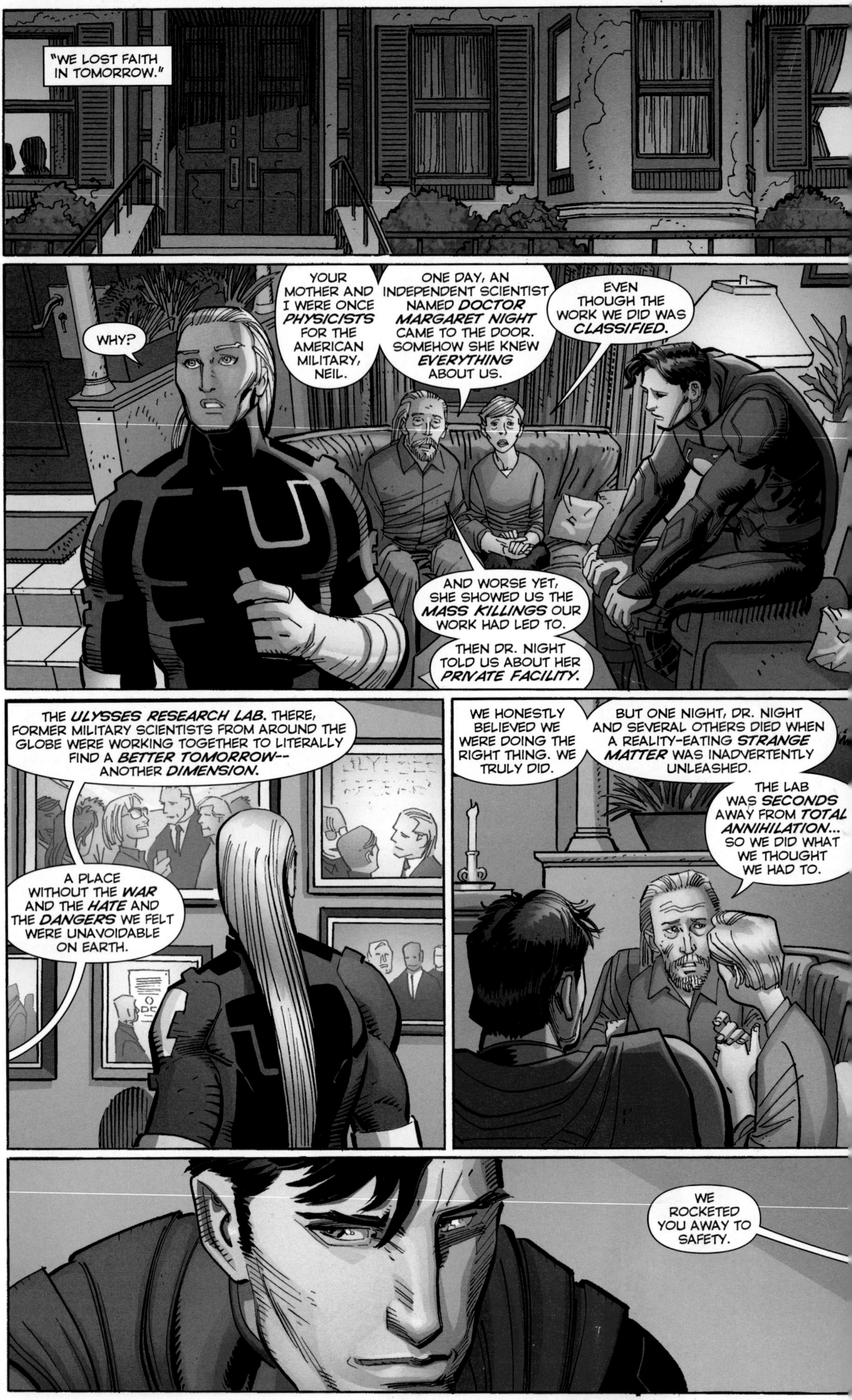

"WE LOST FAITH IN TOMORROW."
WHY?
YOUR MOTHER AND I WERE ONCE PHYSICISTS FOR THE AMERICAN MILITARY, NEIL.
ONE DAY, AN INDEPENDENT SCIENTIST NAMED DOCTOR MARGARET NIGHT CAME TO THE DOOR. SOMEHOW SHE KNEW EVERYTHING ABOUT US.
EVEN THOUGH THE WORK WE DID WAS CLASSIFIED.
AND WORSE YET, SHE SHOWED US THE MASS KILLINGS OUR WORK HAD LED TO.
THEN DR. NIGHT TOLD US ABOUT HER PRIVATE FACILITY.
THE ULYSSES RESEARCH LAB. THERE, FORMER MILITARY SCIENTISTS FROM AROUND THE GLOBE WERE WORKING TOGETHER TO LITERALLY FIND A BETTER TOMORROW-- ANOTHER DIMENSION.
A PLACE WITHOUT THE WAR AND THE HATE AND THE DANGERS WE FELT WERE UNAVOIDABLE ON EARTH.
WE HONESTLY BELIEVED WE WERE DOING THE RIGHT THING. WE TRULY DID.
BUT ONE NIGHT, DR. NIGHT AND SEVERAL OTHERS DIED WHEN A REALITY-EATING STRANGE MATTER WAS INADVERTENTLY UNLEASHED.
THE LAB WAS SECONDS AWAY FROM TOTAL ANNIHILATION... SO WE DID WHAT WE THOUGHT WE HAD TO.
WE ROCKETED YOU AWAY TO SAFETY.

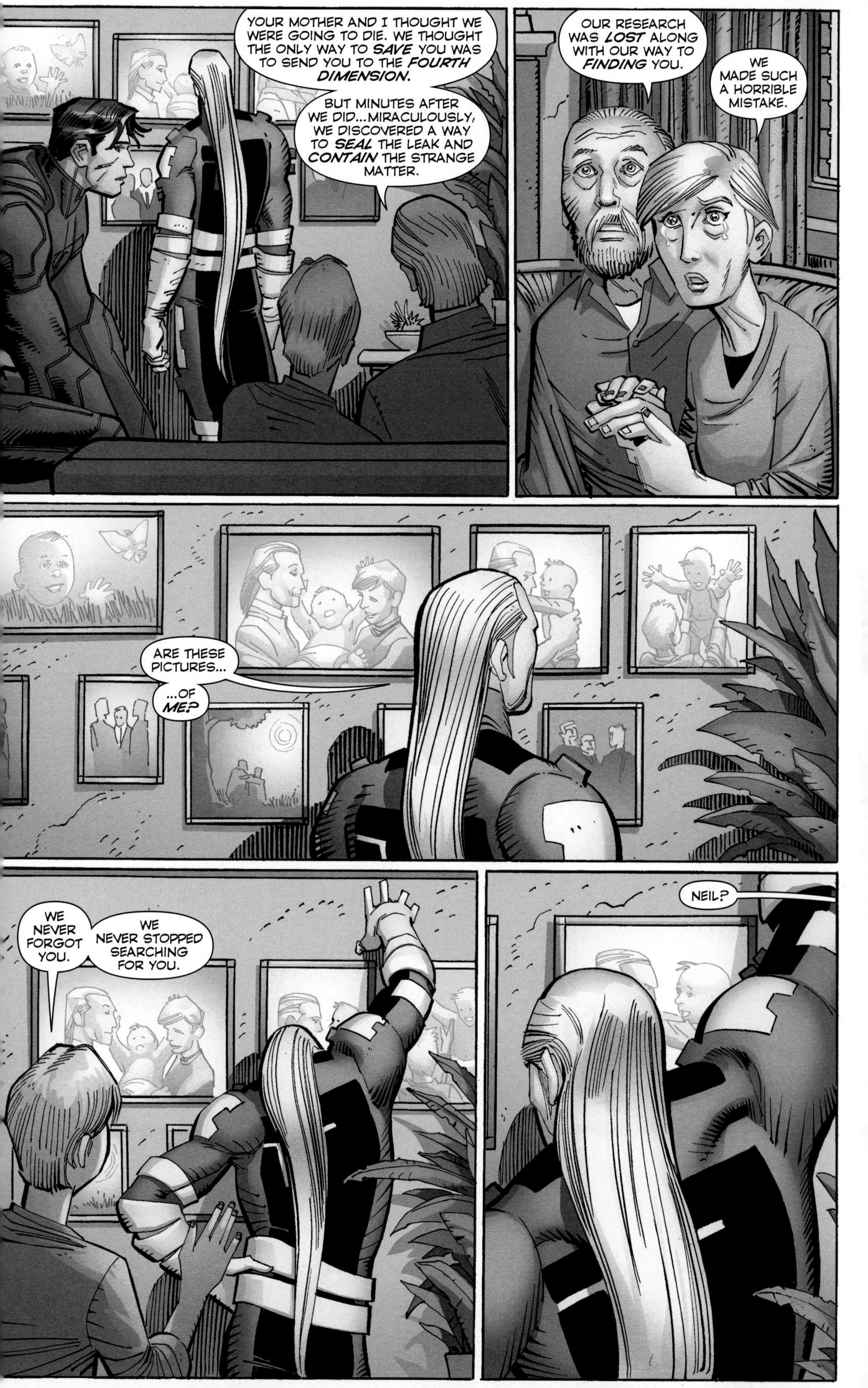
YOUR MOTHER AND I THOUGHT WE WERE GOING TO DIE. WE THOUGHT THE ONLY WAY TO SAVE YOU WAS TO SEND YOU TO THE FOURTH DIMENSION.
BUT MINUTES AFTER WE DID...MIRACULOUSLY, WE DISCOVERED A WAY TO SEAL THE LEAK AND CONTAIN THE STRANGE MATTER.
OUR RESEARCH WAS LOST ALONG WITH OUR WAY TO FINDING YOU.
WE MADE SUCH A HORRIBLE MISTAKE.
ARE THESE PICTURES...
...OF ME?
WE NEVER FORGOT YOU.
WE NEVER STOPPED SEARCHING FOR YOU.
NEIL?

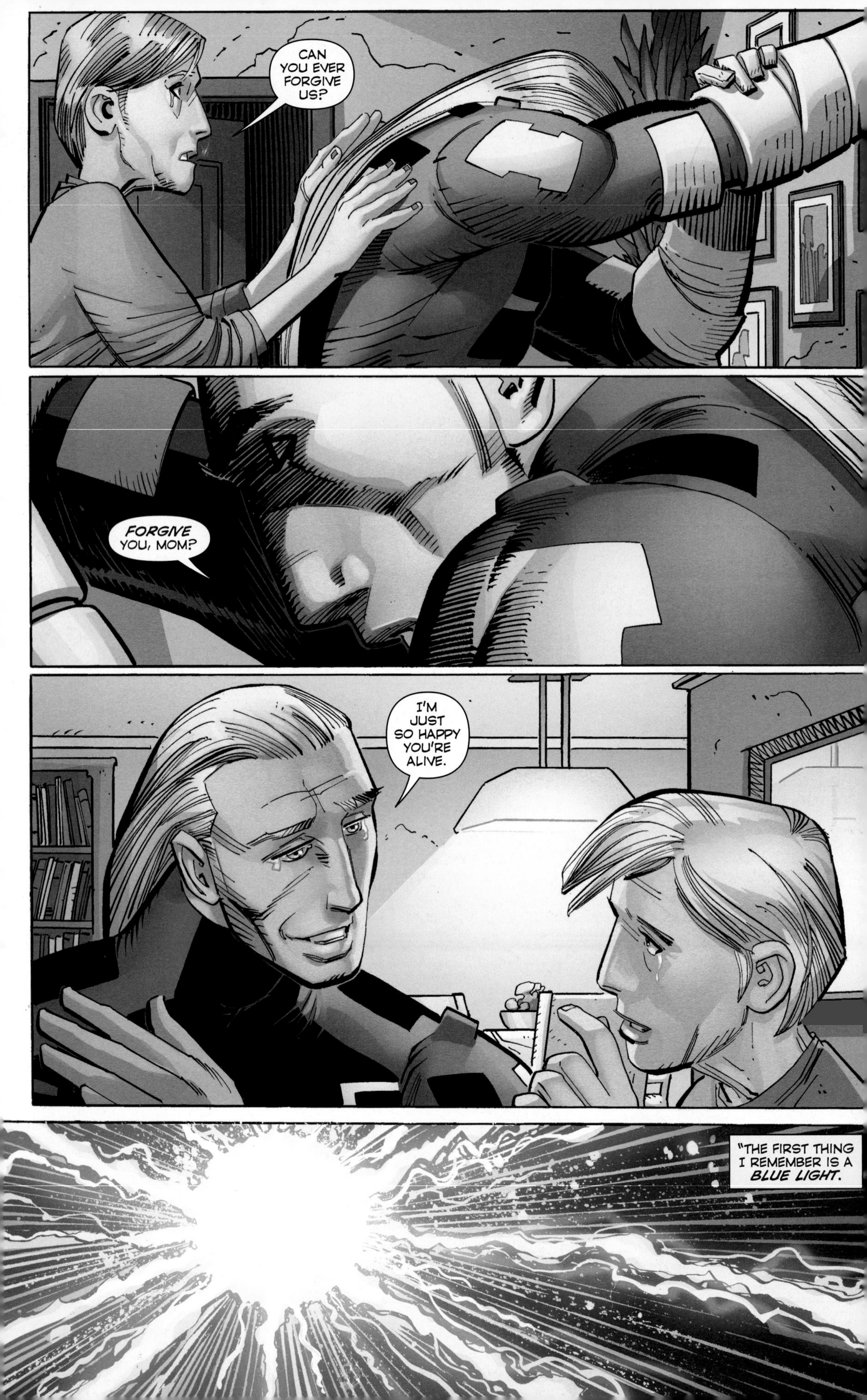
CAN YOU EVER FORGIVE US?
FORGIVE YOU, MOM?
I'M JUST SO HAPPY YOU'RE ALIVE.
"THE FIRST THING I REMEMBER IS A BLUE LIGHT.

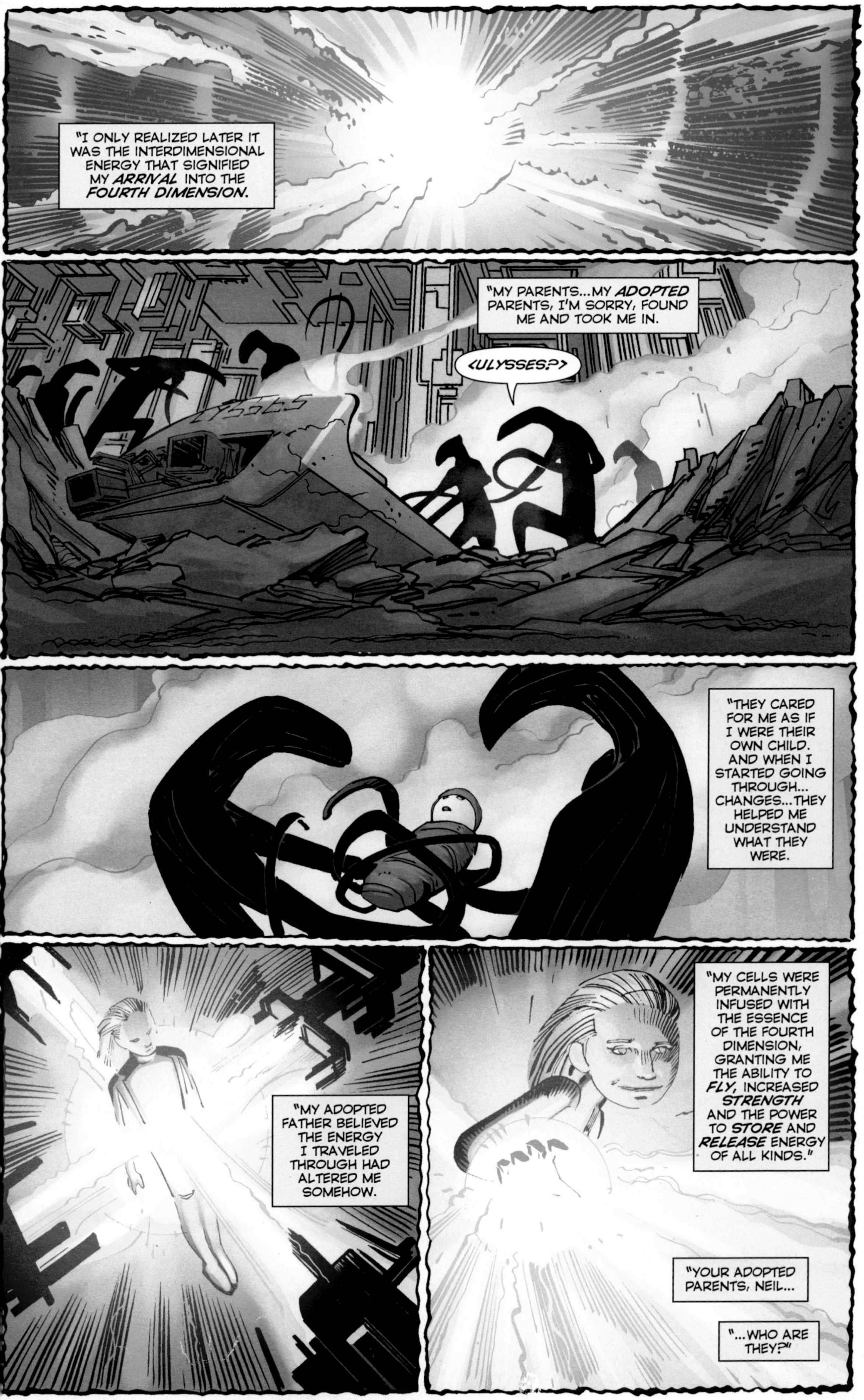
"I ONLY REALIZED LATER IT WAS THE INTERDIMENSIONAL ENERGY THAT SIGNIFIED MY ARRIVAL INTO THE FOURTH DIMENSION.
"MY PARENTS...MY ADOPTED PARENTS, I'M SORRY, FOUND ME AND TOOK ME IN.
<ULYSSES?>
ULYSSES
"THEY CARED FOR ME AS IF I WERE THEIR OWN CHILD. AND WHEN I STARTED GOING THROUGH... CHANGES...THEY HELPED ME UNDERSTAND WHAT THEY WERE.
"MY ADOPTED FATHER BELIEVED THE ENERGY I TRAVELED THROUGH HAD ALTERED ME SOMEHOW.
"MY CELLS WERE PERMANENTLY INFUSED WITH THE ESSENCE OF THE FOURTH DIMENSION, GRANTING ME THE ABILITY TO FLY, INCREASED STRENGTH AND THE POWER TO STORE AND RELEASE ENERGY OF ALL KINDS."
"YOUR ADOPTED PARENTS, NEIL...
"...WHO ARE THEY?"

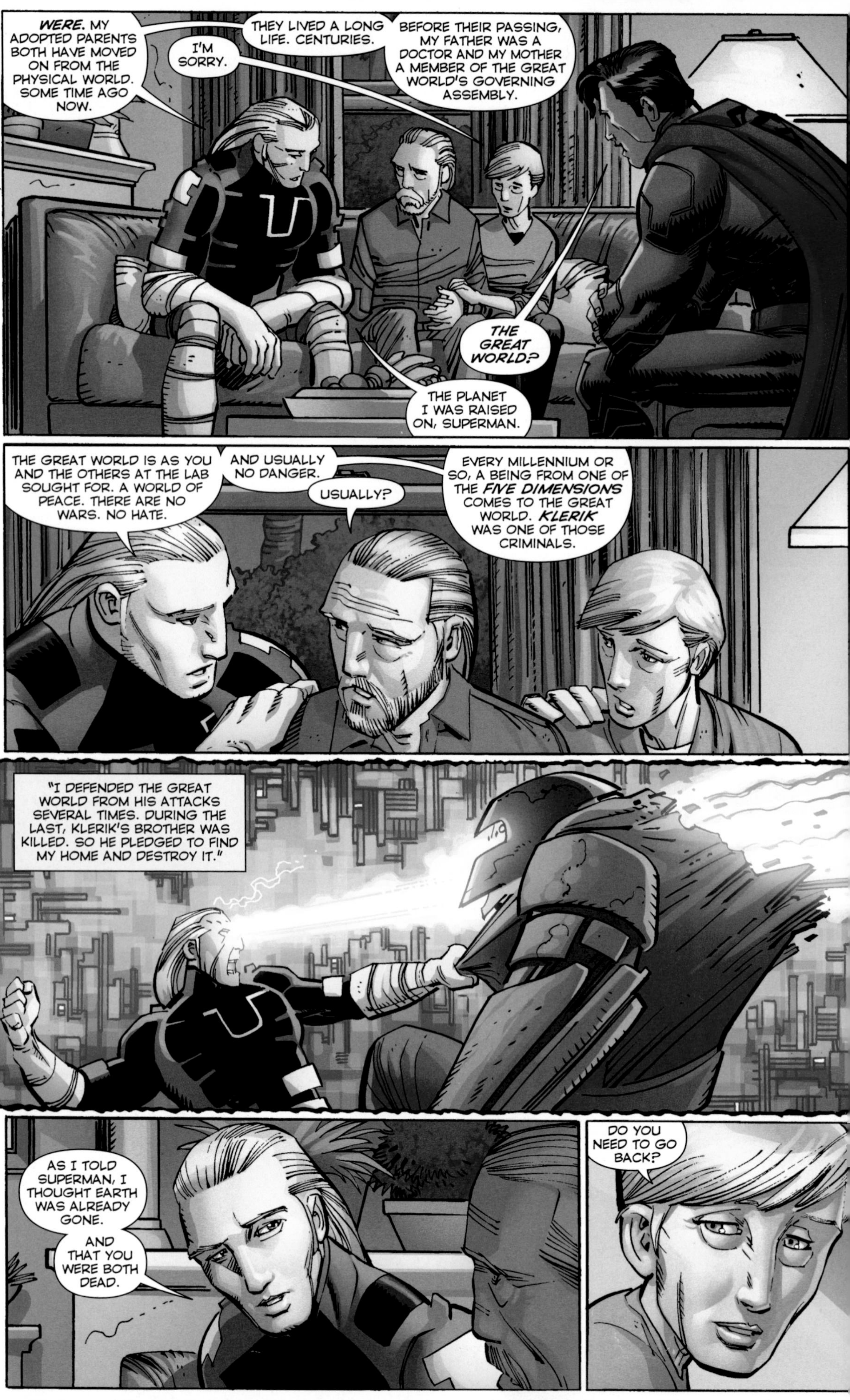
WERE. MY ADOPTED PARENTS BOTH HAVE MOVED ON FROM THE PHYSICAL WORLD. SOME TIME AGO NOW.
I'M SORRY.
THEY LIVED A LONG LIFE. CENTURIES.
BEFORE THEIR PASSING, MY FATHER WAS A DOCTOR AND MY MOTHER A MEMBER OF THE GREAT WORLD'S GOVERNING ASSEMBLY.
THE GREAT WORLD?
THE PLANET I WAS RAISED ON, SUPERMAN.
THE GREAT WORLD IS AS YOU AND THE OTHERS AT THE LAB SOUGHT FOR. A WORLD OF PEACE. THERE ARE NO WARS. NO HATE.
AND USUALLY NO DANGER.
USUALLY?
EVERY MILLENNIUM OR SO, A BEING FROM ONE OF THE FIVE DIMENSIONS COMES TO THE GREAT WORLD. KLERIK WAS ONE OF THOSE CRIMINALS.
"I DEFENDED THE GREAT WORLD FROM HIS ATTACKS SEVERAL TIMES. DURING THE LAST, KLERIK'S BROTHER WAS KILLED. SO HE PLEDGED TO FIND MY HOME AND DESTROY IT."
AS I TOLD SUPERMAN, I THOUGHT EARTH WAS ALREADY GONE.
AND THAT YOU WERE BOTH DEAD.
DO YOU NEED TO GO BACK?

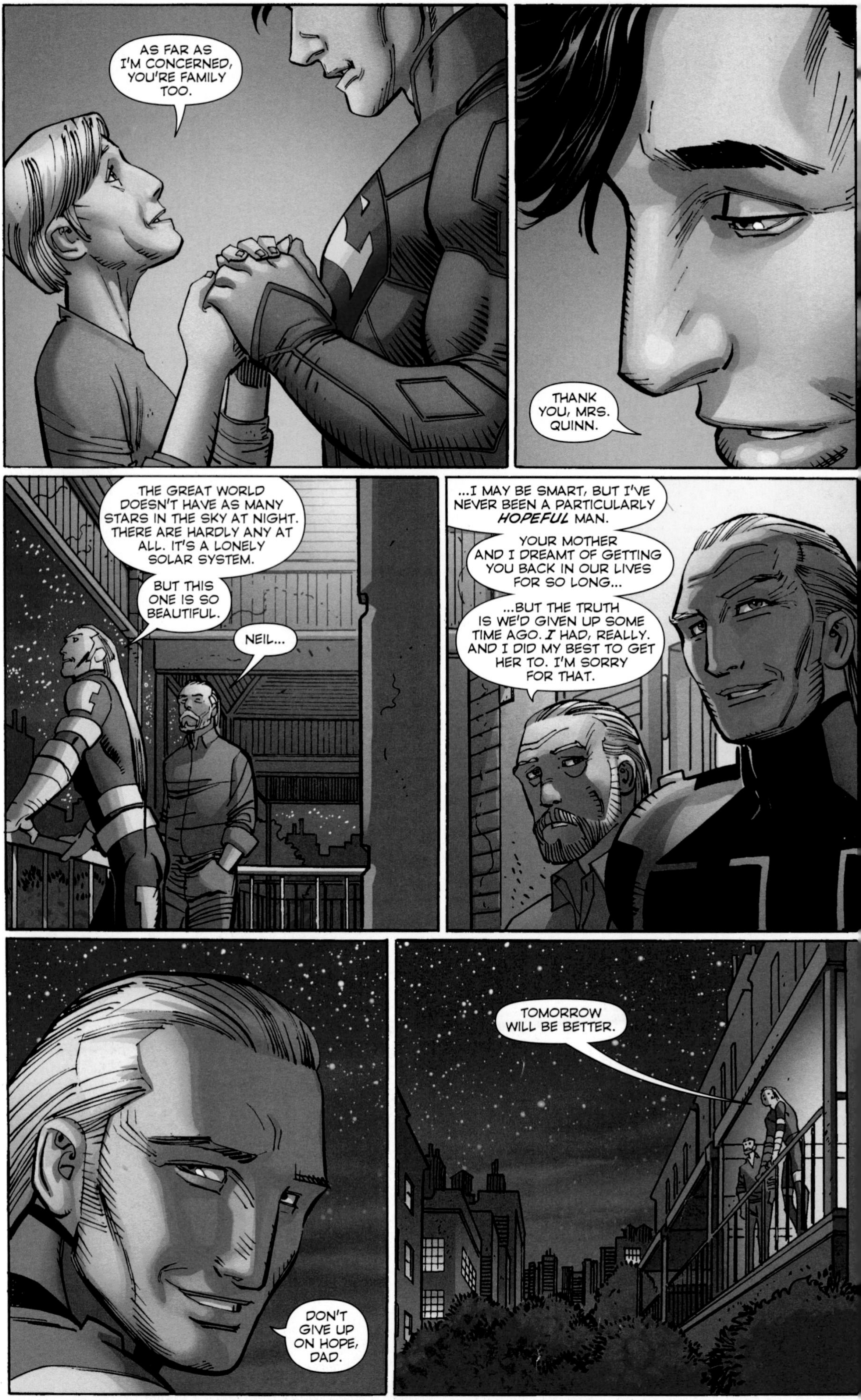
AS FAR AS I'M CONCERNED, YOU'RE FAMILY TOO.
THANK YOU, MRS. QUINN.
THE GREAT WORLD DOESN'T HAVE AS MANY STARS IN THE SKY AT NIGHT. THERE ARE HARDLY ANY AT ALL. IT'S A LONELY SOLAR SYSTEM.
BUT THIS ONE IS SO BEAUTIFUL.
NEIL...
...I MAY BE SMART, BUT I'VE NEVER BEEN A PARTICULARLY HOPEFUL MAN.
YOUR MOTHER AND I DREAMT OF GETTING YOU BACK IN OUR LIVES FOR SO LONG...
...BUT THE TRUTH IS WE'D GIVEN UP SOME TIME AGO. I HAD, REALLY. AND I DID MY BEST TO GET HER TO. I'M SORRY FOR THAT.
DON'T GIVE UP ON HOPE, DAD.
TOMORROW WILL BE BETTER.

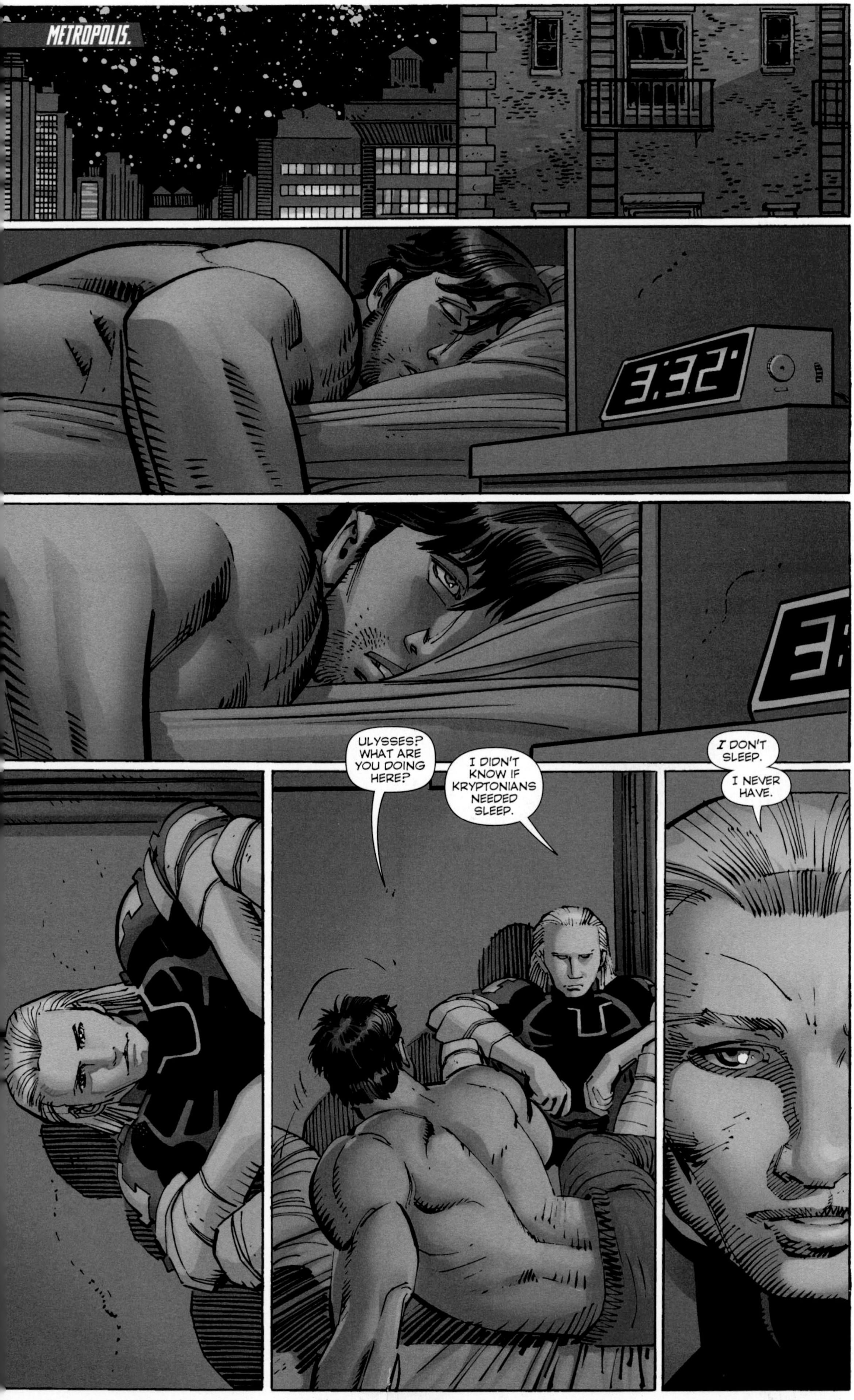
METROPOLIS.
3:32
ULYSSES? WHAT ARE YOU DOING HERE?
I DIDN'T KNOW IF KRYPTONIANS NEEDED SLEEP.
I DON'T SLEEP.
I NEVER HAVE.

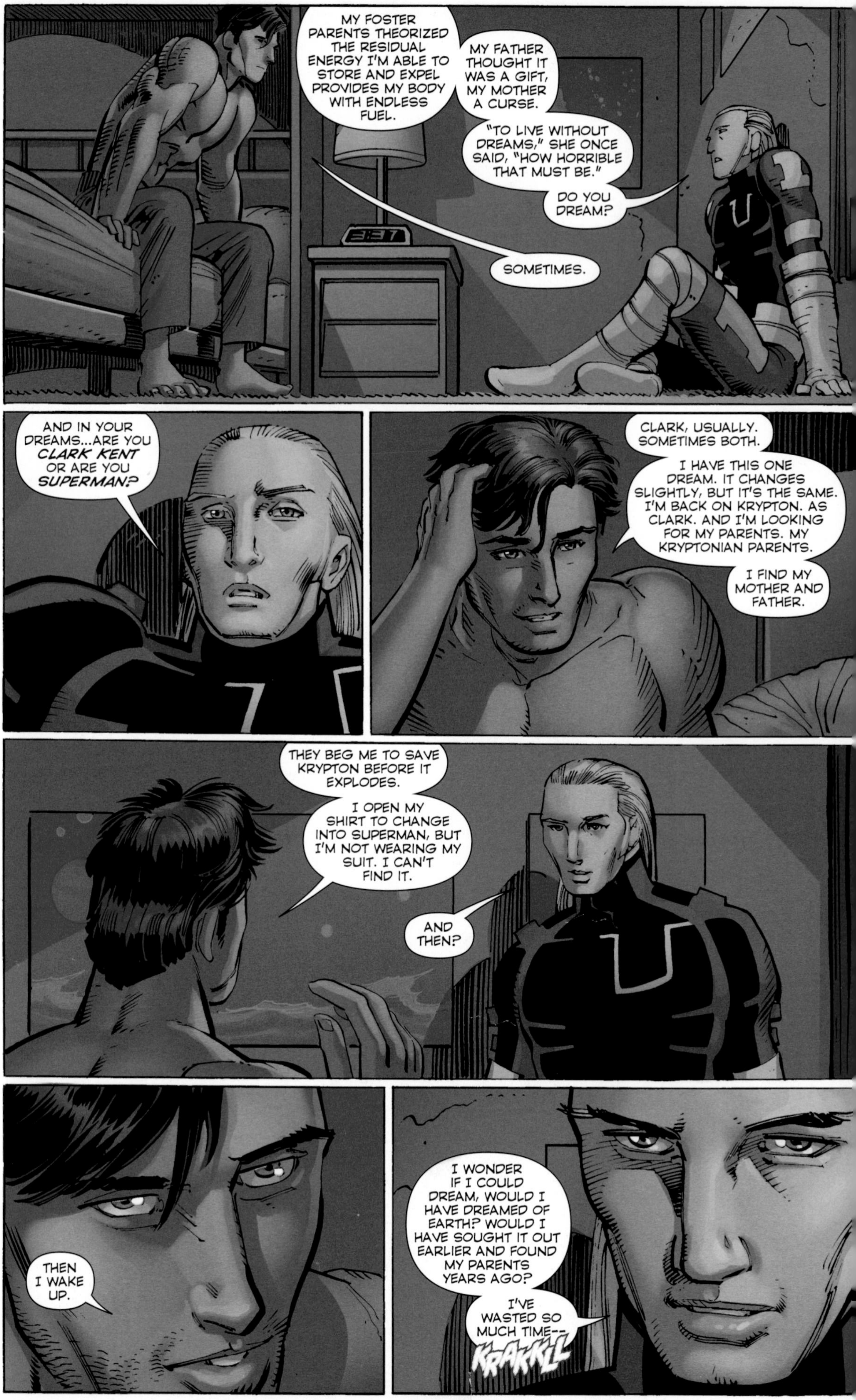

MY FOSTER PARENTS THEORIZED THE RESIDUAL ENERGY I'M ABLE TO STORE AND EXPEL PROVIDES MY BODY WITH ENDLESS FUEL.
MY FATHER THOUGHT IT WAS A GIFT, MY MOTHER A CURSE.
"TO LIVE WITHOUT DREAMS," SHE ONCE SAID, "HOW HORRIBLE THAT MUST BE."
DO YOU DREAM?
SOMETIMES.
AND IN YOUR DREAMS...ARE YOU *CLARK KENT* OR ARE YOU *SUPERMAN?*
CLARK, USUALLY. SOMETIMES BOTH.
I HAVE THIS ONE DREAM. IT CHANGES SLIGHTLY, BUT IT'S THE SAME. I'M BACK ON KRYPTON. AS CLARK. AND I'M LOOKING FOR MY PARENTS. MY KRYPTONIAN PARENTS.
I FIND MY MOTHER AND FATHER.
THEY BEG ME TO SAVE KRYPTON BEFORE IT EXPLODES.
I OPEN MY SHIRT TO CHANGE INTO SUPERMAN, BUT I'M NOT WEARING MY SUIT. I CAN'T FIND IT.
AND THEN?
THEN I WAKE UP.
I WONDER IF I COULD DREAM, WOULD I HAVE DREAMED OF EARTH? WOULD I HAVE SOUGHT IT OUT EARLIER AND FOUND MY PARENTS YEARS AGO?
I'VE WASTED SO MUCH TIME--
KRAKKLL

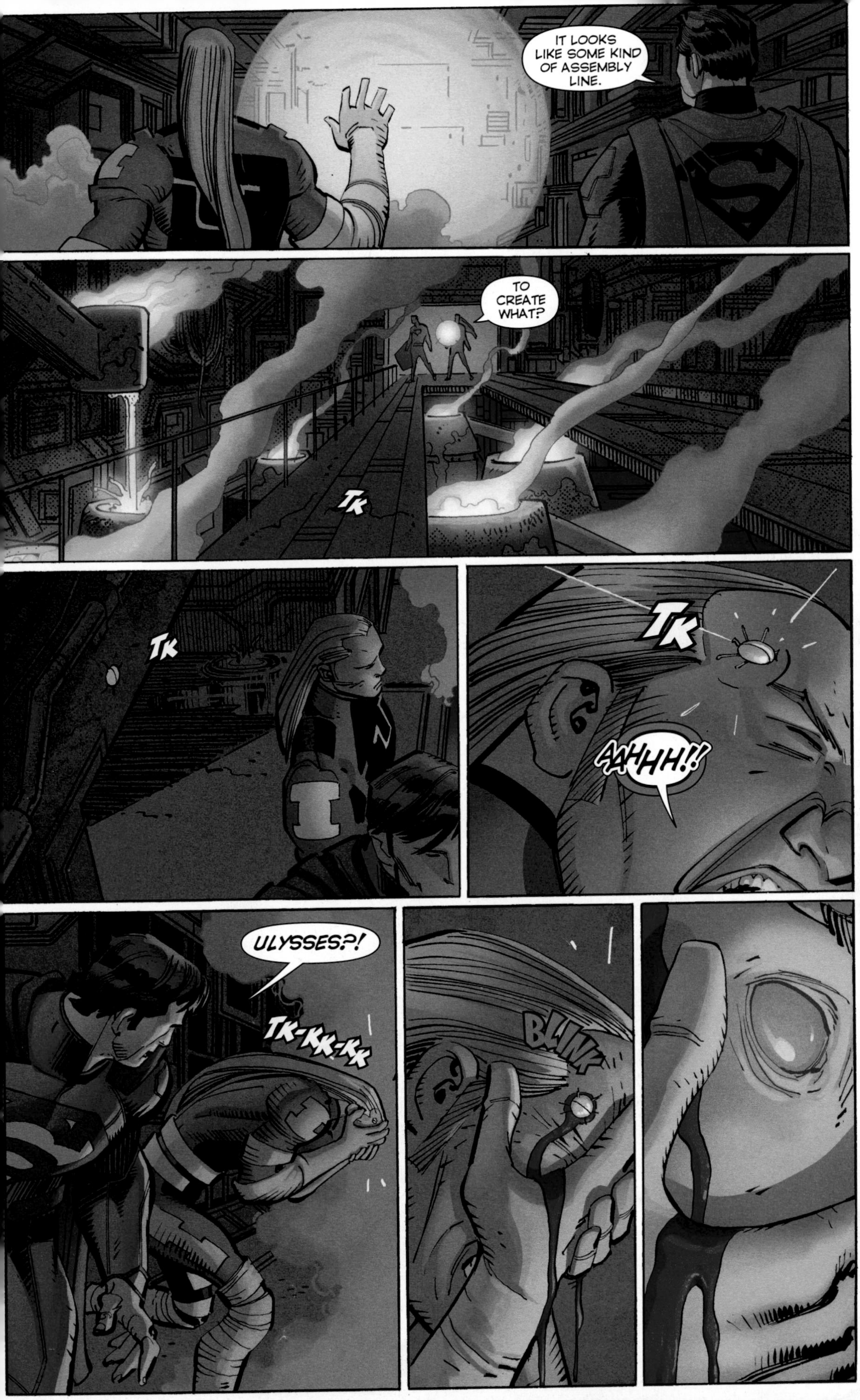
IT LOOKS LIKE SOME KIND OF ASSEMBLY LINE.
TO CREATE WHAT?
TK
TK
TK
AAHHH!!
ULYSSES?!
TK-KK-KK
BLINK

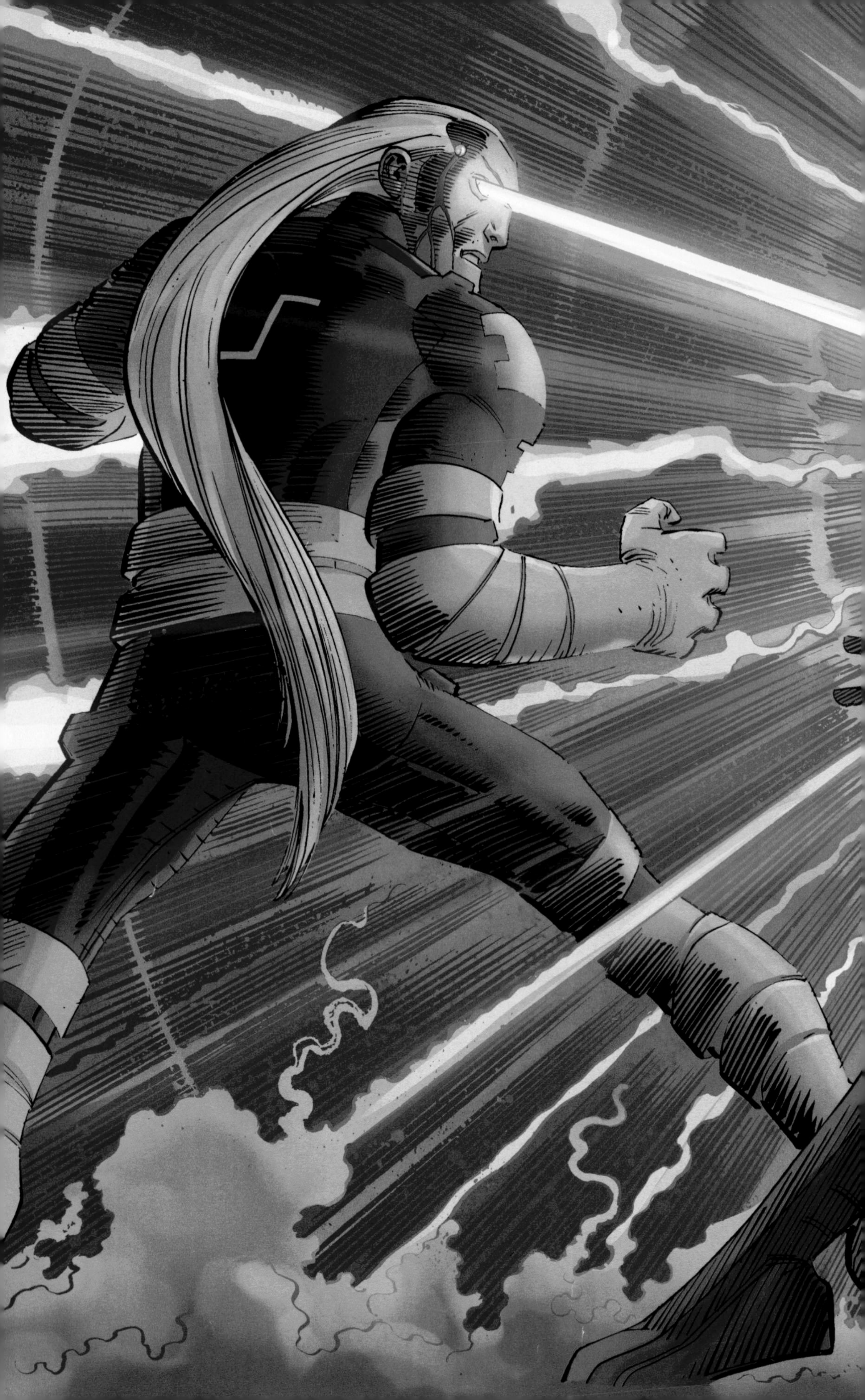

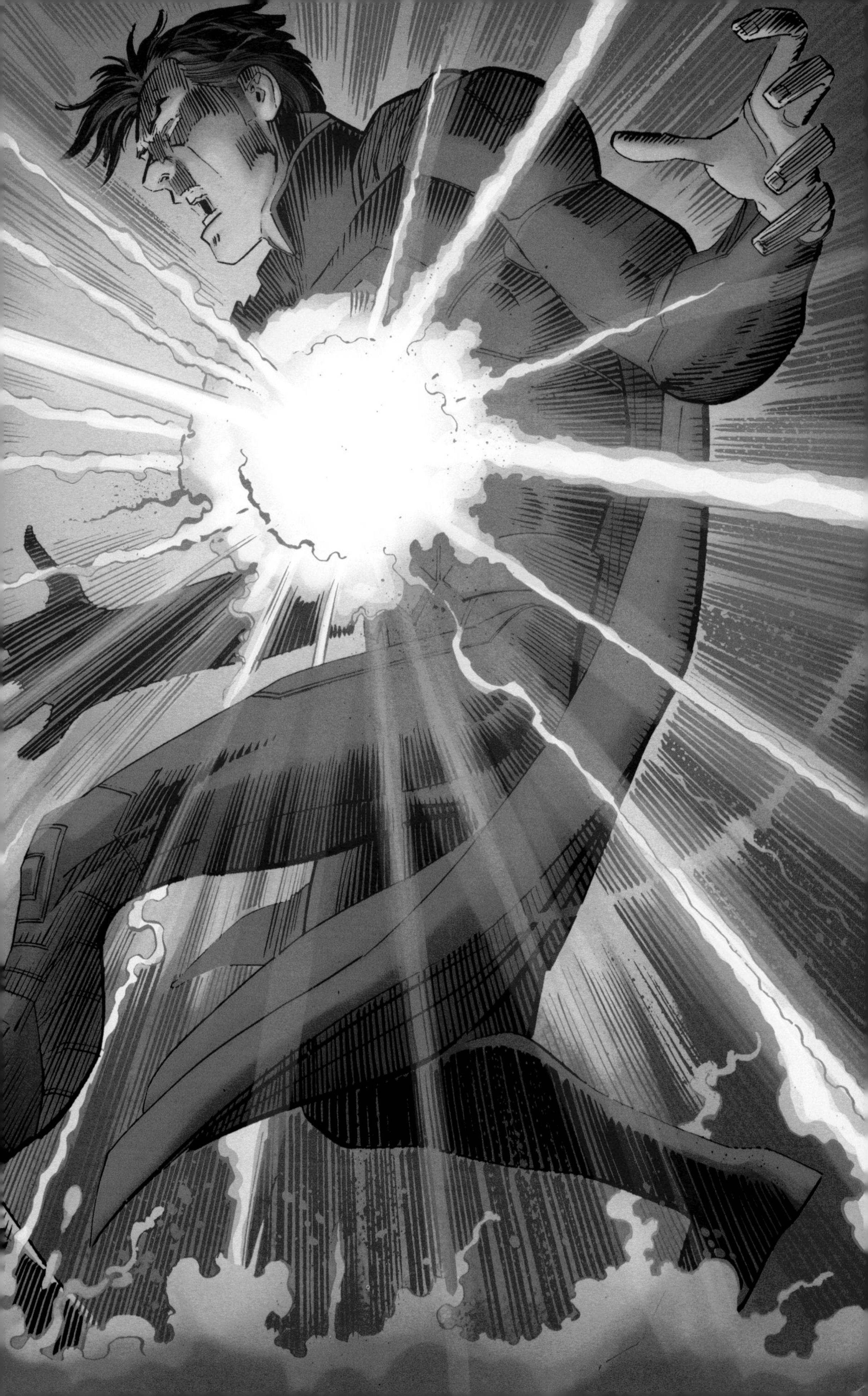

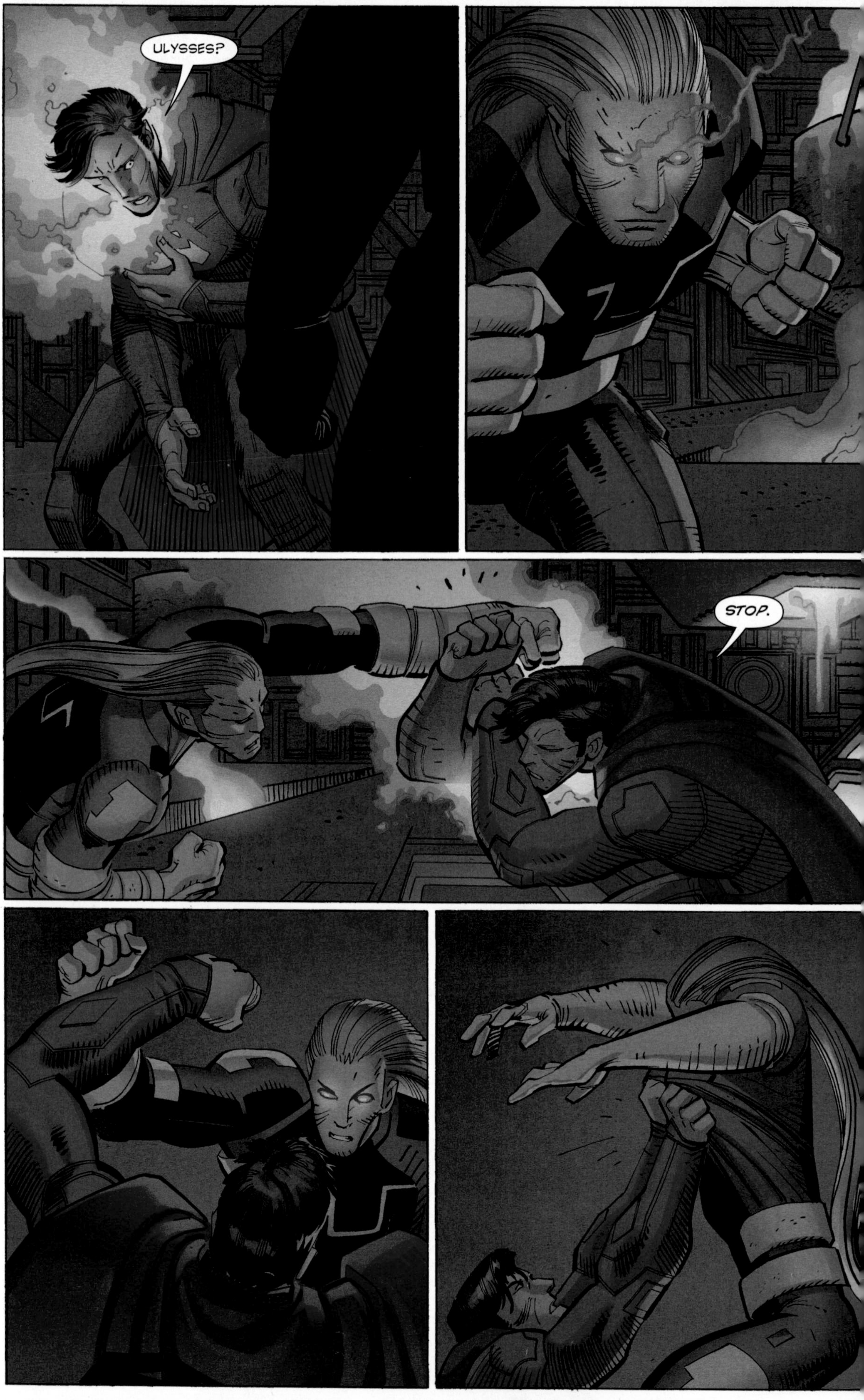
ULYSSES?
STOP.

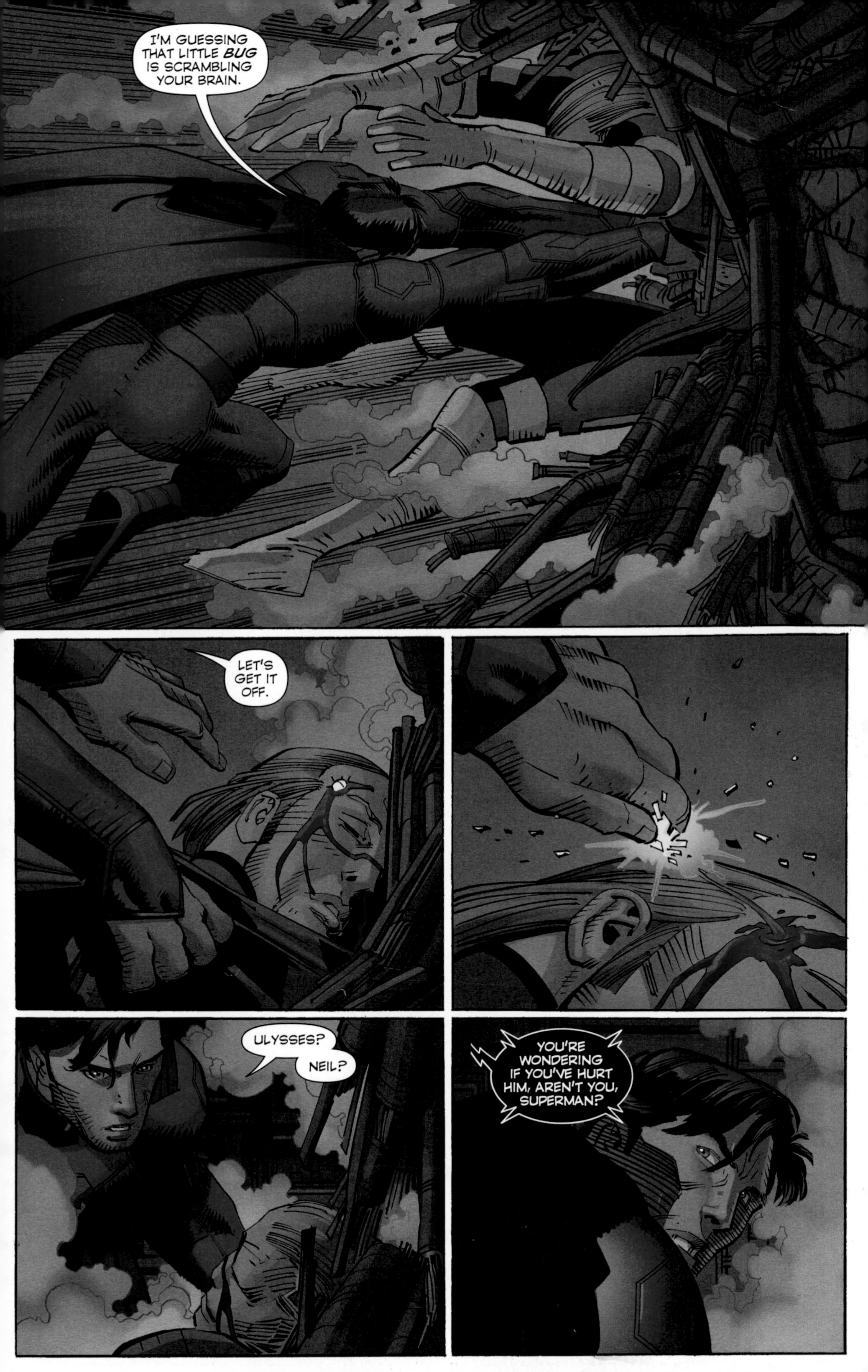
I'M GUESSING THAT LITTLE BUG IS SCRAMBLING YOUR BRAIN.
LET'S GET IT OFF.
ULYSSES?
NEIL?
YOU'RE WONDERING IF YOU'VE HURT HIM, AREN'T YOU, SUPERMAN?

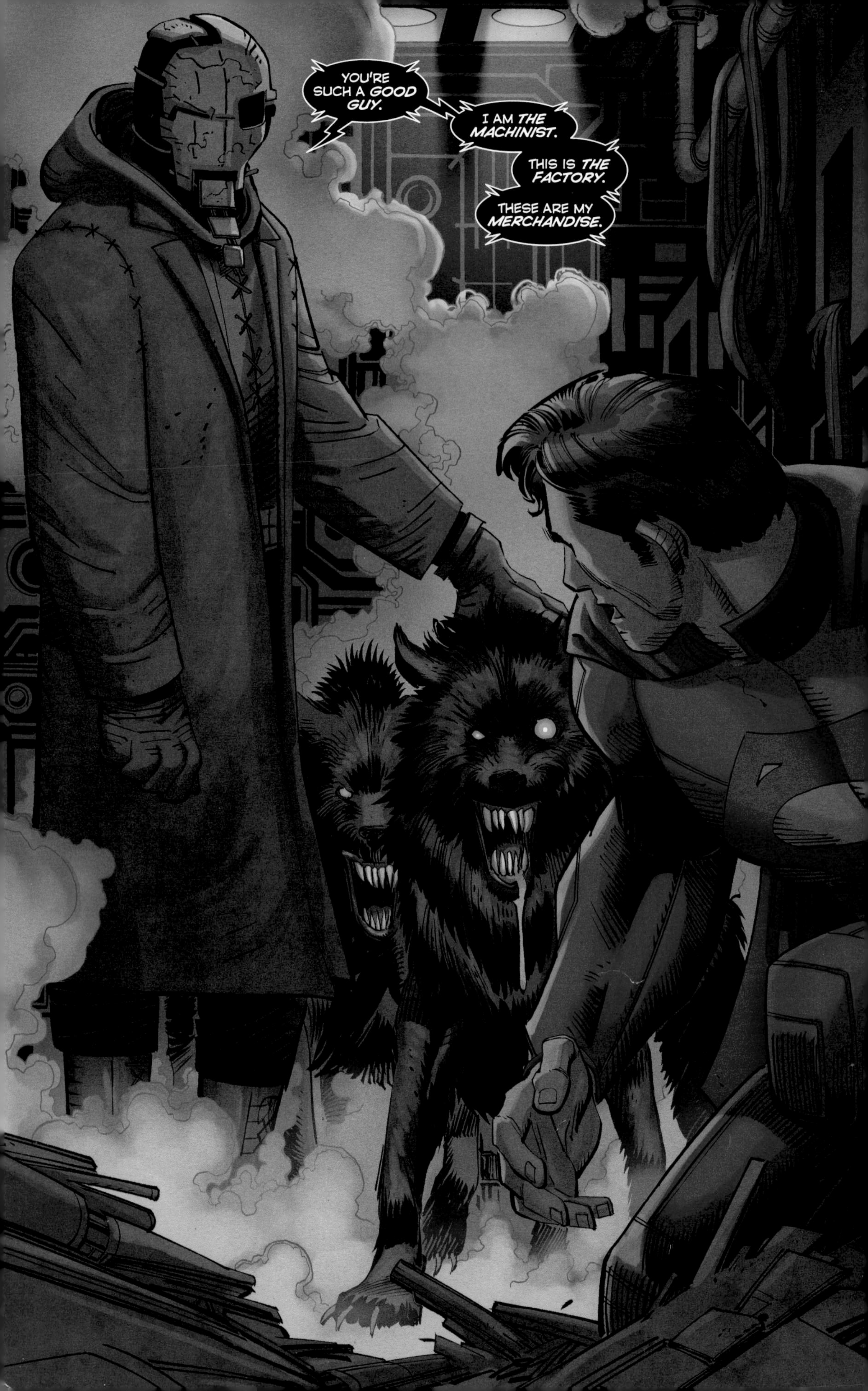
YOU'RE SUCH A GOOD GUY.
I AM THE MACHINIST.
THIS IS THE FACTORY.
THESE ARE MY MERCHANDISE.

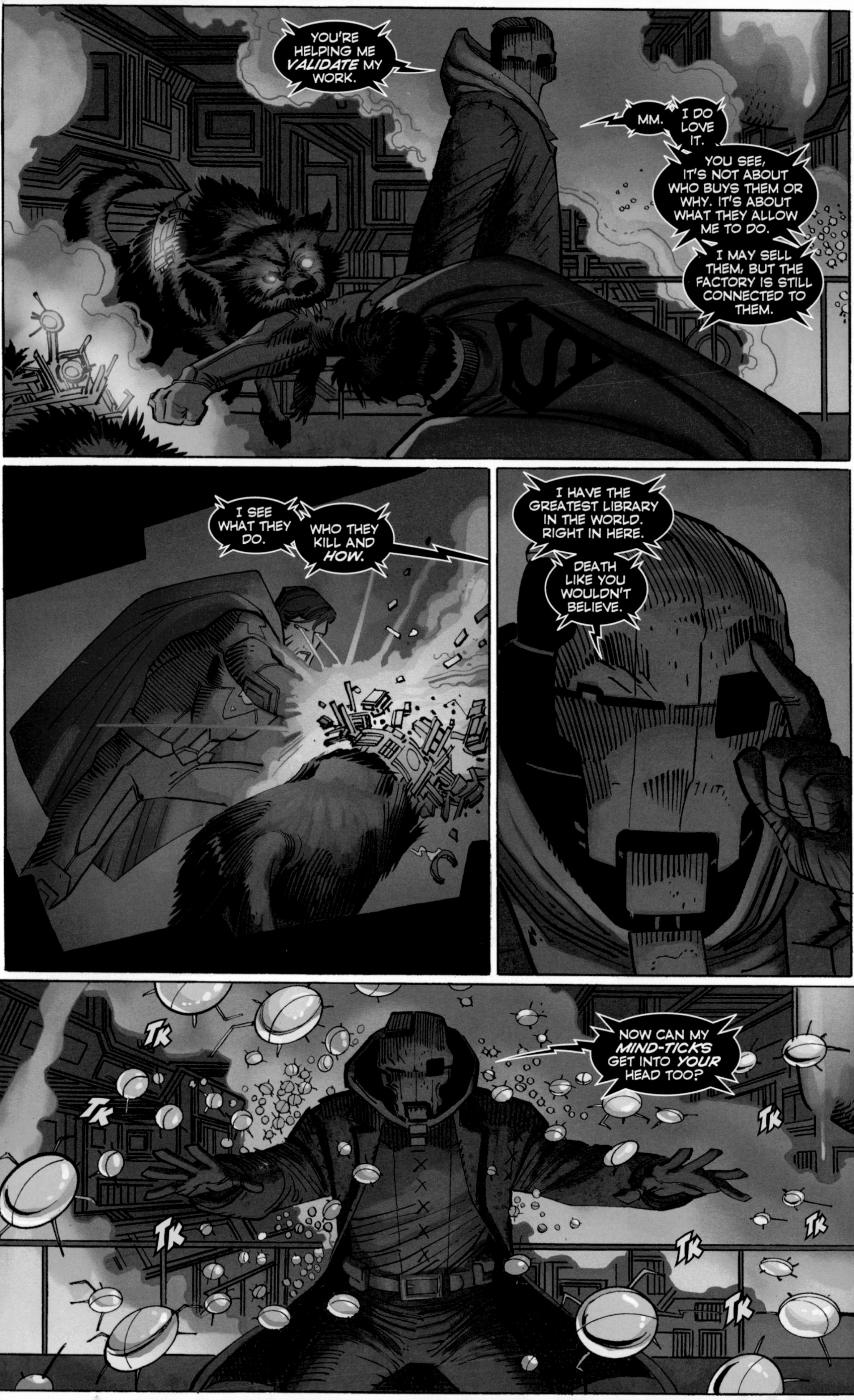
YOU'RE HELPING ME VALIDATE MY WORK.
MM.
I DO LOVE IT.
YOU SEE, IT'S NOT ABOUT WHO BUYS THEM OR WHY. IT'S ABOUT WHAT THEY ALLOW ME TO DO.
I MAY SELL THEM, BUT THE FACTORY IS STILL CONNECTED TO THEM.
I SEE WHAT THEY DO.
WHO THEY KILL AND HOW.
I HAVE THE GREATEST LIBRARY IN THE WORLD. RIGHT IN HERE.
DEATH LIKE YOU WOULDN'T BELIEVE.
NOW CAN MY MIND-TICKS GET INTO YOUR HEAD TOO?
TK
TK
TK
TK
TK
TK
TK

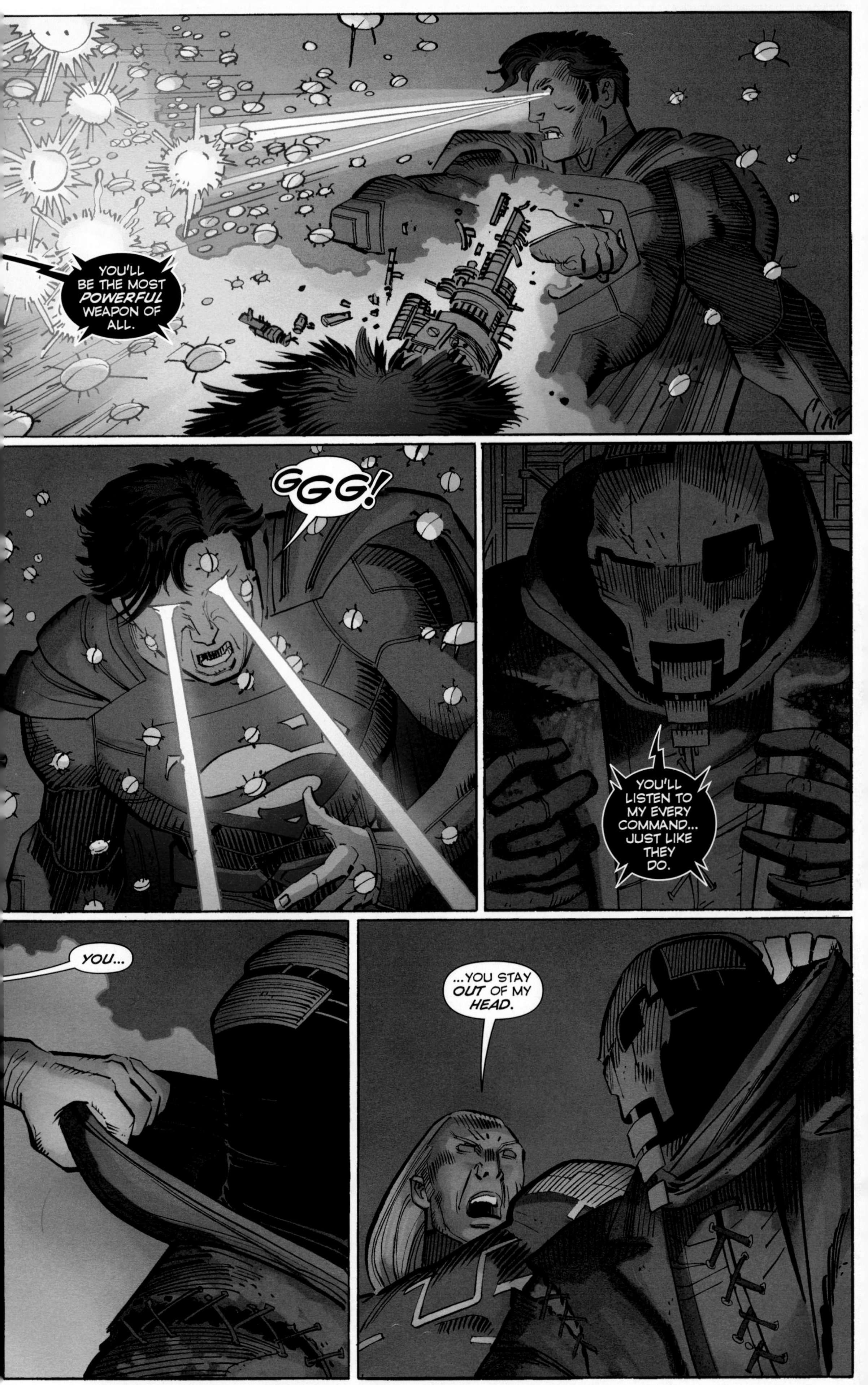
YOU'LL BE THE MOST *POWERFUL* WEAPON OF ALL.
GGG!
YOU'LL LISTEN TO MY EVERY COMMAND... JUST LIKE THEY DO.
YOU...
...YOU STAY *OUT* OF MY *HEAD*.

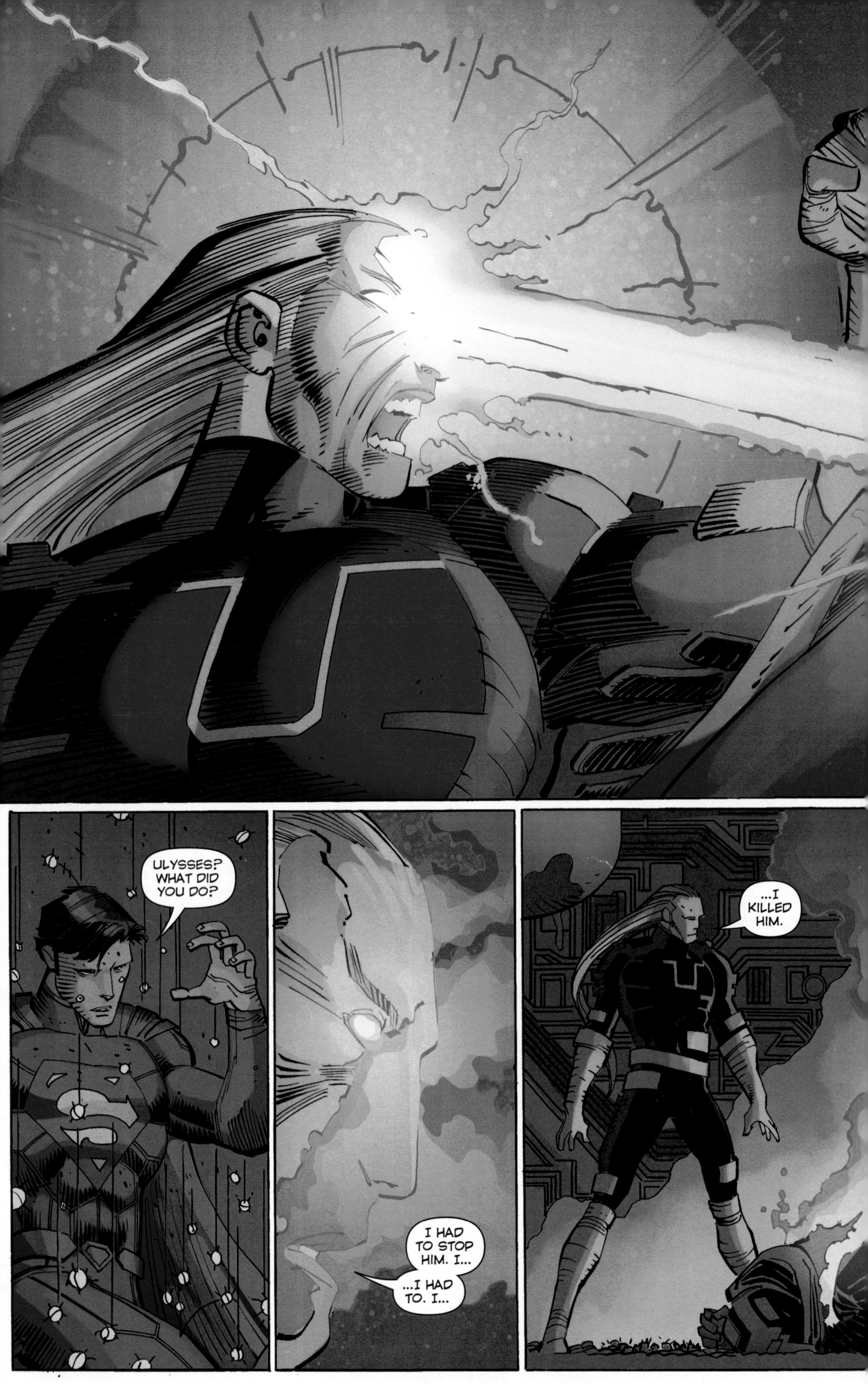
ULYSSES? WHAT DID YOU DO?
I HAD TO STOP HIM. I...
...I HAD TO. I...
...I KILLED HIM.

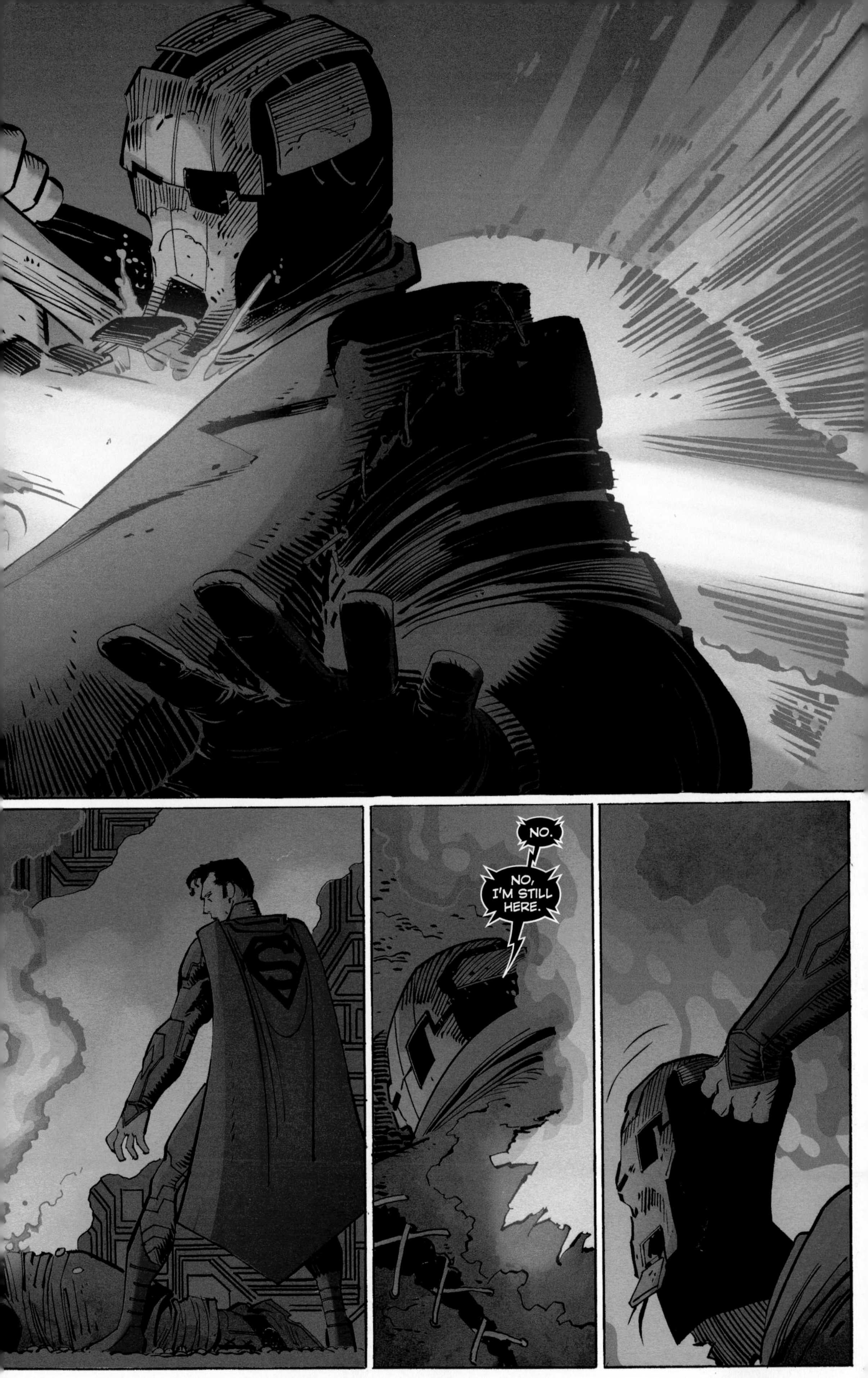
NO.
NO, I'M STILL HERE.

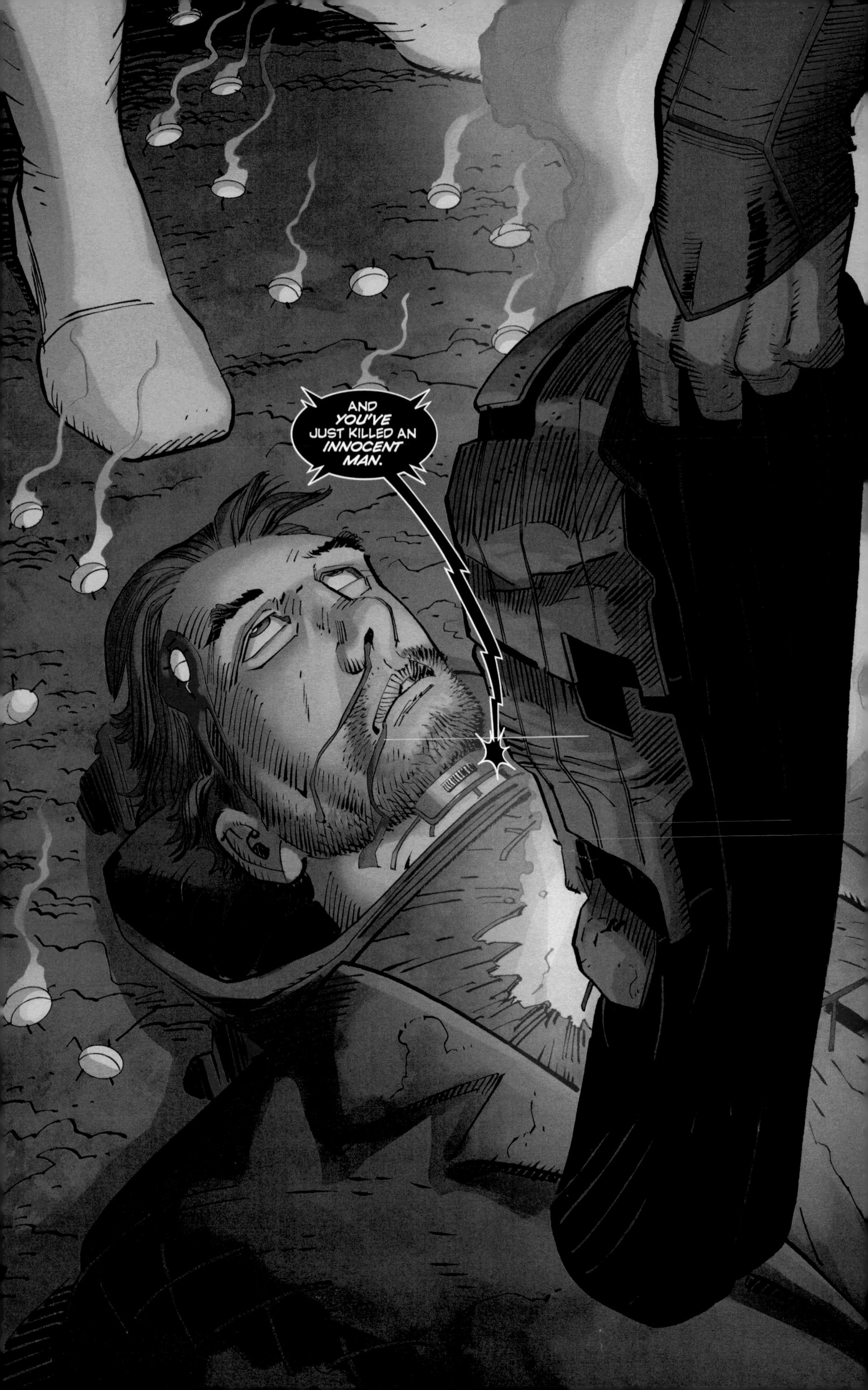
AND *YOU'VE* JUST KILLED AN *INNOCENT MAN.*

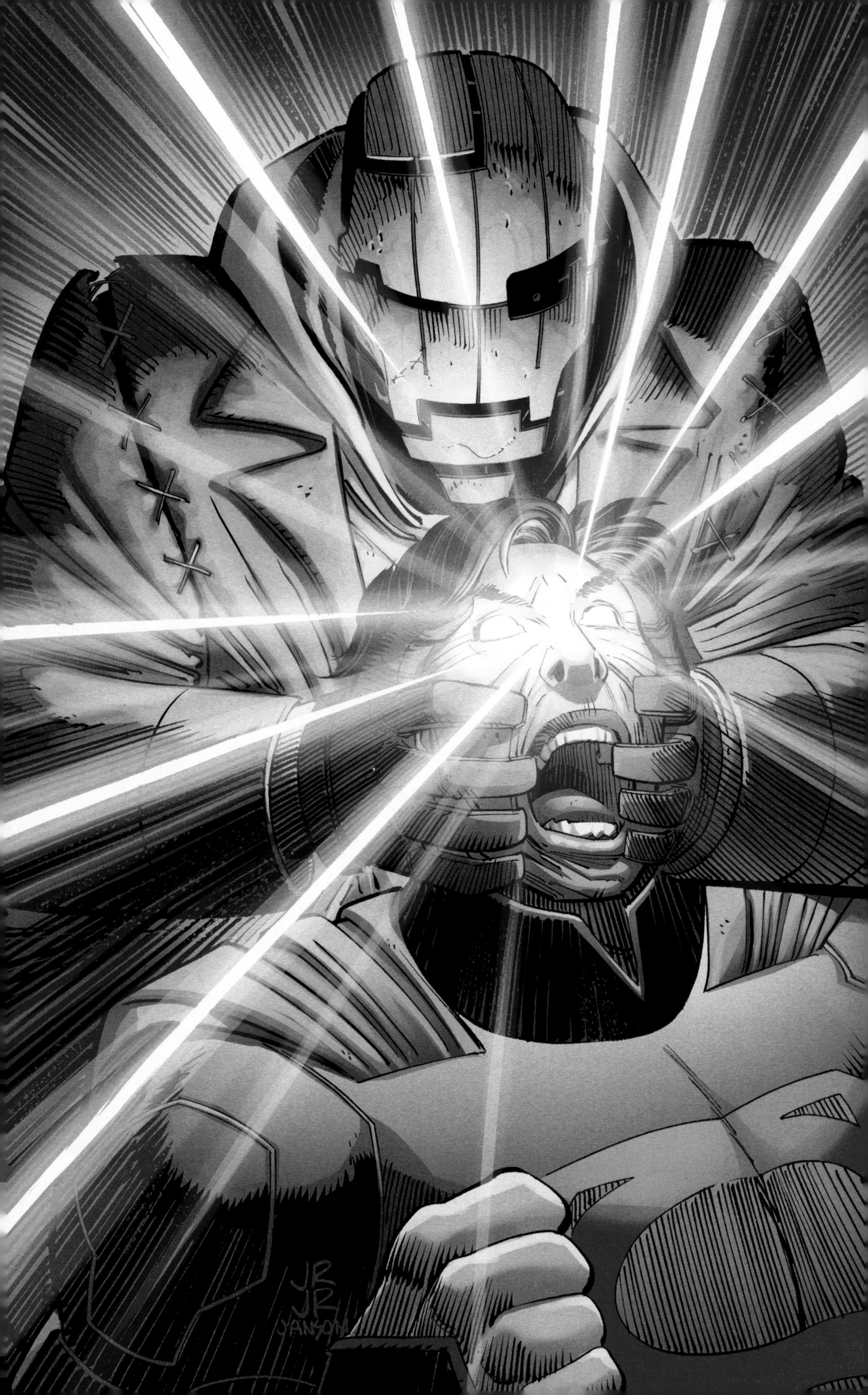
JR
JR
JANSON

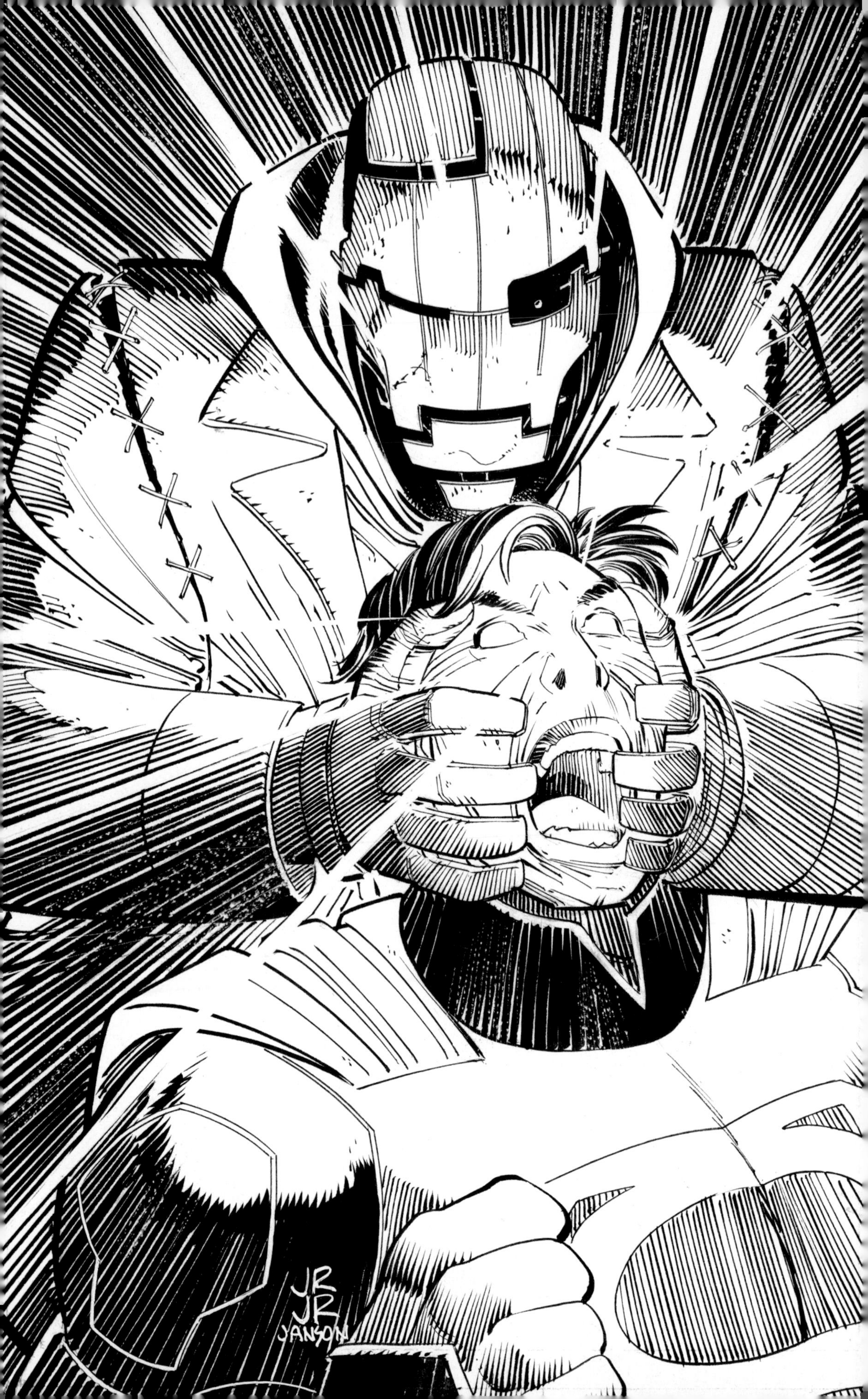
JR
JR
JANSON

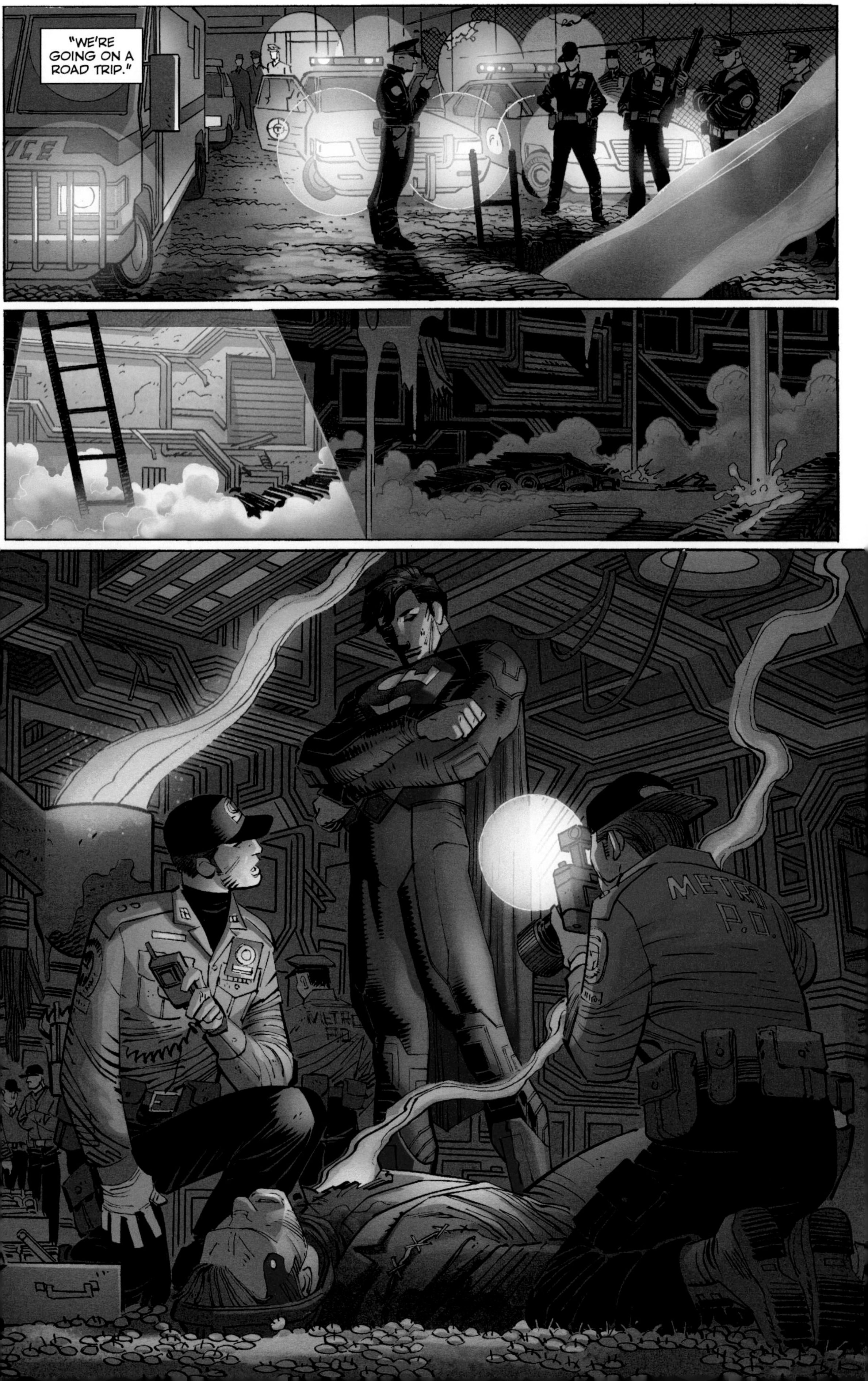
"WE'RE GOING ON A ROAD TRIP."
METRO P.D.

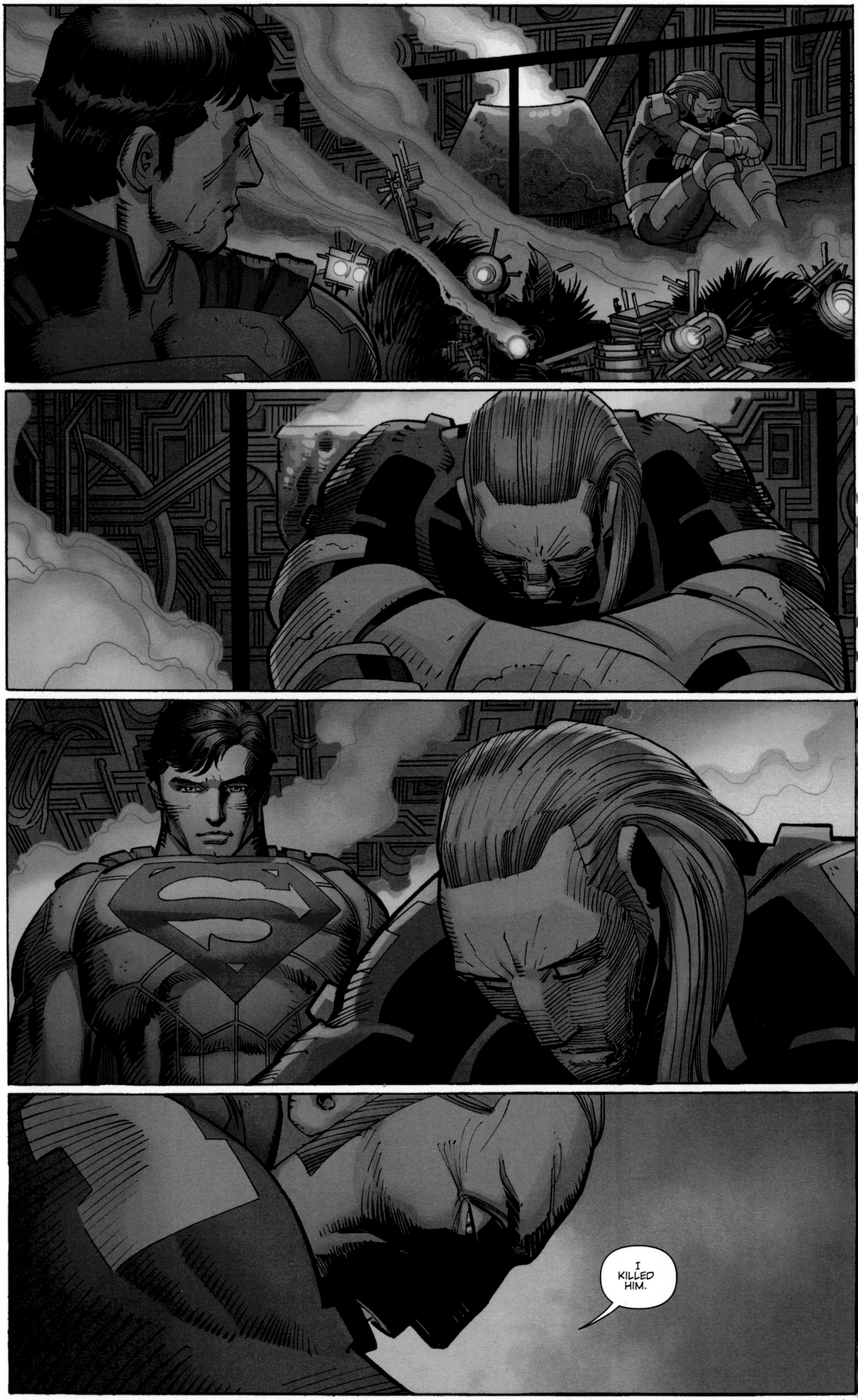
I KILLED HIM.

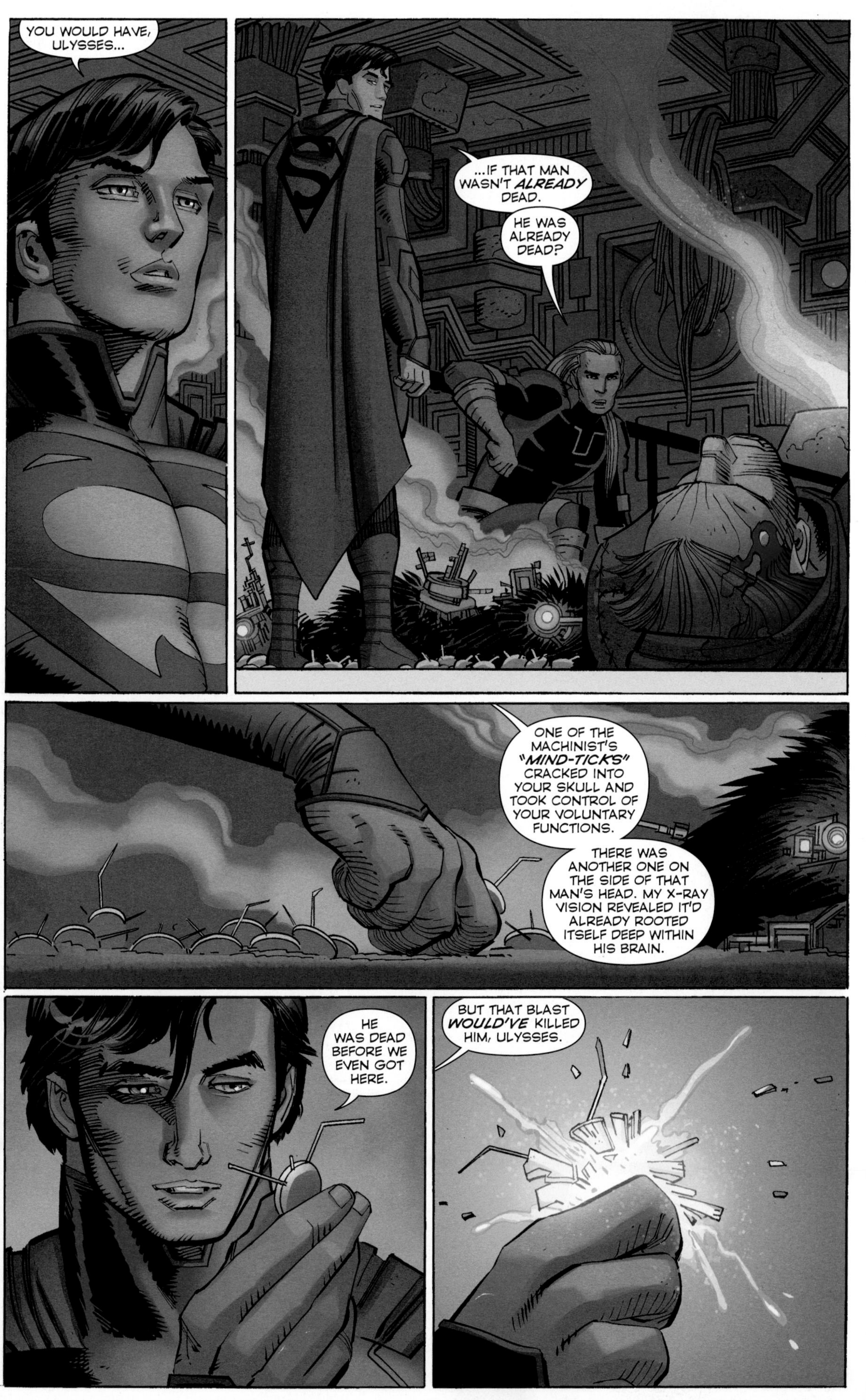
YOU WOULD HAVE, ULYSSES...
...IF THAT MAN WASN'T *ALREADY* DEAD.
HE WAS ALREADY DEAD?
ONE OF THE MACHINIST'S *"MIND-TICKS"* CRACKED INTO YOUR SKULL AND TOOK CONTROL OF YOUR VOLUNTARY FUNCTIONS.
THERE WAS ANOTHER ONE ON THE SIDE OF THAT MAN'S HEAD. MY X-RAY VISION REVEALED IT'D ALREADY ROOTED ITSELF DEEP WITHIN HIS BRAIN.
HE WAS DEAD BEFORE WE EVEN GOT HERE.
BUT THAT BLAST *WOULD'VE* KILLED HIM, ULYSSES.

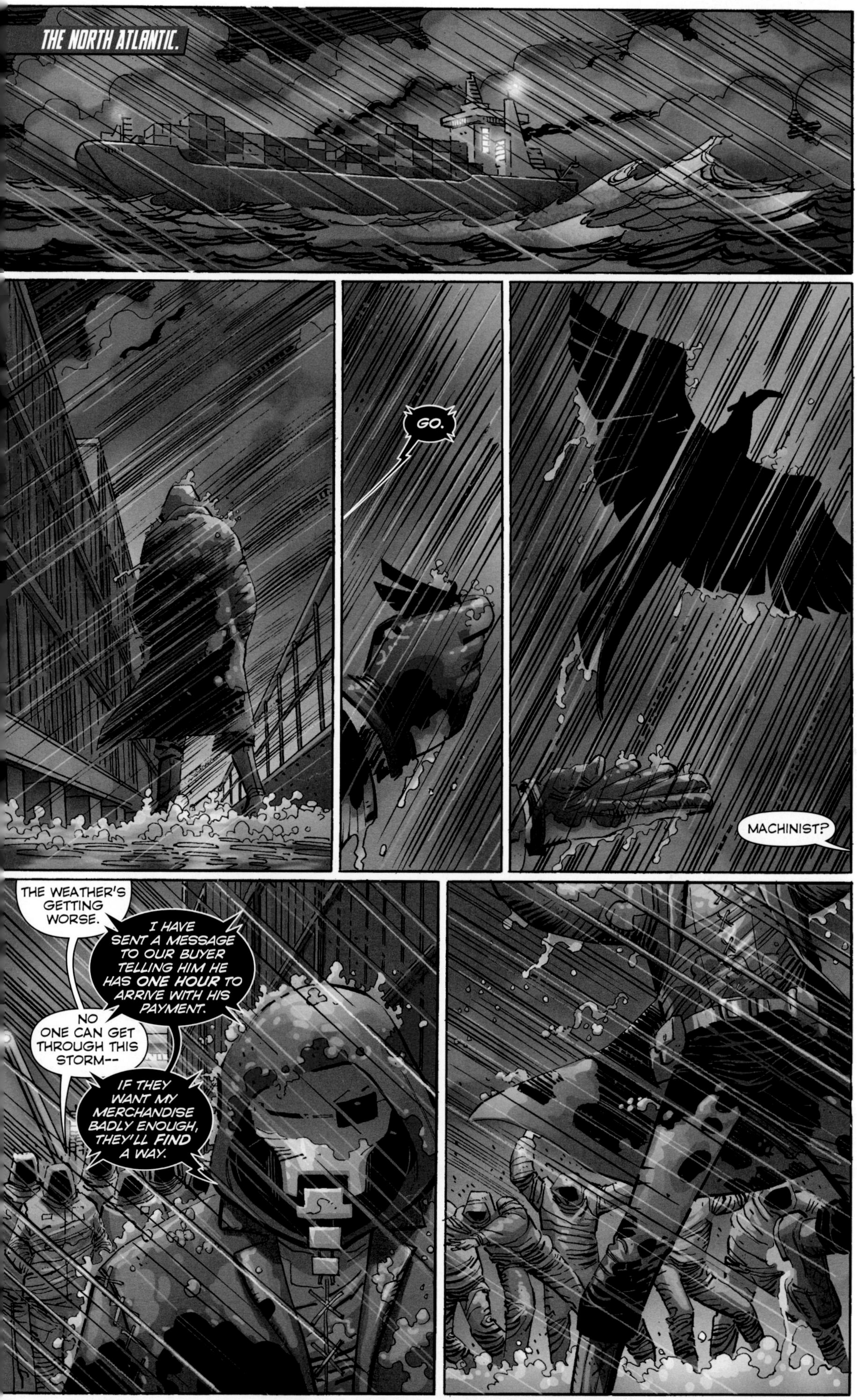
THE NORTH ATLANTIC.
GO.
MACHINIST?
THE WEATHER'S GETTING WORSE.
I HAVE SENT A MESSAGE TO OUR BUYER TELLING HIM HE HAS ONE HOUR TO ARRIVE WITH HIS PAYMENT.
NO ONE CAN GET THROUGH THIS STORM--
IF THEY WANT MY MERCHANDISE BADLY ENOUGH, THEY'LL FIND A WAY.

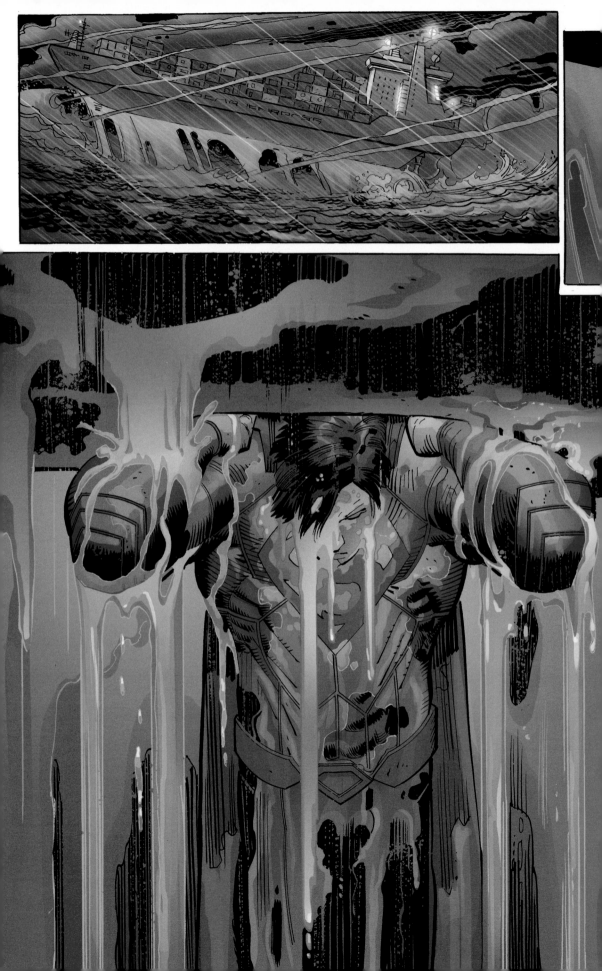

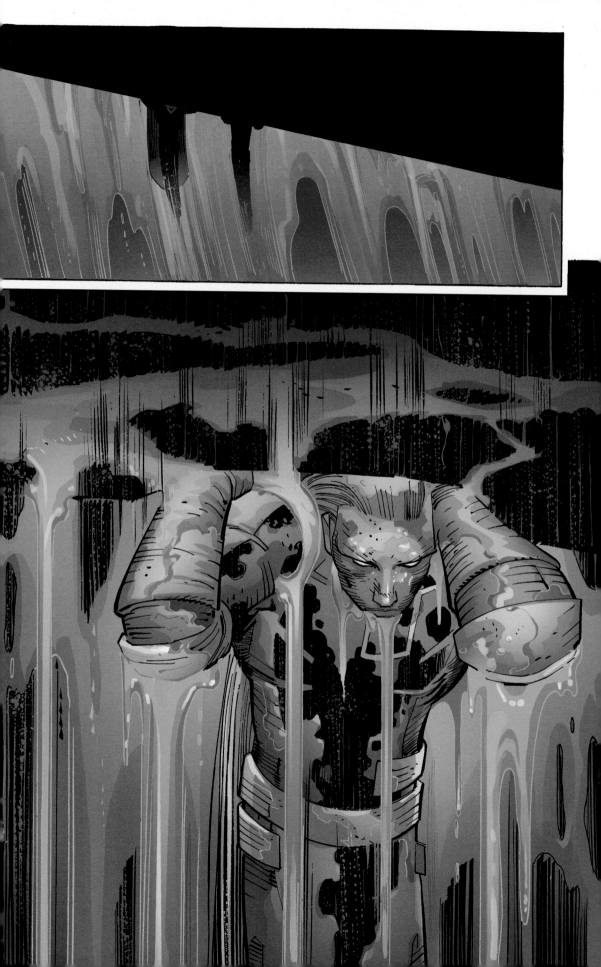

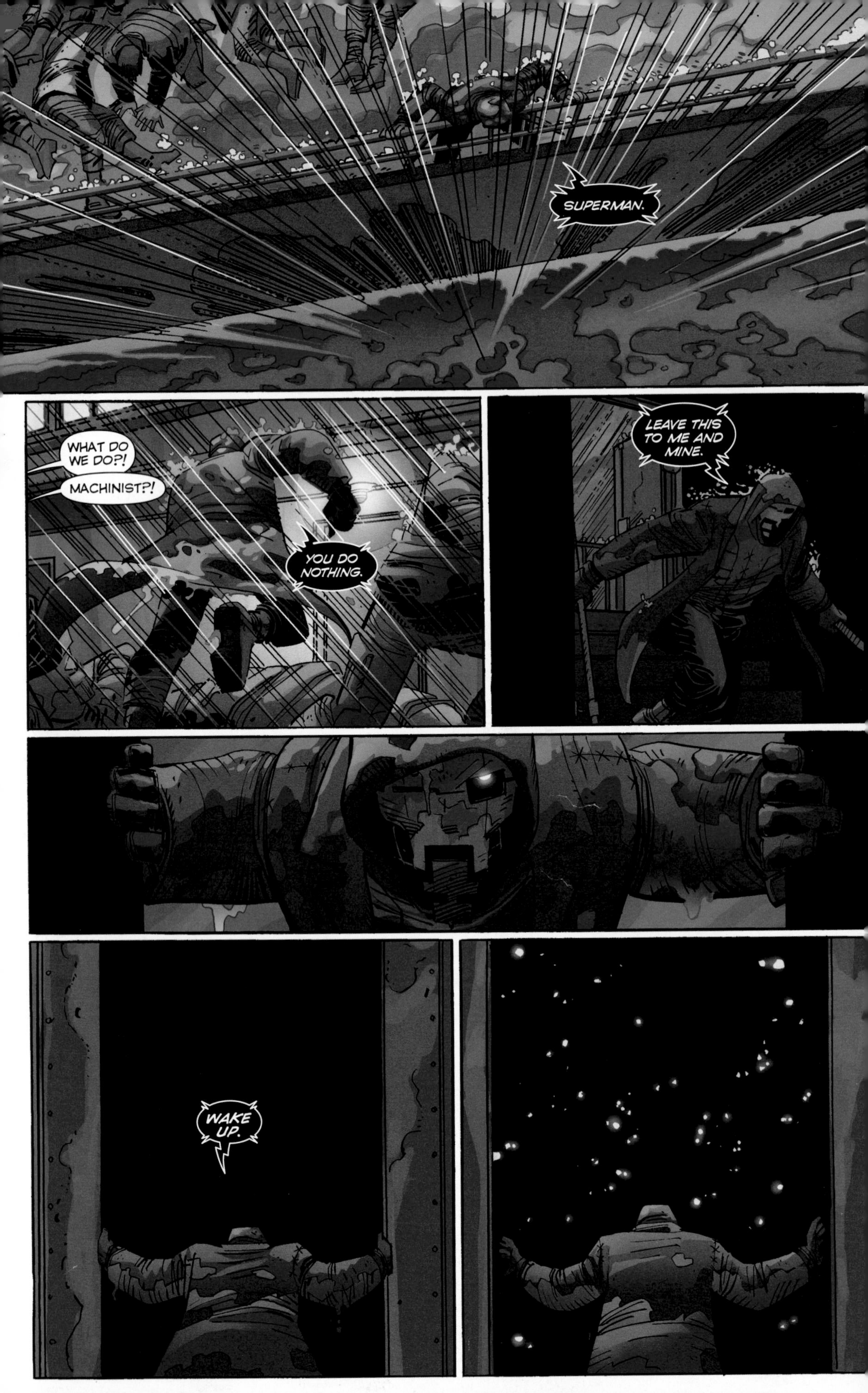
SUPERMAN.
WHAT DO WE DO?!
MACHINIST?!
YOU DO NOTHING.
LEAVE THIS TO ME AND MINE.
WAKE UP.

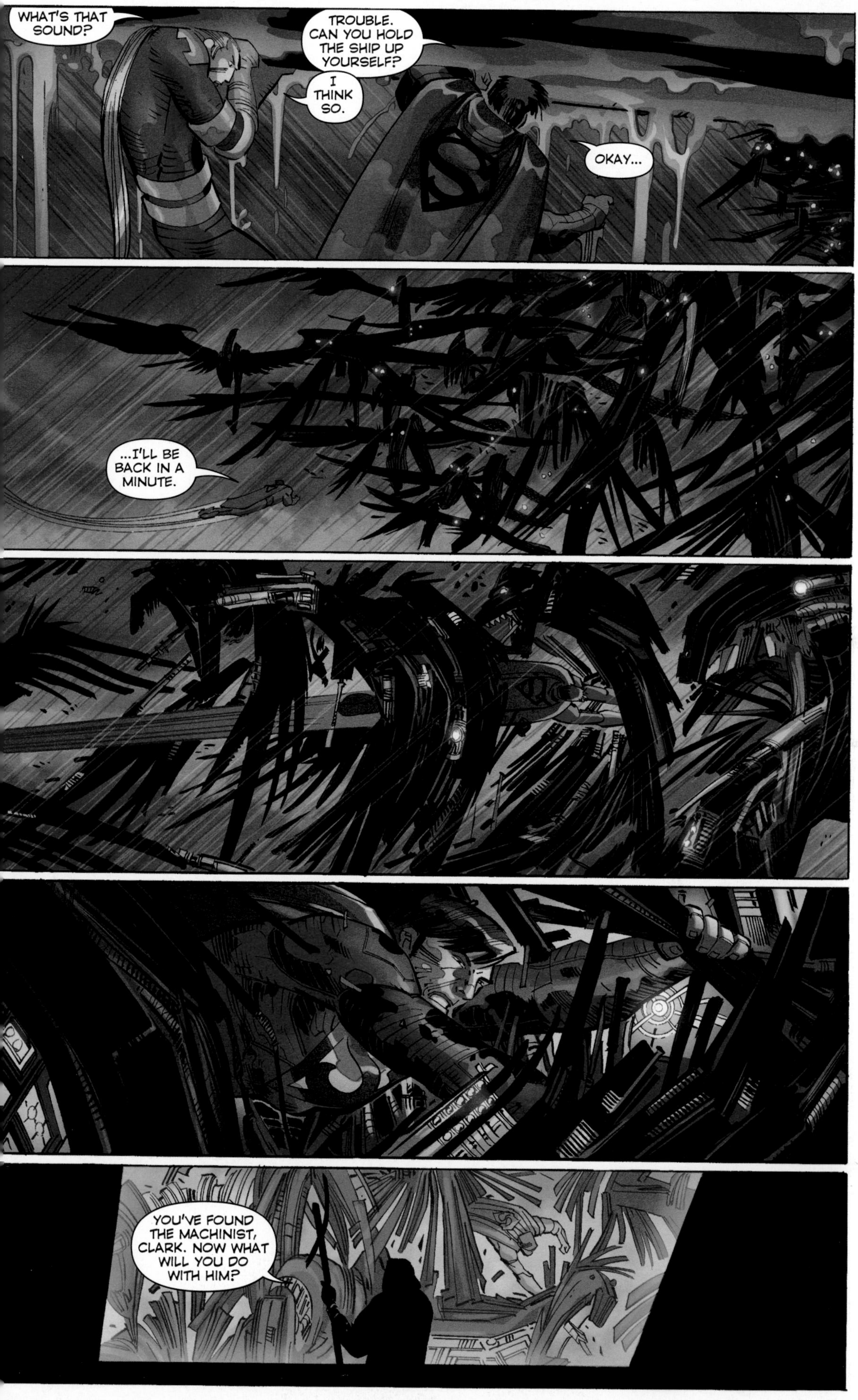
WHAT'S THAT SOUND?
TROUBLE. CAN YOU HOLD THE SHIP UP YOURSELF?
I THINK SO.
OKAY...
...I'LL BE BACK IN A MINUTE.
YOU'VE FOUND THE MACHINIST, CLARK. NOW WHAT WILL YOU DO WITH HIM?

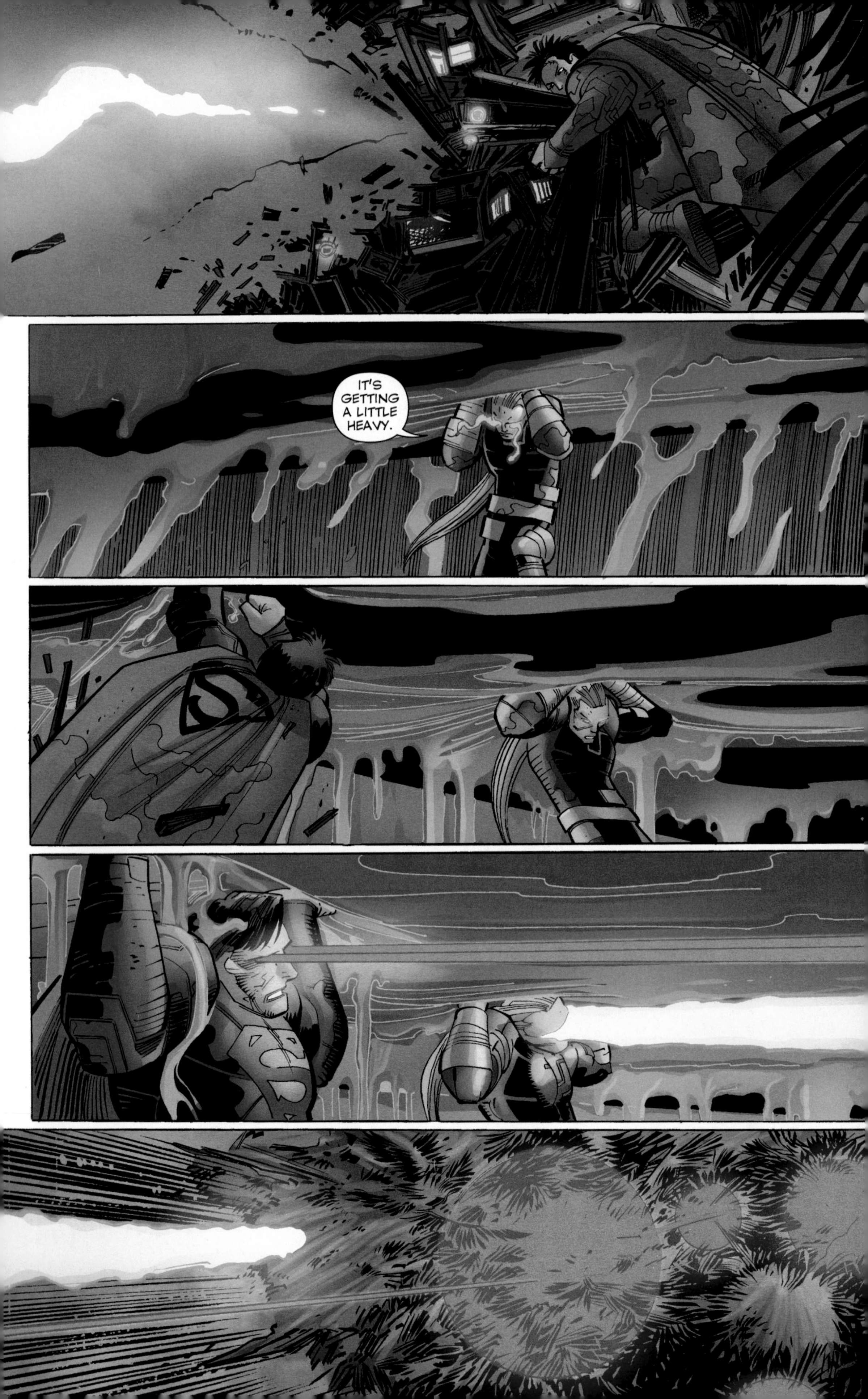
IT'S GETTING A LITTLE HEAVY.

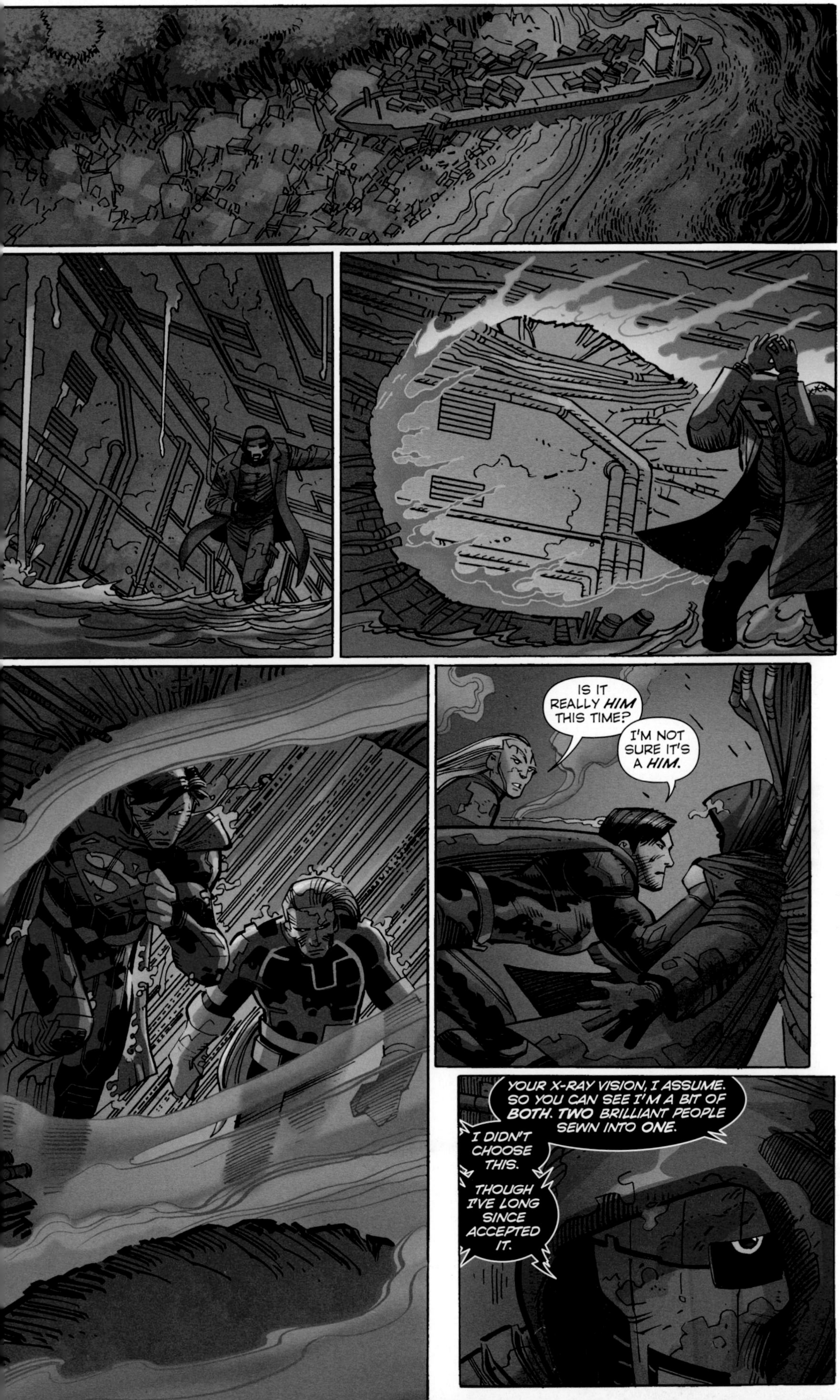
IS IT REALLY HIM THIS TIME?
I'M NOT SURE IT'S A HIM.
YOUR X-RAY VISION, I ASSUME. SO YOU CAN SEE I'M A BIT OF BOTH. TWO BRILLIANT PEOPLE SEWN INTO ONE.
I DIDN'T CHOOSE THIS.
THOUGH I'VE LONG SINCE ACCEPTED IT.

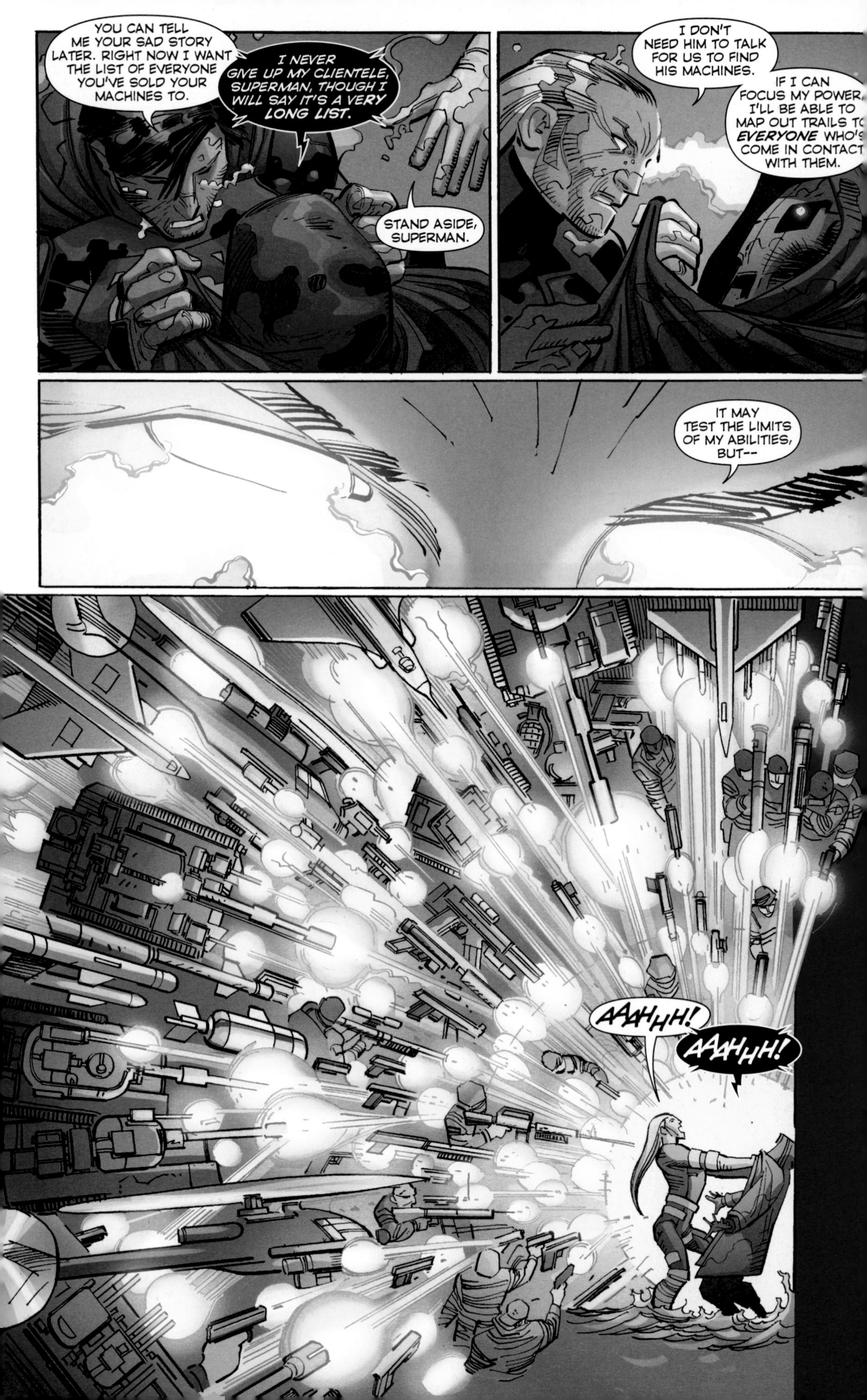
YOU CAN TELL ME YOUR SAD STORY LATER. RIGHT NOW I WANT THE LIST OF EVERYONE YOU'VE SOLD YOUR MACHINES TO.
I NEVER GIVE UP MY CLIENTELE, SUPERMAN, THOUGH I WILL SAY IT'S A VERY LONG LIST.
STAND ASIDE, SUPERMAN.
I DON'T NEED HIM TO TALK FOR US TO FIND HIS MACHINES.
IF I CAN FOCUS MY POWER, I'LL BE ABLE TO MAP OUT TRAILS TO EVERYONE WHO'S COME IN CONTACT WITH THEM.
IT MAY TEST THE LIMITS OF MY ABILITIES, BUT--
AAAHHH!
AAAHHH!

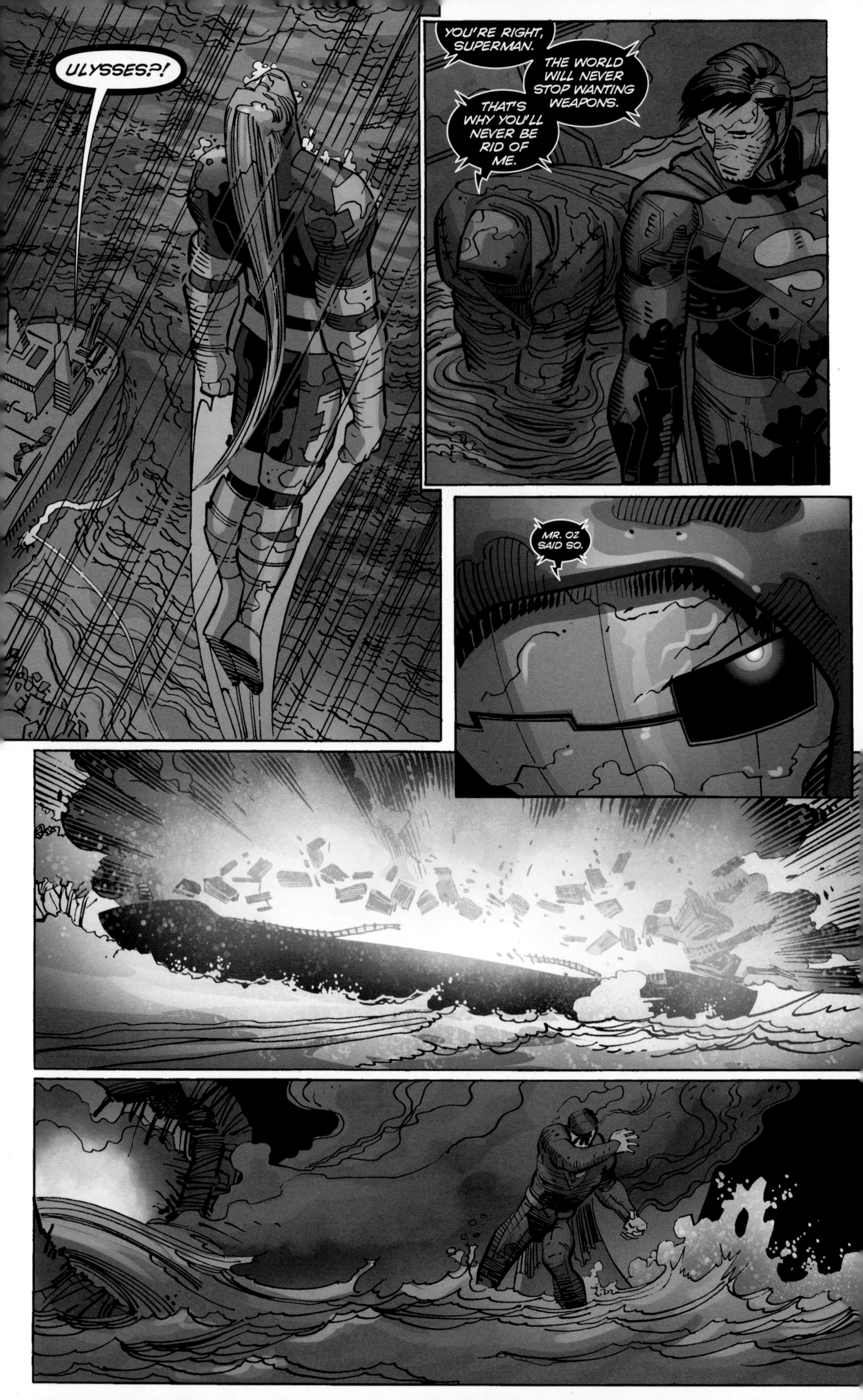
ULYSSES?!
YOU'RE RIGHT, SUPERMAN.
THE WORLD WILL NEVER STOP WANTING WEAPONS.
THAT'S WHY YOU'LL NEVER BE RID OF ME.
MR. OZ SAID SO.

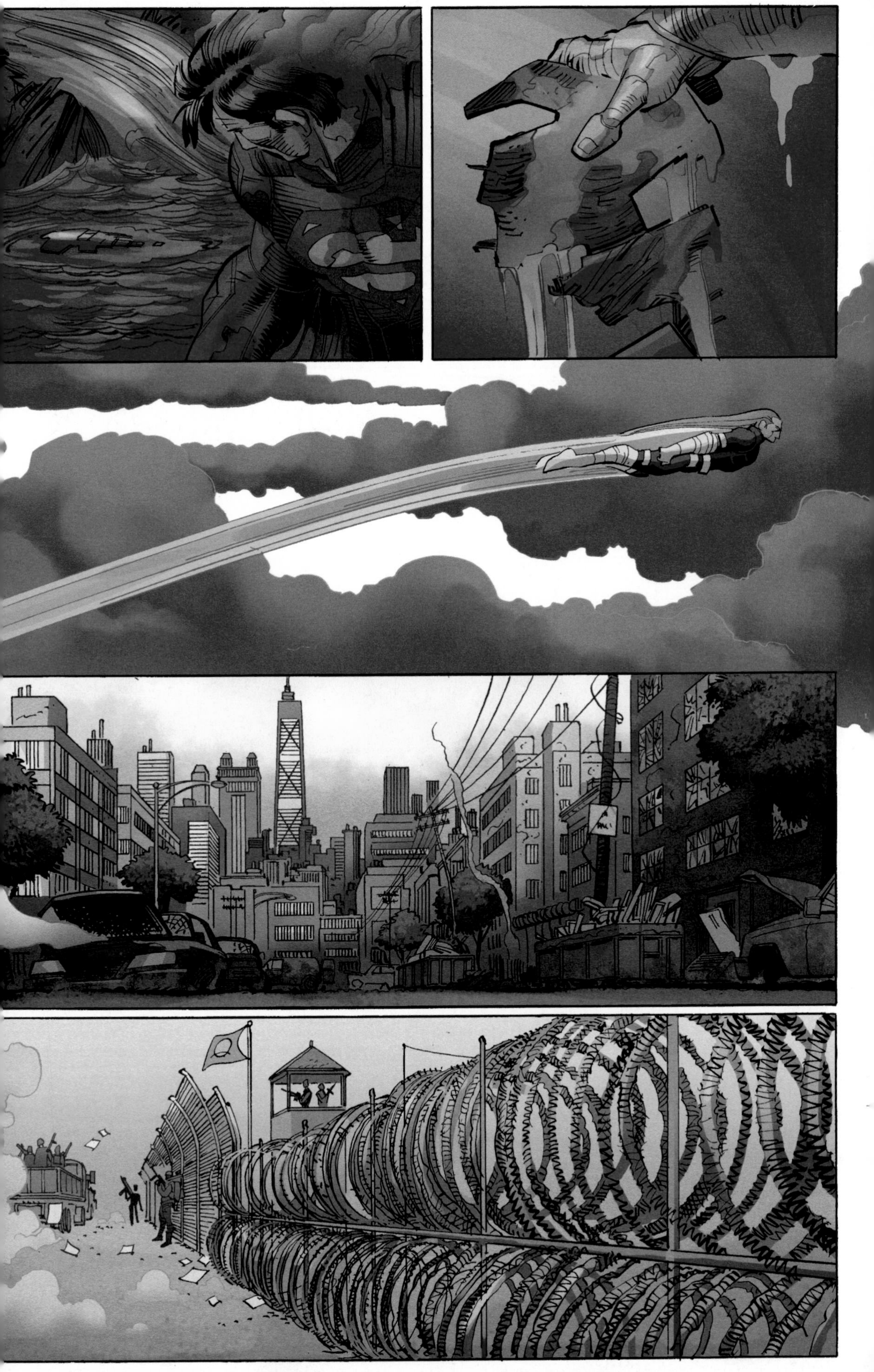

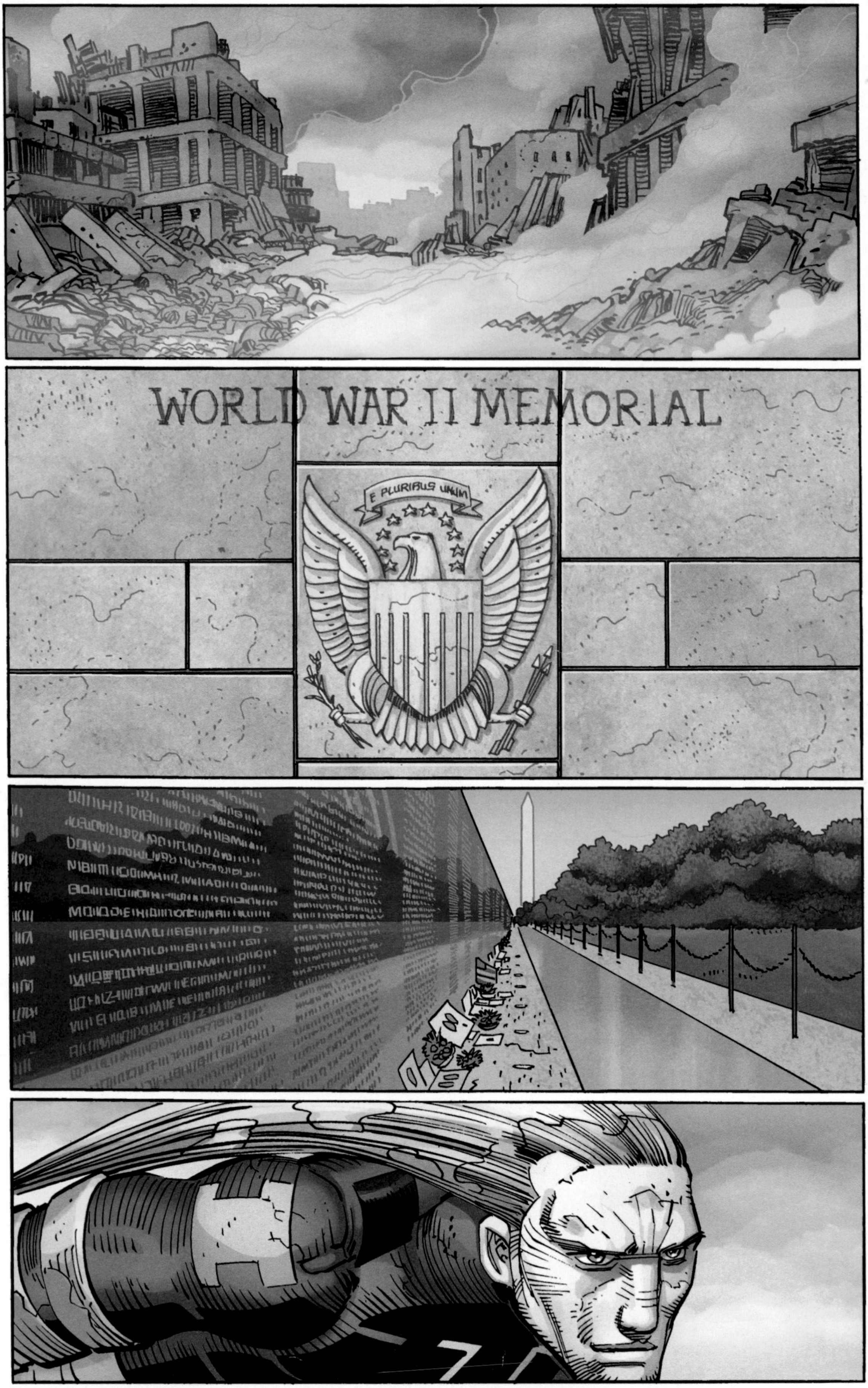
WORLD WAR II MEMORIAL
E PLURIBUS UNUM

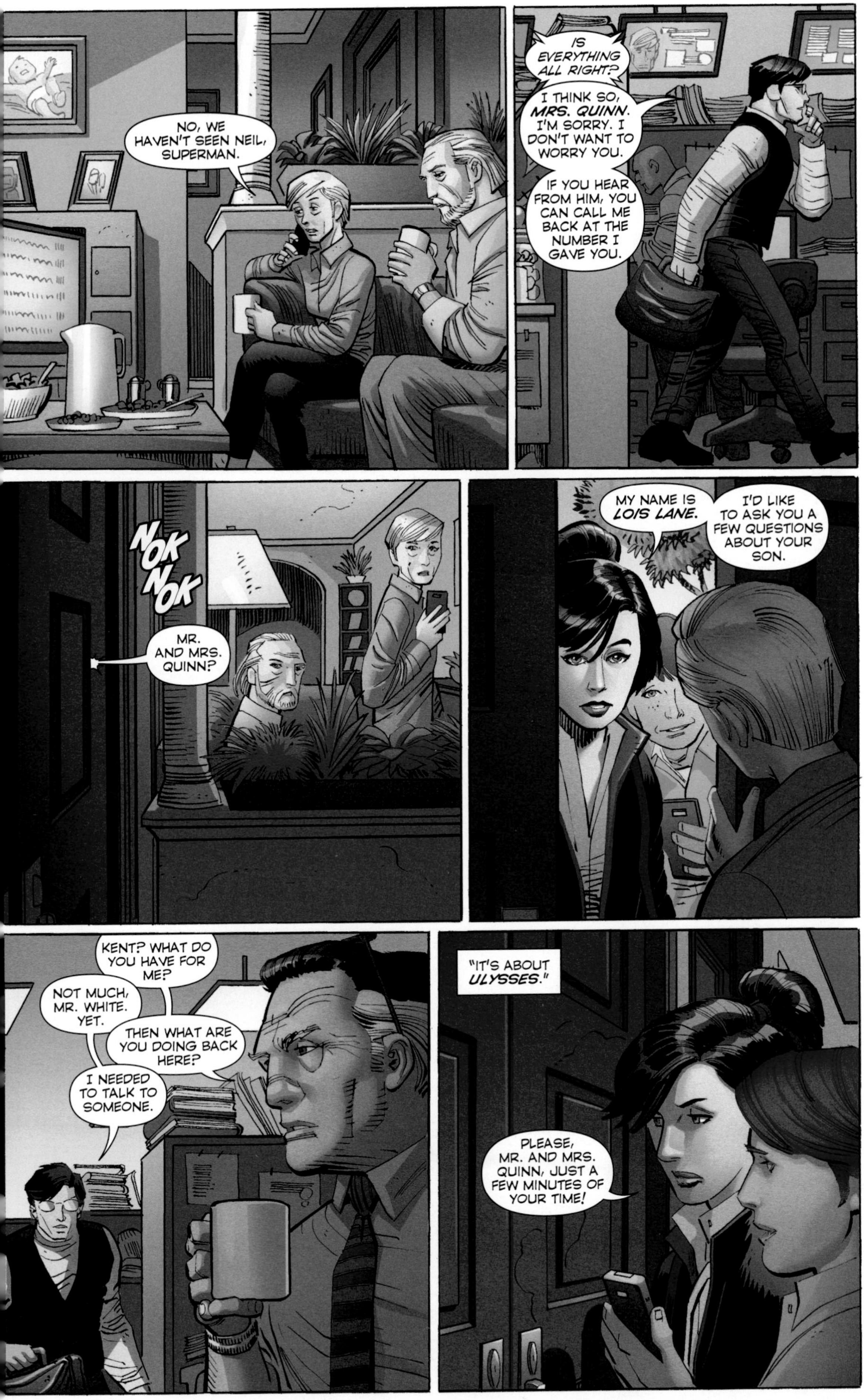
NO, WE HAVEN'T SEEN NEIL, SUPERMAN.
IS EVERYTHING ALL RIGHT?
I THINK SO, MRS. QUINN. I'M SORRY. I DON'T WANT TO WORRY YOU.
IF YOU HEAR FROM HIM, YOU CAN CALL ME BACK AT THE NUMBER I GAVE YOU.
NOK NOK
MR. AND MRS. QUINN?
MY NAME IS LOIS LANE.
I'D LIKE TO ASK YOU A FEW QUESTIONS ABOUT YOUR SON.
KENT? WHAT DO YOU HAVE FOR ME?
NOT MUCH, MR. WHITE. YET.
THEN WHAT ARE YOU DOING BACK HERE?
I NEEDED TO TALK TO SOMEONE.
"IT'S ABOUT ULYSSES."
PLEASE, MR. AND MRS. QUINN, JUST A FEW MINUTES OF YOUR TIME!

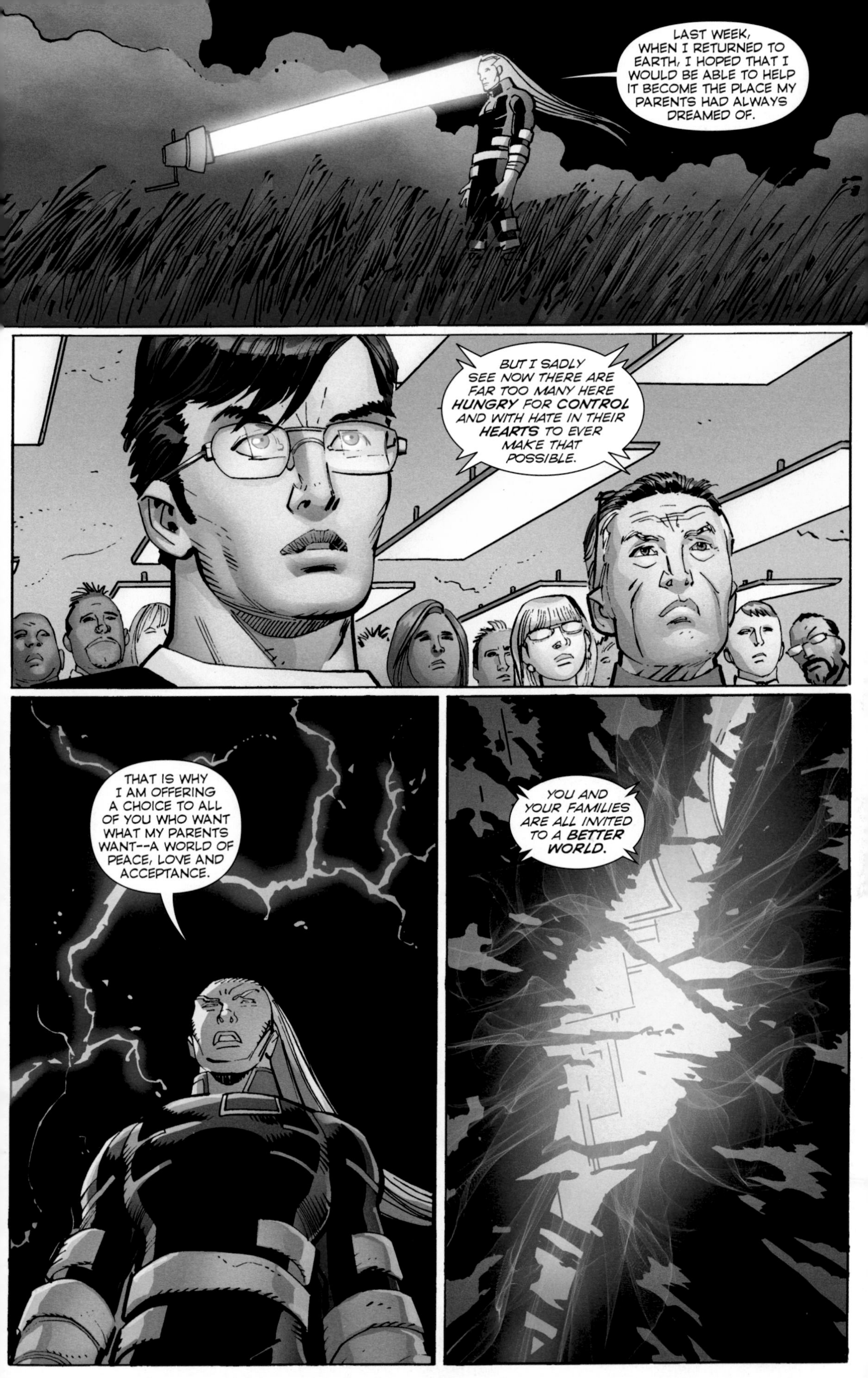
LAST WEEK, WHEN I RETURNED TO EARTH, I HOPED THAT I WOULD BE ABLE TO HELP IT BECOME THE PLACE MY PARENTS HAD ALWAYS DREAMED OF.
BUT I SADLY SEE NOW THERE ARE FAR TOO MANY HERE HUNGRY FOR CONTROL AND WITH HATE IN THEIR HEARTS TO EVER MAKE THAT POSSIBLE.
THAT IS WHY I AM OFFERING A CHOICE TO ALL OF YOU WHO WANT WHAT MY PARENTS WANT--A WORLD OF PEACE, LOVE AND ACCEPTANCE.
YOU AND YOUR FAMILIES ARE ALL INVITED TO A BETTER WORLD.

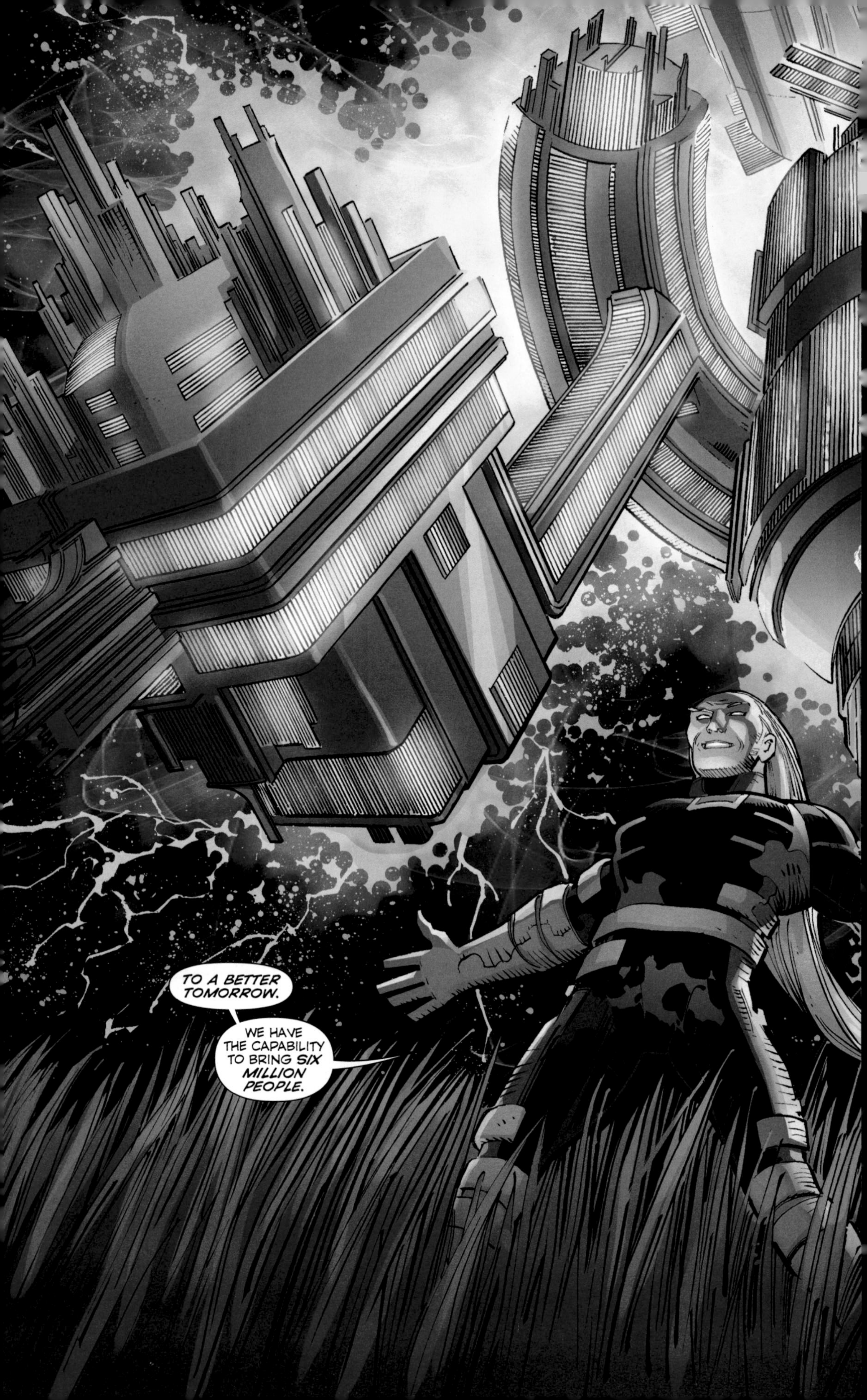
TO A BETTER TOMORROW.
WE HAVE THE CAPABILITY TO BRING SIX MILLION PEOPLE.

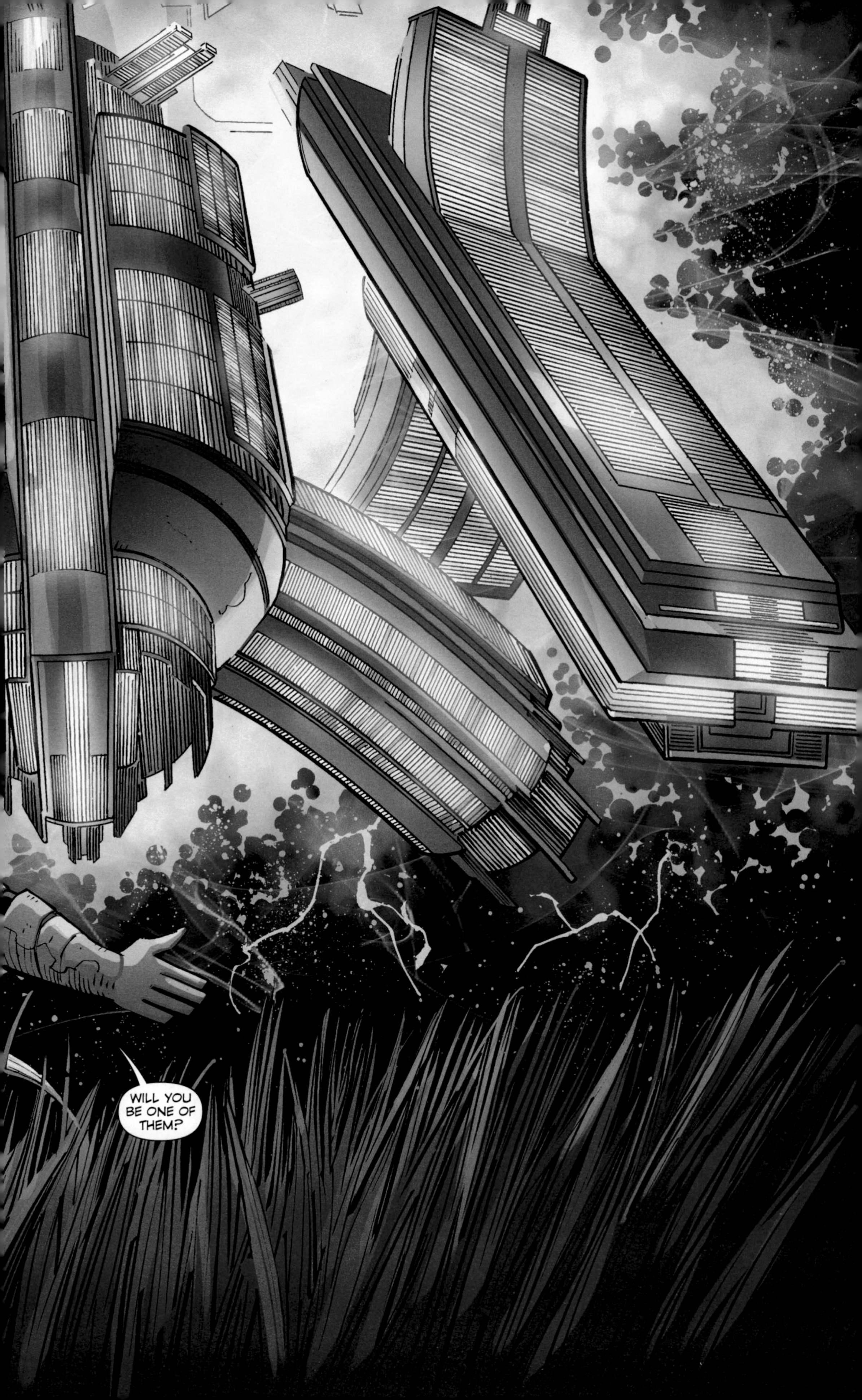
WILL YOU BE ONE OF THEM?

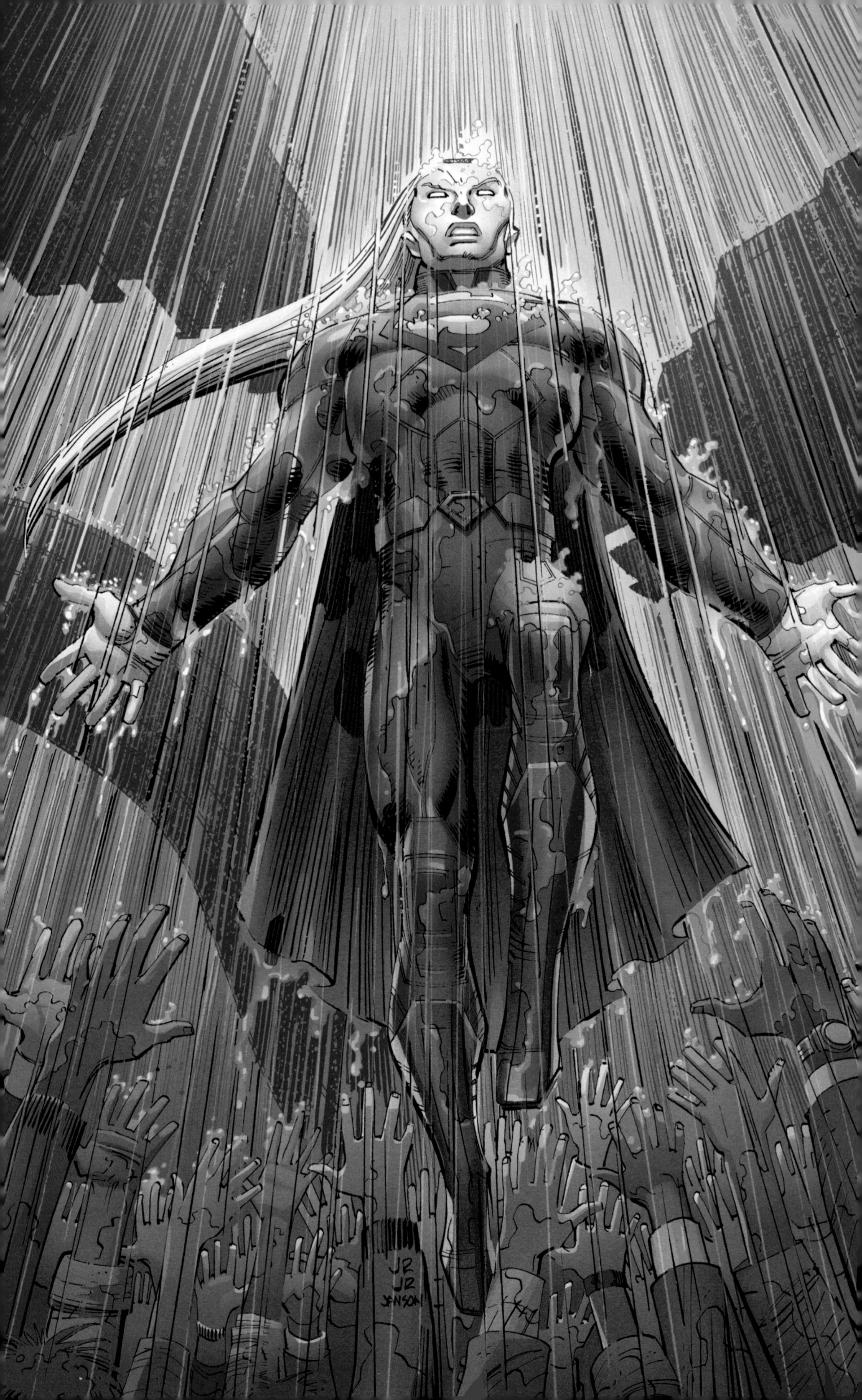
JR
JR
JANSON

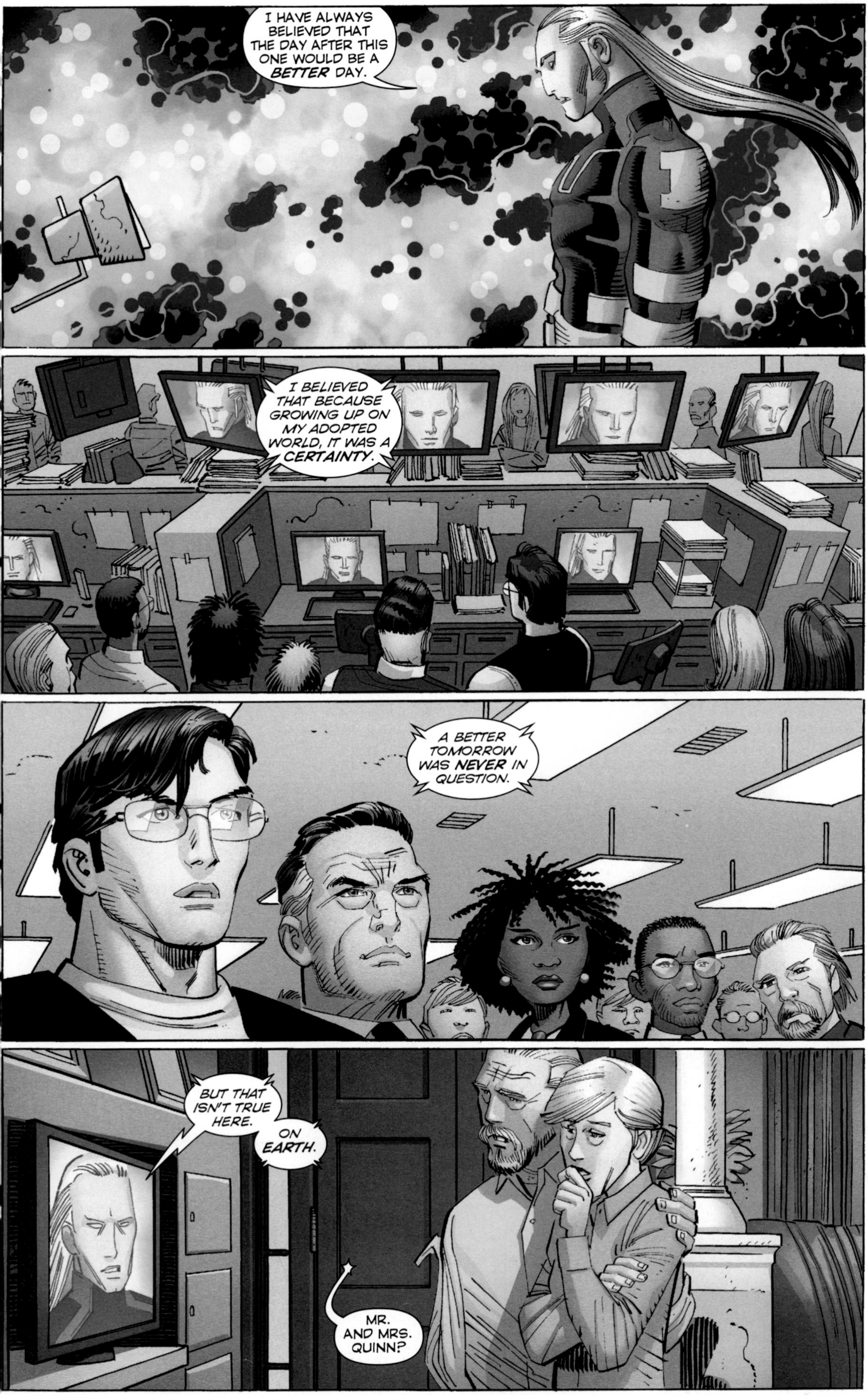
I HAVE ALWAYS BELIEVED THAT THE DAY AFTER THIS ONE WOULD BE A BETTER DAY.
I BELIEVED THAT BECAUSE GROWING UP ON MY ADOPTED WORLD, IT WAS A CERTAINTY.
A BETTER TOMORROW WAS NEVER IN QUESTION.
BUT THAT ISN'T TRUE HERE.
ON EARTH.
MR. AND MRS. QUINN?

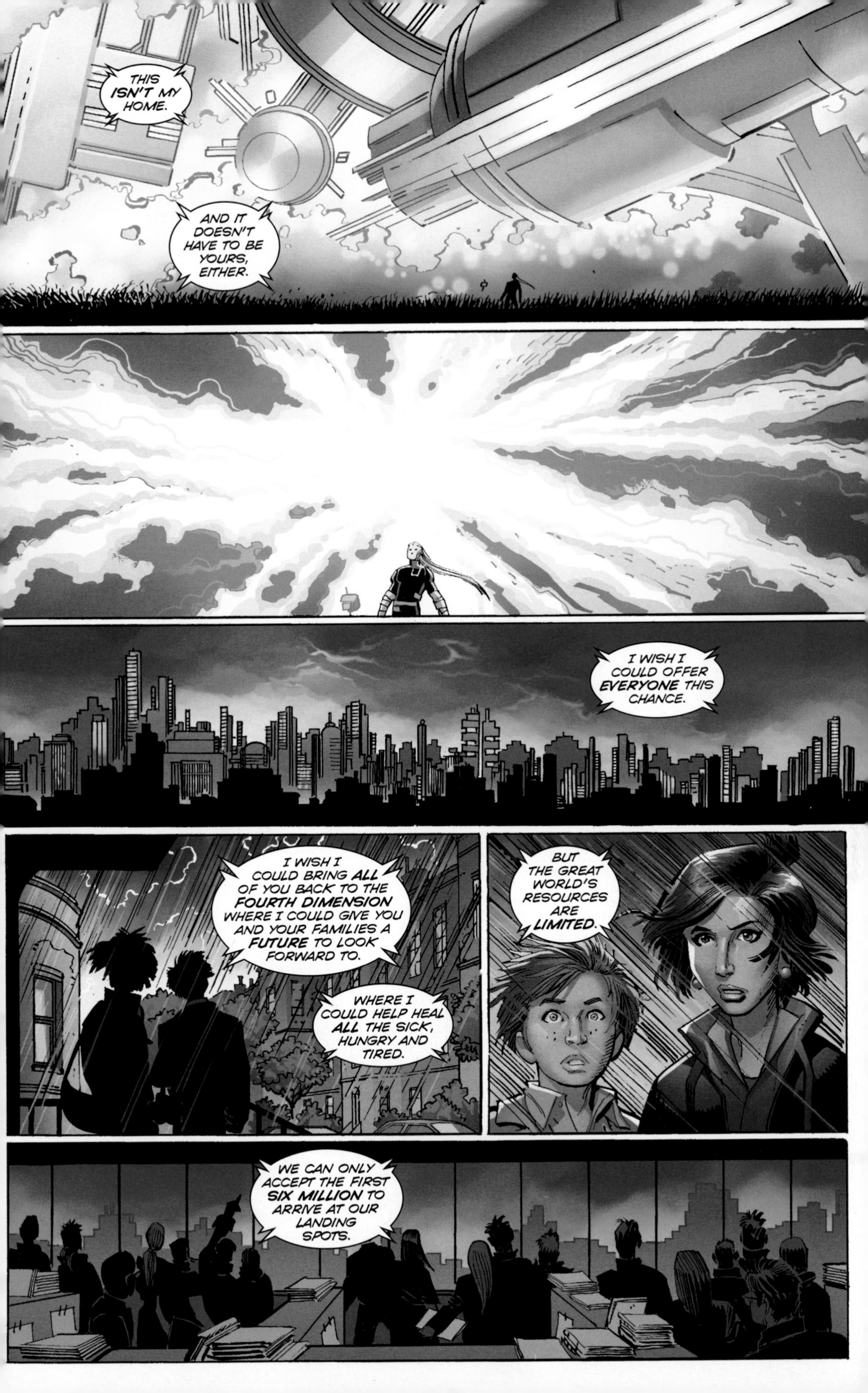
THIS ISN'T MY HOME.
AND IT DOESN'T HAVE TO BE YOURS, EITHER.
I WISH I COULD OFFER EVERYONE THIS CHANCE.
I WISH I COULD BRING ALL OF YOU BACK TO THE FOURTH DIMENSION WHERE I COULD GIVE YOU AND YOUR FAMILIES A FUTURE TO LOOK FORWARD TO.
WHERE I COULD HELP HEAL ALL THE SICK, HUNGRY AND TIRED.
BUT THE GREAT WORLD'S RESOURCES ARE LIMITED.
WE CAN ONLY ACCEPT THE FIRST SIX MILLION TO ARRIVE AT OUR LANDING SPOTS.

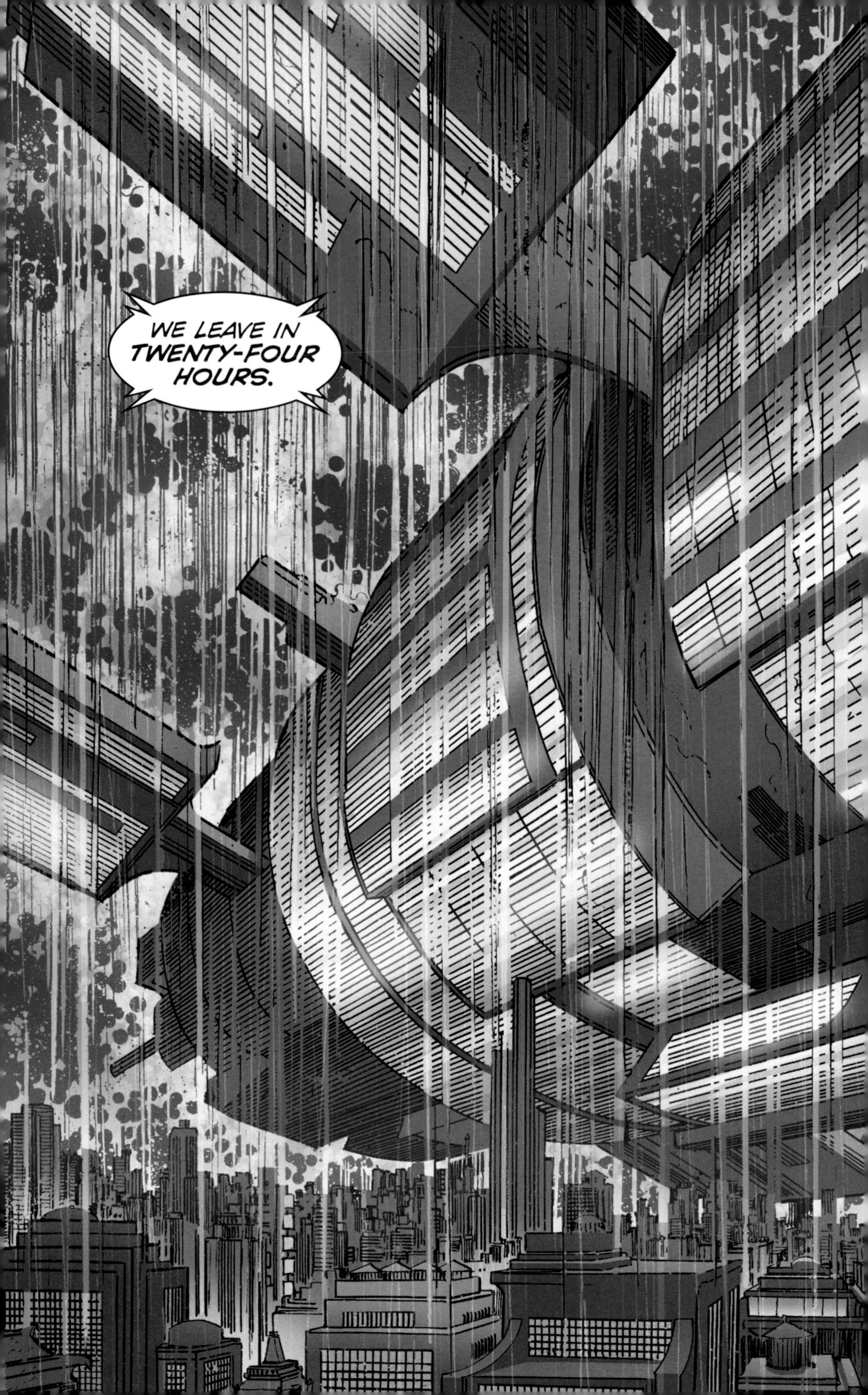
WE LEAVE IN TWENTY-FOUR HOURS.

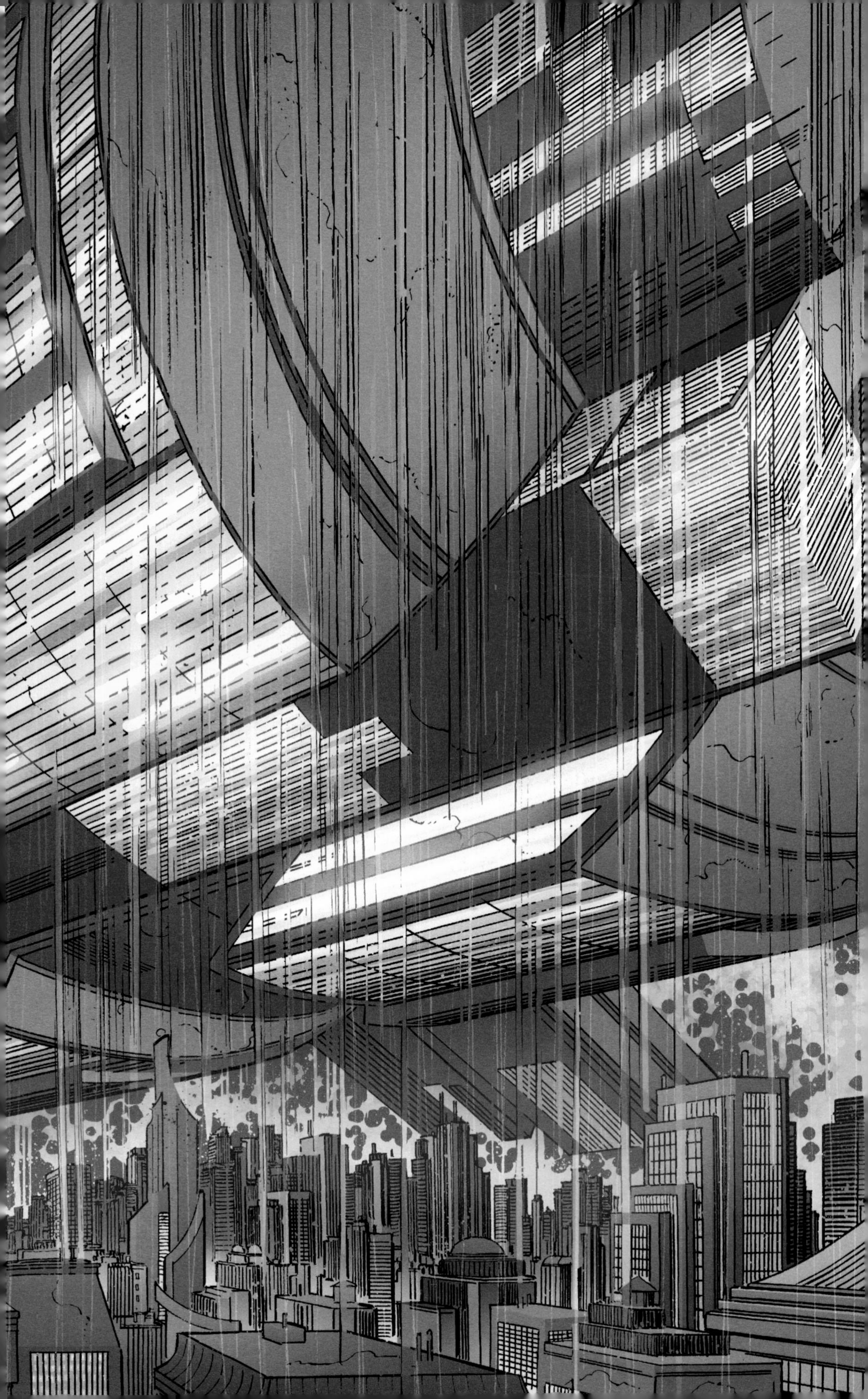

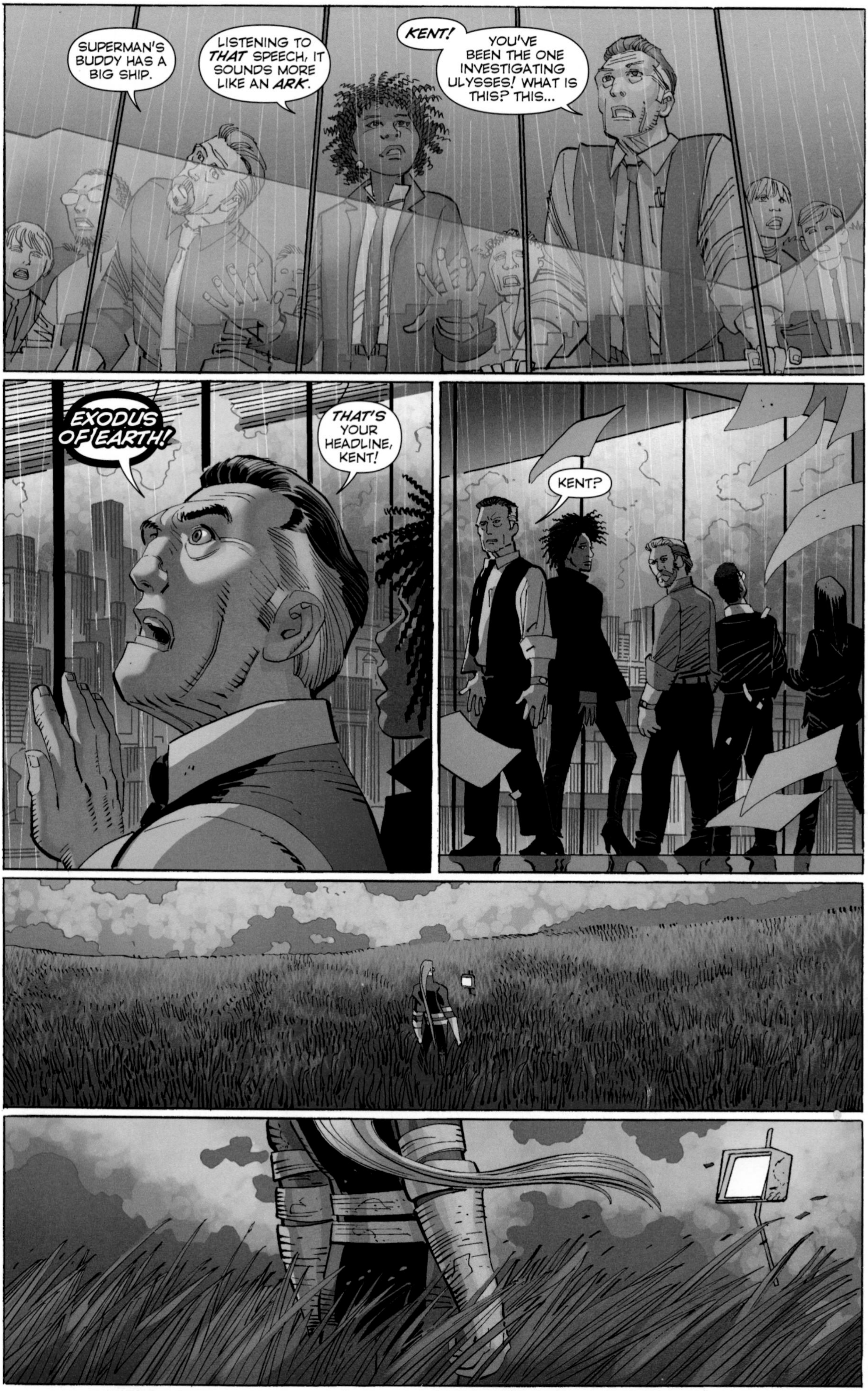
SUPERMAN'S BUDDY HAS A BIG SHIP.
LISTENING TO THAT SPEECH, IT SOUNDS MORE LIKE AN ARK.
KENT!
YOU'VE BEEN THE ONE INVESTIGATING ULYSSES! WHAT IS THIS? THIS...
EXODUS OF EARTH!
THAT'S YOUR HEADLINE, KENT!
KENT?

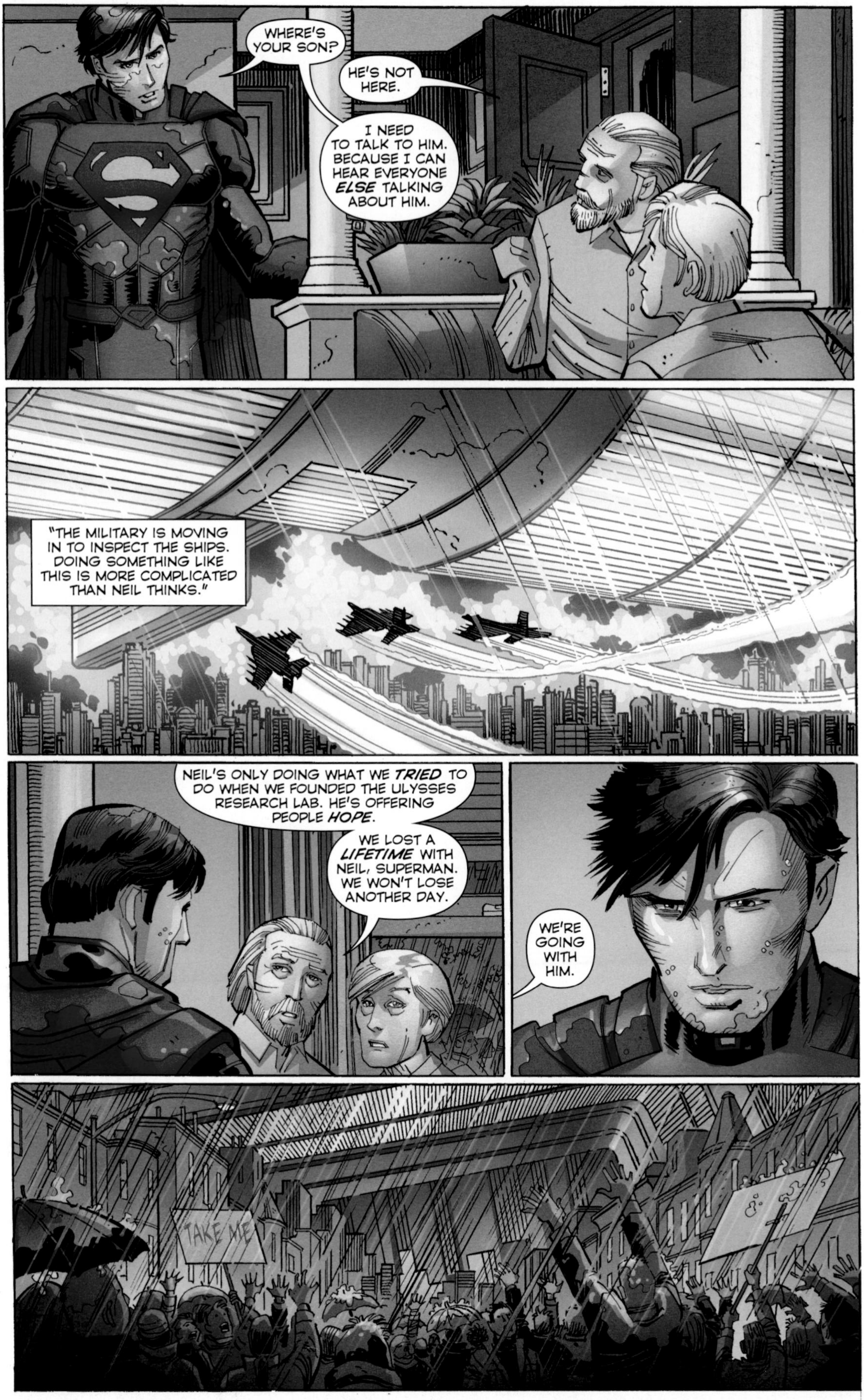
WHERE'S YOUR SON?
HE'S NOT HERE.
I NEED TO TALK TO HIM. BECAUSE I CAN HEAR EVERYONE *ELSE* TALKING ABOUT HIM.
"THE MILITARY IS MOVING IN TO INSPECT THE SHIPS. DOING SOMETHING LIKE THIS IS MORE COMPLICATED THAN NEIL THINKS."
NEIL'S ONLY DOING WHAT WE *TRIED* TO DO WHEN WE FOUNDED THE ULYSSES RESEARCH LAB. HE'S OFFERING PEOPLE *HOPE*.
WE LOST A *LIFETIME* WITH NEIL, SUPERMAN. WE WON'T LOSE ANOTHER DAY.
WE'RE GOING WITH HIM.
TAKE ME

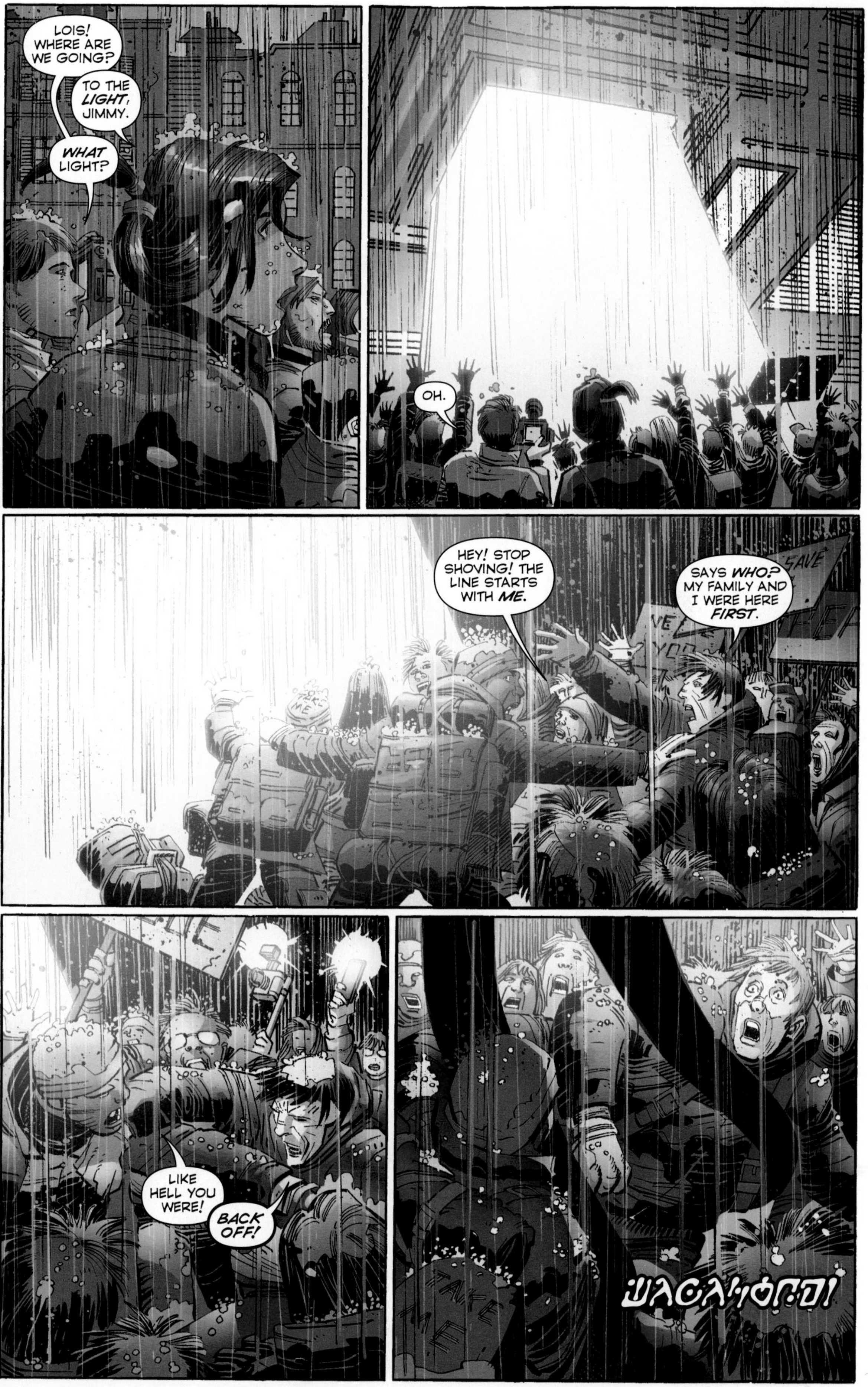
LOIS! WHERE ARE WE GOING?
TO THE LIGHT, JIMMY.
WHAT LIGHT?
OH.
HEY! STOP SHOVING! THE LINE STARTS WITH ME.
SAYS WHO? MY FAMILY AND I WERE HERE FIRST.
SAVE
TAKE ME
LIKE HELL YOU WERE!
BACK OFF!
TAKE ME

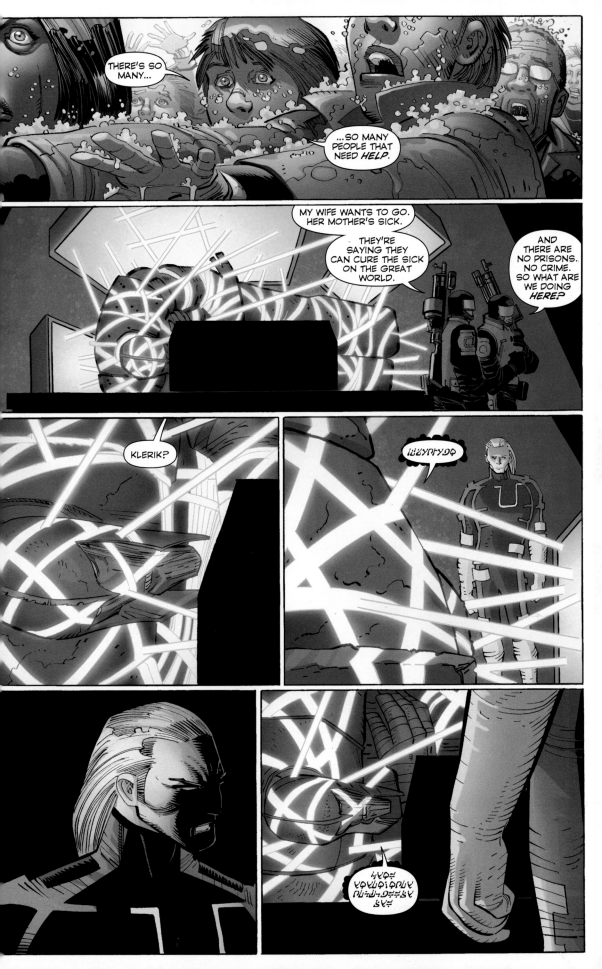

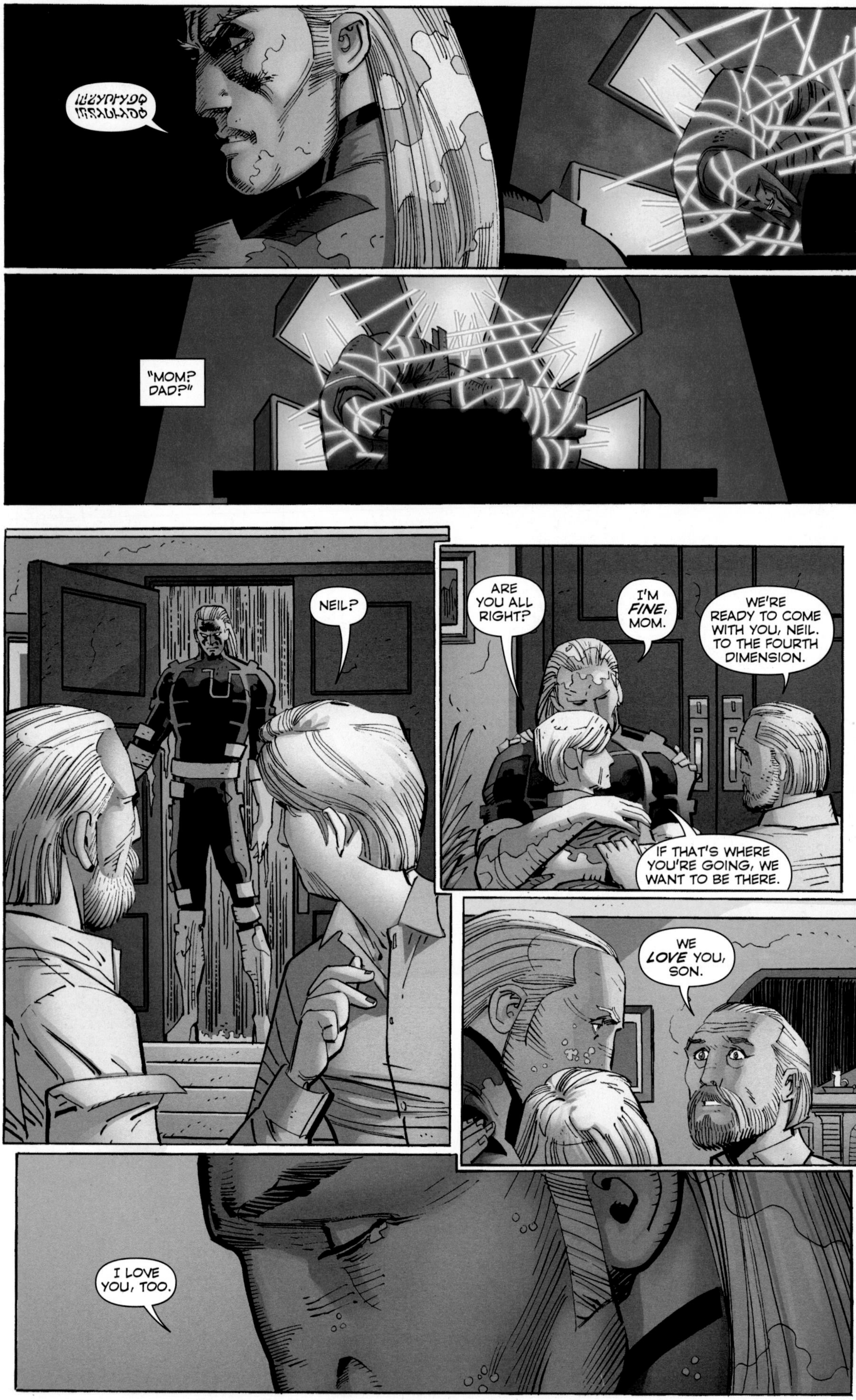
"MOM? DAD?"
NEIL?
ARE YOU ALL RIGHT?
I'M *FINE*, MOM.
WE'RE READY TO COME WITH YOU, NEIL. TO THE FOURTH DIMENSION.
IF THAT'S WHERE YOU'RE GOING, WE WANT TO BE THERE.
WE *LOVE* YOU, SON.
I LOVE YOU, TOO.

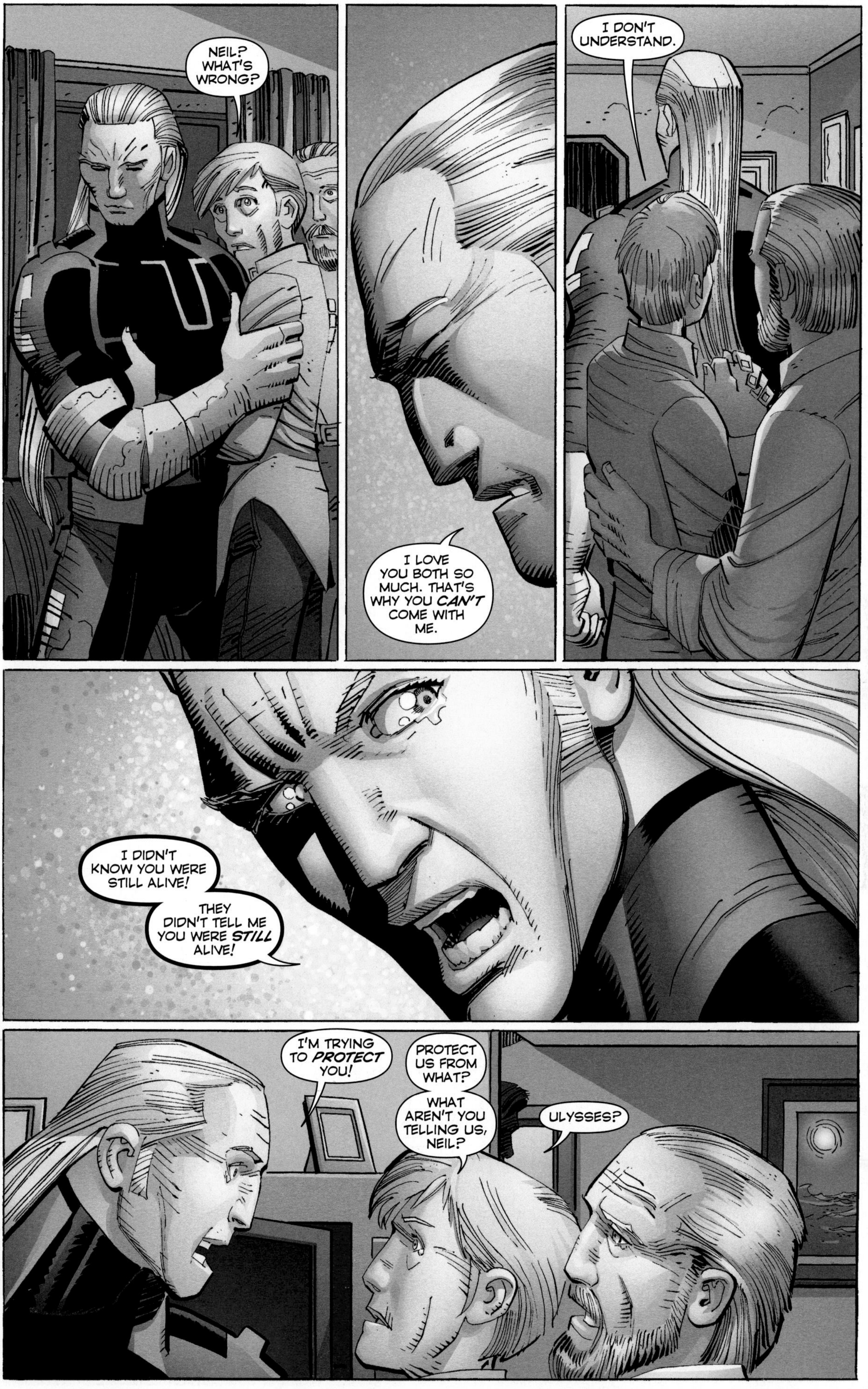
NEIL? WHAT'S WRONG?
I LOVE YOU BOTH SO MUCH. THAT'S WHY YOU *CAN'T* COME WITH ME.
I DON'T UNDERSTAND.
I DIDN'T KNOW YOU WERE STILL ALIVE!
THEY DIDN'T TELL ME YOU WERE *STILL* ALIVE!
I'M TRYING TO *PROTECT* YOU!
PROTECT US FROM WHAT?
WHAT AREN'T YOU TELLING US, NEIL?
ULYSSES?

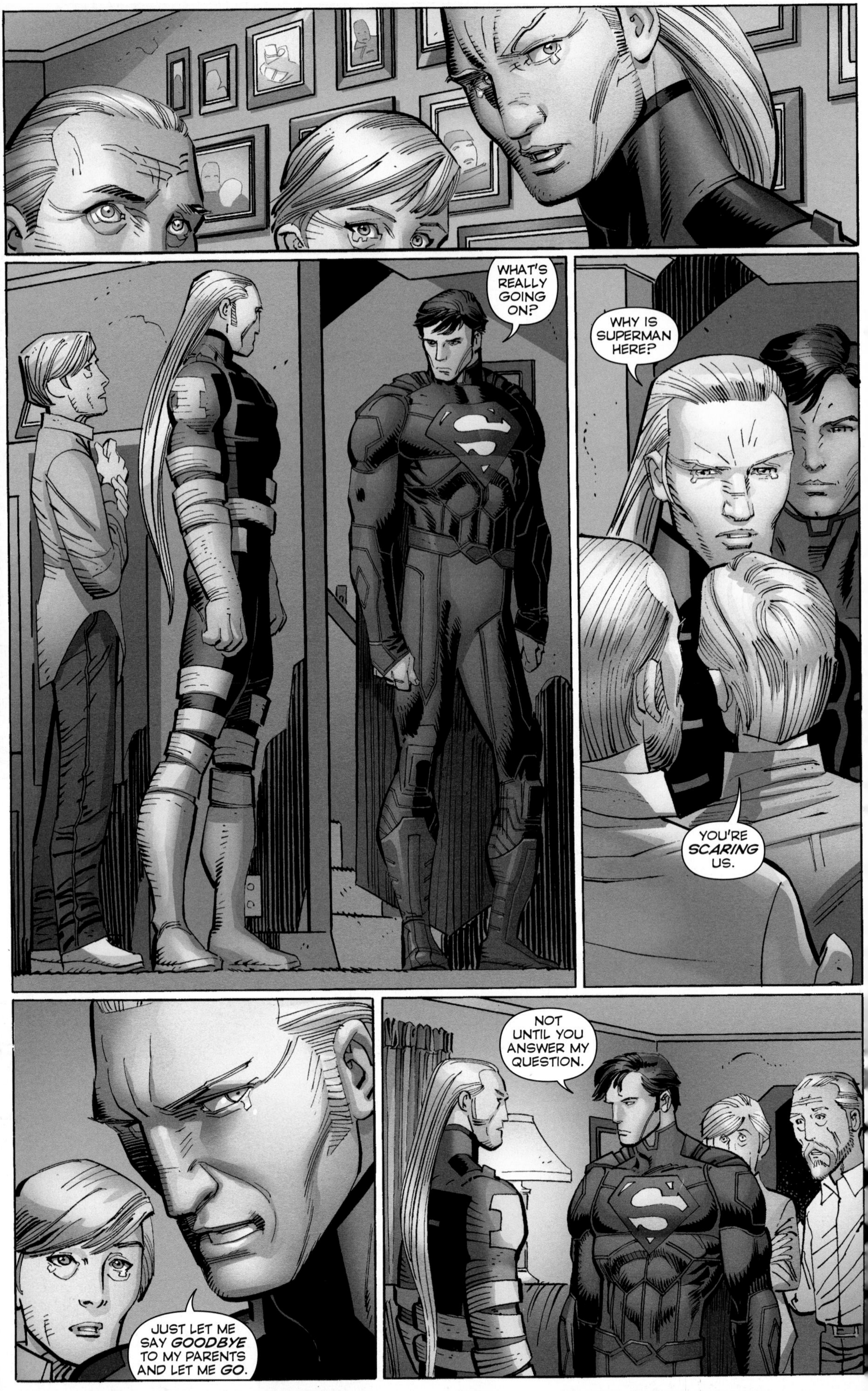
WHAT'S REALLY GOING ON?
WHY IS SUPERMAN HERE?
YOU'RE *SCARING* US.
JUST LET ME SAY *GOODBYE* TO MY PARENTS AND LET ME *GO*.
NOT UNTIL YOU ANSWER MY QUESTION.

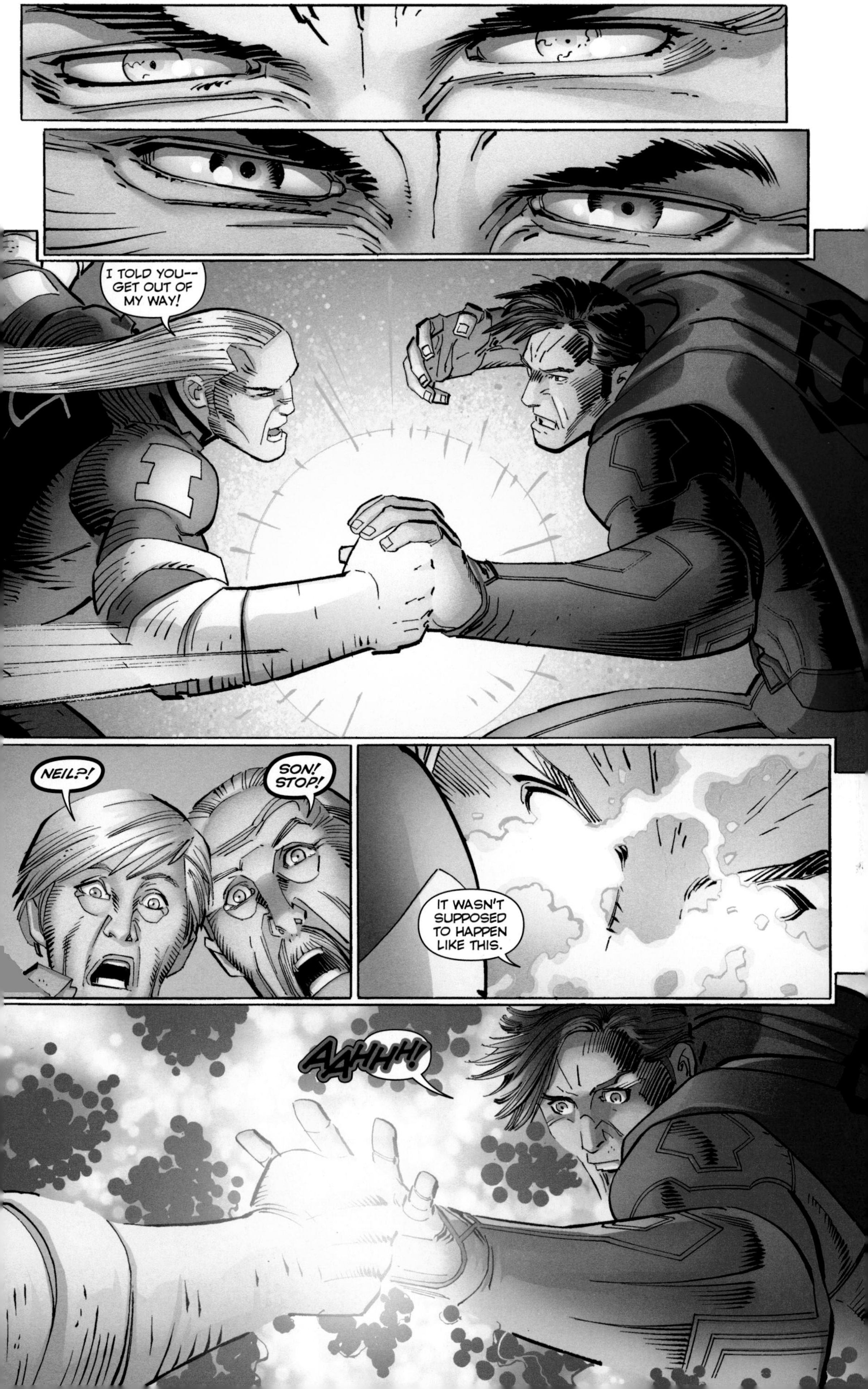
I TOLD YOU--
GET OUT OF
MY WAY!
NEIL?!
SON!
STOP!
IT WASN'T
SUPPOSED
TO HAPPEN
LIKE THIS.
AAHHH!

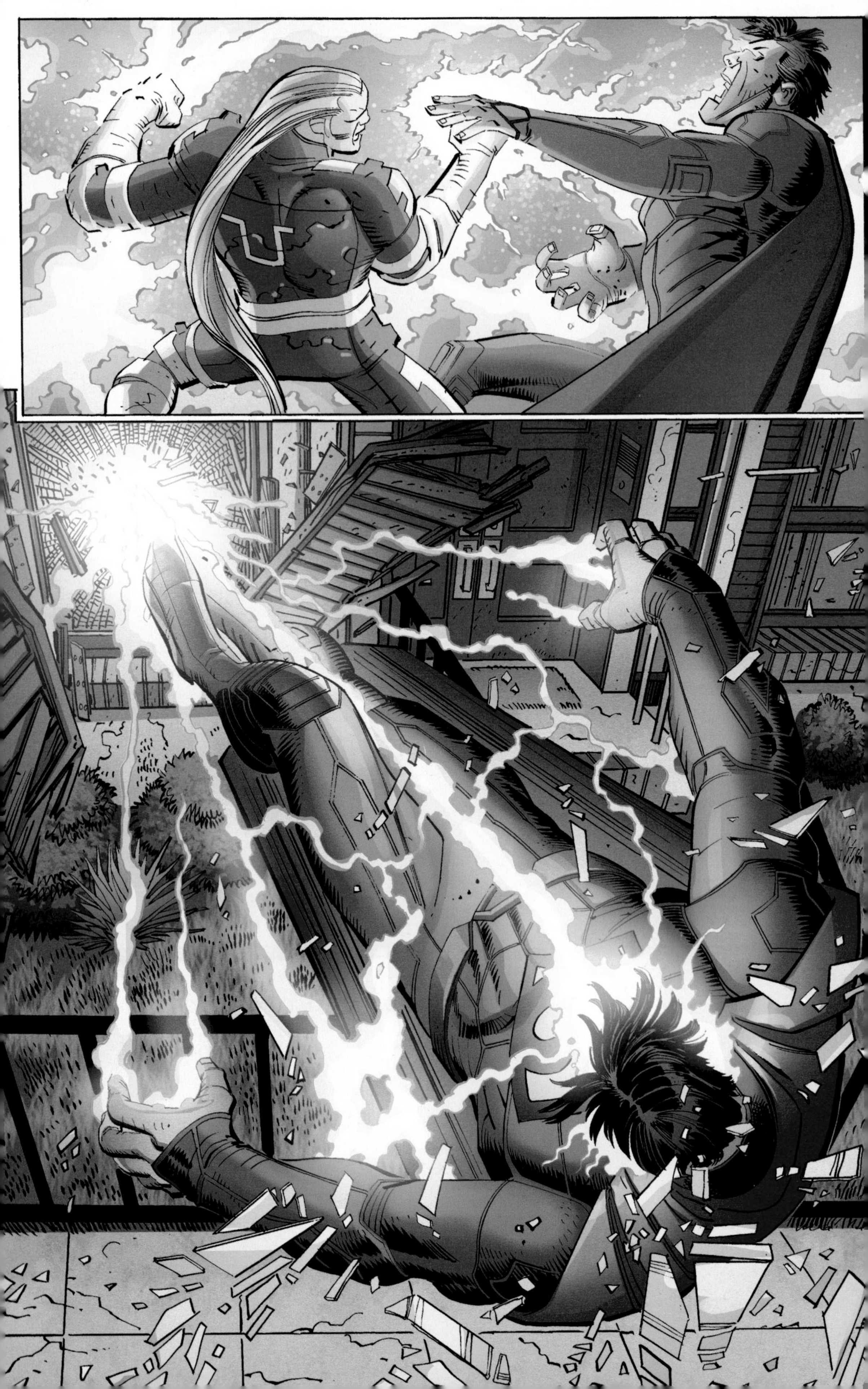

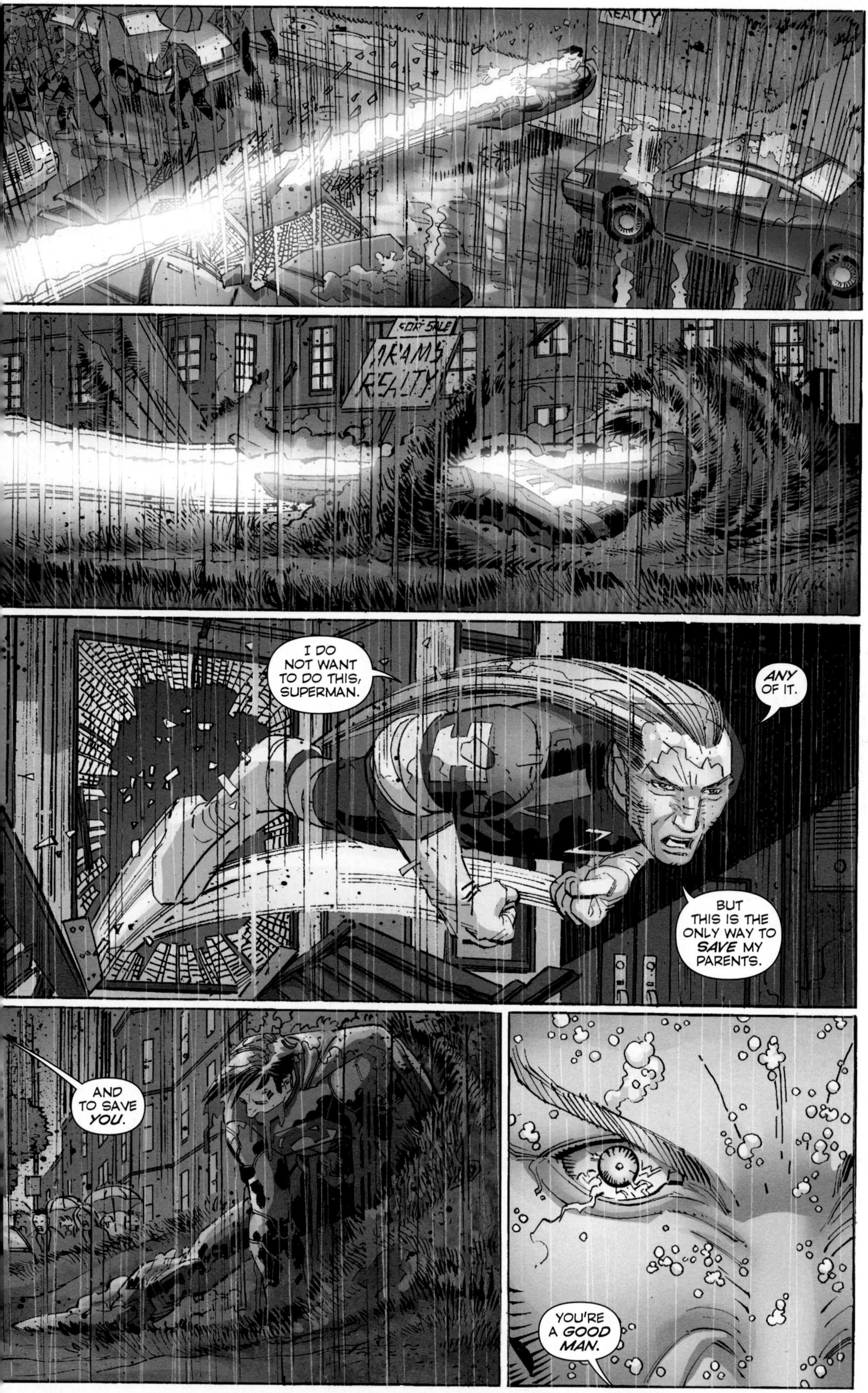
REALTY
FOR SALE
ADAMS REALTY
I DO NOT WANT TO DO THIS, SUPERMAN.
ANY OF IT.
BUT THIS IS THE ONLY WAY TO SAVE MY PARENTS.
AND TO SAVE YOU.
YOU'RE A GOOD MAN.

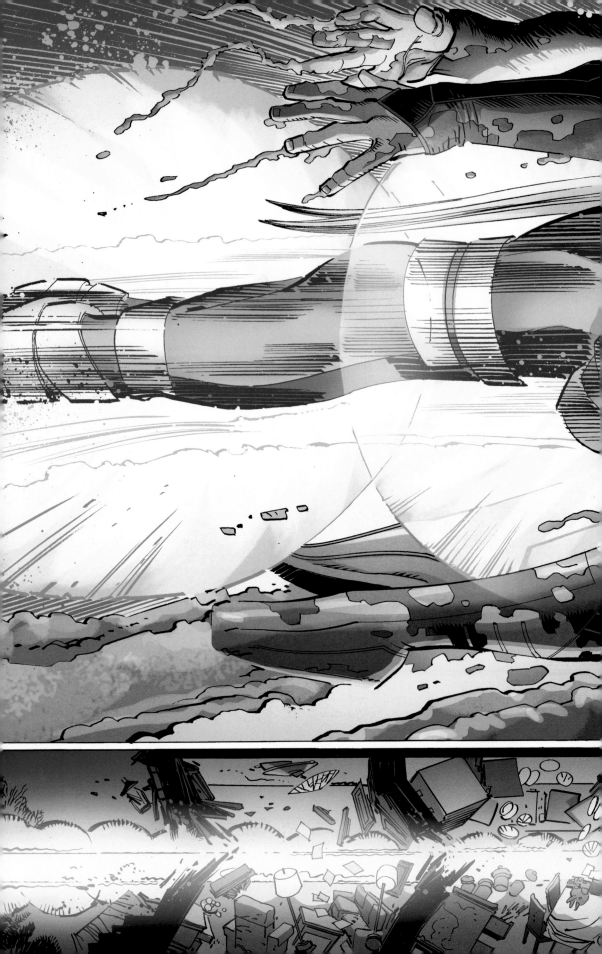

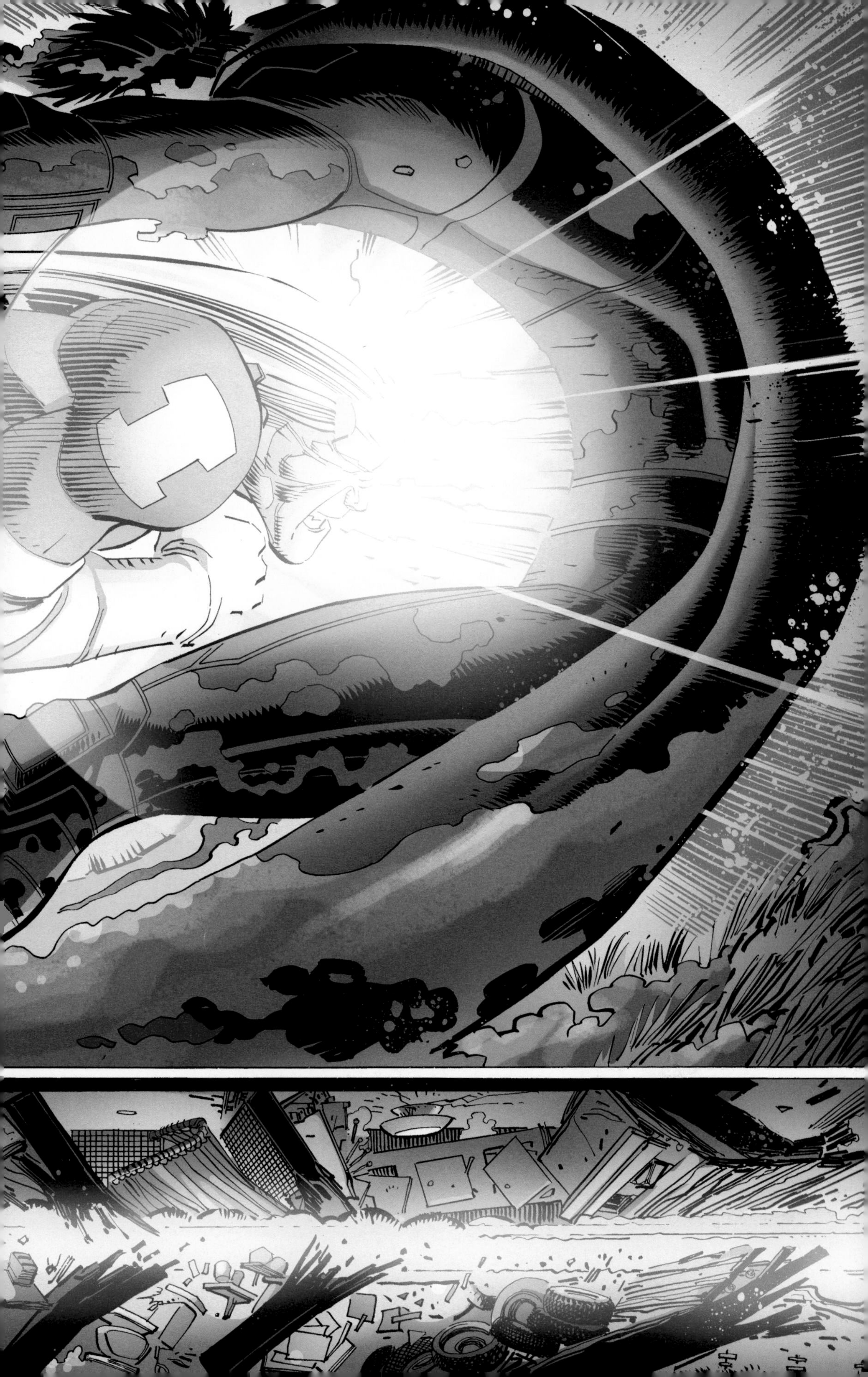

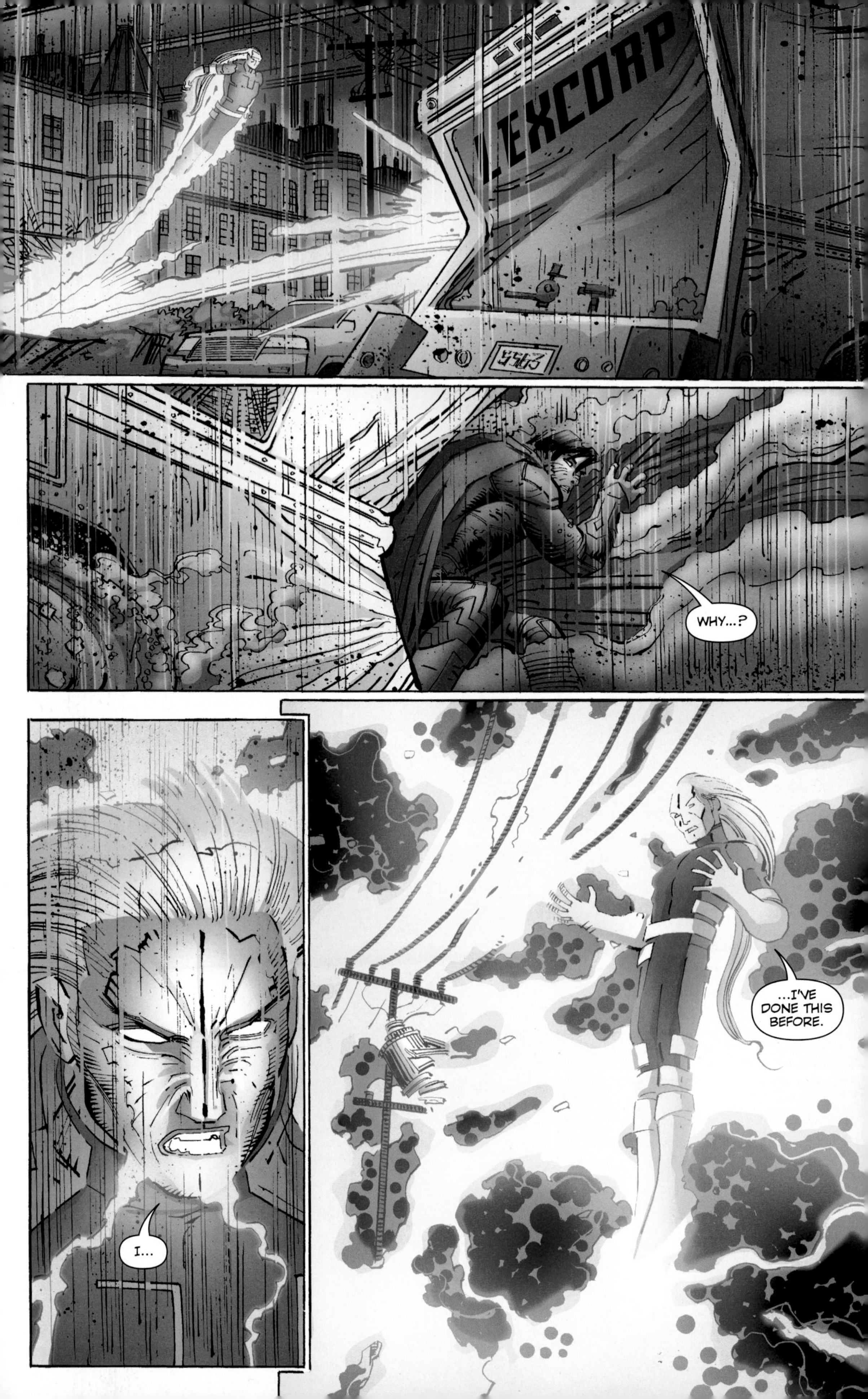
LEXCORP
5563
WHY...?
I...
...I'VE DONE THIS BEFORE.

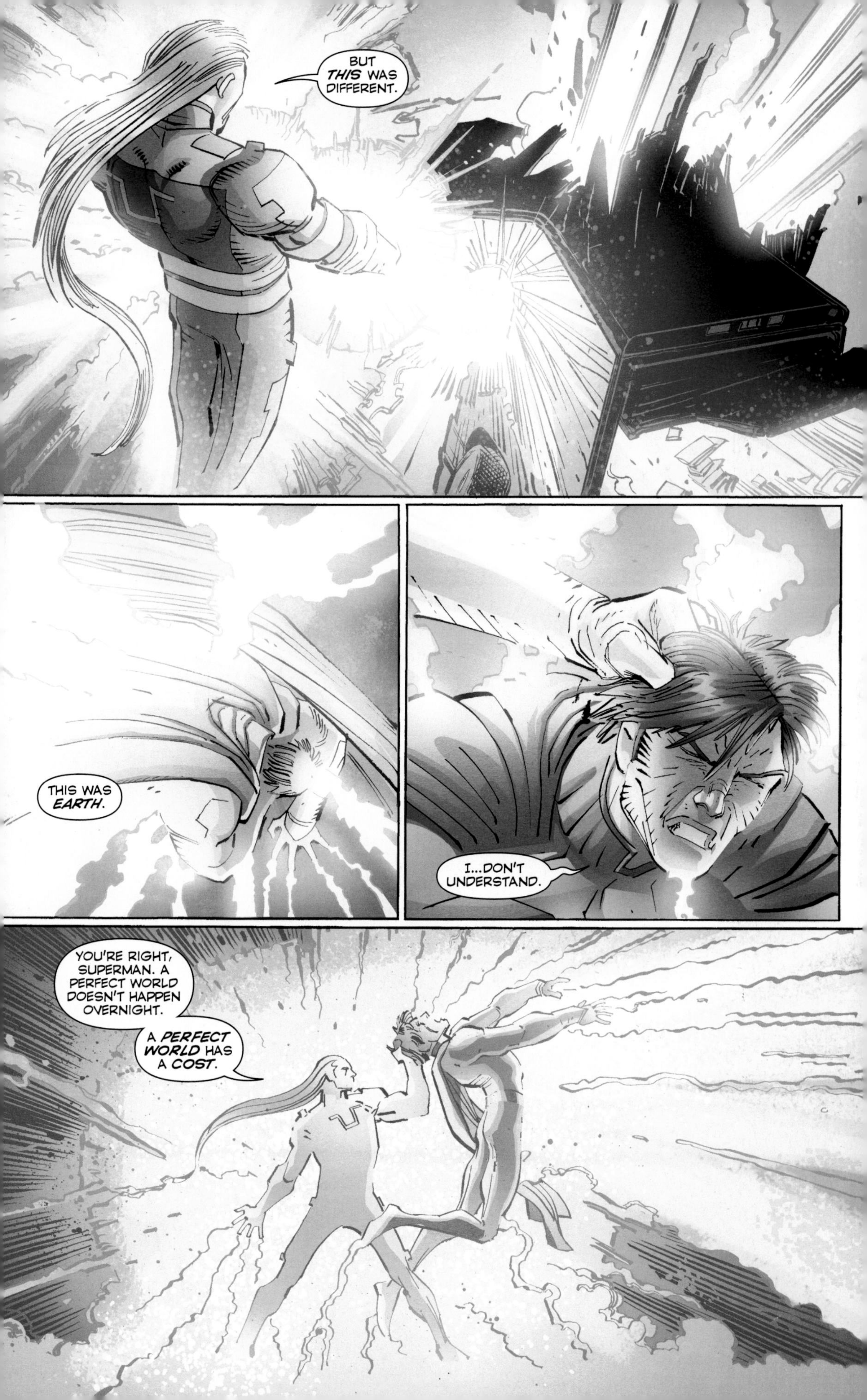
BUT *THIS* WAS DIFFERENT.
THIS WAS *EARTH*.
I...DON'T UNDERSTAND.
YOU'RE RIGHT, SUPERMAN. A PERFECT WORLD DOESN'T HAPPEN OVERNIGHT.
A *PERFECT WORLD* HAS A *COST*.

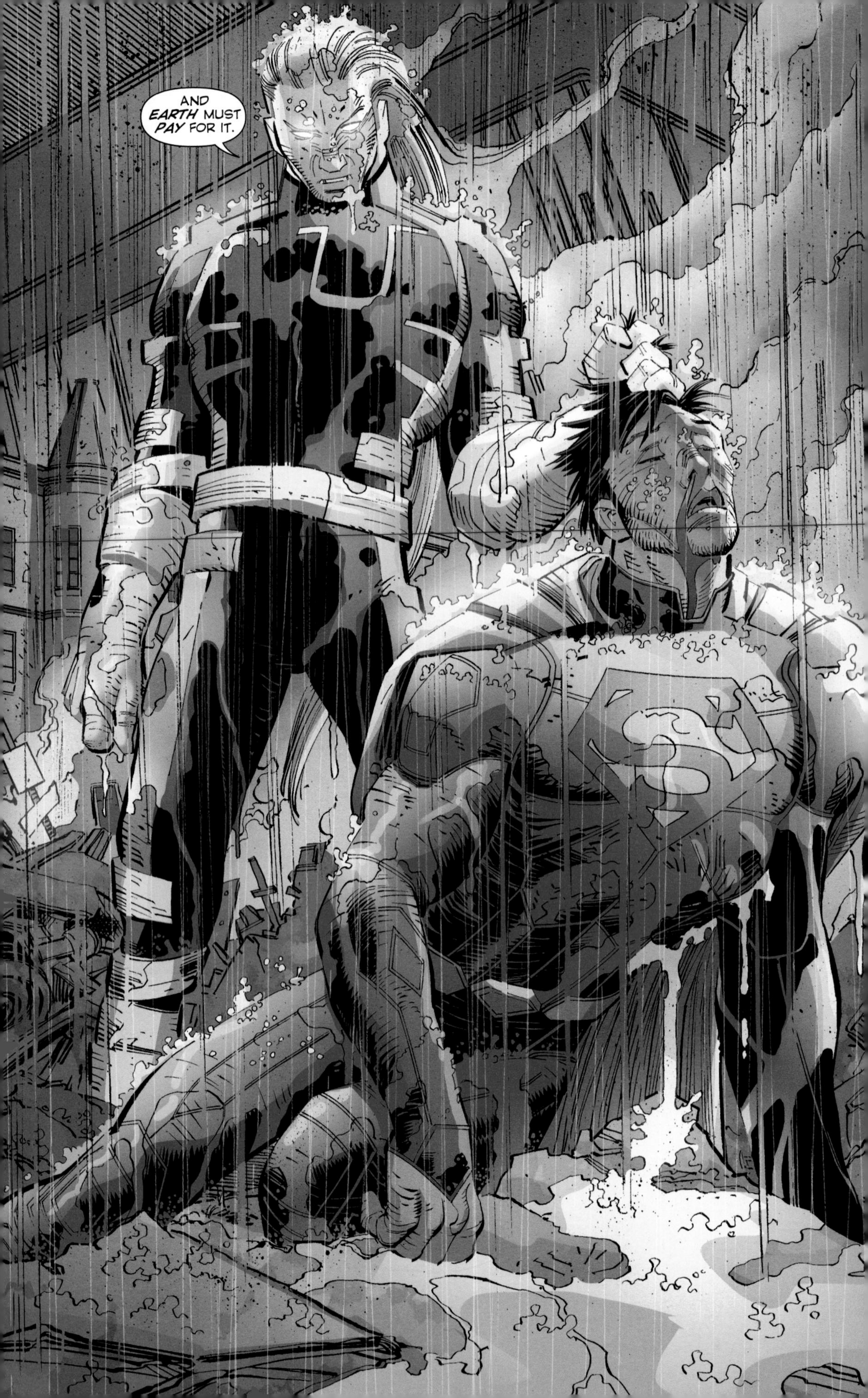
AND EARTH MUST PAY FOR IT.

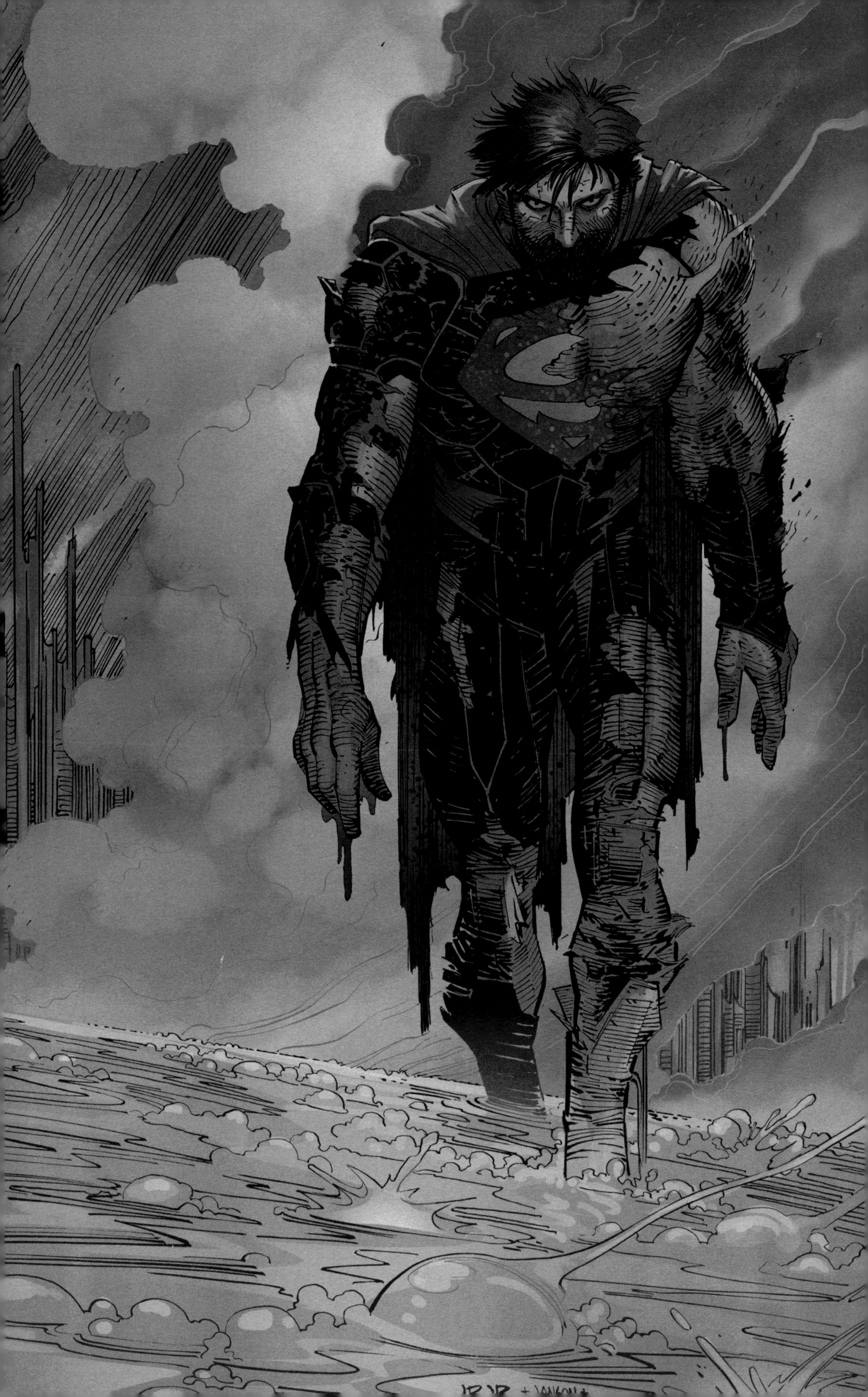

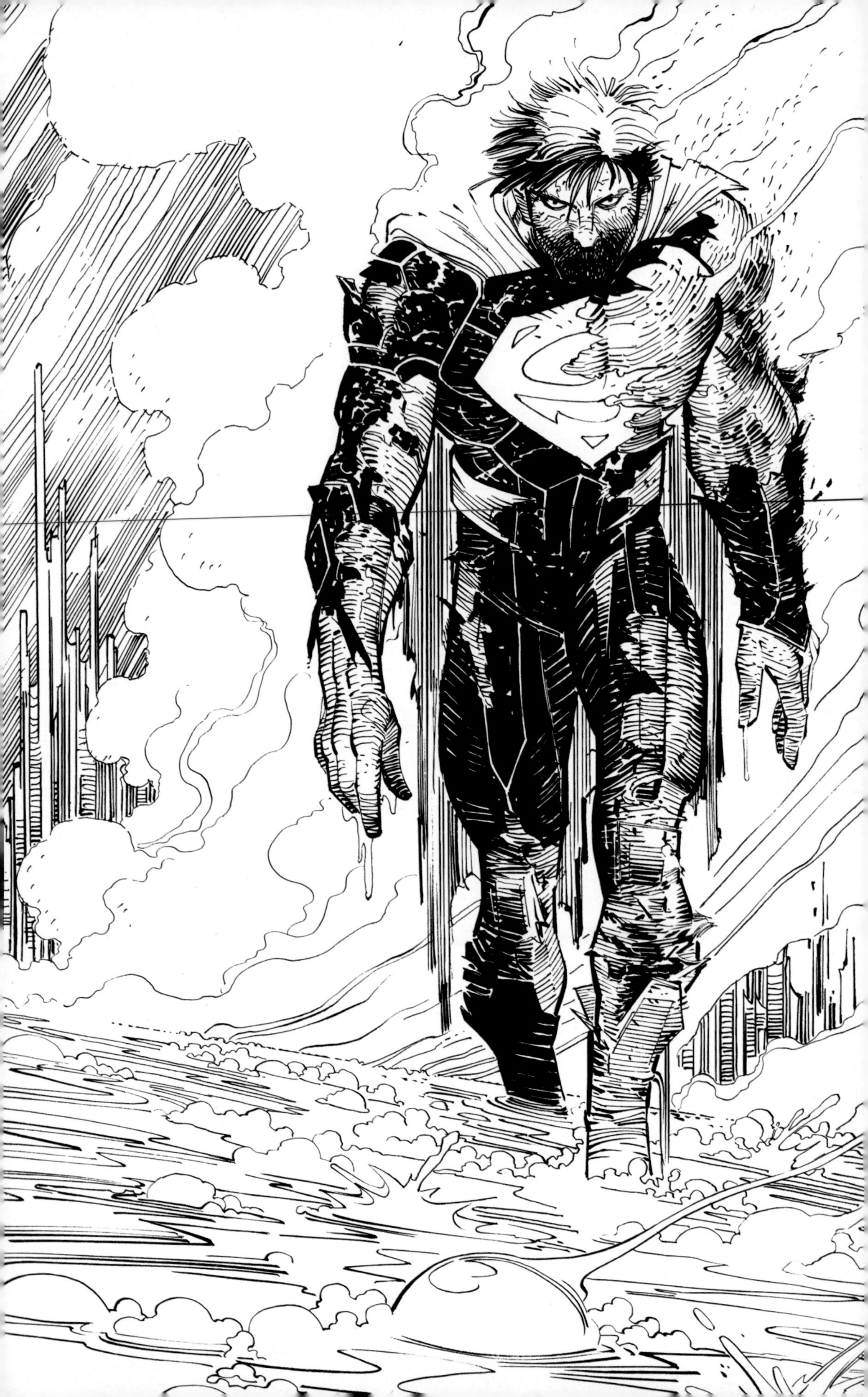

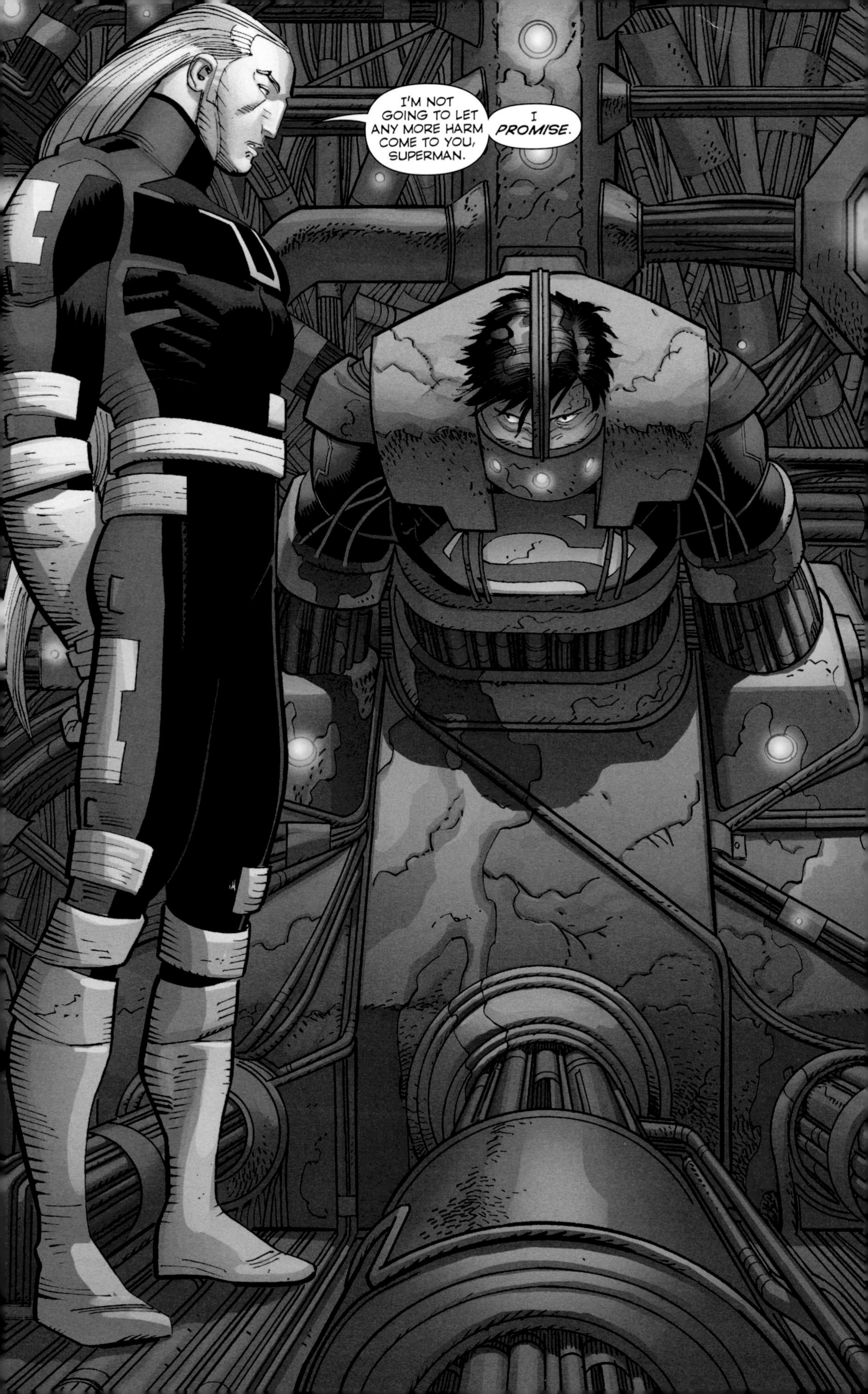

I'M NOT GOING TO LET ANY MORE HARM COME TO YOU, SUPERMAN.
I *PROMISE*.

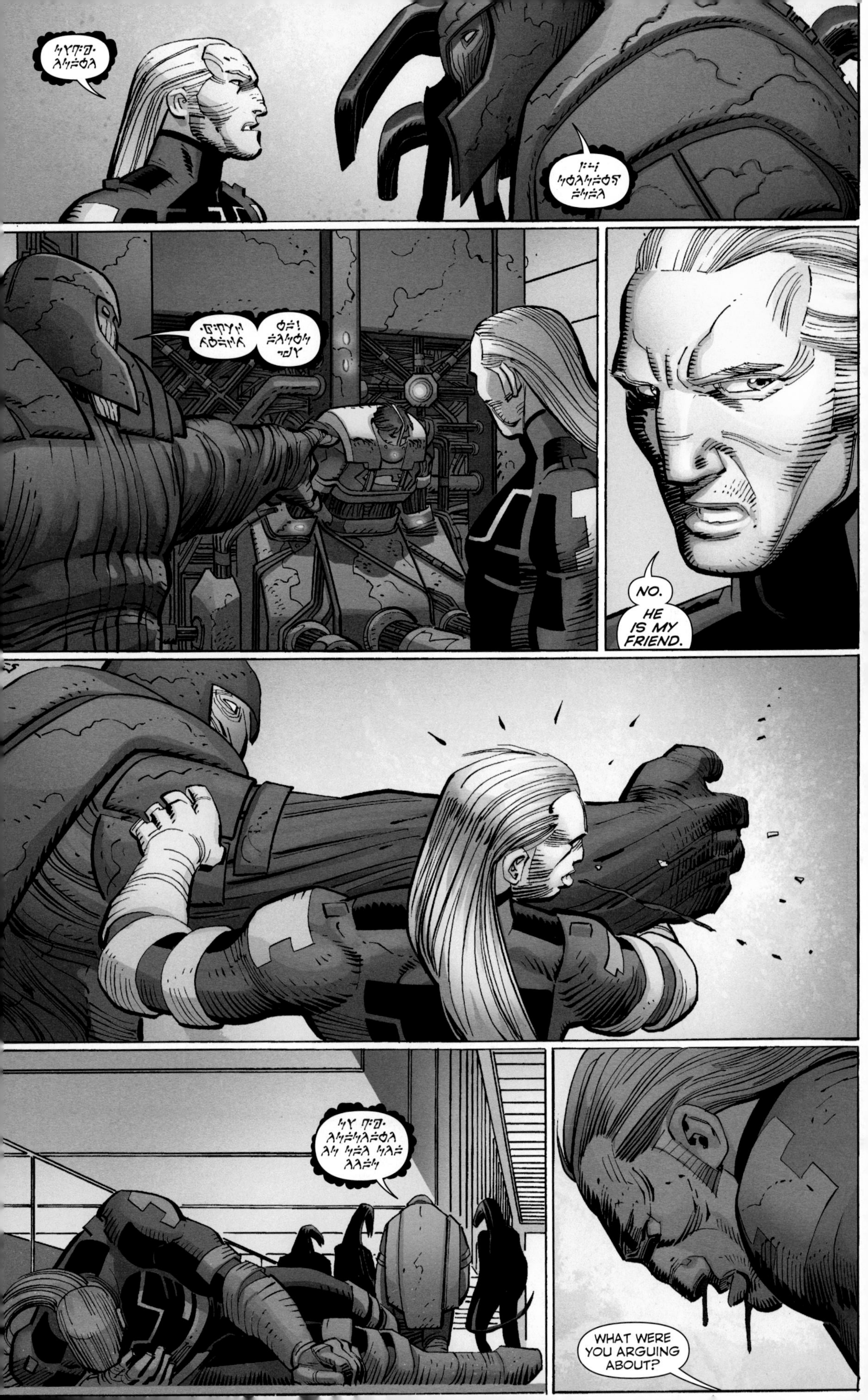
NO. HE IS MY FRIEND.
WHAT WERE YOU ARGUING ABOUT?

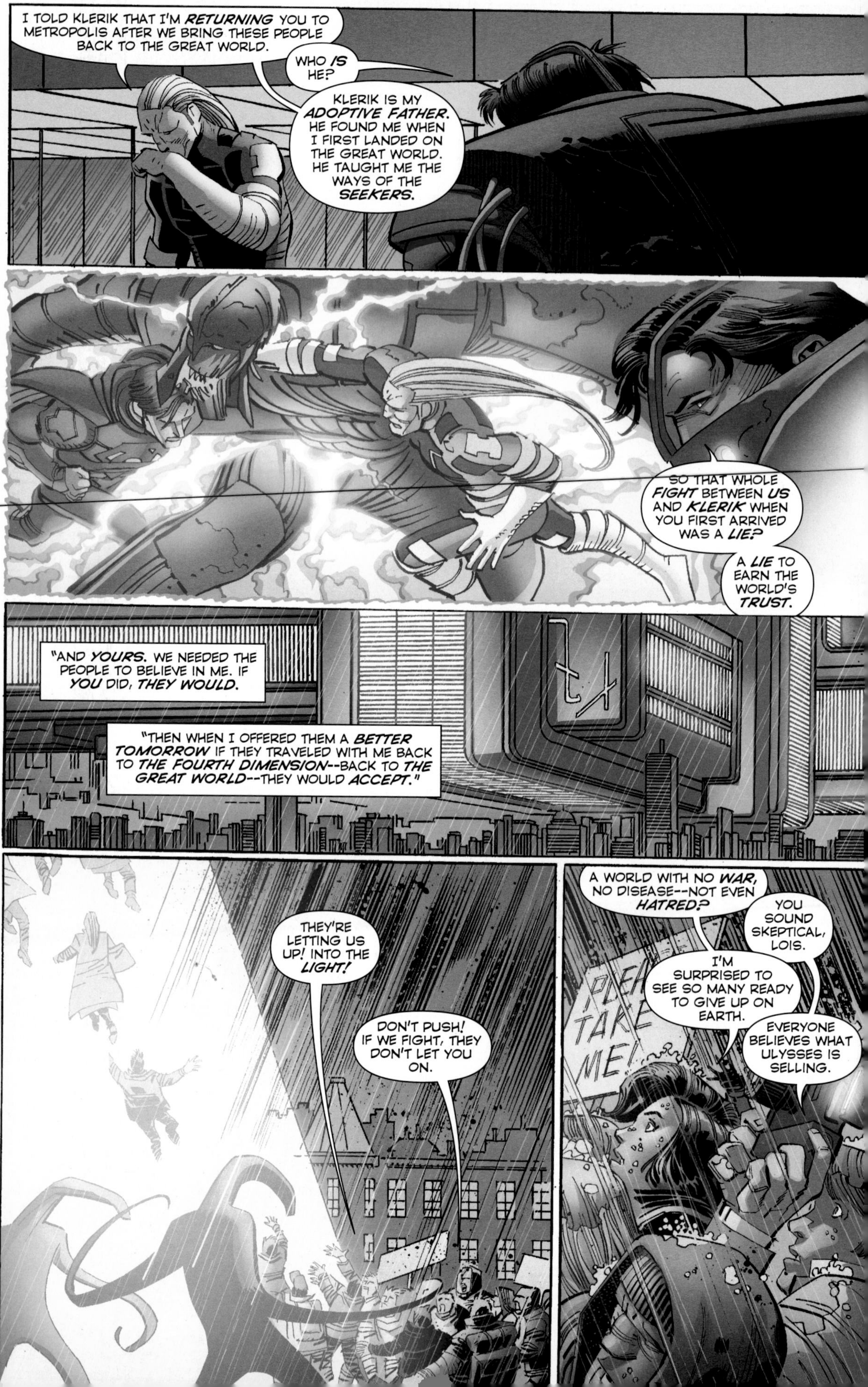
I TOLD KLERIK THAT I'M RETURNING YOU TO METROPOLIS AFTER WE BRING THESE PEOPLE BACK TO THE GREAT WORLD.
WHO IS HE?
KLERIK IS MY ADOPTIVE FATHER. HE FOUND ME WHEN I FIRST LANDED ON THE GREAT WORLD. HE TAUGHT ME THE WAYS OF THE SEEKERS.
SO THAT WHOLE FIGHT BETWEEN US AND KLERIK WHEN YOU FIRST ARRIVED WAS A LIE?
A LIE TO EARN THE WORLD'S TRUST.
"AND YOURS. WE NEEDED THE PEOPLE TO BELIEVE IN ME. IF YOU DID, THEY WOULD.
"THEN WHEN I OFFERED THEM A BETTER TOMORROW IF THEY TRAVELED WITH ME BACK TO THE FOURTH DIMENSION--BACK TO THE GREAT WORLD--THEY WOULD ACCEPT."
THEY'RE LETTING US UP! INTO THE LIGHT!
DON'T PUSH! IF WE FIGHT, THEY DON'T LET YOU ON.
A WORLD WITH NO WAR, NO DISEASE--NOT EVEN HATRED?
YOU SOUND SKEPTICAL, LOIS.
I'M SURPRISED TO SEE SO MANY READY TO GIVE UP ON EARTH.
EVERYONE BELIEVES WHAT ULYSSES IS SELLING.
TAKE ME!

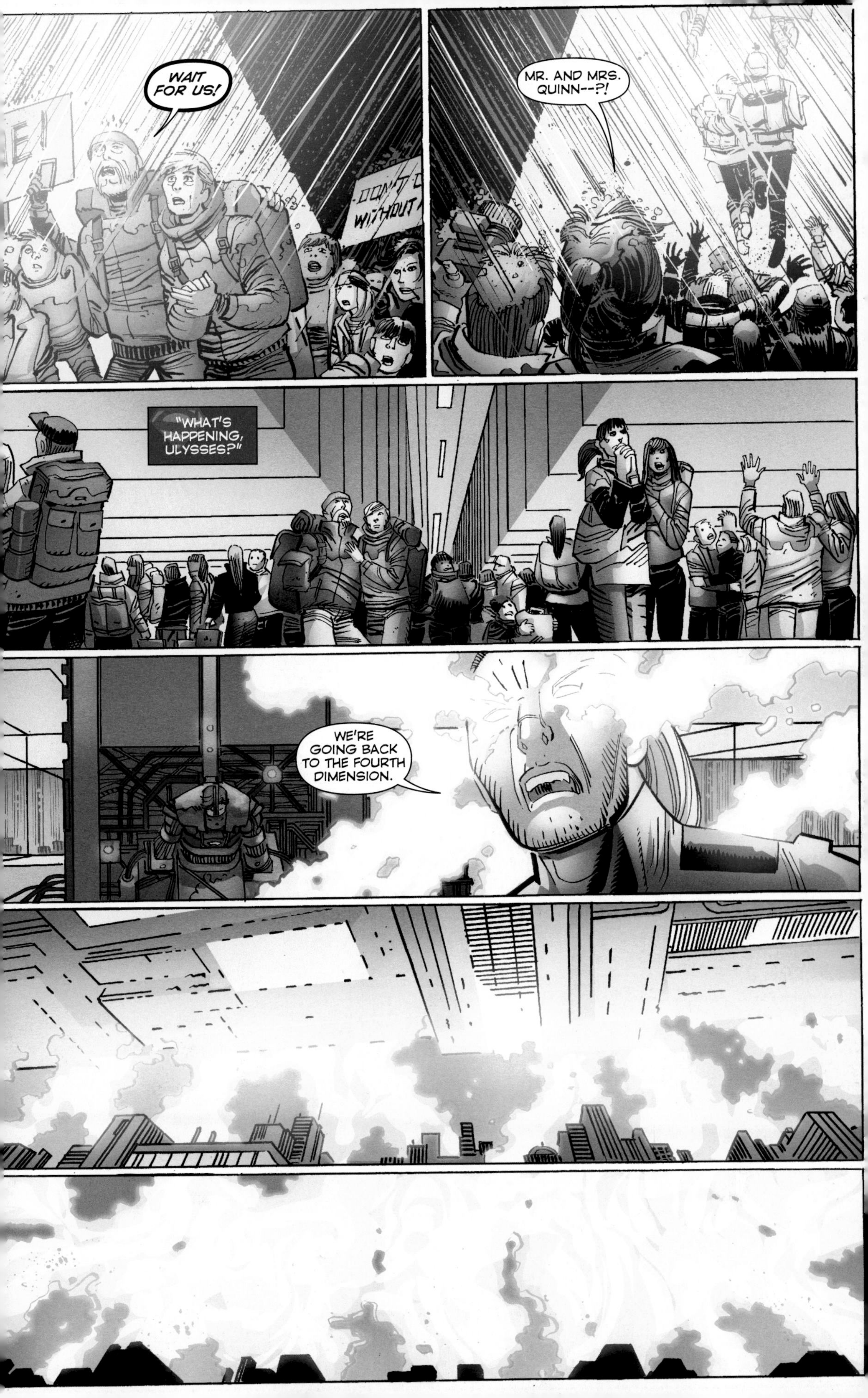
WAIT FOR US!
MR. AND MRS. QUINN--?!
"WHAT'S HAPPENING, ULYSSES?"
WE'RE GOING BACK TO THE FOURTH DIMENSION.

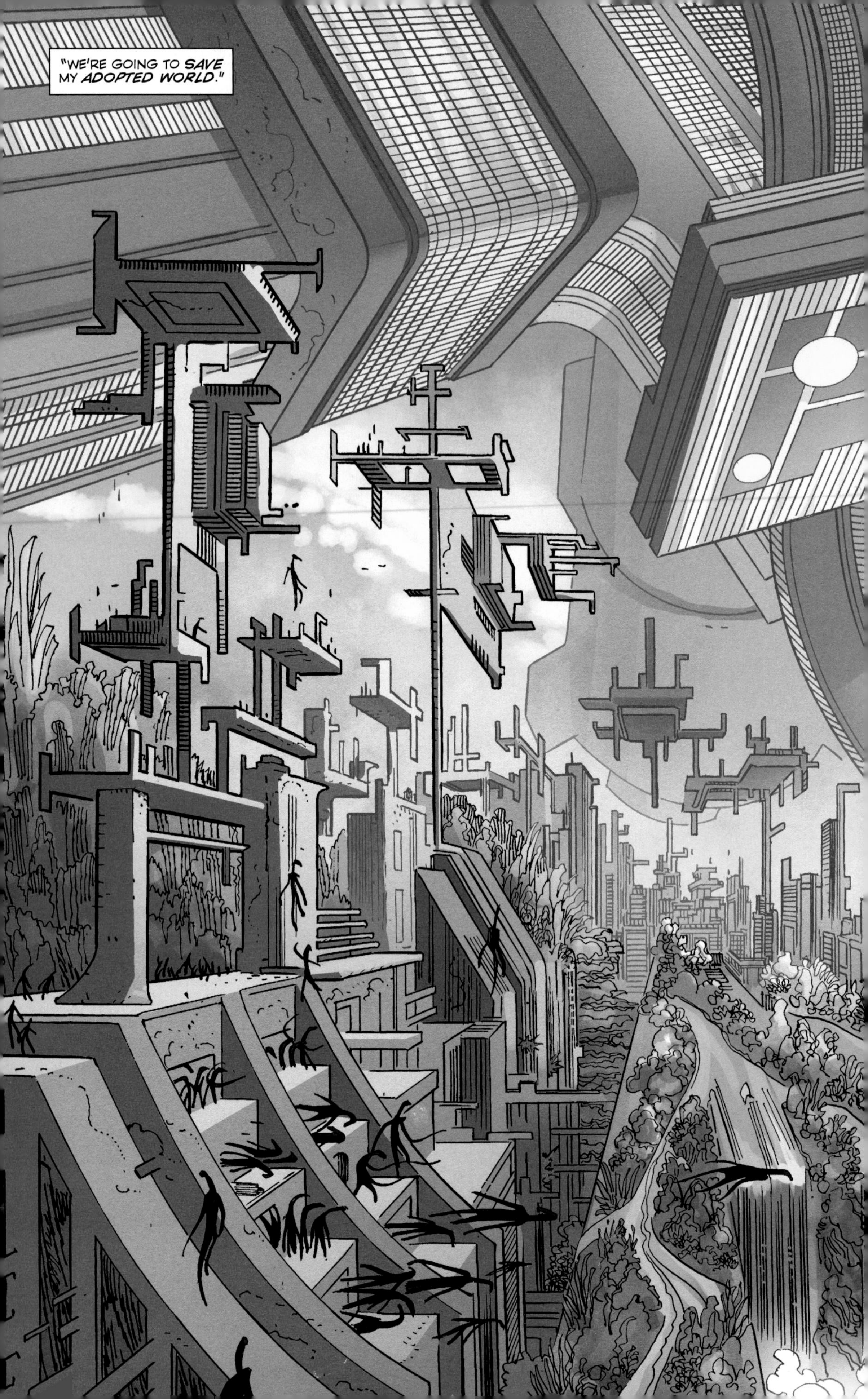
"WE'RE GOING TO SAVE MY ADOPTED WORLD."

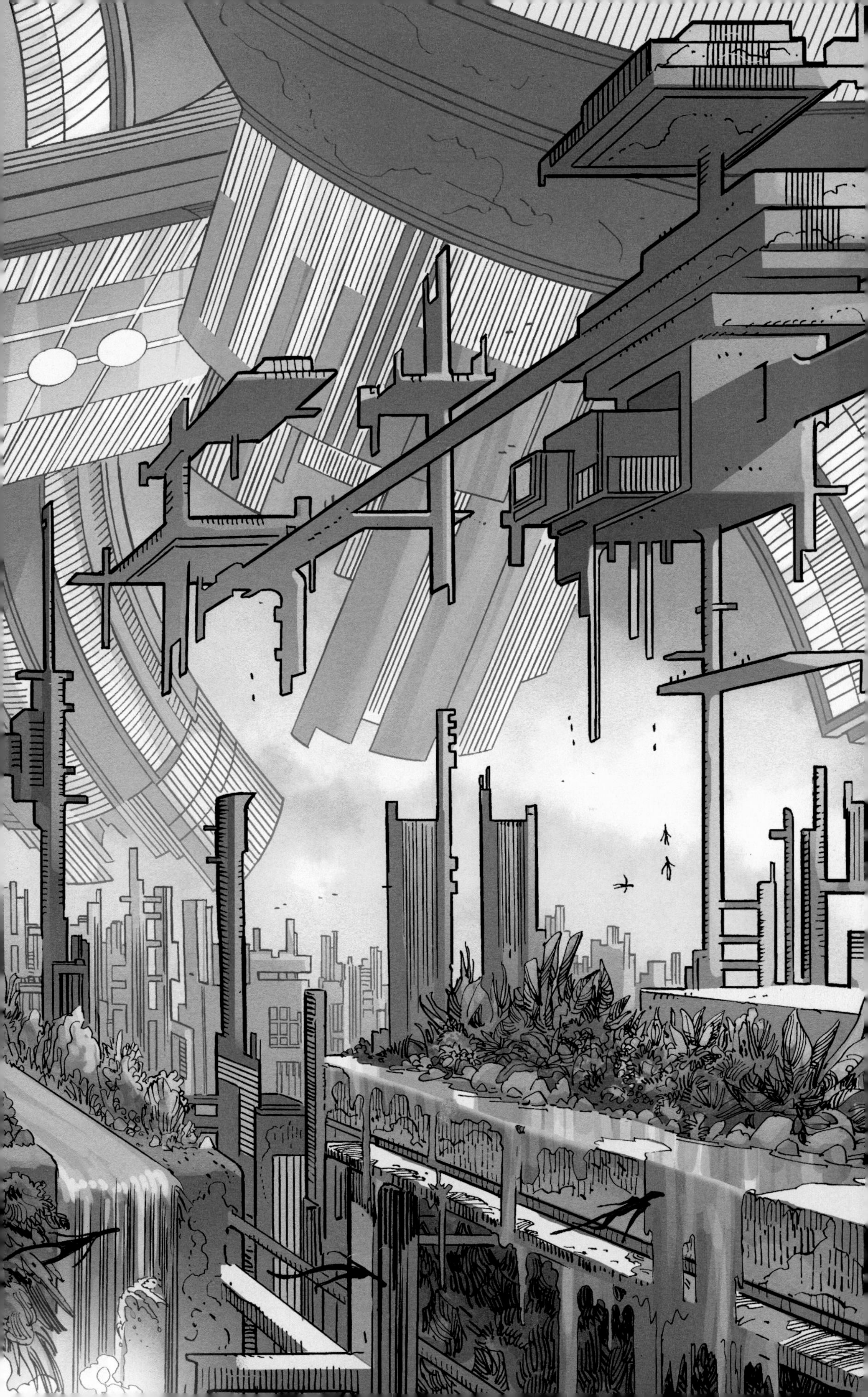

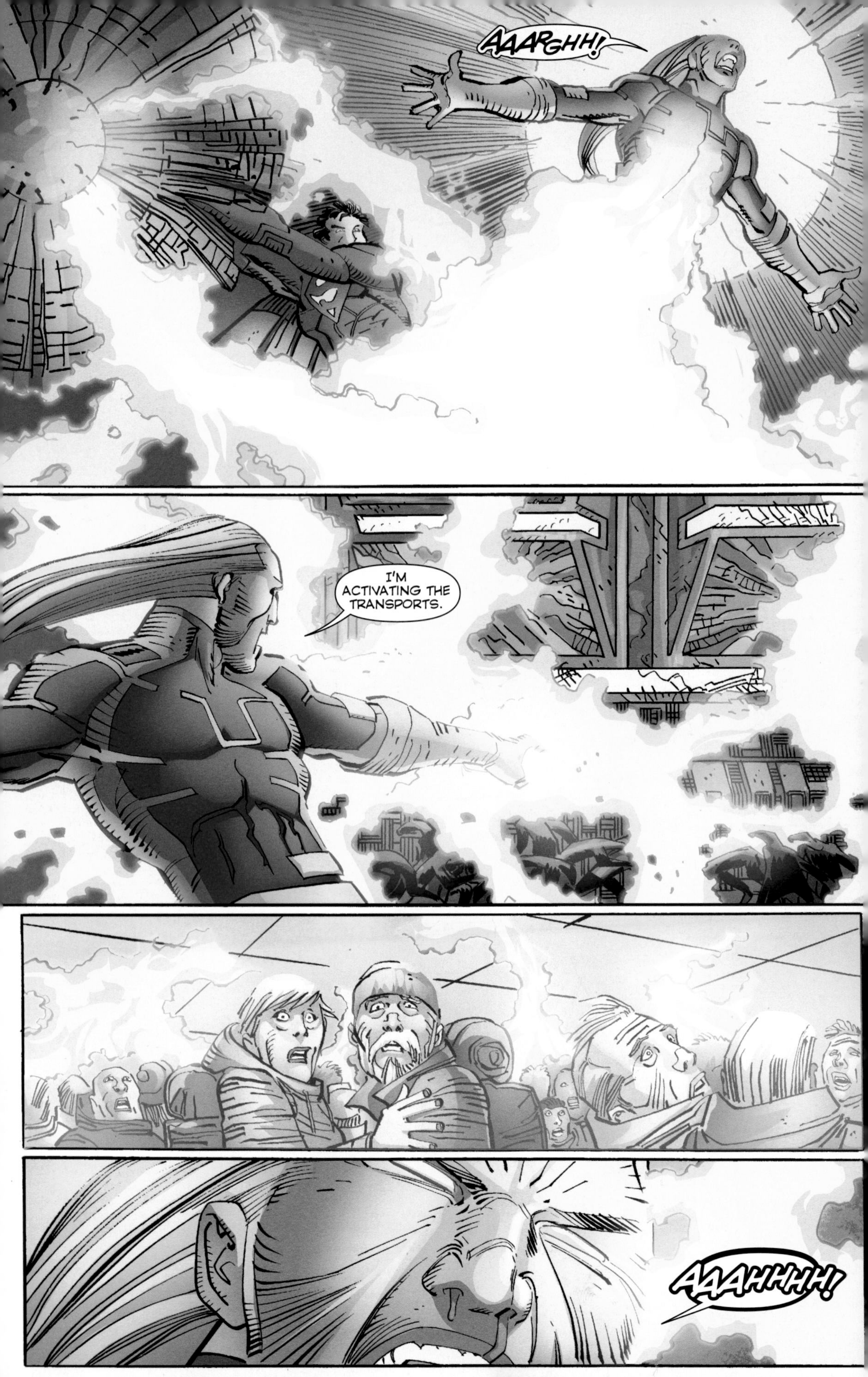
AAARGHH!
I'M ACTIVATING THE TRANSPORTS.
AAAHHHH!

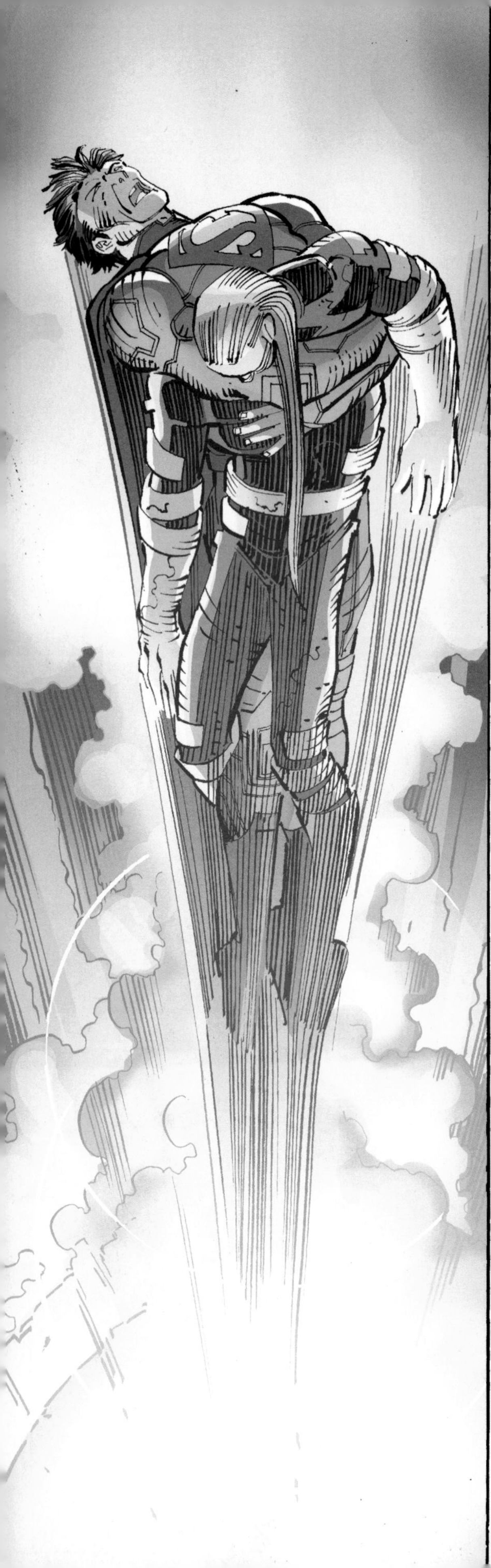
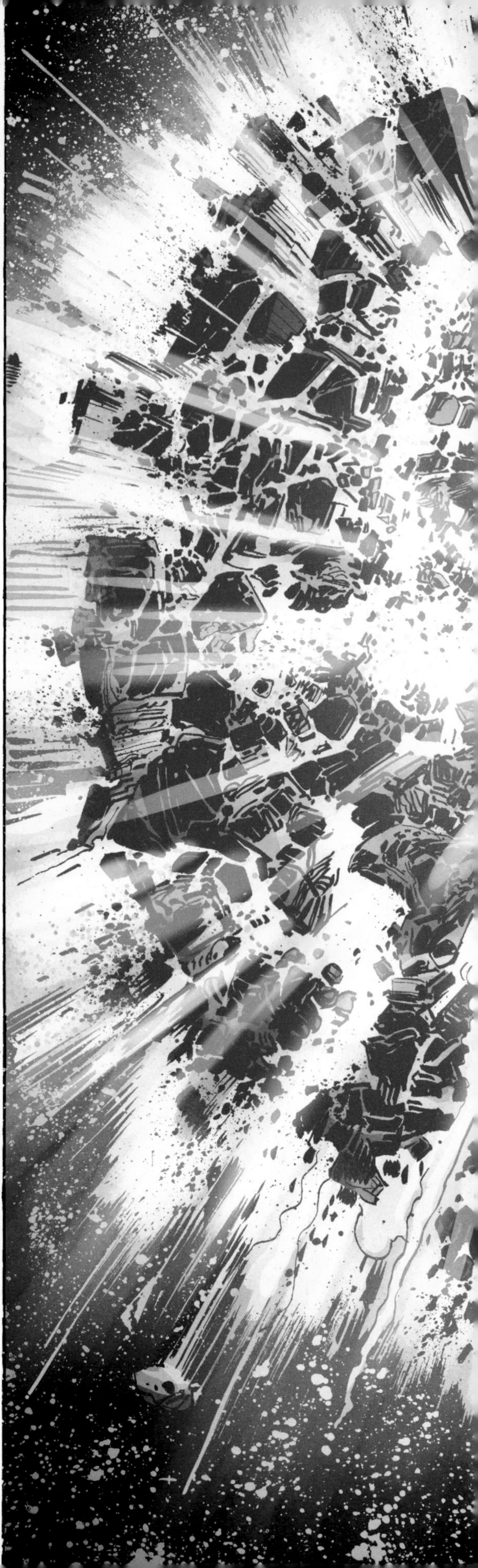

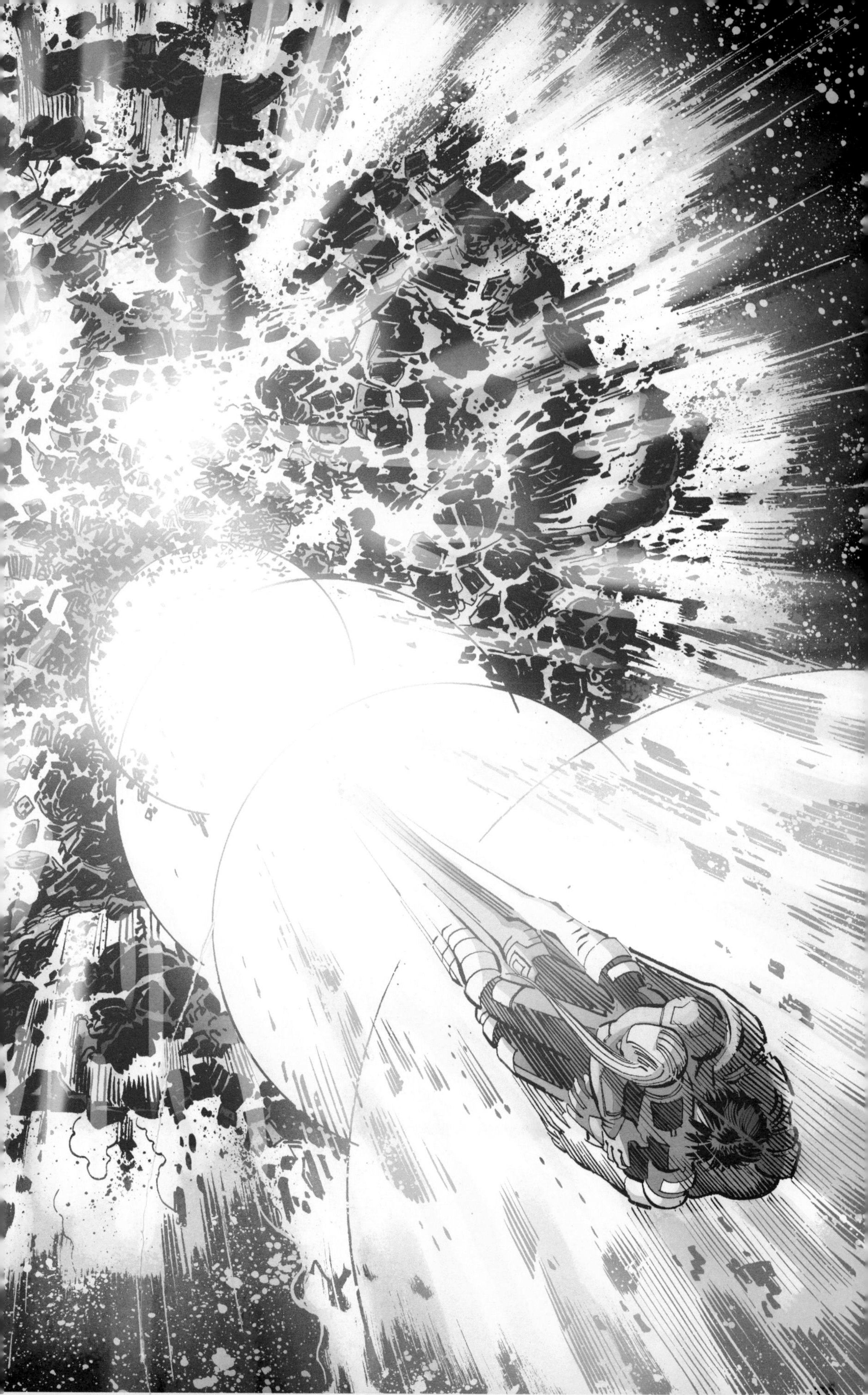

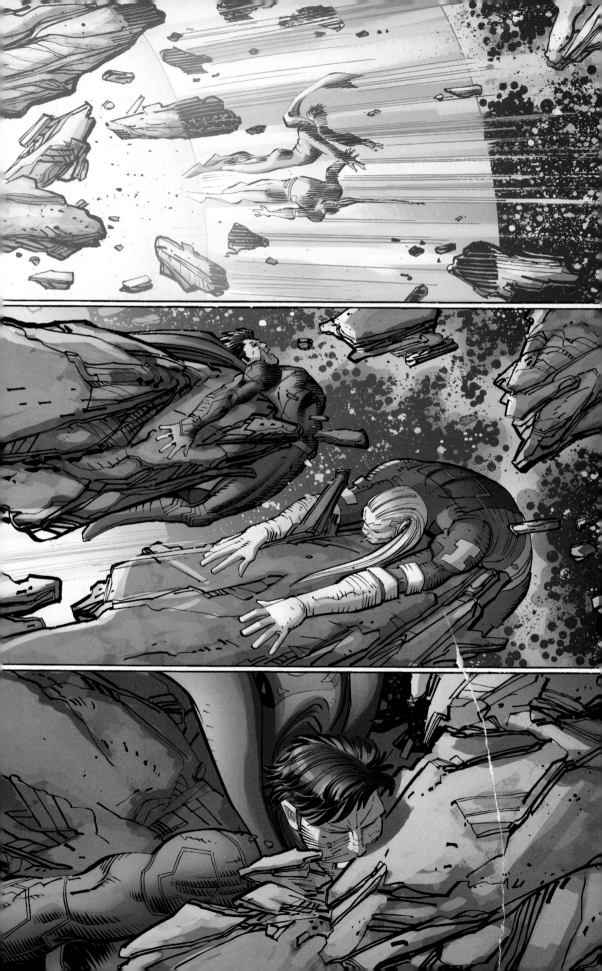

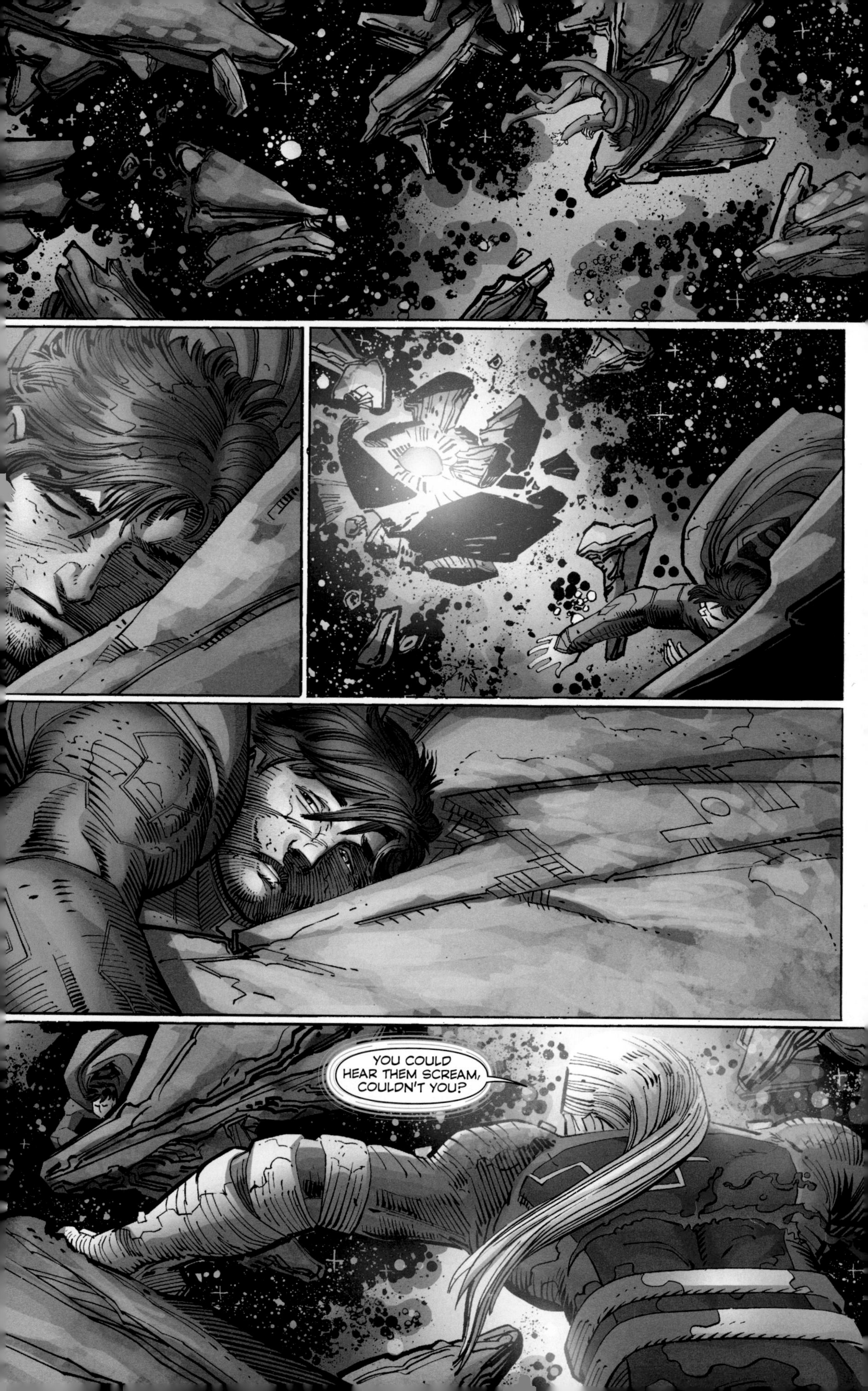
YOU COULD HEAR THEM SCREAM, COULDN'T YOU?

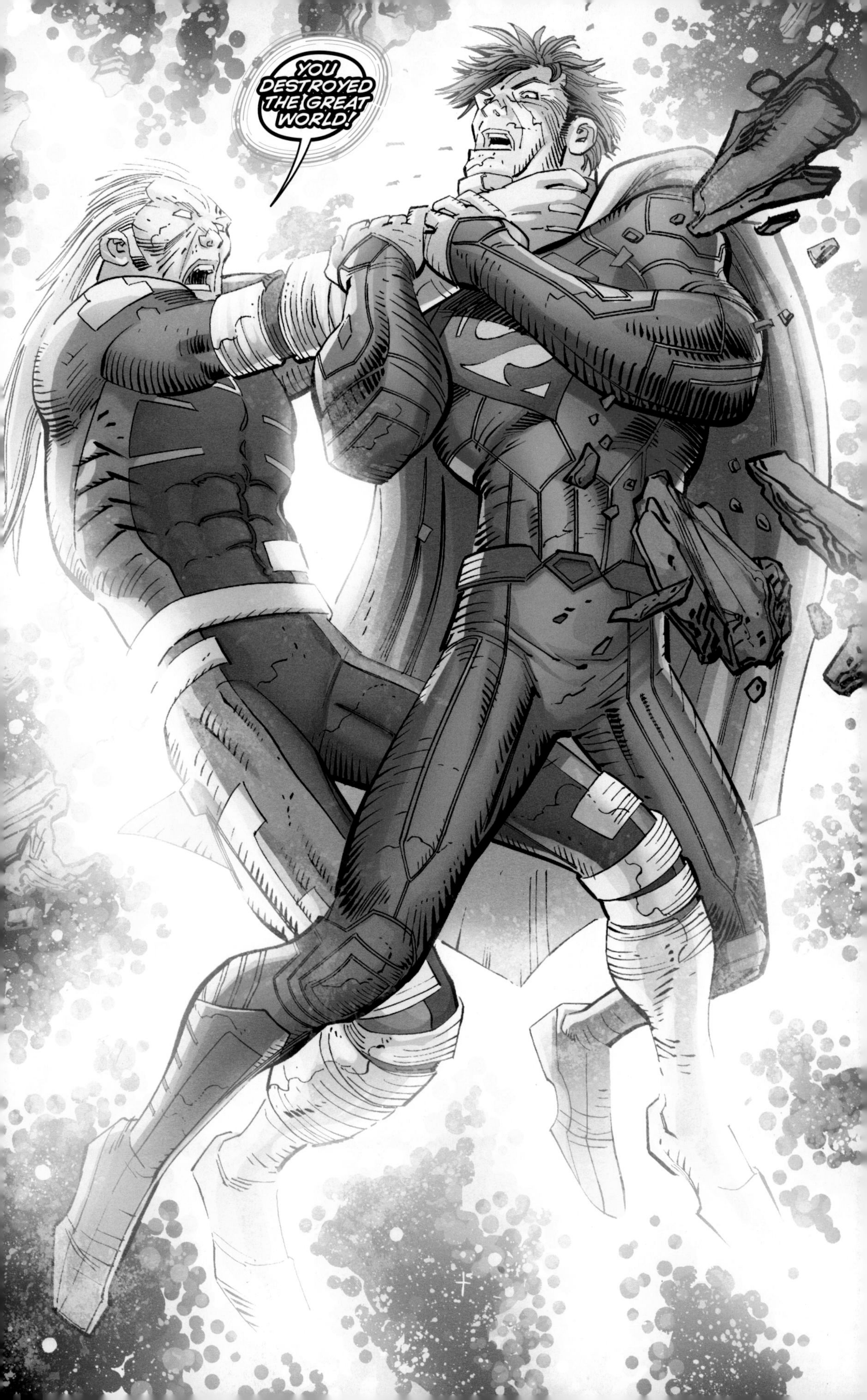
YOU DESTROYED THE GREAT WORLD!

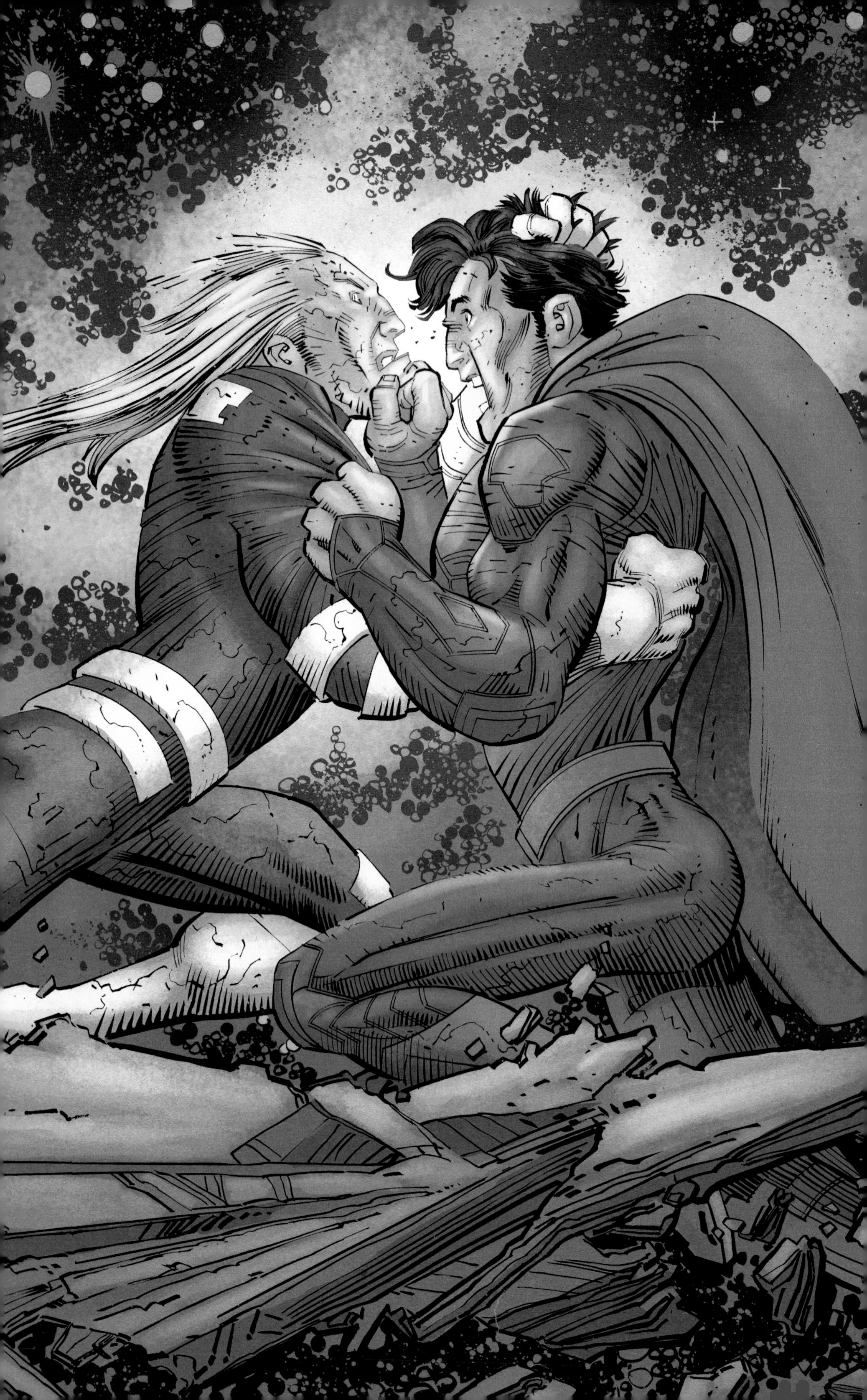

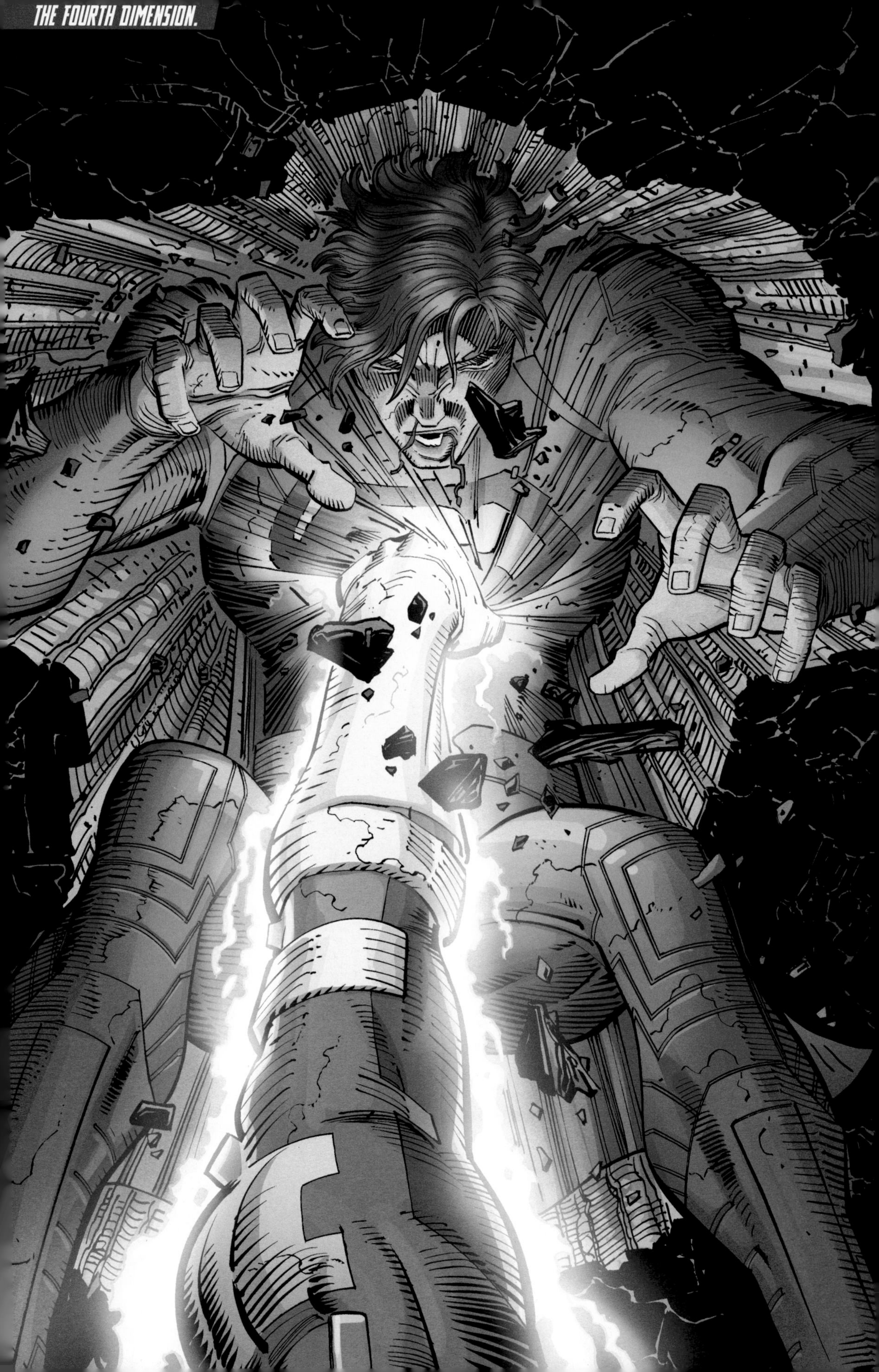
THE FOURTH DIMENSION.

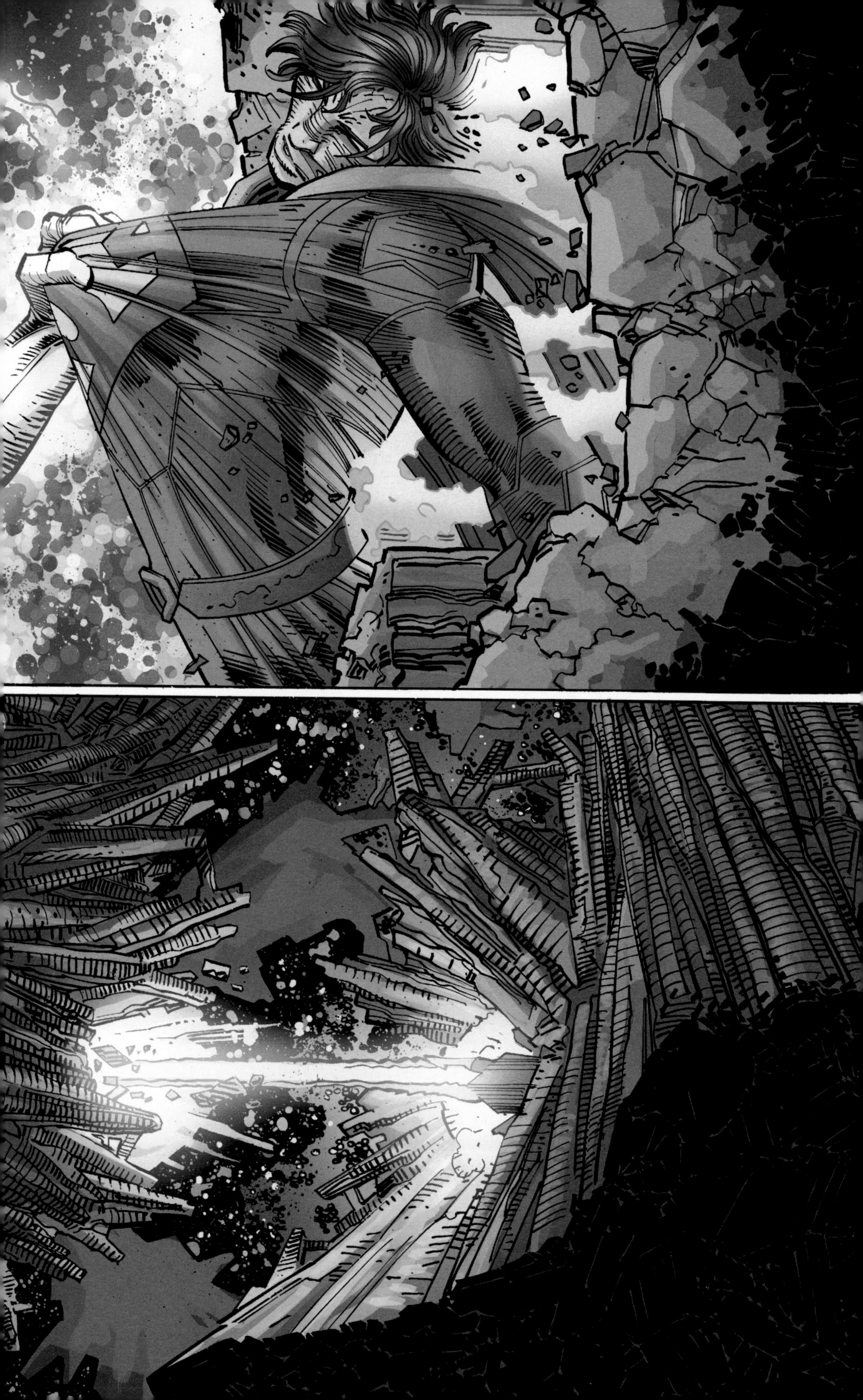

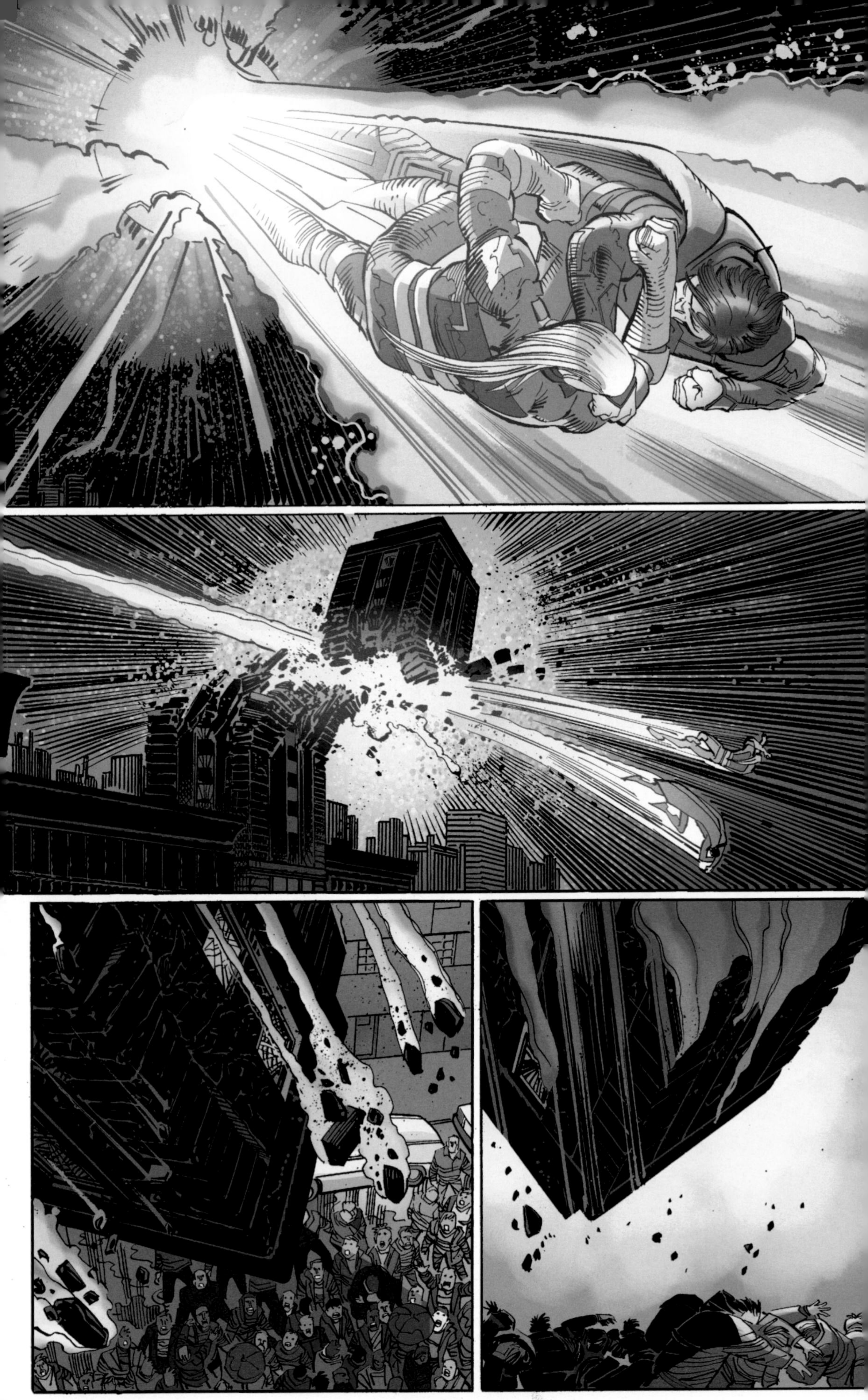

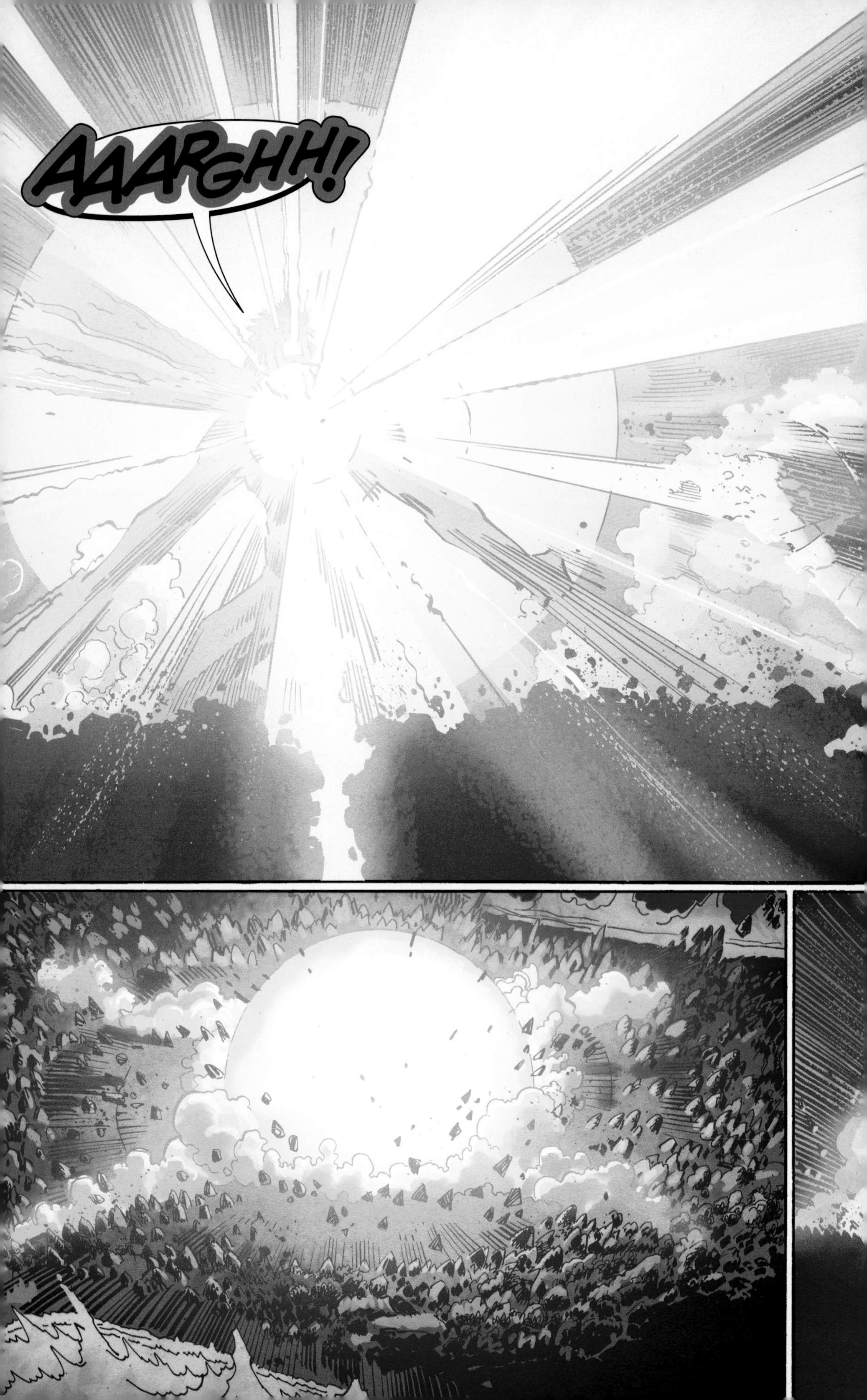
AAARGHH!

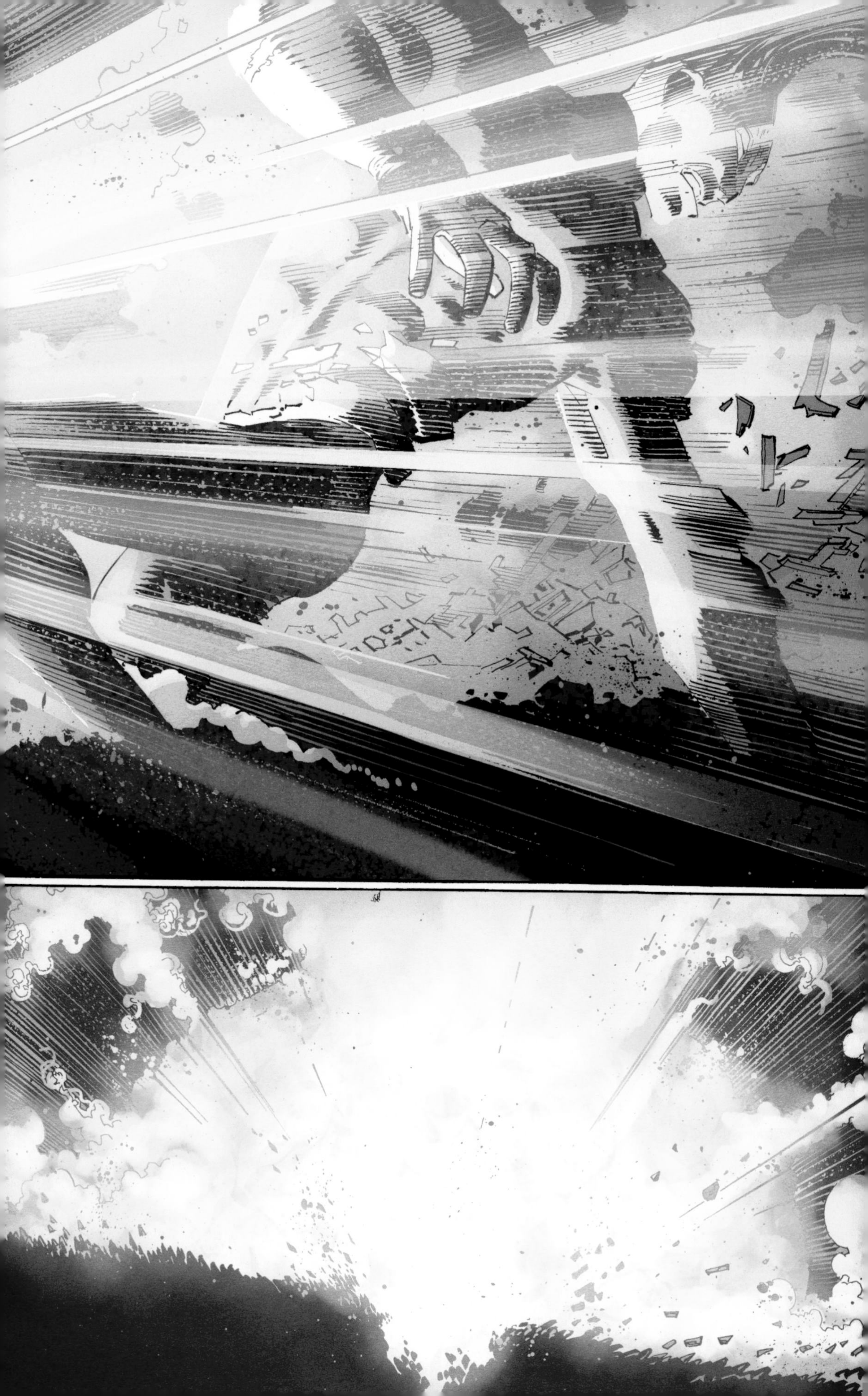

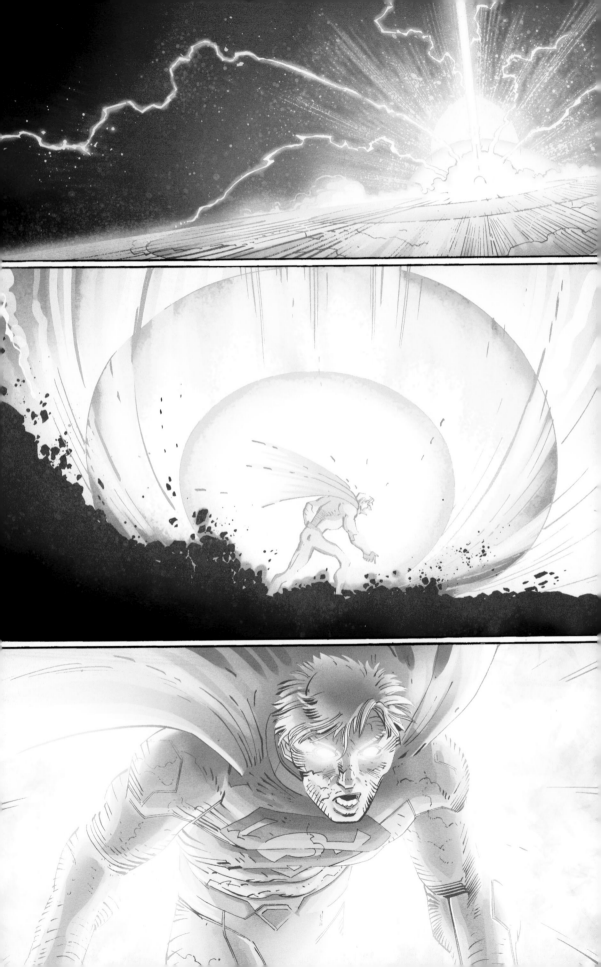

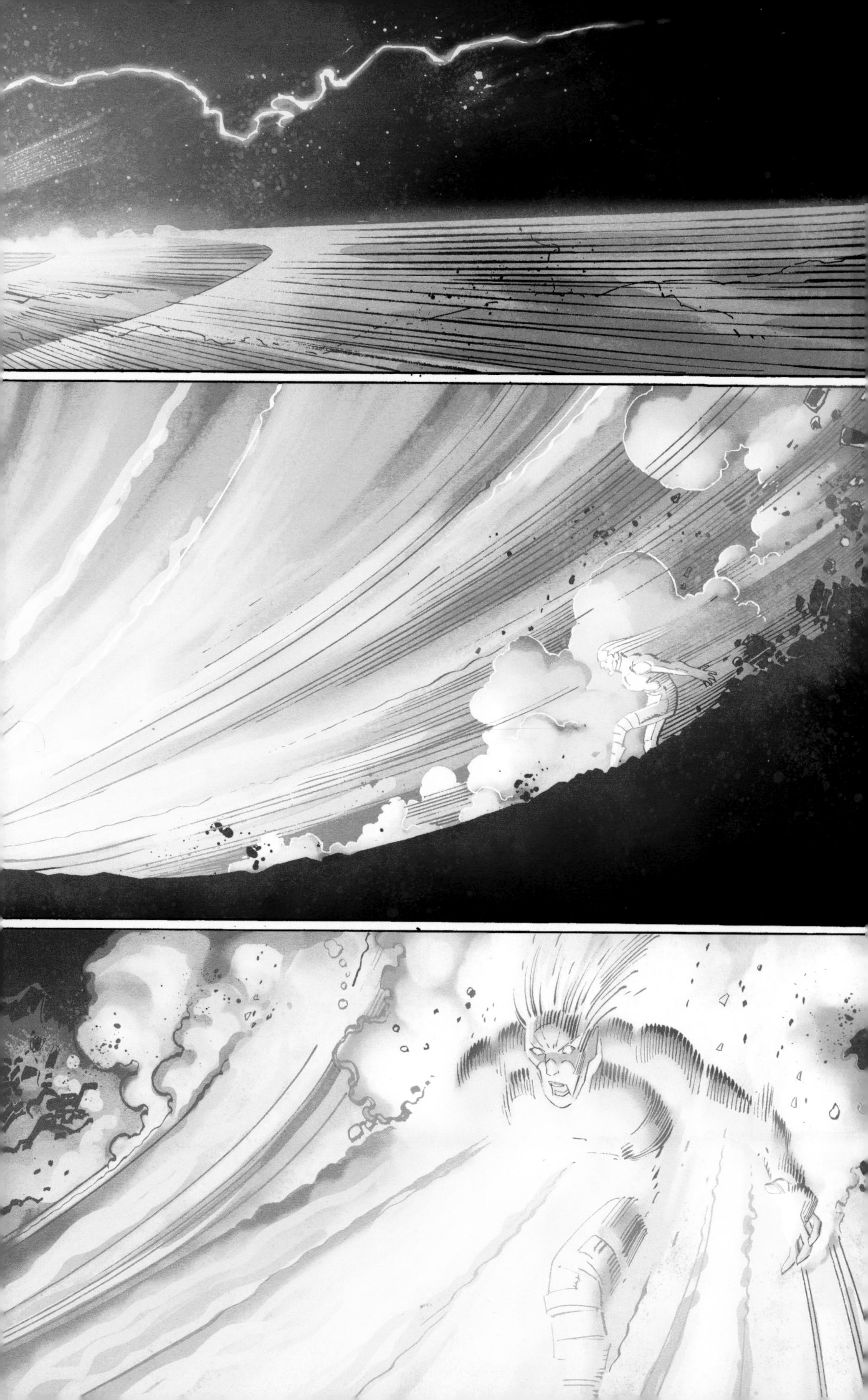

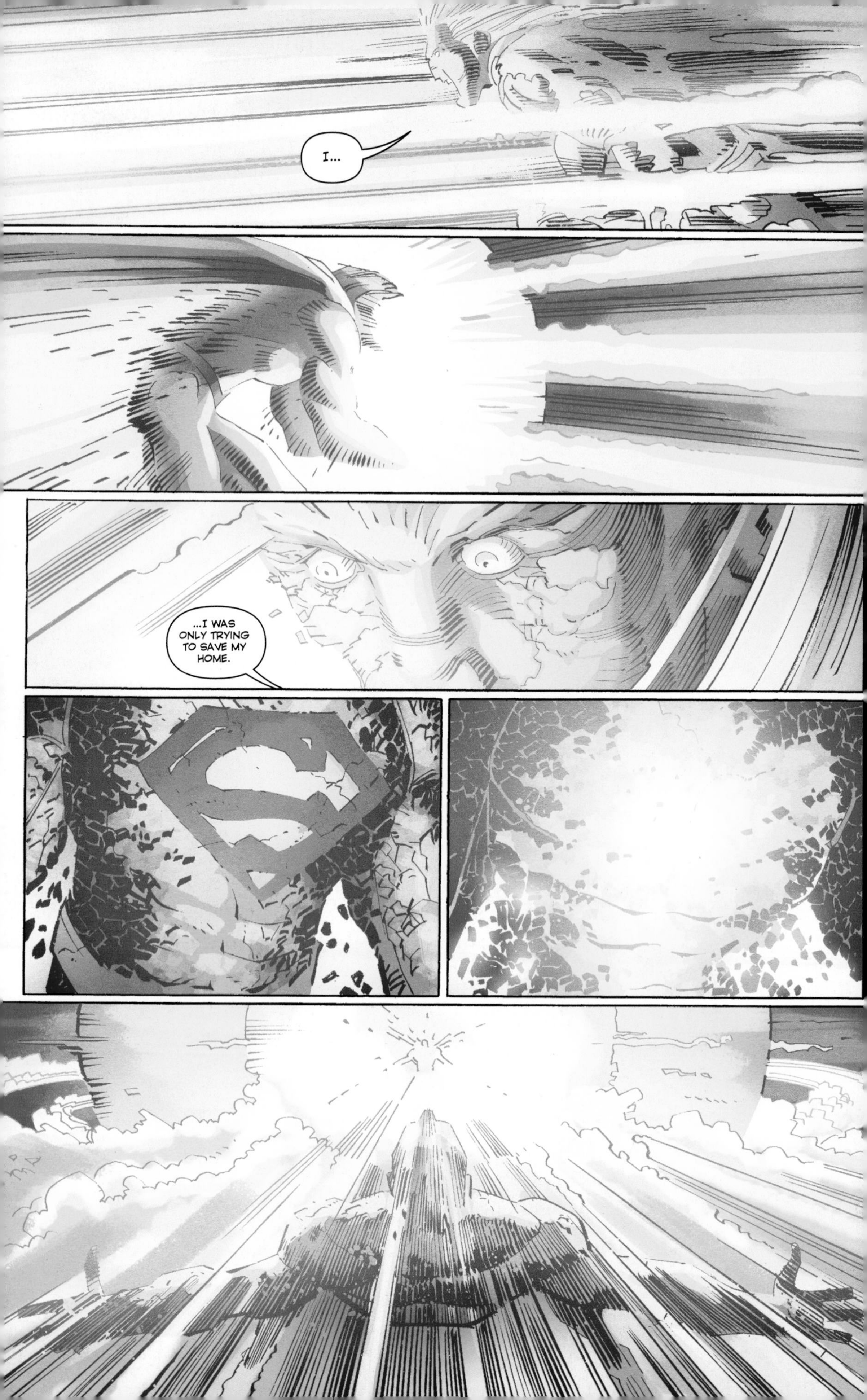
I...
...I WAS ONLY TRYING TO SAVE MY HOME.

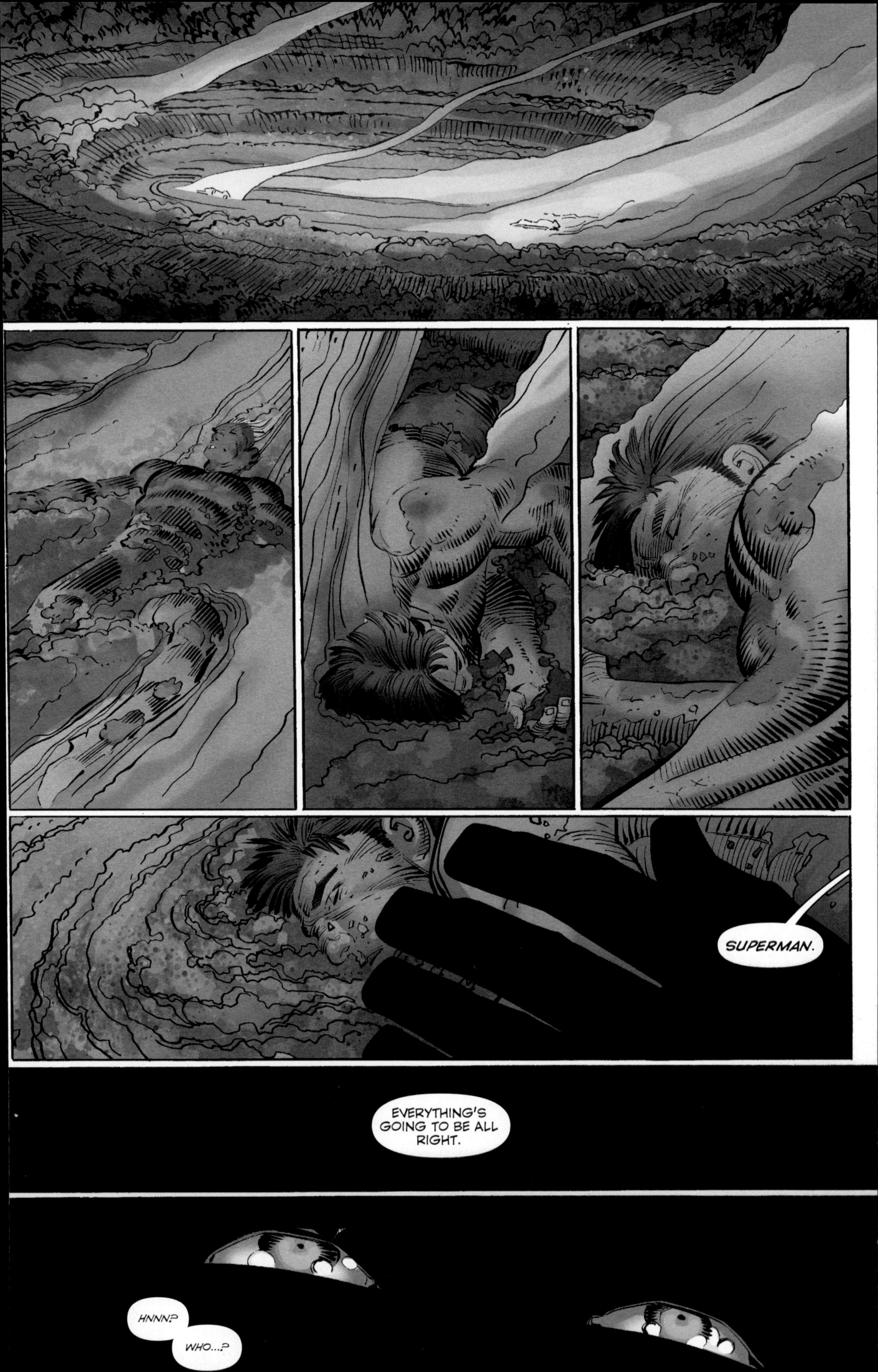
SUPERMAN.
EVERYTHING'S GOING TO BE ALL RIGHT.
HNNN?
WHO...?

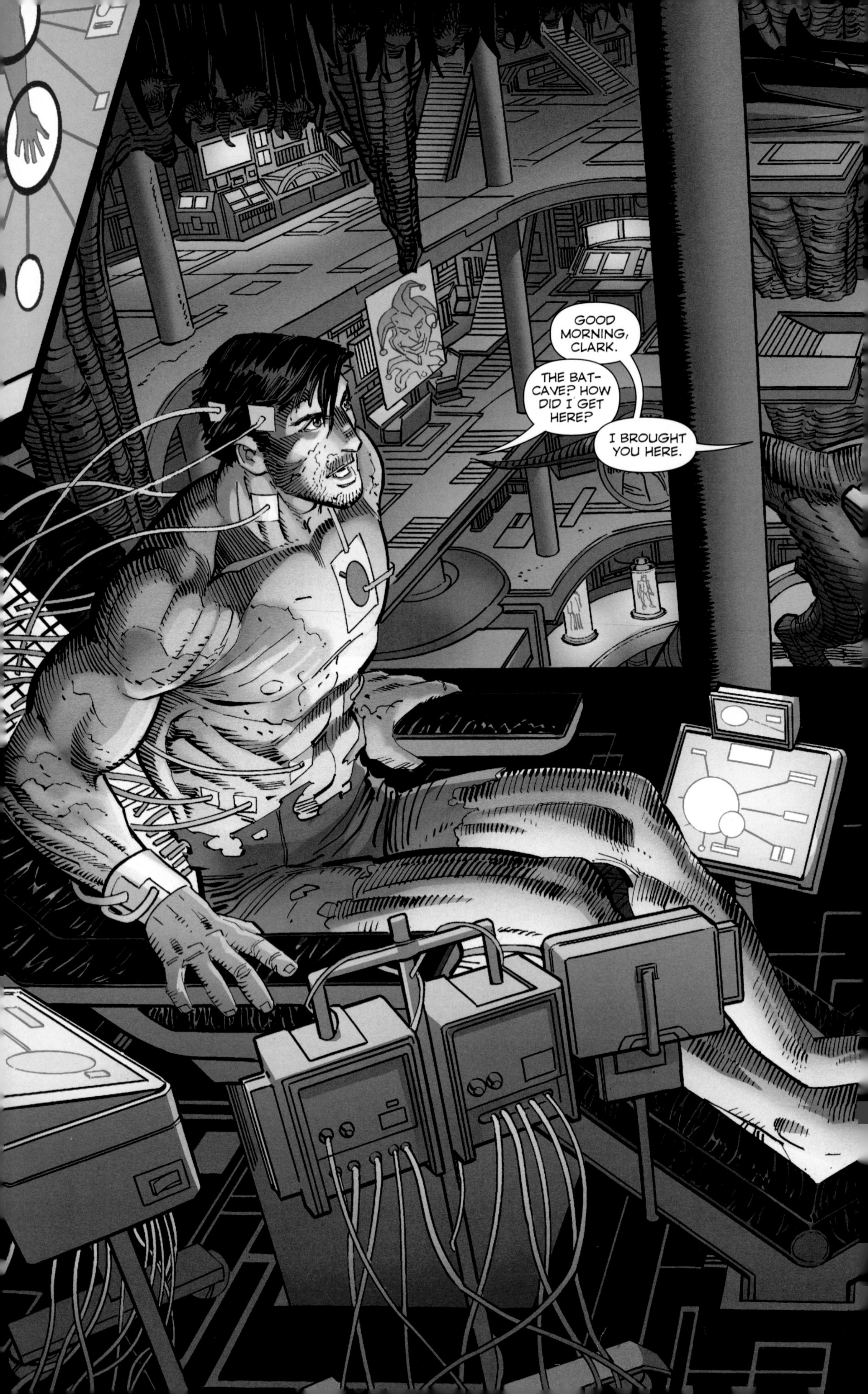

THE BAT-CAVE? HOW DID I GET HERE?
GOOD MORNING, CLARK.
I BROUGHT YOU HERE.

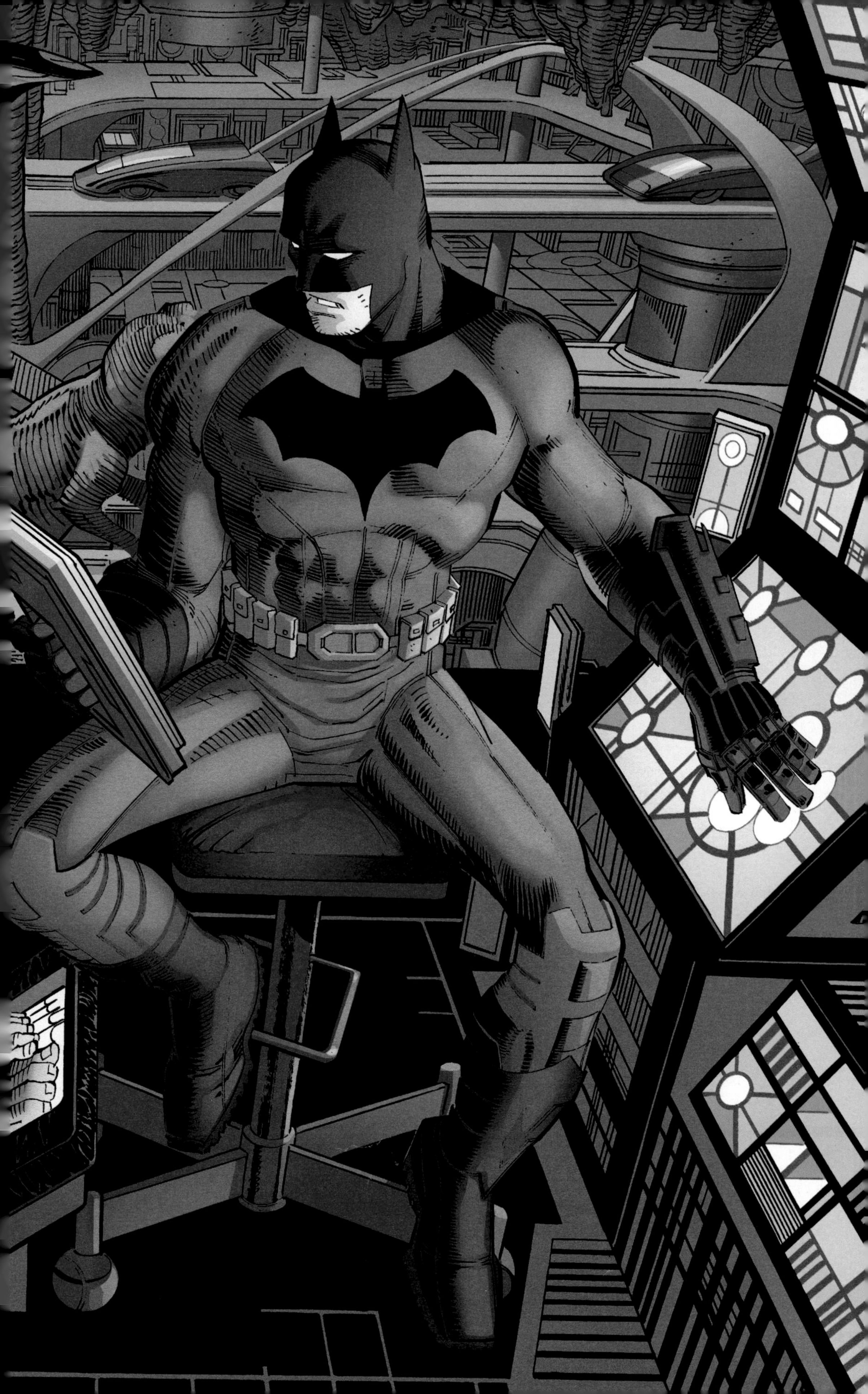

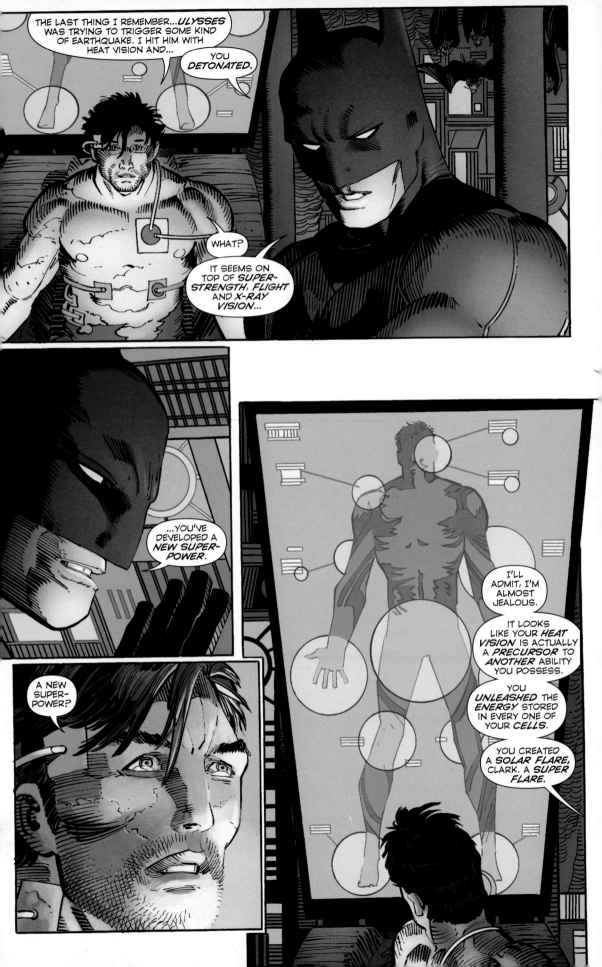

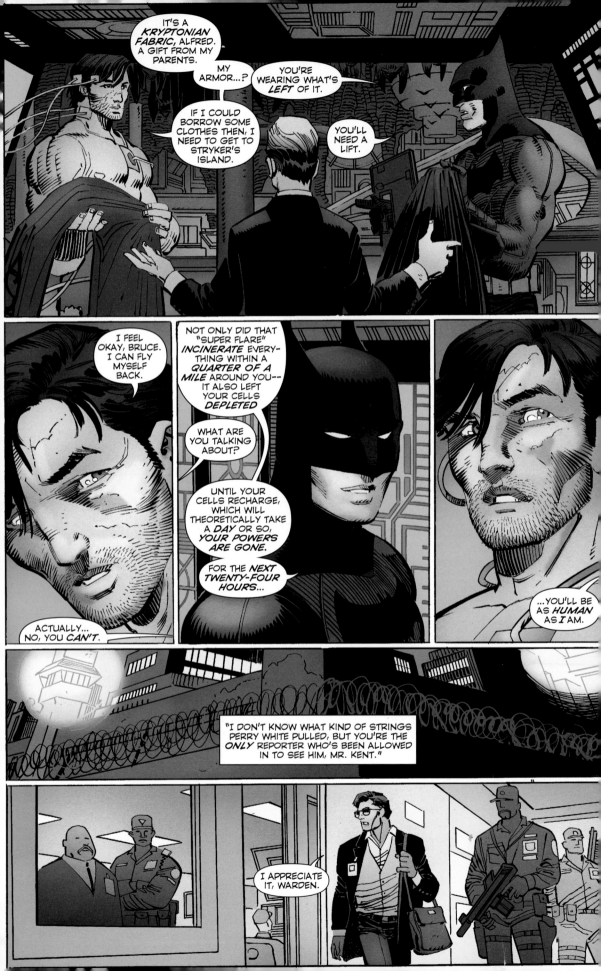

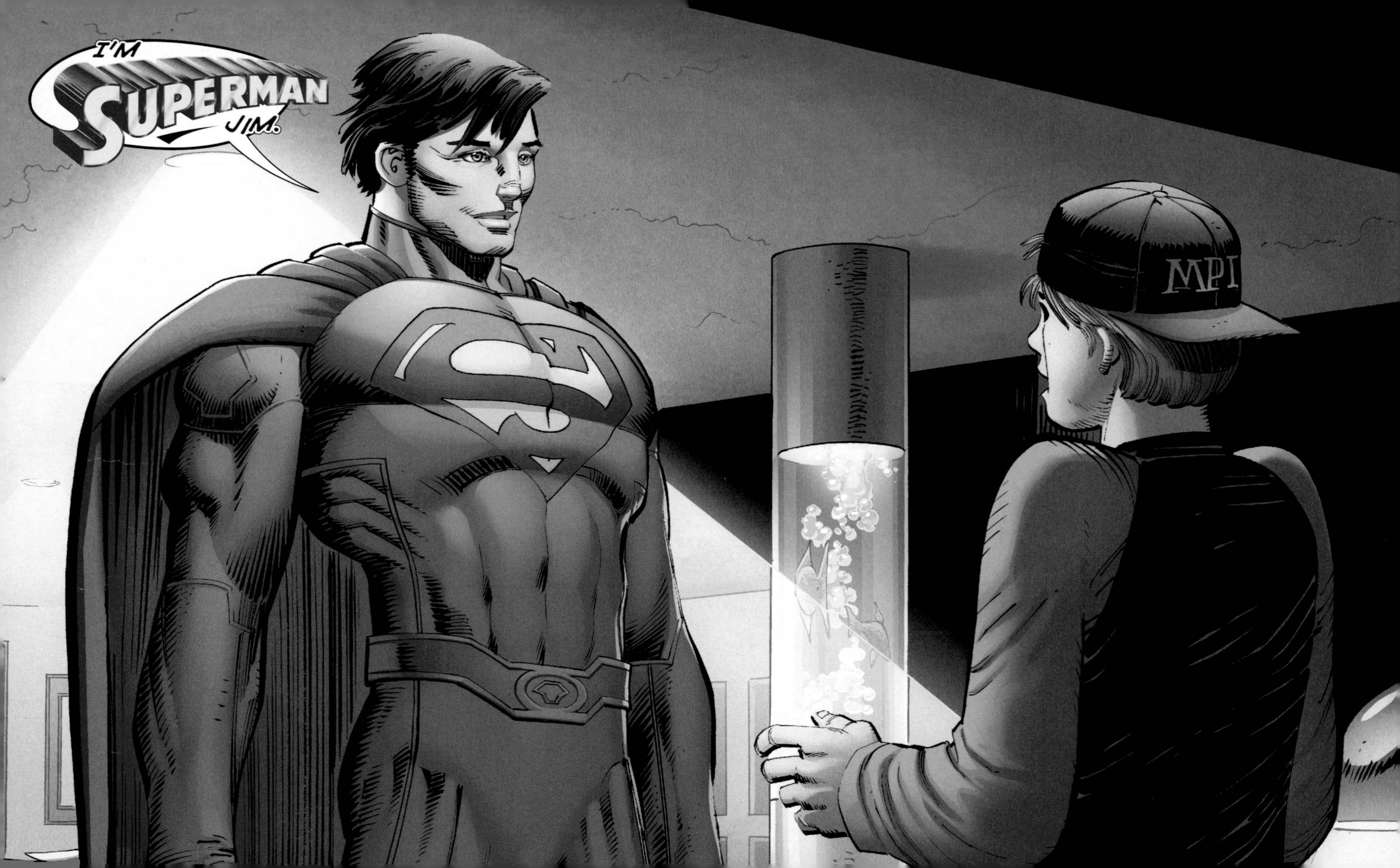
I'M SUPERMAN JIM.
MPI

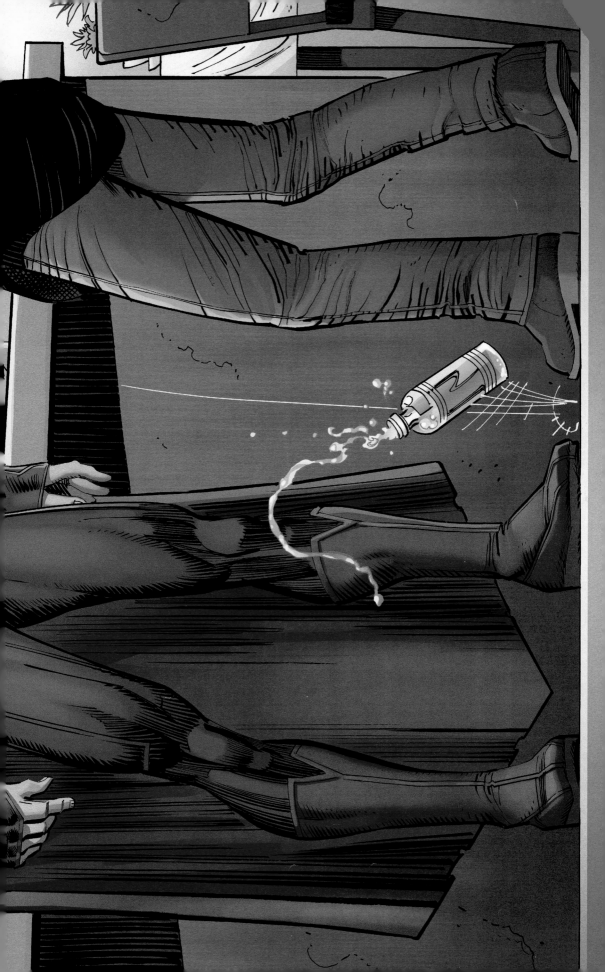

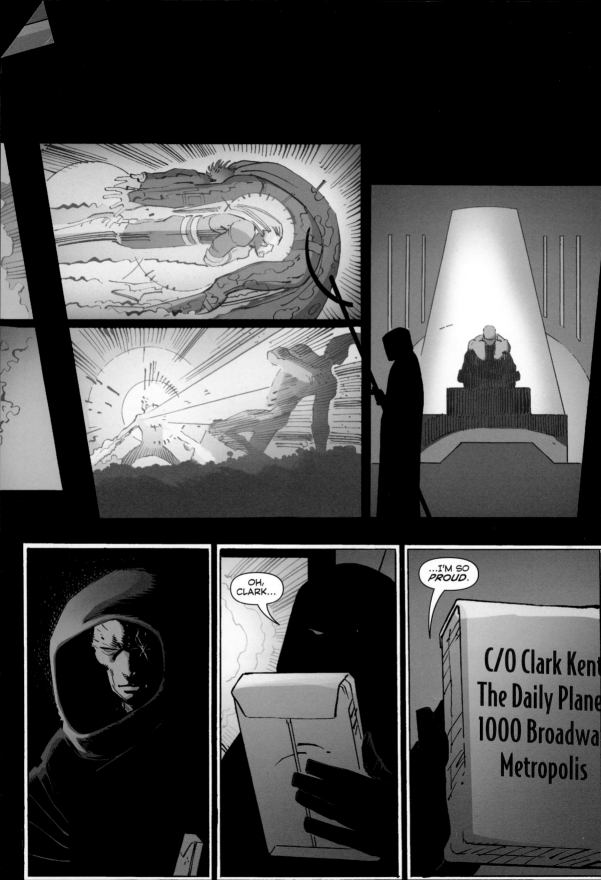

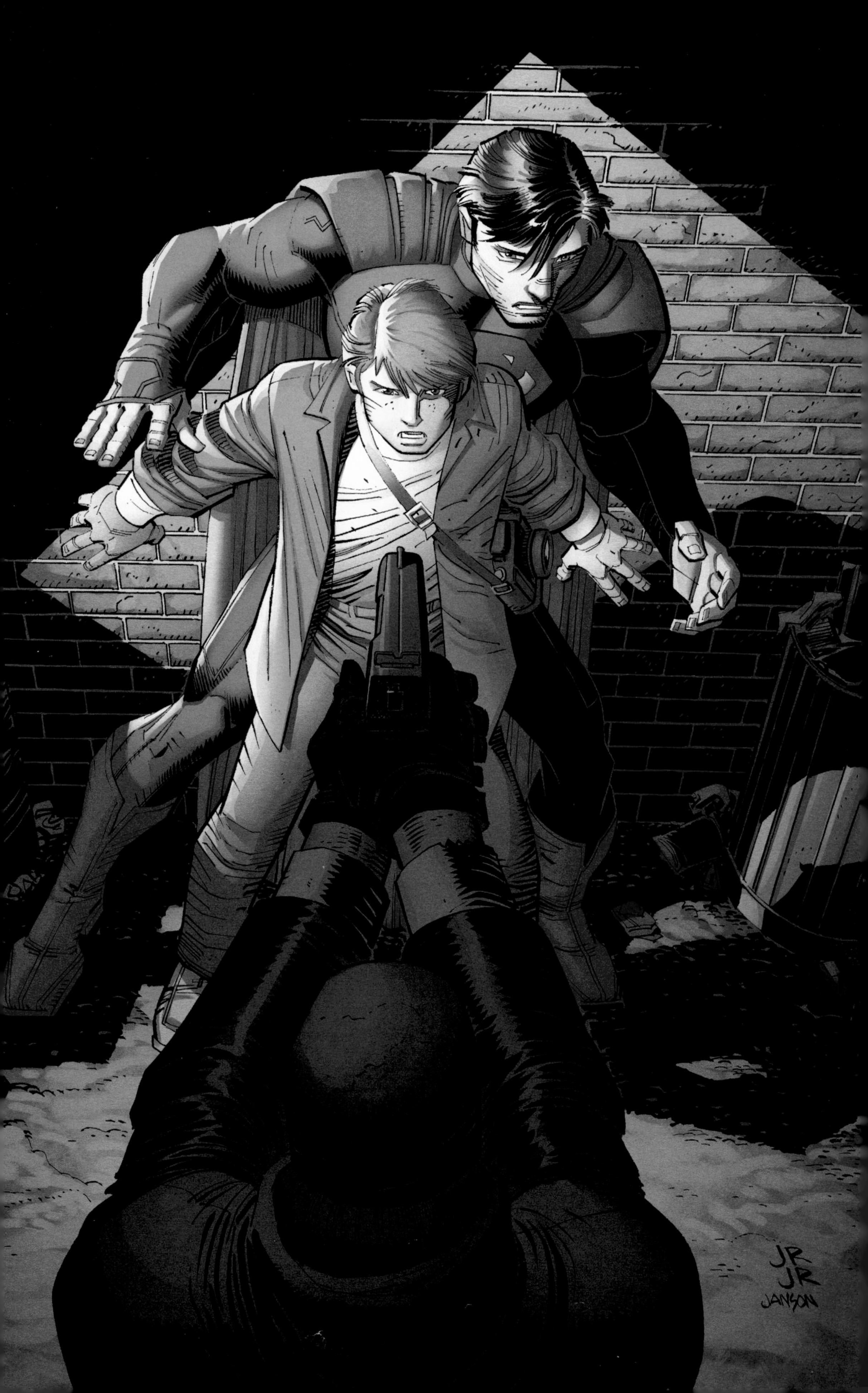
JR JR
JANSON

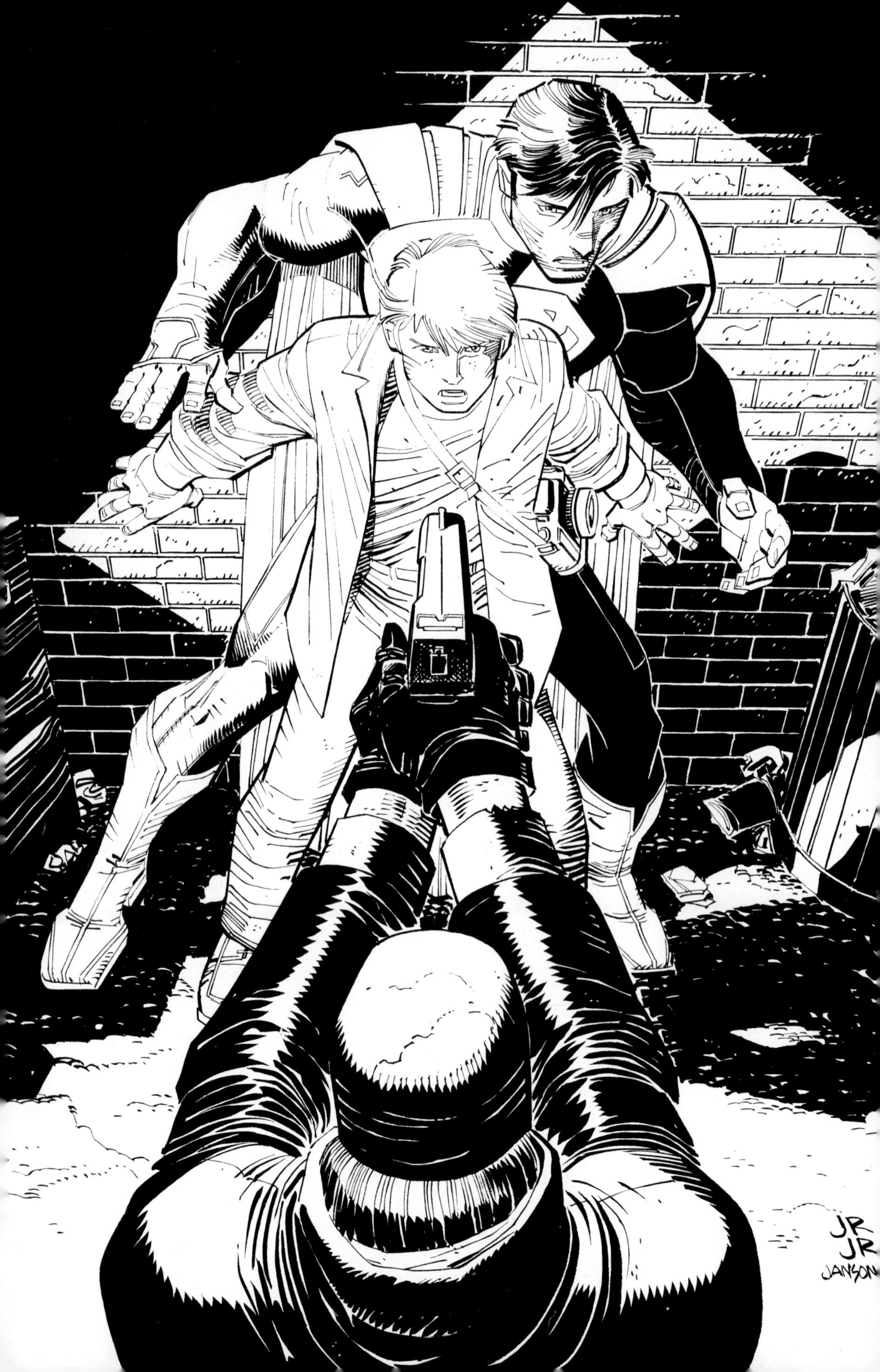
JR JR
JANSON

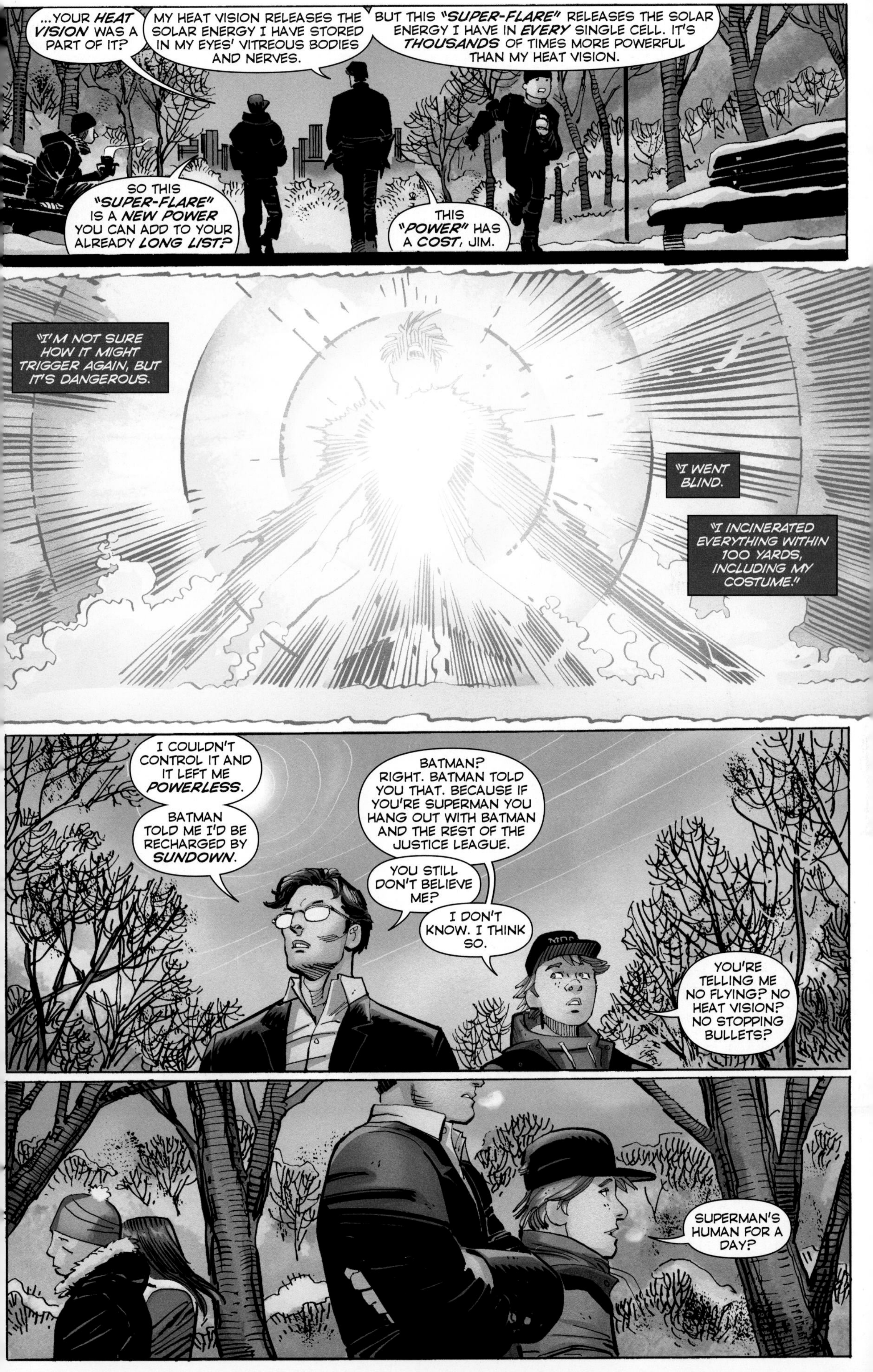
...YOUR HEAT VISION WAS A PART OF IT?
MY HEAT VISION RELEASES THE SOLAR ENERGY I HAVE STORED IN MY EYES' VITREOUS BODIES AND NERVES.
BUT THIS "SUPER-FLARE" RELEASES THE SOLAR ENERGY I HAVE IN EVERY SINGLE CELL. IT'S THOUSANDS OF TIMES MORE POWERFUL THAN MY HEAT VISION.
SO THIS "SUPER-FLARE" IS A NEW POWER YOU CAN ADD TO YOUR ALREADY LONG LIST?
THIS "POWER" HAS A COST, JIM.
"I'M NOT SURE HOW IT MIGHT TRIGGER AGAIN, BUT IT'S DANGEROUS.
"I WENT BLIND.
"I INCINERATED EVERYTHING WITHIN 100 YARDS, INCLUDING MY COSTUME."
I COULDN'T CONTROL IT AND IT LEFT ME POWERLESS.
BATMAN TOLD ME I'D BE RECHARGED BY SUNDOWN.
BATMAN? RIGHT. BATMAN TOLD YOU THAT. BECAUSE IF YOU'RE SUPERMAN YOU HANG OUT WITH BATMAN AND THE REST OF THE JUSTICE LEAGUE.
YOU STILL DON'T BELIEVE ME?
I DON'T KNOW. I THINK SO.
YOU'RE TELLING ME NO FLYING? NO HEAT VISION? NO STOPPING BULLETS?
SUPERMAN'S HUMAN FOR A DAY?

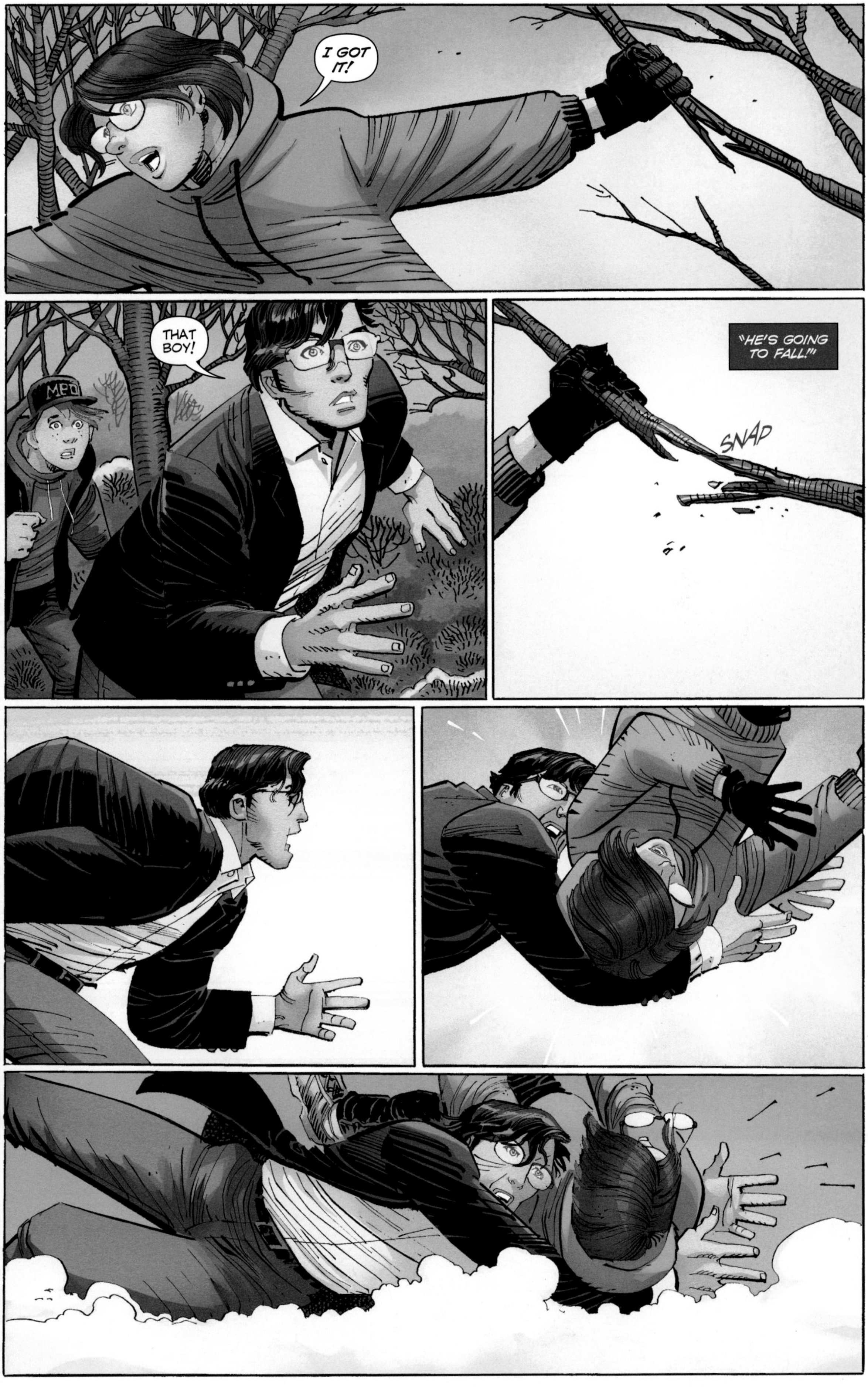
I GOT IT!
THAT BOY!
"HE'S GOING TO FALL!"
SNAP

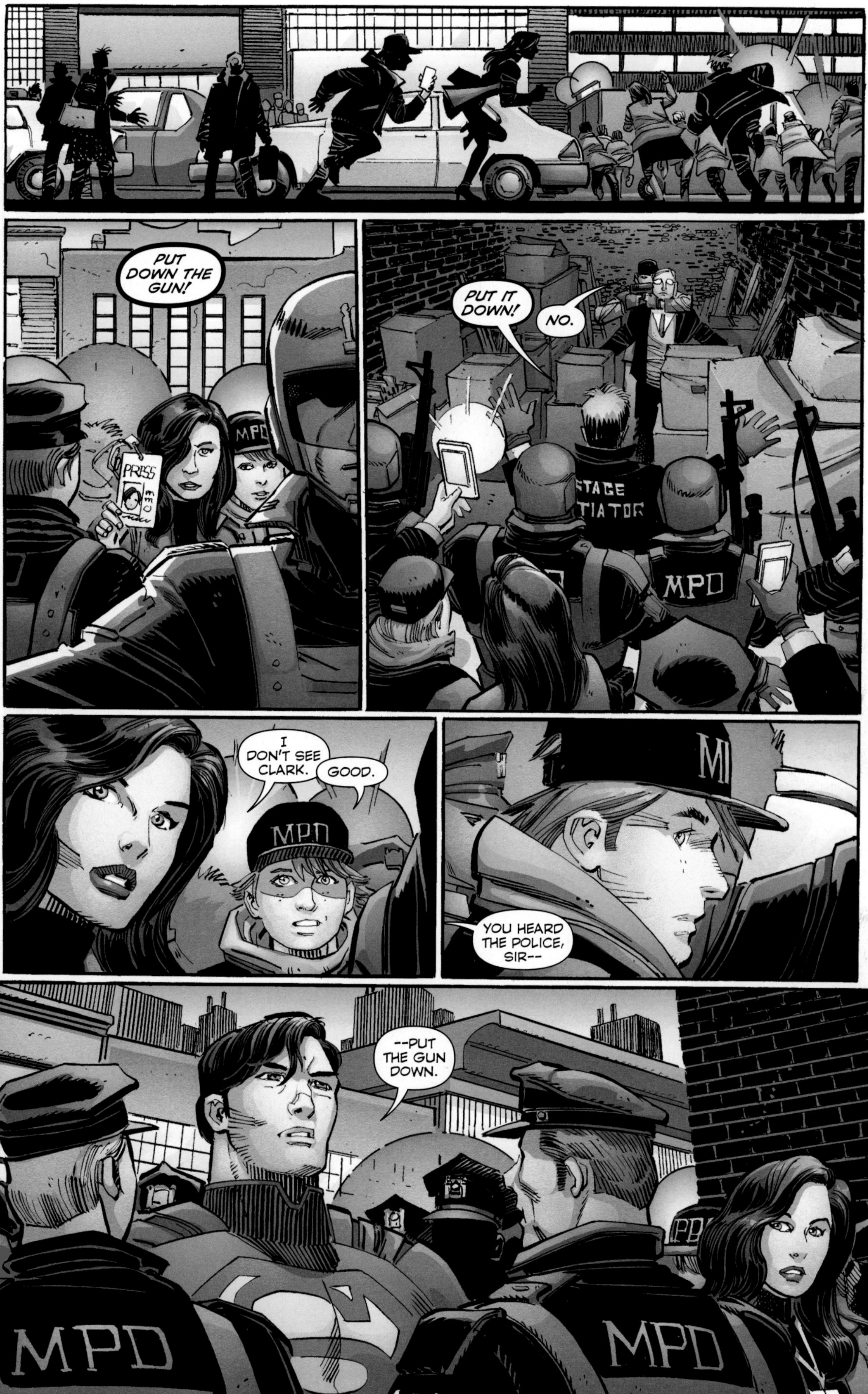

PUT DOWN THE GUN!
PUT IT DOWN!
NO.
PRESS
STAGE
TIATOR
MPD
I DON'T SEE CLARK.
GOOD.
YOU HEARD THE POLICE, SIR--
--PUT THE GUN DOWN.
MPD
MPD

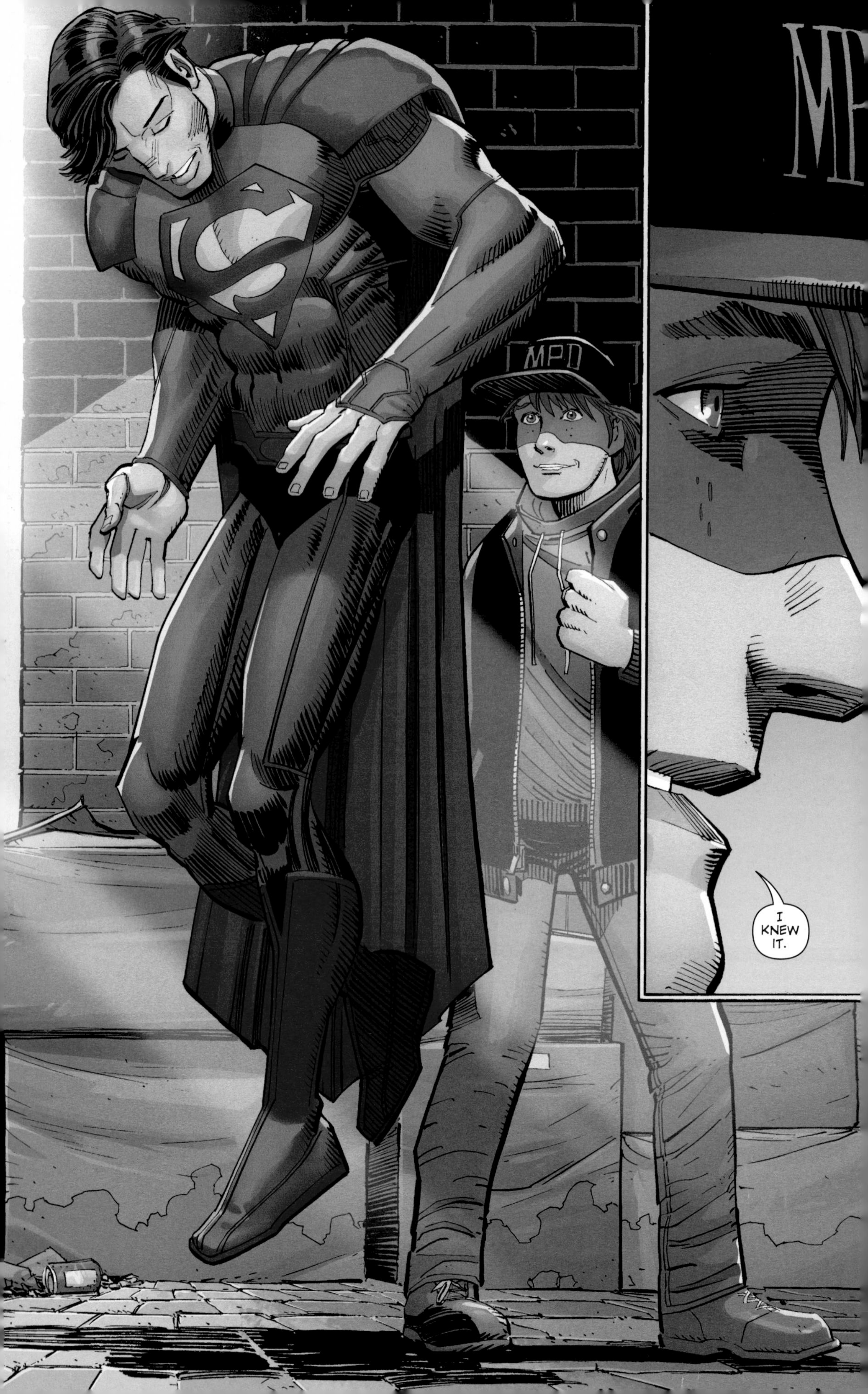
MPD
I KNEW IT.

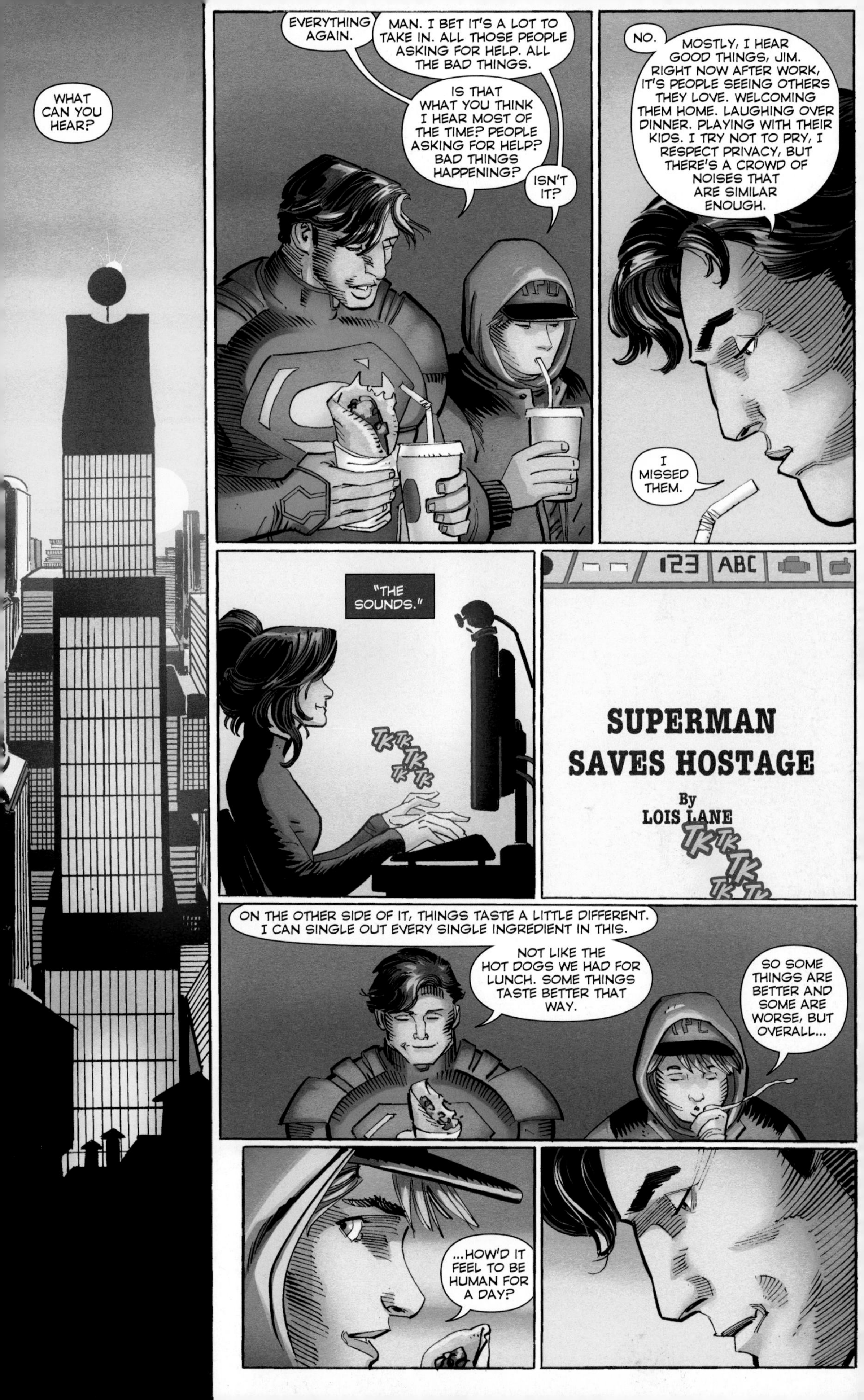
WHAT CAN YOU HEAR?
EVERYTHING AGAIN.
MAN. I BET IT'S A LOT TO TAKE IN. ALL THOSE PEOPLE ASKING FOR HELP. ALL THE BAD THINGS.
IS THAT WHAT YOU THINK I HEAR MOST OF THE TIME? PEOPLE ASKING FOR HELP? BAD THINGS HAPPENING?
ISN'T IT?
NO.
MOSTLY, I HEAR GOOD THINGS, JIM. RIGHT NOW AFTER WORK, IT'S PEOPLE SEEING OTHERS THEY LOVE. WELCOMING THEM HOME. LAUGHING OVER DINNER. PLAYING WITH THEIR KIDS. I TRY NOT TO PRY, I RESPECT PRIVACY, BUT THERE'S A CROWD OF NOISES THAT ARE SIMILAR ENOUGH.
I MISSED THEM.
"THE SOUNDS."
TK TK TK TK TK
123 ABC
SUPERMAN SAVES HOSTAGE
By LOIS LANE
TK TK TK TK
ON THE OTHER SIDE OF IT, THINGS TASTE A LITTLE DIFFERENT. I CAN SINGLE OUT EVERY SINGLE INGREDIENT IN THIS.
NOT LIKE THE HOT DOGS WE HAD FOR LUNCH. SOME THINGS TASTE BETTER THAT WAY.
SO SOME THINGS ARE BETTER AND SOME ARE WORSE, BUT OVERALL...
...HOW'D IT FEEL TO BE HUMAN FOR A DAY?

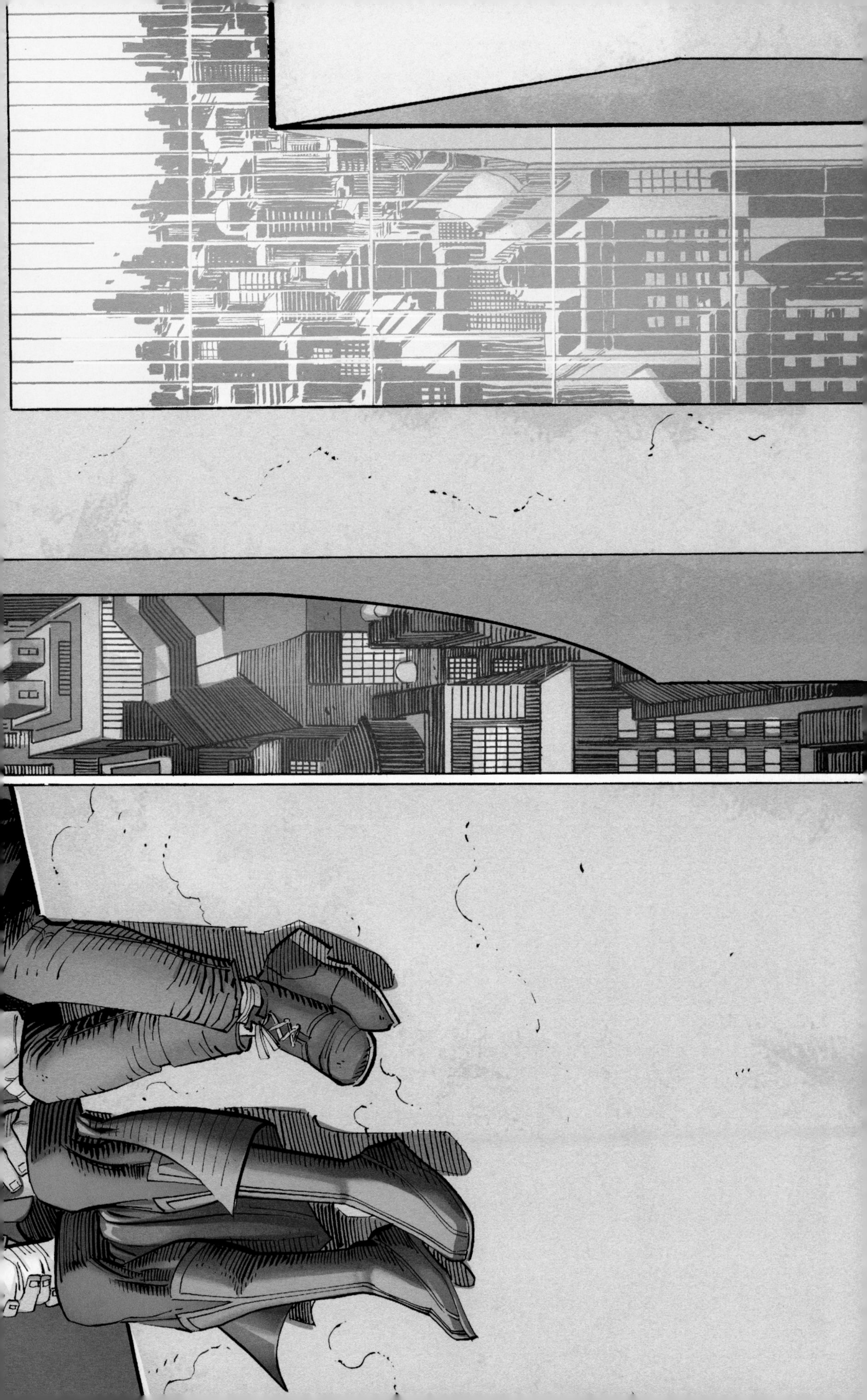

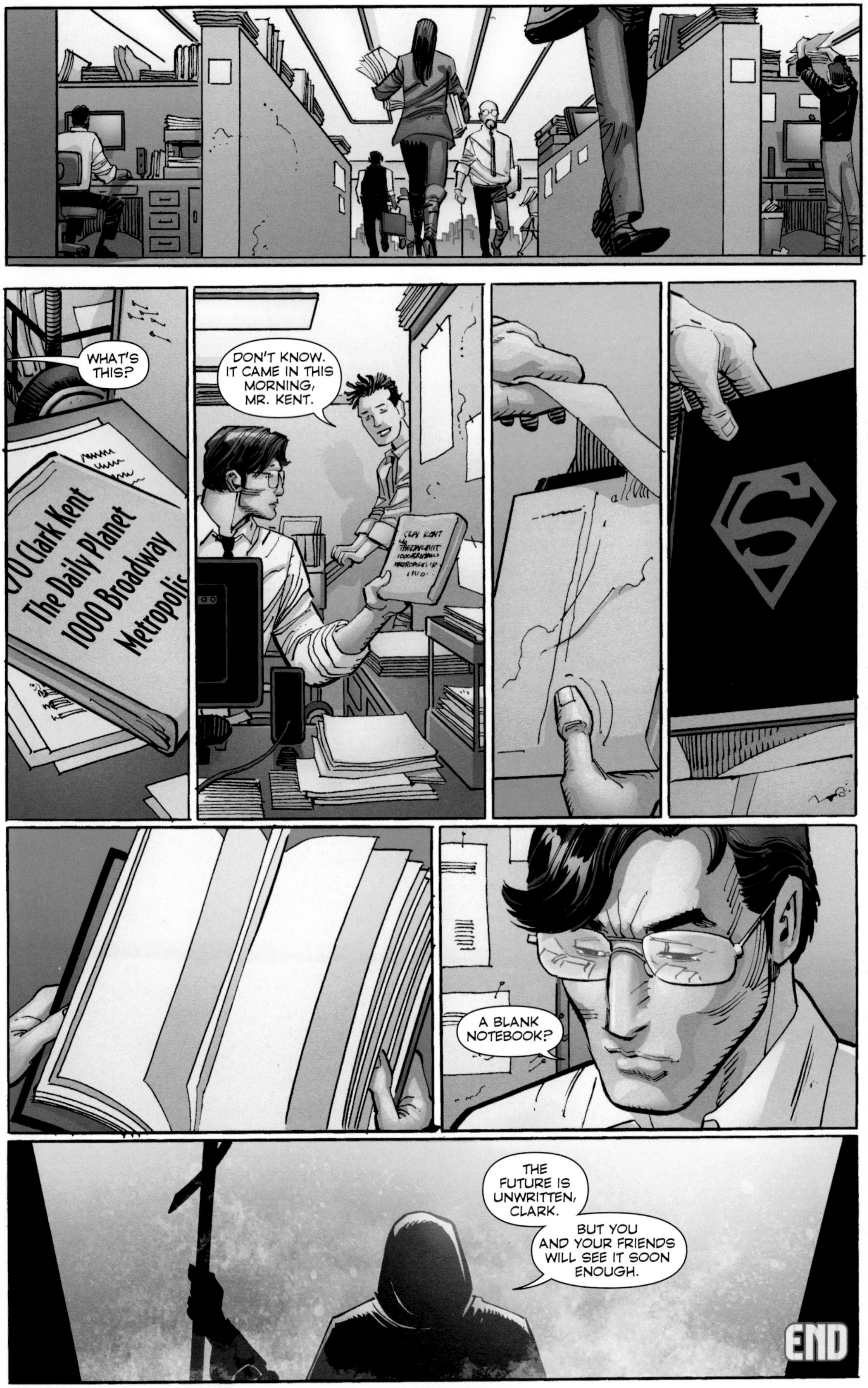
WHAT'S THIS?
c/o Clark Kent
The Daily Planet
1000 Broadway
Metropolis
DON'T KNOW. IT CAME IN THIS MORNING, MR. KENT.
A BLANK NOTEBOOK?
THE FUTURE IS UNWRITTEN, CLARK.
BUT YOU AND YOUR FRIENDS WILL SEE IT SOON ENOUGH.
END

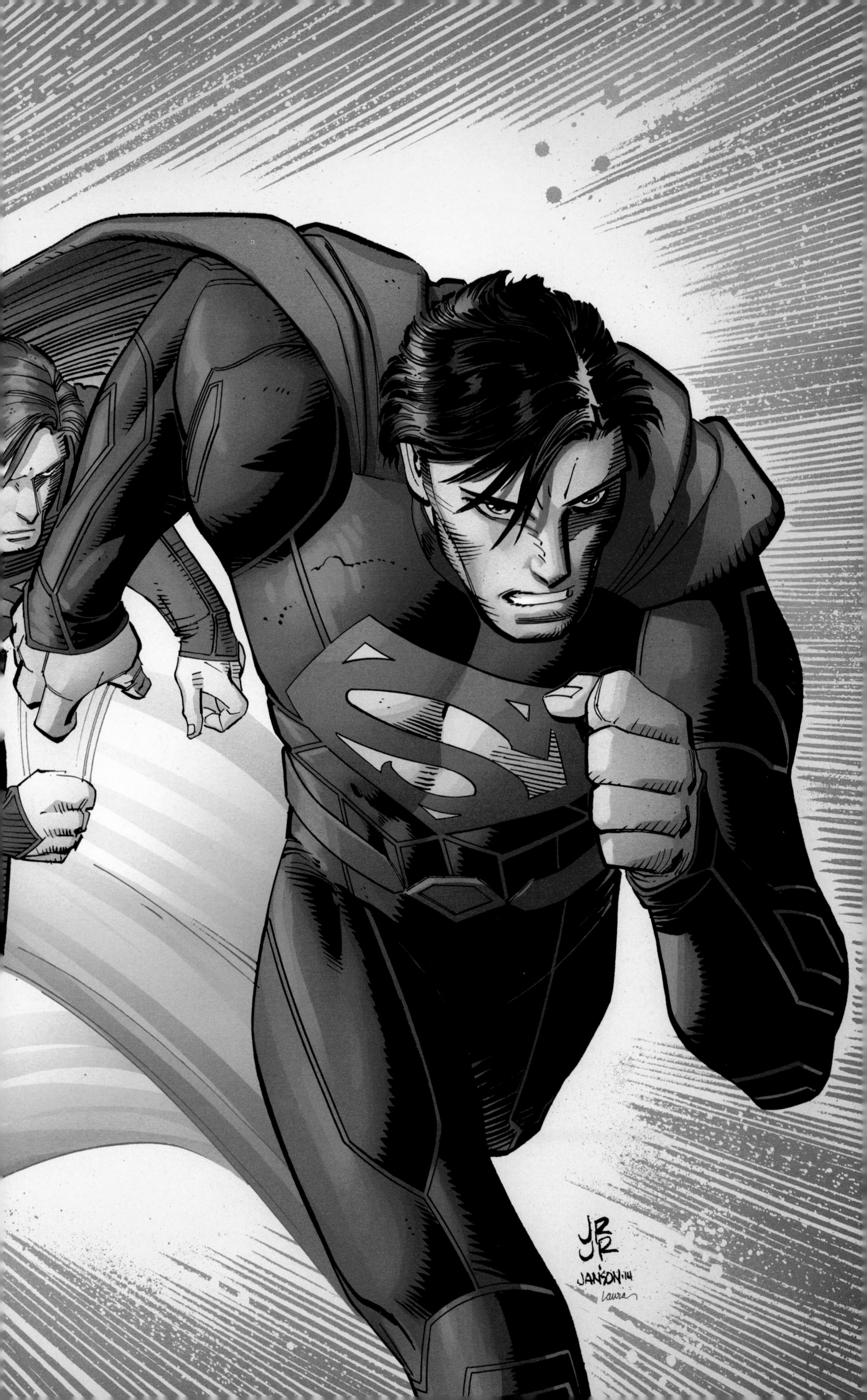
JANSON·14

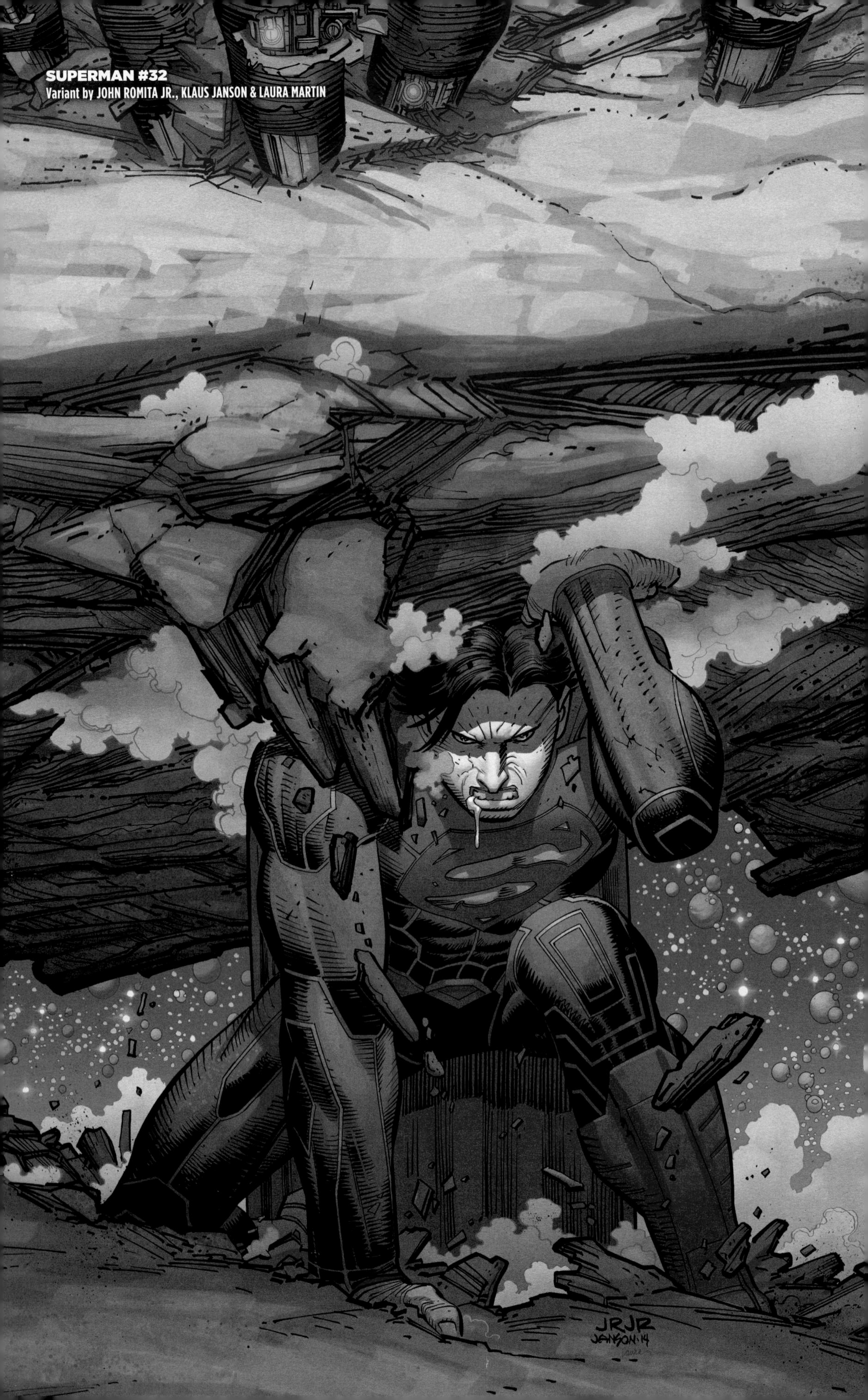
JRJR
JANSON·14

SUPERMAN #32
Variant by JOHN ROMITA JR., KLAUS JANSON & LAURA MARTIN

SUPERMAN #32

San Diego Comic-Con variant by JOHN ROMITA JR., KLAUS JANSON & LAURA MARTIN

SUPERMAN #33
Variant by JOHN ROMITA JR., KLAUS JANSON & LAURA MARTIN

SUPERMAN #33
Batman 75th anniversary variant by ERIK LARSEN

SUPERMAN #34
Variant by JOHN ROMITA JR., KLAUS JANSON & LAURA MARTIN

SUPERMAN #34
Variant by JOHN ROMITA, KLAUS JANSON & LAURA MARTIN

SUPERMAN #34

Selfie variant by NEIL EDWARDS, DANNY MIKI & ALEX SINCLAIR

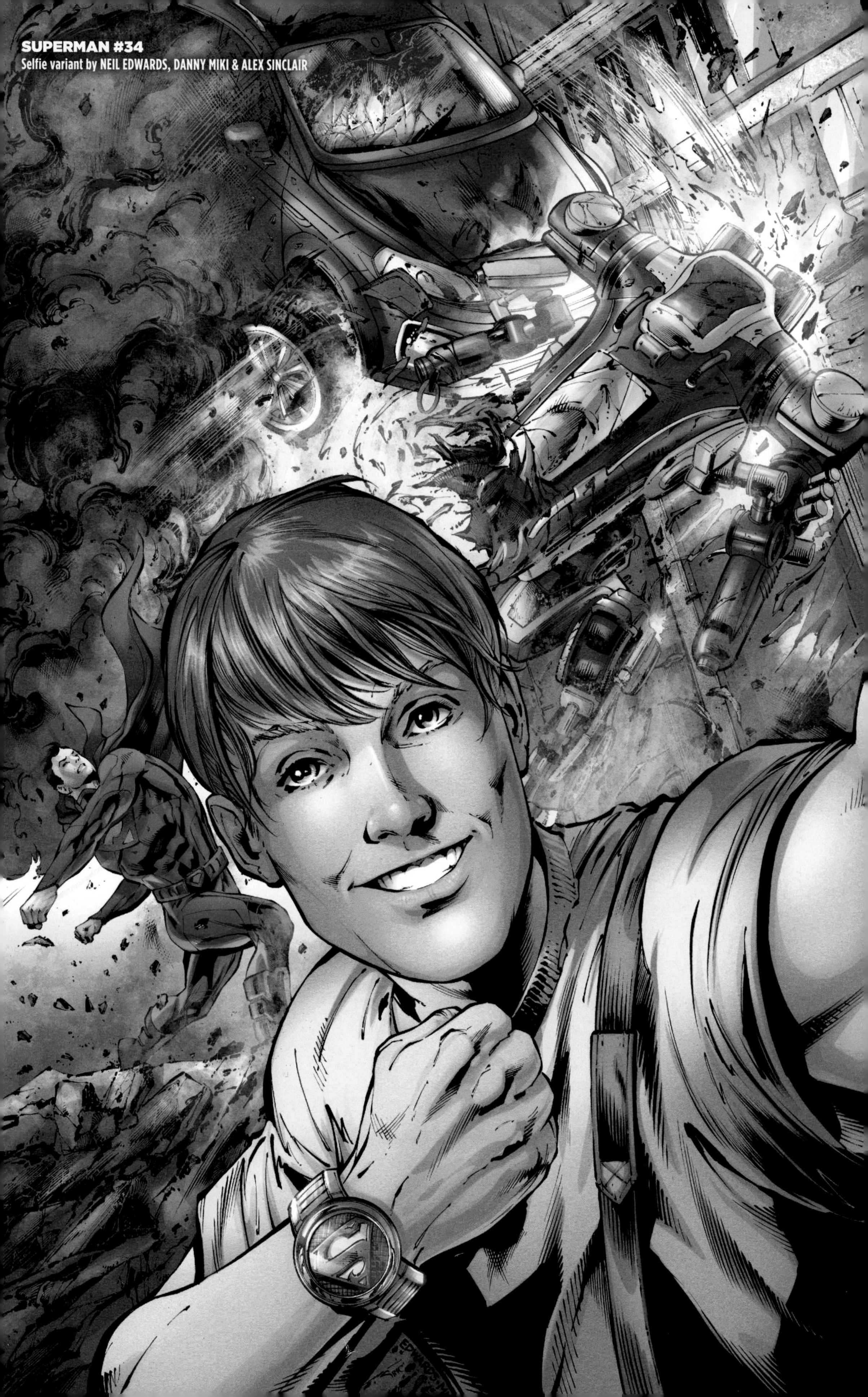

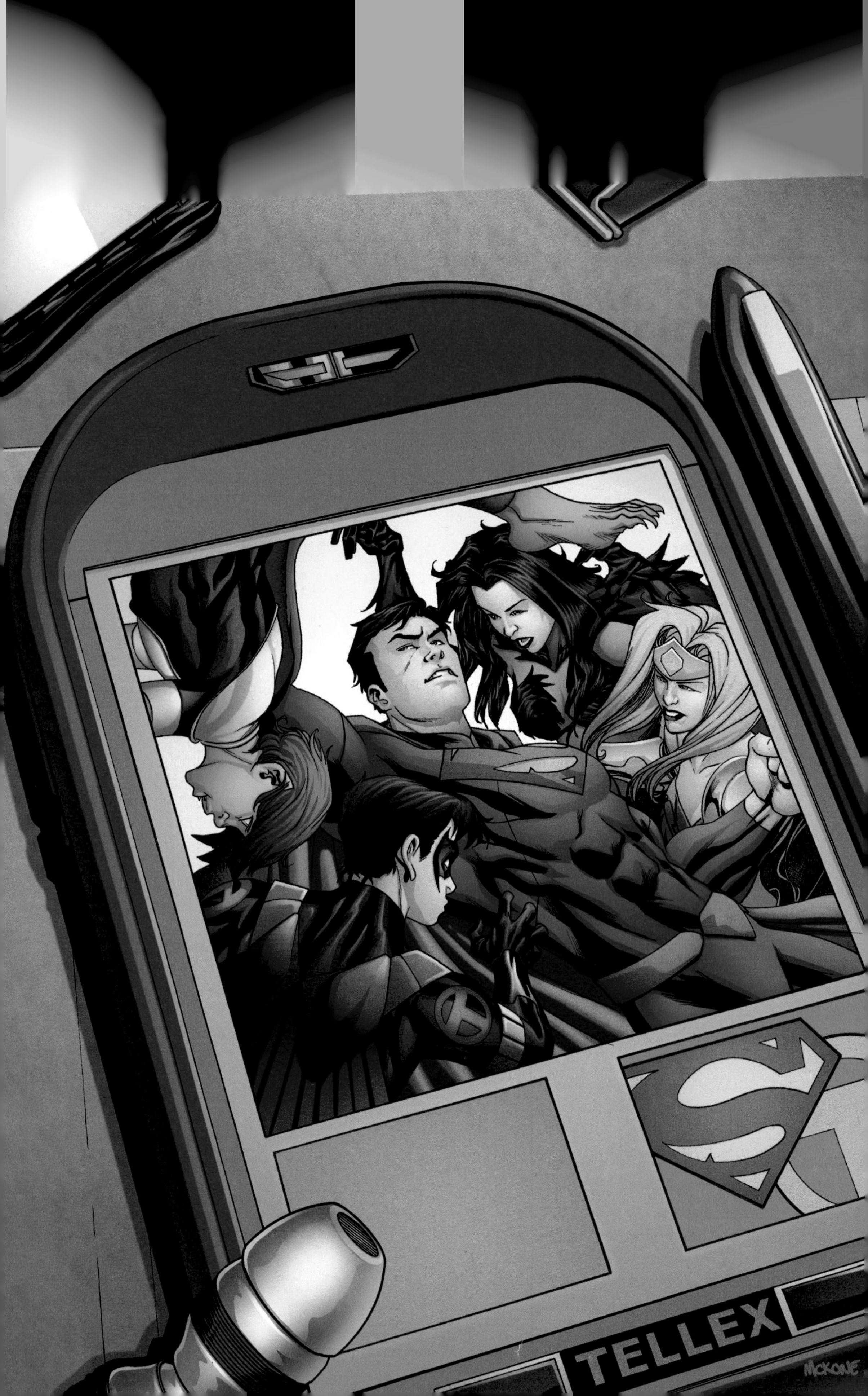
TELLEX
MCKONE

SUPERMAN #35
Variant by JOHN ROMITA JR., KLAUS JANSON & LAURA MARTIN

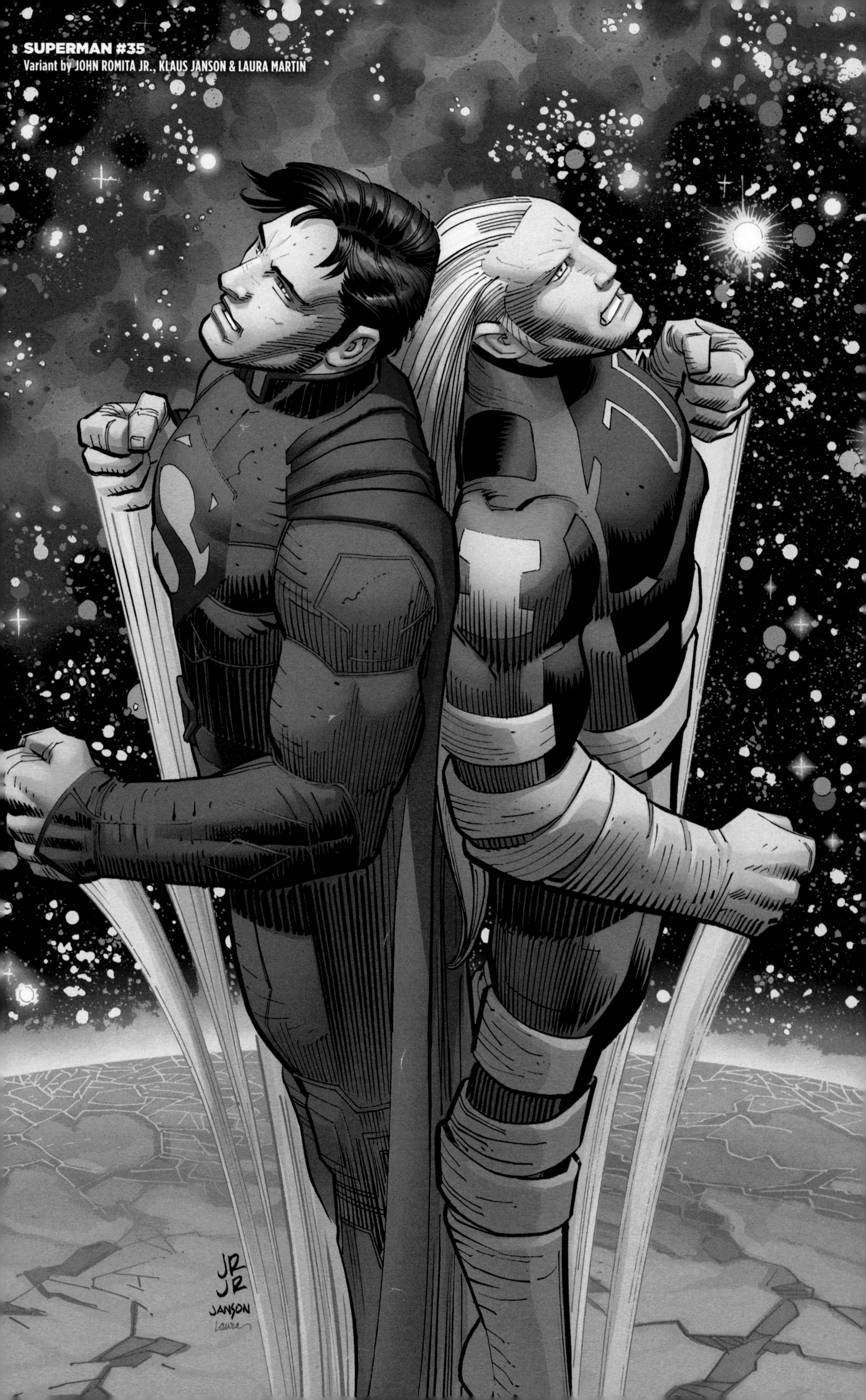
JR JR
JANSON
Laura

SUPERMAN #35
Monster variant by JASON PEARSON

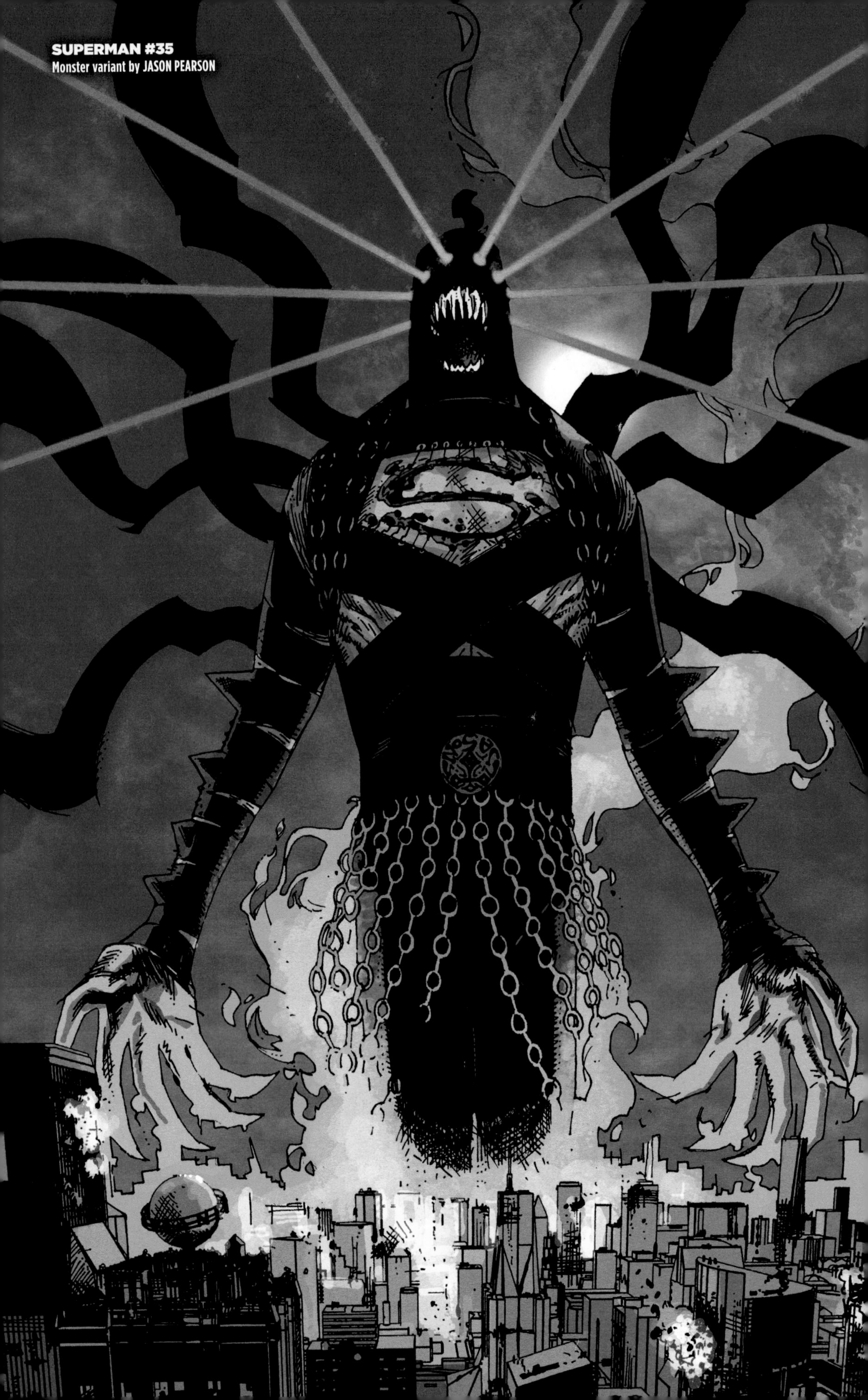

SUPERMAN #36
Variant by FRANCIS MANAPUL

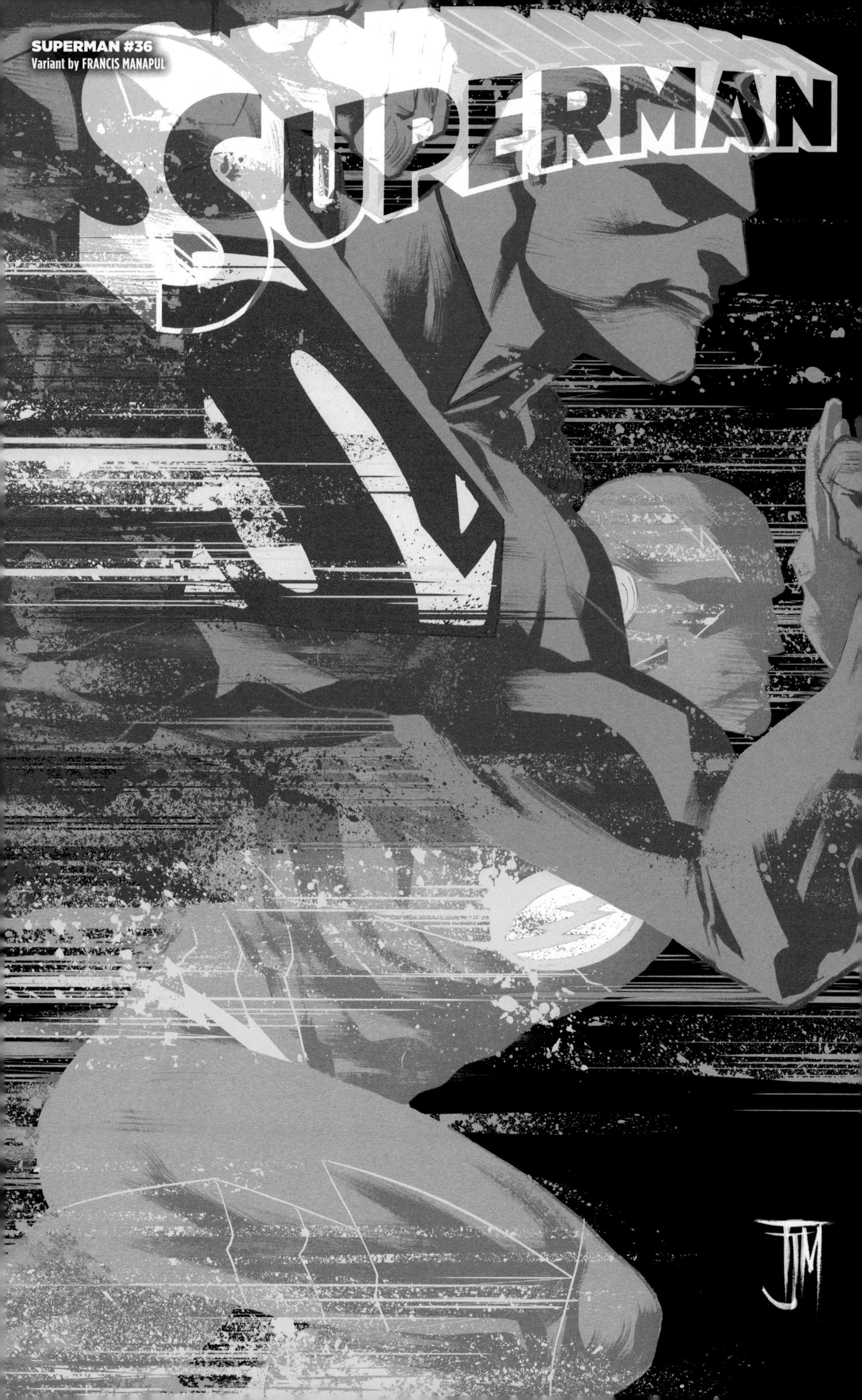
SUPERMAN

SUPERMAN #36
Variant by JOHN ROMITA JR., KLAUS JANSON & LAURA MARTIN

SUPERMAN #36
LEGO variant

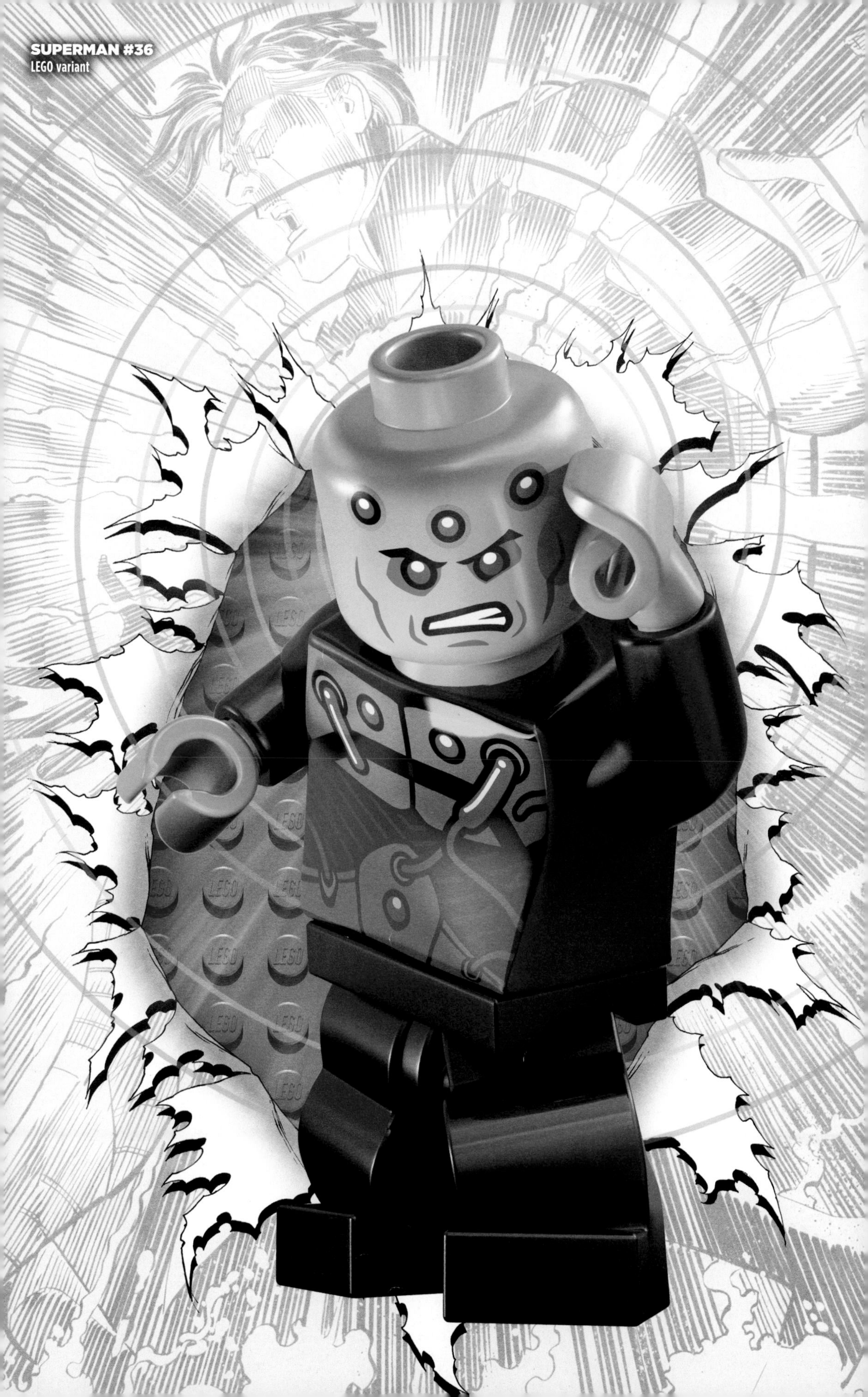
LEGO

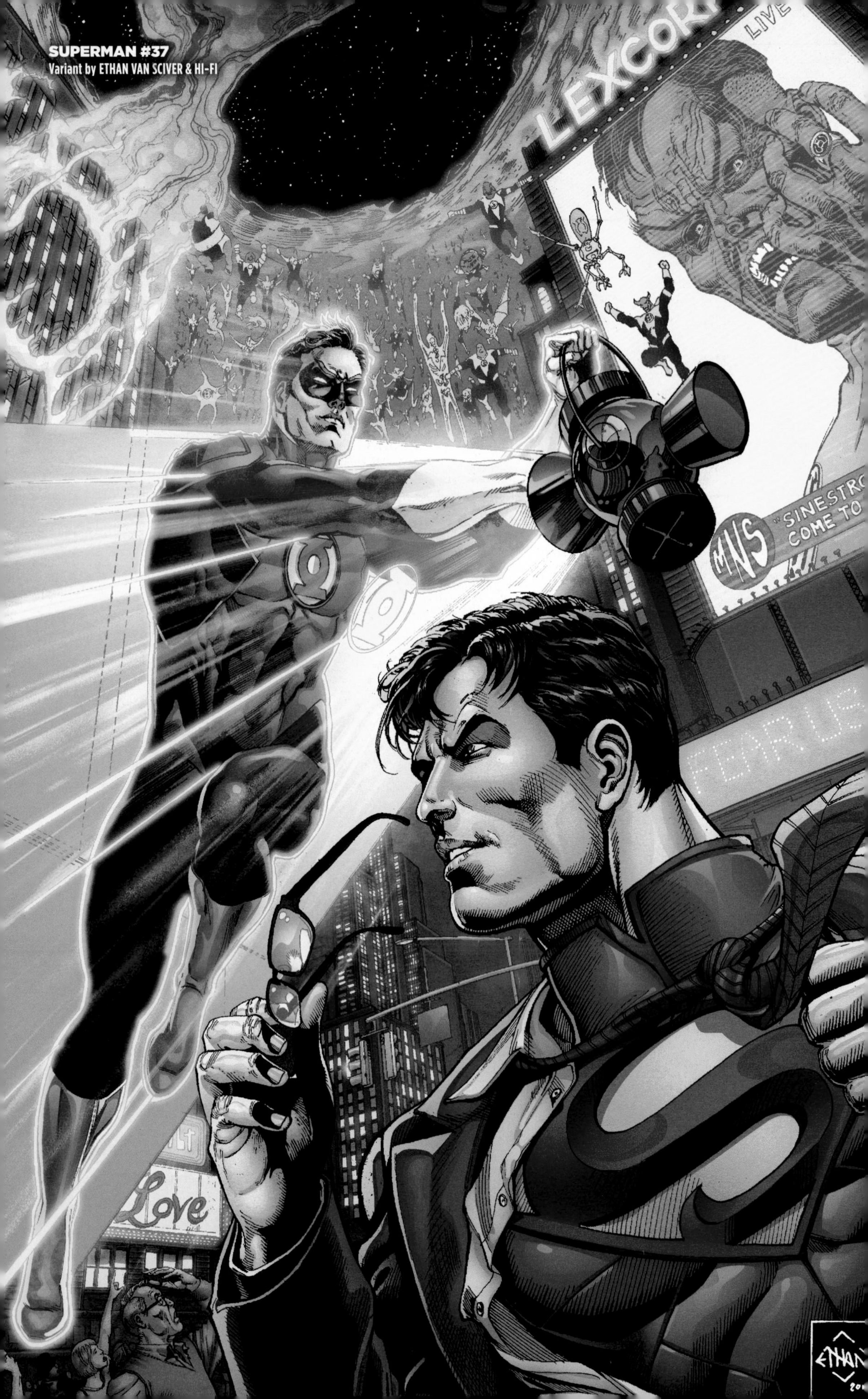
LEXCOR
LIVE
MNS
"SINESTRO
COME TO
Love
ETHAN

SUPERMAN #37
Variant by ETHAN VAN SCIVER & HI-FI

SUPERMAN #37
Variant by JOHN ROMITA JR., KLAUS JANSON & LAURA MARTIN

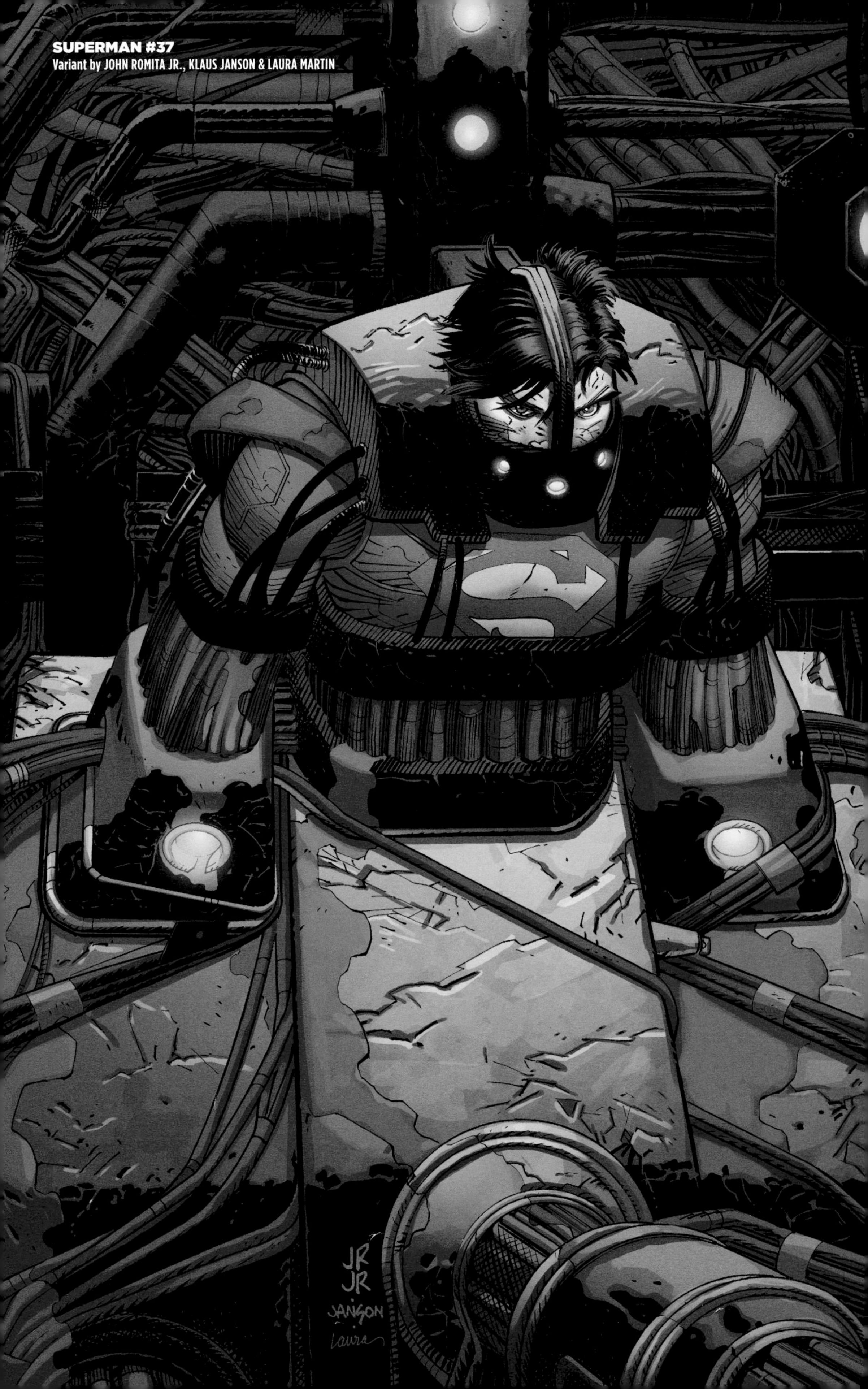
JR
JR
JANSON
laura

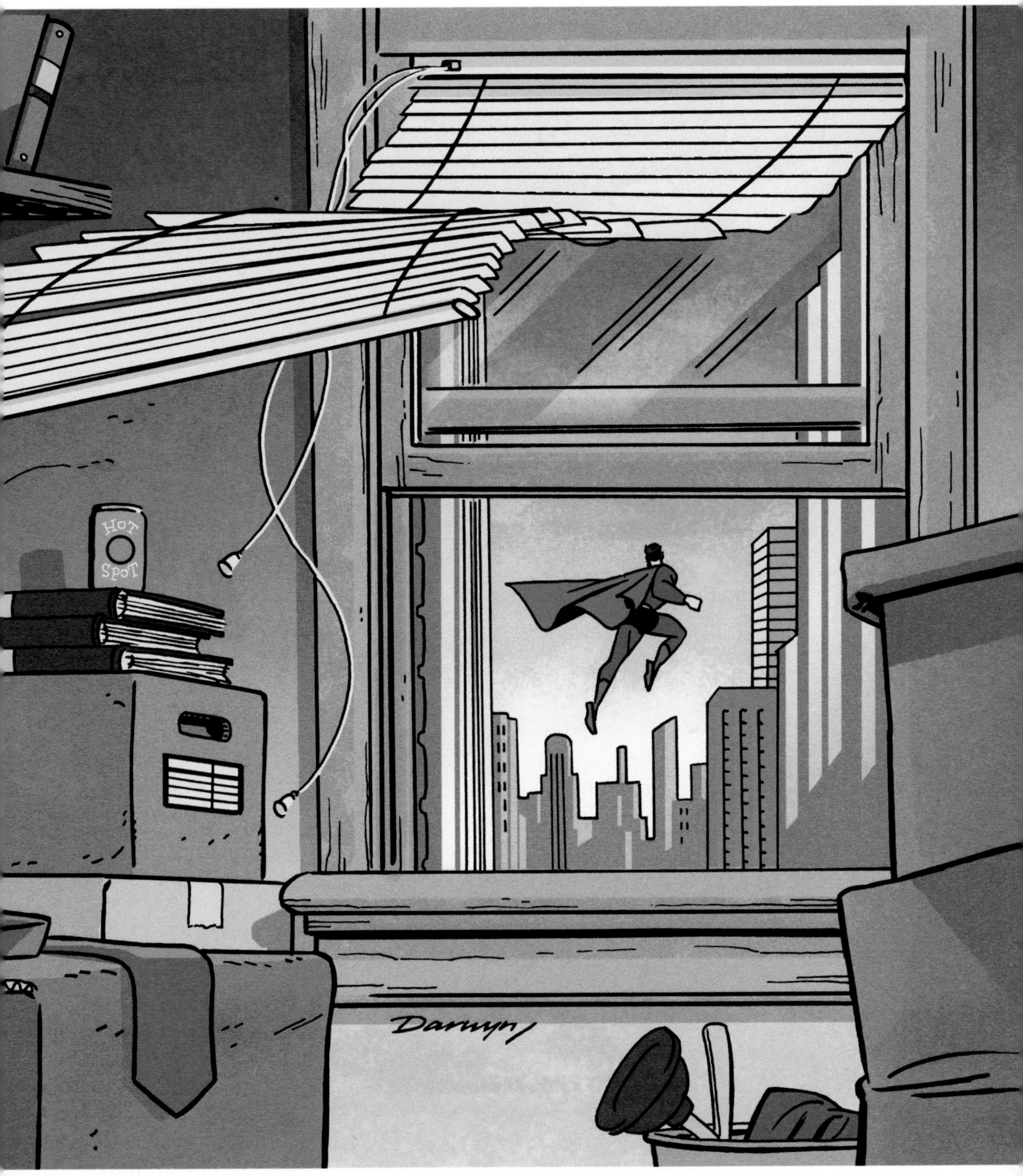
HOT SPOT
Darwyn

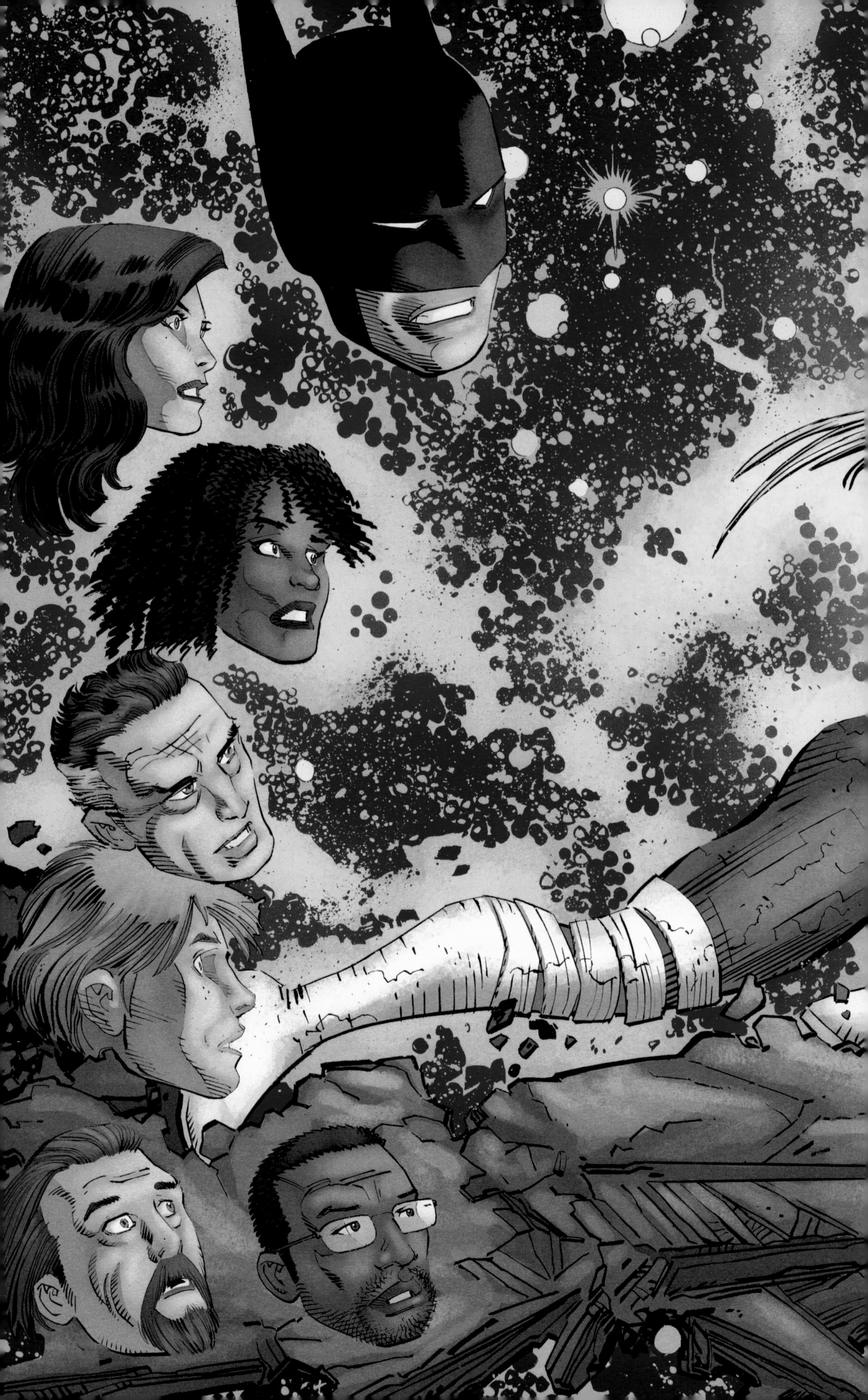

SUPERMAN #38
Full wrap-around cover by JOHN ROMITA JR., KLAUS JANSON & LAURA MARTIN

SUPERMAN #38
Variant cover by LEE MODER & MIKE ATIYEH

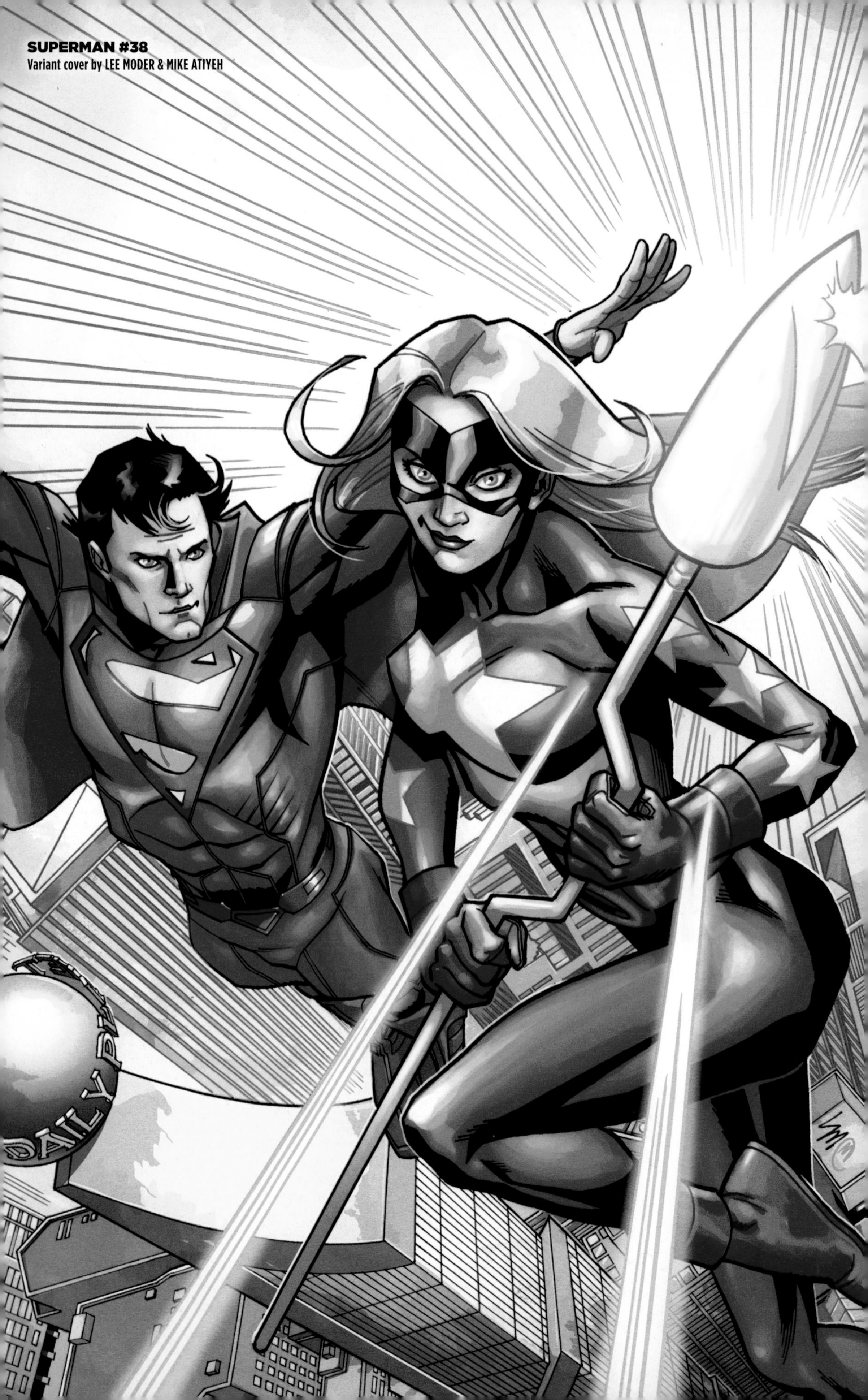
DAILY

SUPERMAN #38
Variant by JOHN ROMITA JR., KLAUS JANSON & LAURA MARTIN

SUPERMAN #39
Variant by JOHN ROMITA JR., KLAUS JANSON & LAURA MARTIN

SUPERMAN #39

Variant by SHANE DAVIS, MICHELLE DELECKI & BARBARA CIARDO

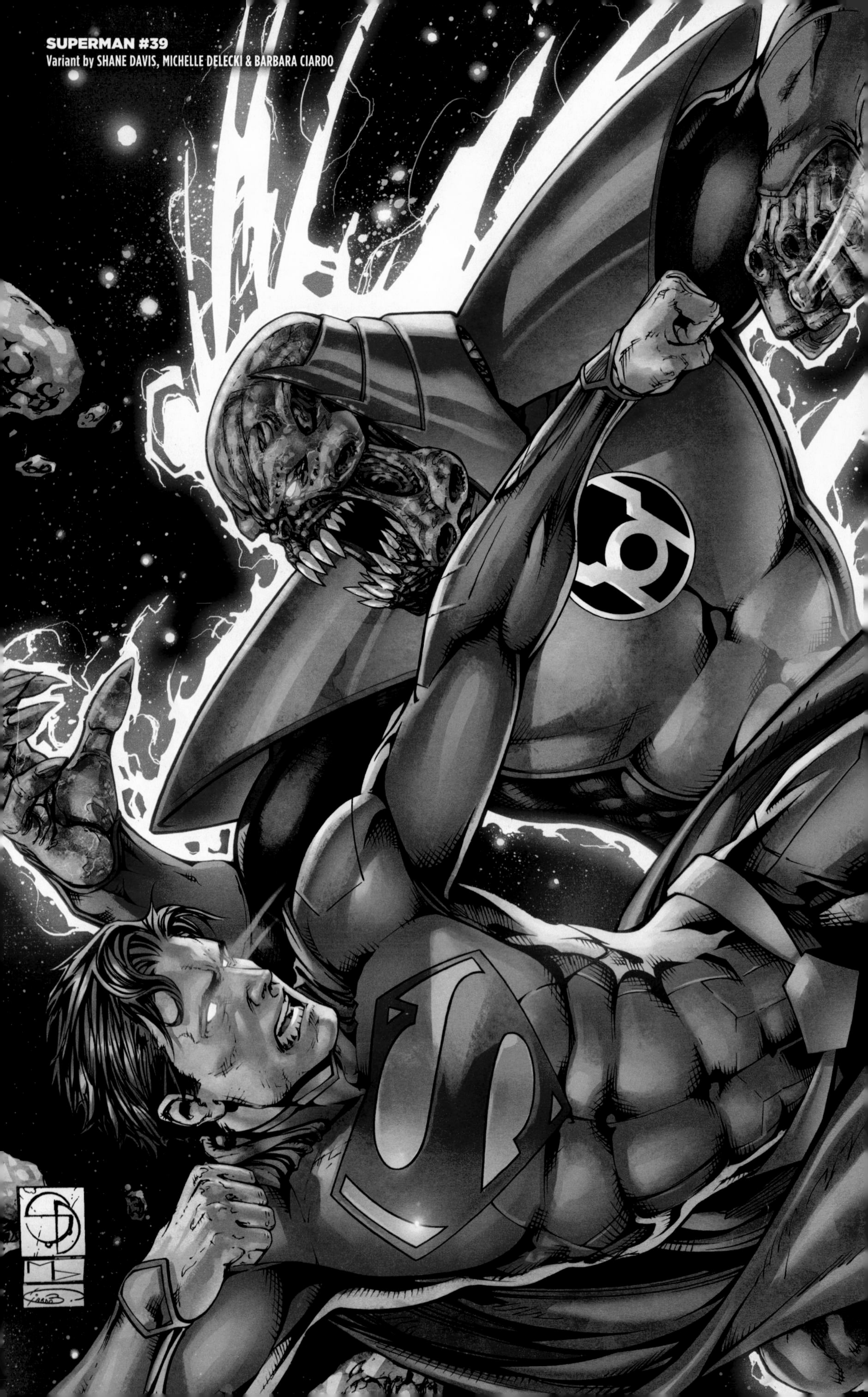

SUPERMAN #39
Harley Quinn variant by AMANDA CONNER & PAUL MOUNTS

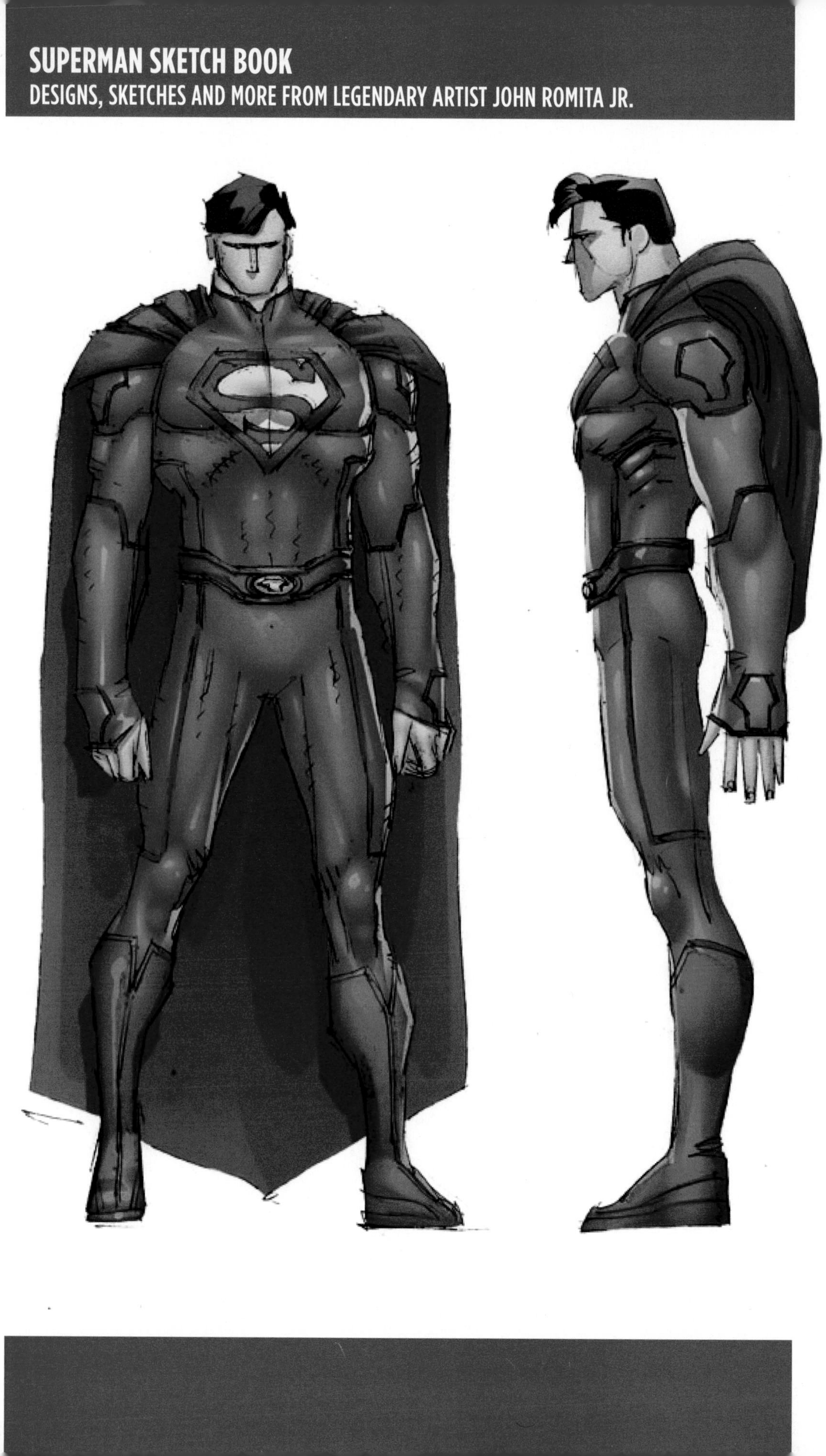

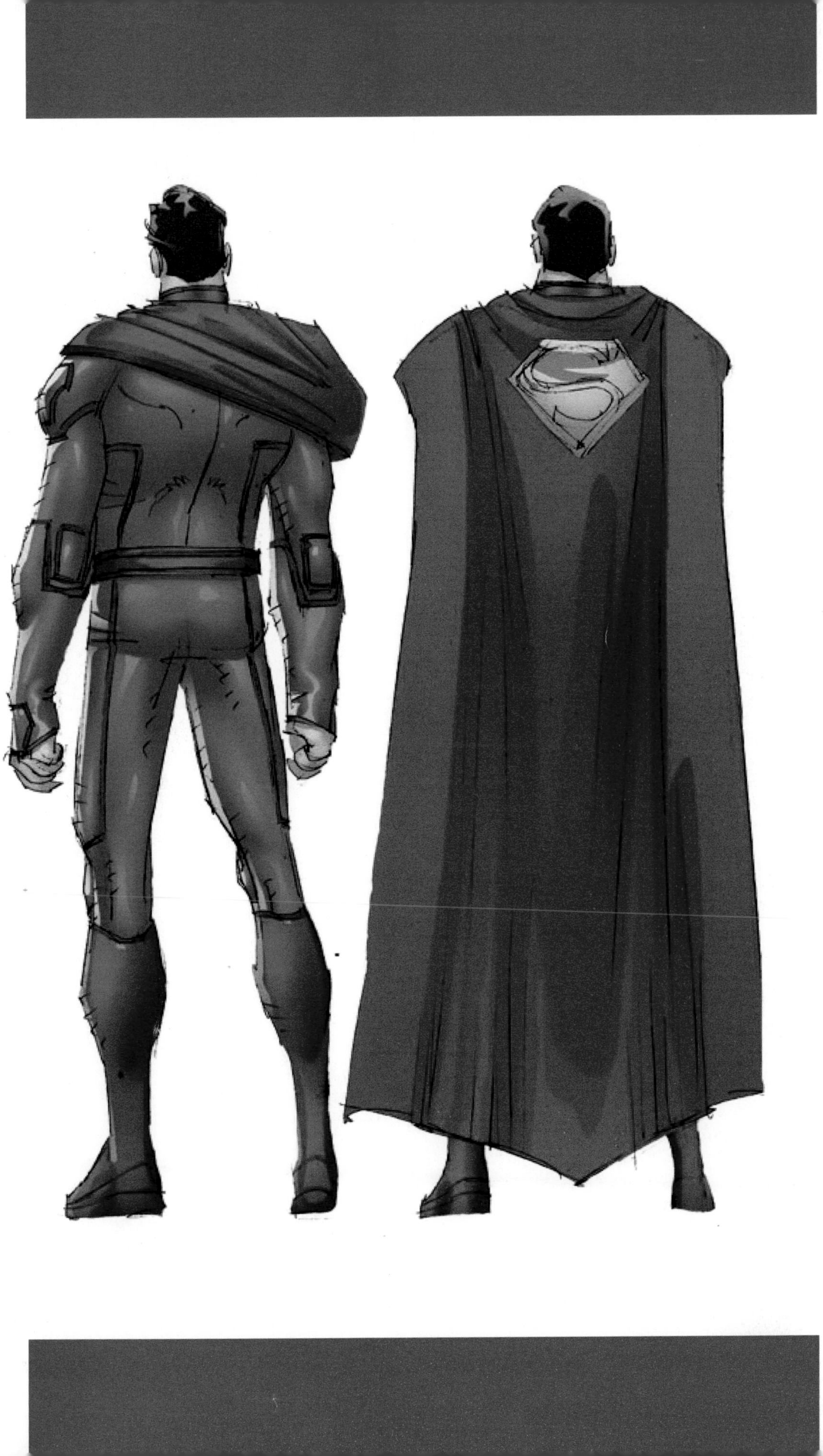

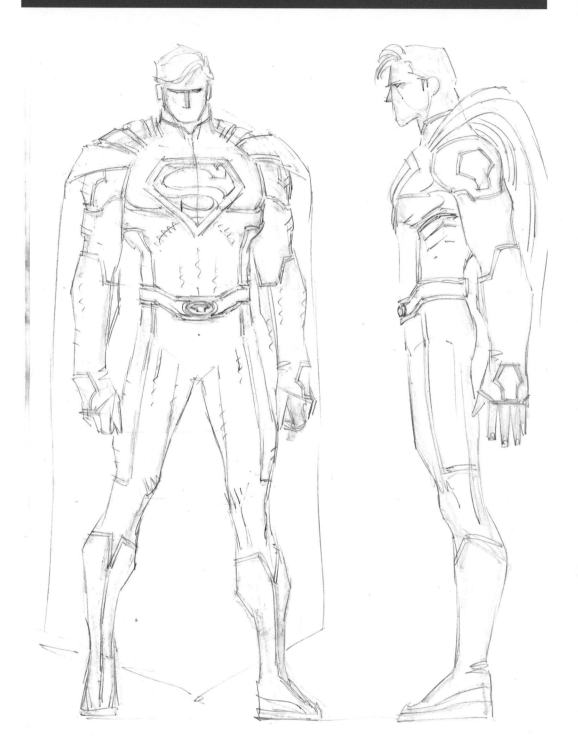

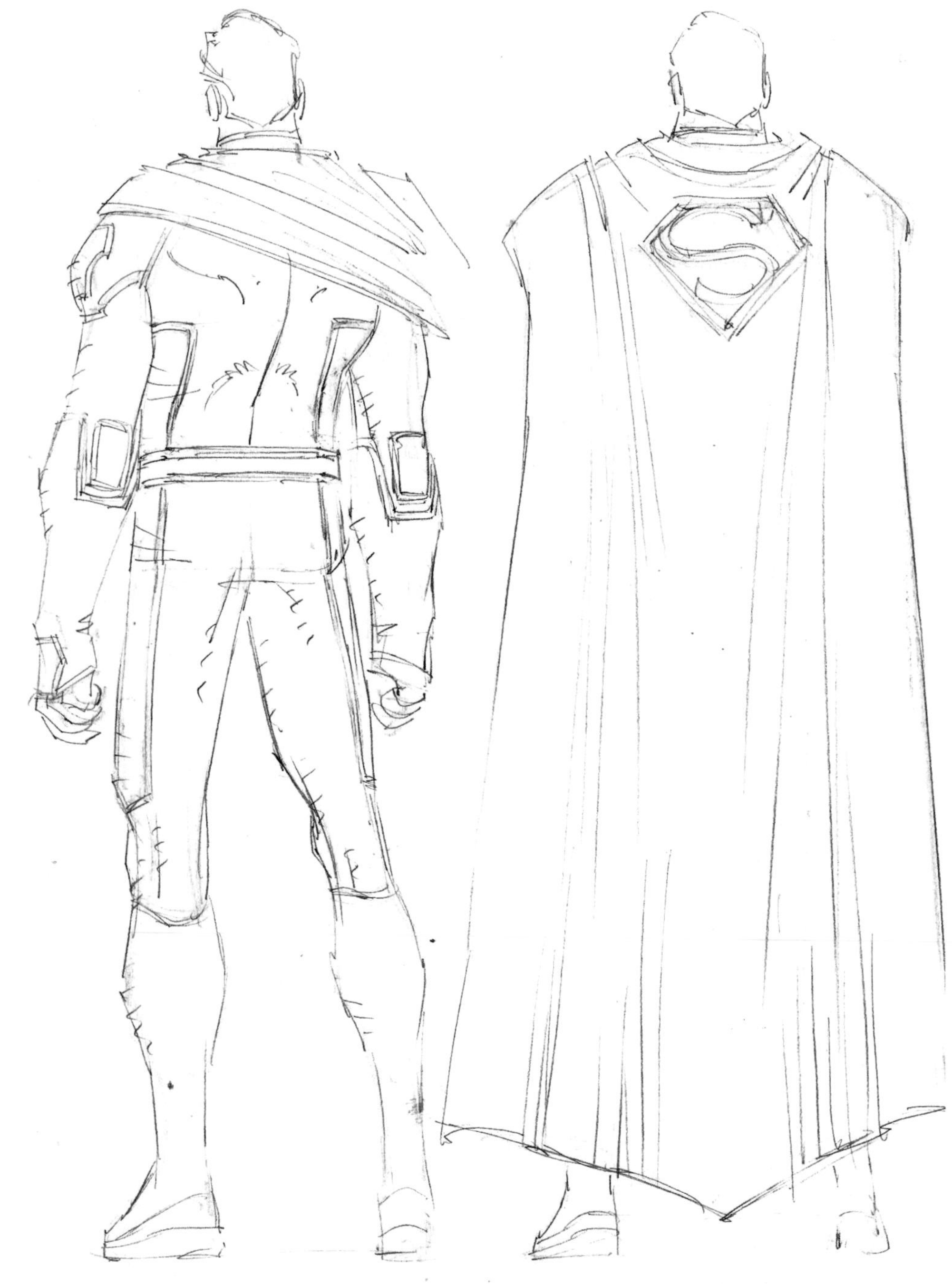

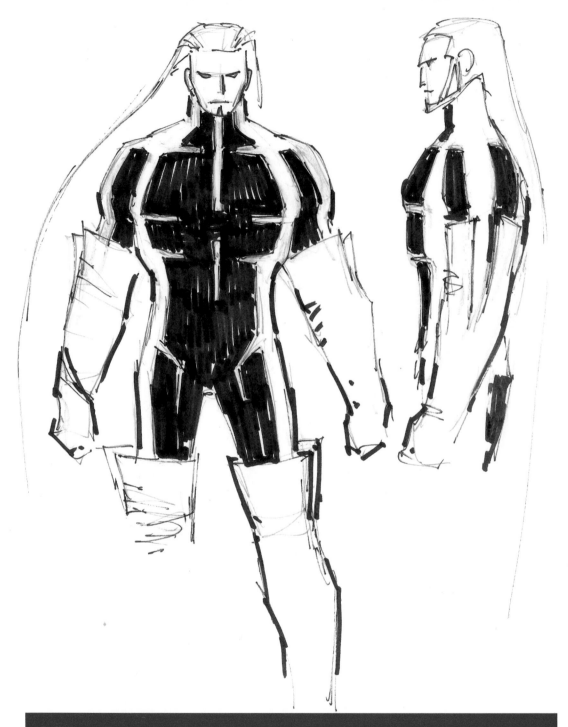

Geoff's note to John—
"I'm envisioning someone that reflects Superman in some way, it shouldn't simply mirror him. I'm not sure if he needs a cape—maybe when he first shows up he doesn't have one and then gets one after being influenced by Superman.

Does he have a beard? He should have a great hero's smile. For the first few issues we will think and portray him as a hero. He only gets dark later.

Physically, I'm thinking he's much like Superman at least in terms of size. He should have a different hair color obviously. I'm envisioning blonde, but am open."

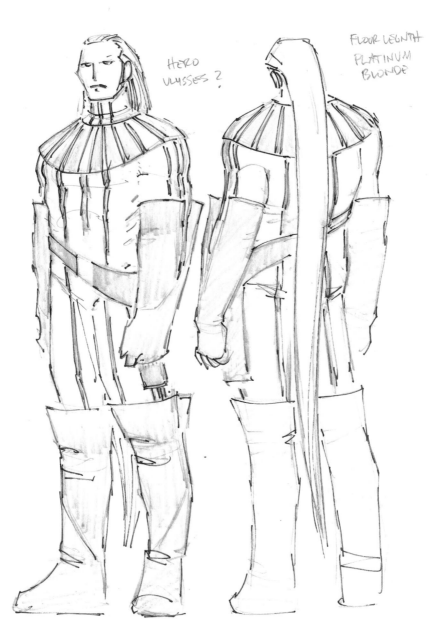

VILLAIN
COSTUME

HERO
FACE

VILLAIN
ULYSSES

-- DIFFERENT FROM HERO VERSION?

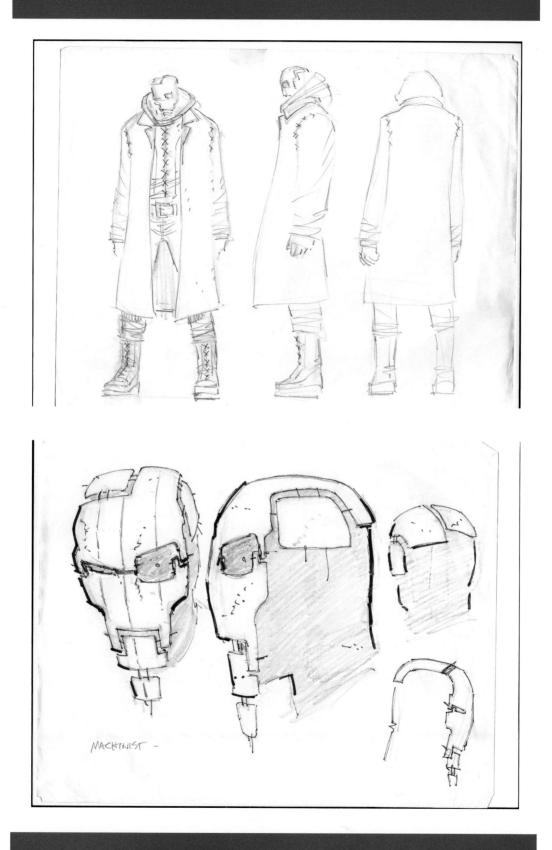

MACHINIST -

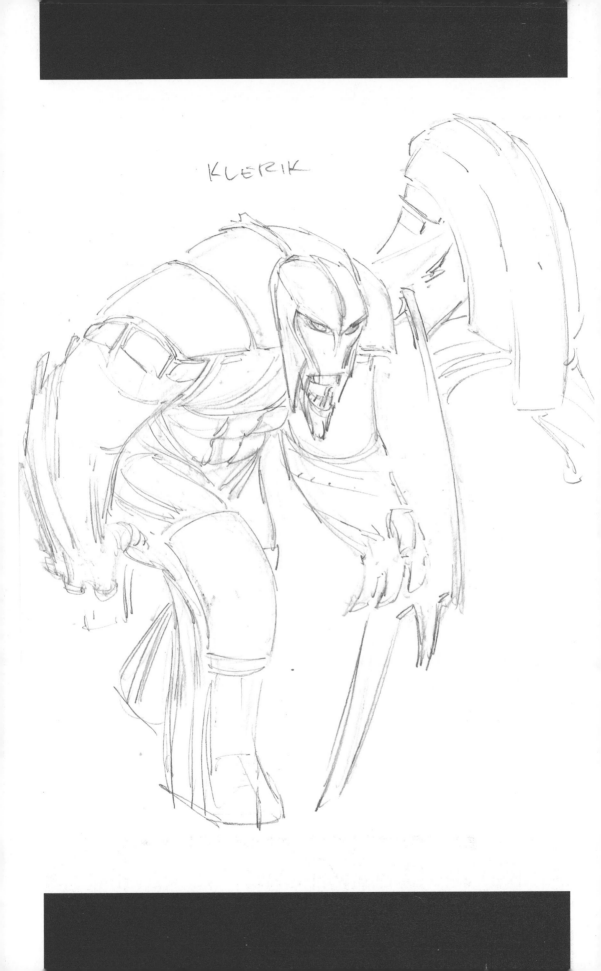

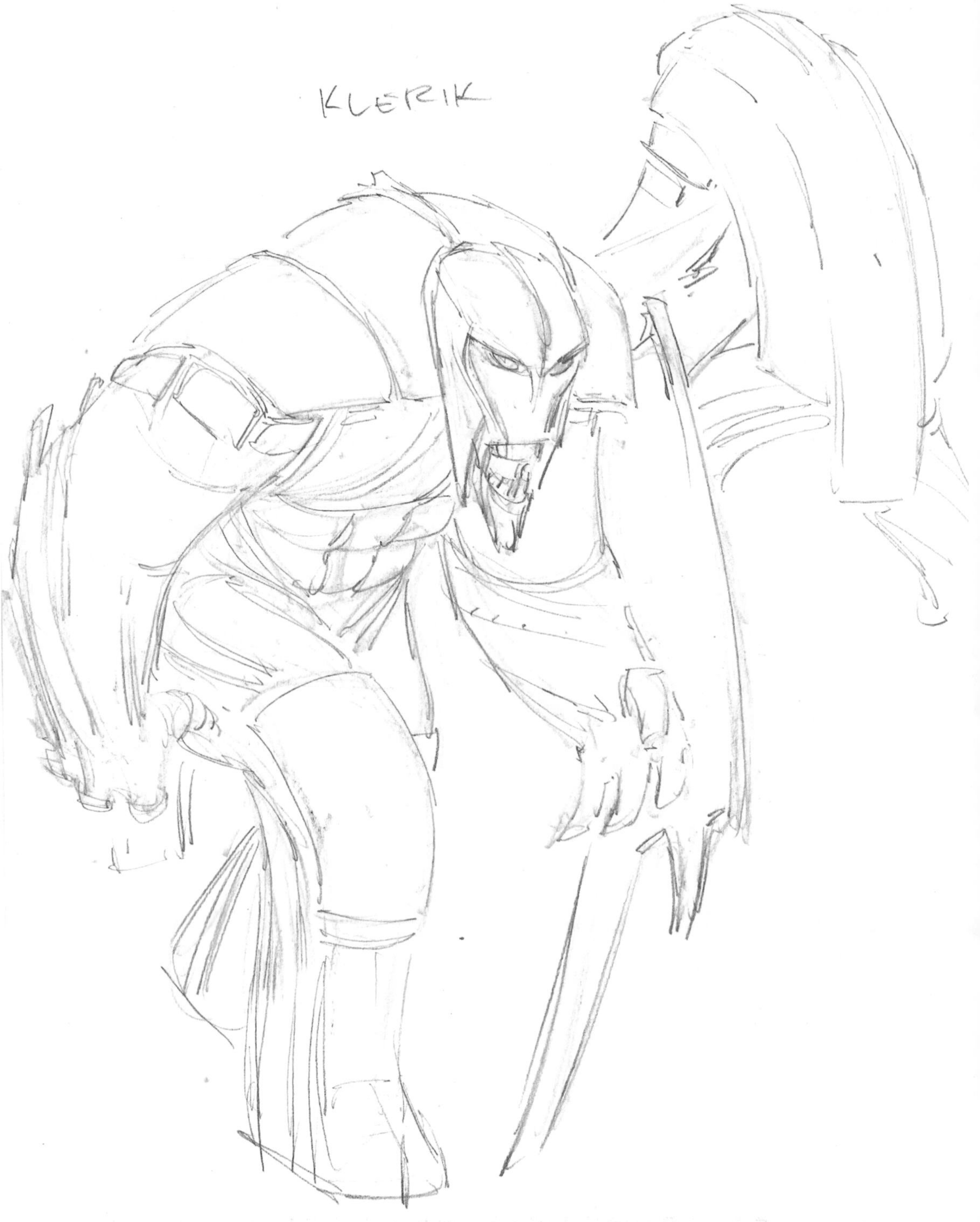
KLERIK

JACKIE

Brand-new character introduced at The Side Car bar with Lois. Jackee smiles more often times than not, never loses her cool, unassuming but incredibly shrewd. She asks the hard questions and tears into the answers.

But there are rumors that Jackee was once involved with groups like Wikileaks. That she has made enemies in high places. She has a past that could catch up with her. And she knows it.

Friend to Lois. Tech-savvy with multiple smartphones, including one that's totally off the grid. Coffee drinker.

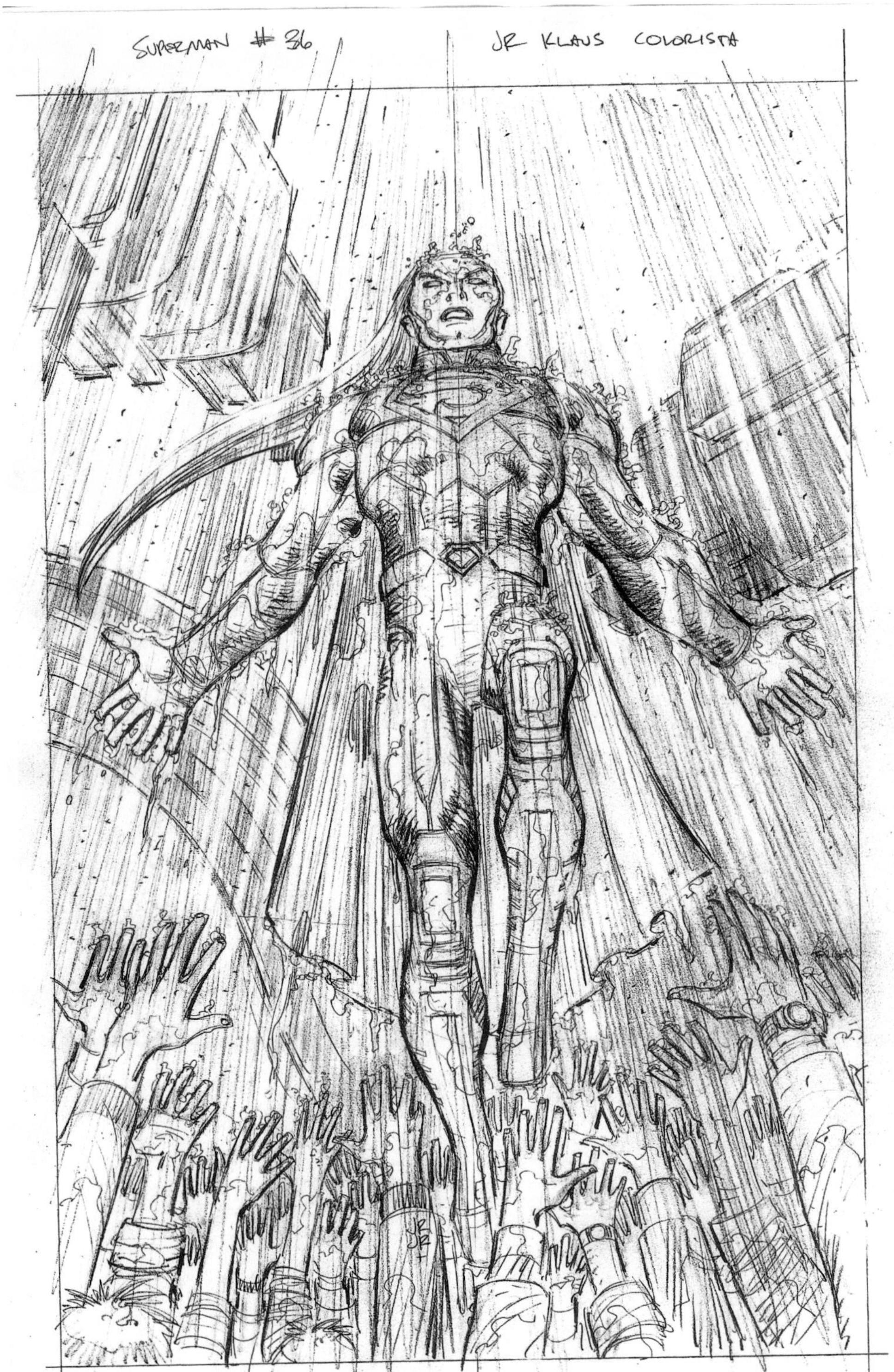
SUPERMAN #36
JR KLAUS COLORISTA